Morton A. Lieberman
Leonard D. Borman
and Associates

with special contributions by
Gary R. Bond, Paul Antze,
and Leon H. Levy

Self-Help Groups for Coping with Crisis

Origins, Members,
Processes, and Impact

 Jossey-Bass Publishers
San Francisco • Washington • London • 1979

SELF-HELP GROUPS FOR COPING WITH CRISIS
Origins, Members, Processes, and Impact
      by Morton A. Lieberman, Leonard D. Borman, and Associates

Copyright © 1979 by: Jossey-Bass Inc., Publishers
                      433 California Street
                      San Francisco, California 94104

                              &

                      Jossey-Bass Limited
                      28 Banner Street
                      London EC1Y 8QE

Library of Congress Cataloging in Publication Data

Lieberman, Morton A.   1931–
    Self-help groups for coping with crisis.

    Bibliography: p.
    Includes index.
    1. Self-help groups—United States—Addresses,
essays, lectures. I. Borman, Leonard D., joint
author. II. Title.
HV547.L53   361.7   79–88772
ISBN 0–87589–435–6

Manufactured in the United States of America

JACKET DESIGN BY WILLI BAUM

FIRST EDITION

Code 7938

The Jossey-Bass
Social and Behavioral Science Series

Acknowledgments

We are indebted to a number of colleagues, students, and staff who have contributed directly to the studies that form the basis of this book. In all, three distinct projects are represented. The study of women's consciousness-raising groups was initiated while Morton A. Lieberman was at the University of Wisconsin with help from funds provided by that university. When he returned to the University of Chicago he was joined by Gary R. Bond, Janet Reibstein, and Nancy Solow in carrying out the studies of women's consciousness-raising groups. The project examining Mended Hearts included Lieberman and Leonard D. Borman as principal investigators, with Bond as project director, and involved Steven Daiter, Elizabeth A. Bankoff, Nancy Solow, and Lynn M. Videka as participants. We are grateful to the University of Chicago Cancer Control Center for providing funding from a grant, PHS #3, R18–CA1640–0151.

Our major project study of self-help groups began in 1977 with a grant from the National Institute of Mental Health (Self-Help and Urban Problems: Alternative Help Systems,

PHS #5, R01–MH30742). Lieberman and Borman were the co-principal investigators, with Bond as project director. The study was also helped by a Research Scientist Award (Processes and Outcomes of People-Changing Groups, #1, K05–MH20342) to Lieberman. During the two years that the project has been in existence, three teams have been studying various groups representing widowhood, child loss, and motherhood. The widowhood team consists of Elizabeth A. Bankoff, Penny Burdette, Mark Steinberg, and Carrie Miles; child loss, Harriet Davidson, Marsha Kornfield, Brant Serxner, Barry Sherman, Lynn Videka, and Michael Wax; motherhood, Kristin Glaser, Jacqueline Kieff, Nancy Klein, Janet Reibstein, Susan Shore, Nancy Solow, and Beverly Sweny.

Without the assistance of a number of other supporting staff members, these projects and this book would not have been possible. We are indebted to Gail Cassel, Cathy Geers, Pamela Strauss, Lauren Furst, Susan Pasco, Mary Videka, Ceci Bohn, and Claudia Springer, who provided secretarial services; and to Minnie R. Hardy and Suann Strickland, who provided the administrative support. To our respective universities, the University of Chicago and Northwestern University (The Center for Urban Affairs and the Epilepsy in the Urban Environment Project), we owe a debt beyond the ordinary institutional acknowledgment. They provided not only the facilities and encouragement but occasional material support for these studies. Above all, we are indebted to individuals too numerous to mention from the various self-help groups represented in our studies. They gave of their time and their interests and permitted the sometimes unfortunate intrusion that must accompany research such as ours. They lent their heads and their hearts to aiding us in developing our studies. For that we are grateful.

October 1979   MORTON A. LIEBERMAN
                                        Chicago, Illinois

                                        LEONARD D. BORMAN
                                        Evanston, Illinois

Contents

Part Four: Evaluating the Impact of Self-Help Groups

The Authors

MORTON A. LIEBERMAN is professor in the Committee on Human Development, Department of Behavioral Sciences, and in the Department of Psychiatry at the University of Chicago. He was awarded the Ph.D. degree in social psychology from the University of Chicago (1958). He has been a faculty member at the University of Chicago since 1957 and a research career investigator (National Institute of Mental Health) since 1963. He was a visiting professor at the University of Wisconsin during 1968–69.

One of his major interests over the past twenty years has been solving the puzzle of what conditions in a group setting lead to change in participants; he has pursued this interest through a variety of studies, with emphasis on comparative analyses of such "people-changing" groups as psychotherapy, encounter, drug abuse, women's consciousness raising, and a variety of self-help groups. His other major interest has been in the psychology of adulthood, where his goal has been to determine the effects of various changes on people in the latter half of their lifespans.

Lieberman is the author of *Psychotherapy Through the Group Process* (with D. S. Whitaker, 1964), *Encounter Groups: First Facts* (with I. Yalom and M. Miles, 1973), and *Last Home for the Aged* (with S. Tobin, 1976). He has also edited special issues of the *Journal of Applied Behavioral Science* focusing on the self-help movement (with L. D. Borman, 1976) and of the *American Journal of Community Psychology* on helping processes (with J. Glidewell, 1978).

LEONARD D. BORMAN is director of the Self-Help Institute and research associate in the Center for Urban Affairs, Northwestern University. He was awarded both the M.A. and Ph.D. degrees in anthropology from the University of Chicago (1952 and 1965, respectively).

Borman was director of Education and Recreation at the Friends Neighborhood Guild in Philadelphia (1954–1956); was chief of the Anthropology Service, Veterans Administration Hospital, in Downey, Illinois (1958–1965); served with the planning division of Chicago's Board of Health (1965–1966); and was program director first of the Stone-Brandel Center and then of the W. Clement and Jessie V. Stone Foundation in Chicago (1966–1974). He has conducted field work with North American Indians, Kalmuk Buddhist Mongols who resettled in the United States, hospitalized mental patients, and many self-help groups.

Borman has published numerous articles, and much of his work has been based on the developing "action anthropology tradition," which combines learning with helping. He edited the proceedings of a self-help exploratory conference (*Explorations in Self-Help and Mutual Aid*, 1975) and a special issue of the *Journal of Applied Behavioral Science* focusing on the self-help movement (with M. A. Lieberman, 1976).

PAUL ANTZE is assistant professor, Division of Social Science, York University, Downsview, Ontario.

ELIZABETH A. BANKOFF is a graduate student in the Committee on Human Development, Department of Behavioral Science, University of Chicago.

GARY R. BOND is assistant professor, Institute of Psychiatry, Northwestern University, and research associate, Committee on Human Development, Department of Behavioral Science, University of Chicago.

STEVEN DAITER is a graduate student in the Committee on Human Development, Department of Behavioral Science, University of Chicago.

HARRIET DAVIDSON is a graduate student in the School of Social Service Administration, University of Chicago.

NANCY GOURASH is a graduate student in the Committee on Human Development, Department of Behavioral Science, University of Chicago.

LEON H. LEVY is professor and chairman, Department of Psychology, University of Maryland, Catonsville.

CARRIE MILES is a graduate student in the Committee on Human Development and the Committee on Social and Organizational Behavior, Department of Behavioral Science, University of Chicago.

JANET REIBSTEIN is a graduate student in the Committee on Human Development, Department of Behavioral Science, University of Chicago.

BARRY SHERMAN is a graduate student in the Committee on Human Development and the Committee on Social and Organizational Behavior, Department of Behavioral Science, University of Chicago.

NANCY SOLOW is a graduate student in the Committee on Human Development, Department of Behavioral Science, University of Chicago.

MARK STEINBERG is a graduate student in the School of Social Service Administration, University of Chicago.

LYNN M. VIDEKA is a graduate student in the School of Social
Service Administration, University of Chicago.

In memory of
Samuel Lieberman (1900–1979)
William Borman (1888–1979)

Self-Help Groups for Coping with Crisis

Origins, Members,
Processes, and Impact

Overview: The Nature of Self-Help Groups

*Morton A. Lieberman &
Leonard D. Borman*

The purpose of this book is to provide a current perspective on self-help or mutual aid groups through the use of empirical research and theory generated from that research. Despite the relatively long history of self-help organizations, disciplined investigation is still in an embryonic stage. Little useful information exists about what factors in society determine the emergence of self-help groups and why people join them. We have only a rudimentary understanding of their relationship to the helping professionals and less knowledge about whom they serve. How do they work? How effective are they for their members? What makes certain self-help groups thrive? What makes others show an early demise? These are the questions that demand answers, the questions that have only recently begun to be examined in a scientific framework. Our goal is to provide some initial findings responsive to these questions. This book builds on our earlier publication, Special Issue, *Journal of Applied Behavioral Science*, 1976, a collection of articles oriented toward theory and policy for the self-help movement.

1

The first task confronting investigators of self-help groups is to define boundaries for inclusion. The range of activities and organizations that have been so labeled is, indeed, diverse. Friendship, community, shared afflictions, status, and political-social goals are all sources of organizational affiliation for self-help groups. Some of these groups are small, grass-roots affiliations unrelated to external structures; others are part of large, well-organized, national organizations. Traditionally, they have been defined as being composed of members who share a common condition, situation, heritage, symptom, or experience. They are largely self-governing and self-regulating. They emphasize self-reliance and generally offer a face-to-face or phone-to-phone fellowship network, available and accessible without charge. They tend to be self-supporting rather than dependent on external funding. The flavor of diversity and the problems that social scientists have experienced in categorizing self-help groups is best expressed by Killilea (1976), whose extensive review of the literature suggests some of the following perspectives for defining self-help organizations. Self-help groups have been seen as support systems; as social movements; as spiritual movements and secular religions; as systems of consumer participation; as alternative, care-giving systems adjunct to professional helping systems; as intentional communities; as subcultural entities that represent a way of life; as supplementary communities; as expressive-social influence groups; and as organizations of the deviant and stigmatized. Examples of actual organizations that fit these perspectives are plentiful. In short, taxonomies are nearly as plentiful as the actual groups.

Our studies of self-help groups reported in this volume certainly do not cover the range of such systems. In selecting organizations for study we sought to focus on groups that effect change in their members, as well as on groups that enable their members to adapt to life changes. The first type of group centers on the need to modify or control members' behaviors, attitudes, and effects. Examples of this type include Alcoholics Anonymous, Parents Anonymous, TOPS, Recovery, Inc., and women's consciousness-raising groups. These organizations provide intensive support systems that uphold the importance of the members' change and behavior. Support is available, not just at regularly scheduled meetings but as often as the members need it. Such groups often specify clear and concrete guidelines through which to obtain desired change. The second type of self-help group of interest to us focuses much more on adaptation and coping through internal behavioral, attitudinal, or affective changes. These groups provide a variety of helping methods to their members, their goal being adaption from major life changes which may range from a medical condition to the catastrophic event of parents' coping with their child's terminal illness.

As noted, the interest of social scientists in a scientific study of self-help groups is much more recent than the beginnings of such organizations. Early social theorists concentrated on kinship and family groups, social classes, or nation states, ignoring social support systems, such as self-help and other common interest groups. Researchers of small groups were preoccupied with those that could be studied in the laboratory or clinic, or with such "captive populations" as those available in college classrooms, prisons, and mental hospitals. To what may we attribute this new interest among ourselves and our colleagues? We believe that a number of issues within the general society as well as the scientific community have led to this renaissance. Policy concern among social scientists and helping professionals is paramount. Increased attention to the real world of service delivery, dissatisfaction with current methods, and a recognition of limited resources have all served to refocus interest on alternative modes of helping. Studies on the limitations of professional resources and their frequent ineffectiveness also play a role, as does awareness that the provision of helping services in our society must not be examined in isolation but as embedded in complex systems.

The increased sensitivity and examination of the role of informal social networks—the kith, kin, and surrounding community in mitigating crises—have become major themes in scientific investigation and theoretical conceptualization. Another factor influencing scientific interest in self-help groups is the potential they offer for genuine discovery of new methods for inducing change. Fundamental theoretical issues concerning how people change have broadened beyond the confines of professionally generated intentional systems for such change. Perhaps this is akin to the parallel of pharmacology where studies of traditional medications outside of medical sciences have led to important discoveries based upon the "wisdom" of nonscientifically generated knowledge. Self-help groups and their development through experience of what helps individuals cope and change can provide new input into a very complex human process.

In setting out to answer the major questions considered in this book—the origins, growth, and development of self-help groups, the kinds of needs they serve, for whom, and under what conditions; the factors that make for effectiveness of self-help groups and, of course, how effective they are—we found ourselves drawing upon a wide diversity of intellectual disciplines. Included were macrosociology, organizational theory, urban anthropology, small-group theory, social network analysis, and psychotherapy. This range of intellectual context is testimony to the diversity and complexity of self-help groups. As we have indicated, they are institutions that cannot be easily fitted into the current pathways of the social sciences. One example of this "problem" can be found in our attempt to understand such groups in terms of the more general issue of helping resources in our society. The numerous investigations that have directed their attention to institutional structures providing solace and aid in times of distress have ordinarily followed two clear pathways: examination of formal legitimized structures (professional systems) and their functions, analysis of their impacts on individuals who utilize them. An increasingly popular area of investigation, however, is concerned with informal social networks and their role in both the mitigation of stress and the avoidance of life's dilemmas. Self-help groups do not fit easily into one or the other; they are not professional systems as usually defined, nor are they analogous to informal social networks. They are organizations usually composed of strangers, having a structure and requiring those wishing to utilize their resources to spend effort and energy much as they would had they sought professional systems. In short, the disciplined examination of self-help groups requires some conceptual adjustments on the part of investigators in their attempt to understand them.

Indeed, we have found that just as those professionals who founded or supported self-help groups needed to go beyond the conventional boundary lines of their disciplines, so too has this applied to research investigators. Such a concern with the limitations of our own disciplines provided a major impetus to our collaboration as social psychologist and anthropologist. As the social psychologist needed to go beyond the model of the laboratory and clinic into the community, so too the anthropologist needed to be informed on issues of survey design, sampling, and outcome measures. Where the psychologist was more comfortable with quantitative knowing, including the rigorous measurement of individuals, the anthropologist was more bent on the humanistic discernment of patterns. We needed to find ways to learn from each other in order to combine quantitative with qualitative knowing.

This book is concerned not only with substance but also with methods. We address what we see as some of the major considerations that must be grappled with by those who desire to investigate self-help groups. Our methods are some of the usual tools of our respective disciplines: ethnography, survey research, the clinical interview, psychotherapy process, and outcome strategies. The unique contributions of and dilemmas faced by each approach will become clearer as one reads the following chapters. Since we are still in the midst of our studies of self-help groups, many findings reported in this volume are preliminary.

One aspect of method that is worth more than a passing nod in this introductory chapter concerns the issue of collaboration with self-help organizations. Much of analytic social science requires some degree of control or influence over the phenomenon being studied. Such control is of particular concern when considering questions of individual differences, whether differences with regard to the fact of participation in self-help groups, the modes through which such participation leads to effectiveness, or the question of effectiveness itself. Problems of analytic statistics come to the fore when we attempt to answer such questions using quantitative data. The composition of the population relevant for sampling is a major unknown facing the self-help investigator. Beyond such method problems, however, lies the issue of the appropriate and realistic affiliations that an investigator of self-help groups needs and desires to establish with the organizations studied. The potential for investigator effects is maximized in the study of self-help groups, but realistic collaborative arrangements are required to gain access and maintain active involvement with them. We believe we have gained an unusual degree of meaningful collaboration with the groups studied. Since self-help groups are not conventional forms of helping developed by professionals under the auspices of human service delivery agencies, access to groups may present some special problems. In the Special Issue of the *Journal of Applied Behavioral Science* (1976), we suggested that "models of meaningful collaboration can be developed and executed, but they will involve the researcher in activities that do not entirely fit with an archetypical view of what research is and how one conducts it" (p. 461). Our experience since that time, borne out in many of the reports in this volume, indicates that mutual collaboration between researcher and self-help group has been productive for both. Two of the groups reported on here at some length took the initiative in approaching the researchers. Mended Hearts, in seeking to understand the needs and problems of its growing membership, contacted one of us (Leonard Borman) early in 1976 for some help in the construction and implementation of a questionnaire. We were also asked to meet with their developing chapter in the Chicago area. In a similiar way, Compassionate Friends approached us in 1977. They wanted to be listed in any roster of self-help groups that we were compiling so that they could reach more bereaved parents. The local Chicago area group also requested specific help concerning organizational development, fund raising, publicity, and its efforts to host the first national convention. Such requests have been echoed by other groups as well. Parents Anonymous and GROW have contacted us about similar issues of organization and chapter development, recruitment, and fund raising.

There have been times in the history of our project when, as investigators, we raised concerns about our own level of involvement with the self-help groups. To what extent was it appropriate, given our goal and our perspective as investigators, to influence what we were studying? The conflict between minimizing investigator effects and the normal human response to individuals in deep distress required considerable balancing. The loss of appropriate perspectives was a frequent topic of discussion at our team meetings. Our basic contract was to provide feedback and to invite the self-help groups' influence on the instruments we used to assess membership and the effectiveness of their settings. At times, such feedback had major impact on the workings of the self-help group system. The clearest example was a radical change in methods of recruitment and operation used by some of the consciousness-raising groups we examined. Our results had indicated to the organizers of such groups that goals of the women's movement were clearly not being met by their groups.

Our identification and involvement in the organizations we were studying soon spilled across boundaries we had set for ourselves. This may have been caused in part by an overlapping or differentiation of roles in our research team. One of us (Leonard Borman) established a center or institute that would serve as a clearinghouse of information about self-help groups, including the provision of some technical assistance. It may be too early in our experience with the studies to evaluate the impact of such forms of collaboration on the nature of the research itself. We do know that such deep involvement provided us with an intimate portrait of the issues and problems faced by self-help groups. We became closely acquainted with their problems of leadership, chapter formation and development, building of a national organization, articulation with professionals and voluntary agencies, recruitment, funding, and so forth.

Clearly, researchers who set out to study self-help groups must recognize that a greater degree of involvement may be required than they are accustomed to. If the cost of "collaboration" is measured primarily in terms of time and resources, then it is perhaps a small price to pay for the strengthening of such collaborative bonds and the opportunity for an insider's view of these groups. If the cost is reflected in ways that would jeopardize our understanding of self-help groups or cause the loss of an important perspective, then the cost may be too high and future researchers should be alerted to the dilemma.

Nonetheless, we should identify one important outcome that resulted from our close collaboration with self-help groups. Often researchers, as well as those who support research endeavors, are ineffective in providing for the dissemination and utilization of their findings, which are frequently relegated to the back shelves of resource libraries. Yet we have found that self-help groups are eager to receive feedback reports; they frequently invited us to address their conventions and their boards of directors and to meet with their chapters. In addition, several self-help systems we studied chose to alter their practice and/or programs based on the research. Such interest and sensitivity to our findings can only lead to our becoming more responsible and perceptive researchers.

Plan of This Book

The book is divided into four parts. Part One—How Groups Are Started and Structured—looks at self-help groups from an organizational perspective. Part Two—Who Participates in Self-Help Groups—examines the participants in self-help groups: Why do they come, what are their goals, and what are the pathways through which they reach these groups? Part Three—How Self-Help Groups Work—addresses the issue of what helps participants in self-help groups:What characteristics effect change and provide relief to their participants? Part Four —Evaluating the Impact of Self-Help Groups—deals with the problem of outcomes: What is the impact on the participants?

Part One: How Groups Are Started and Structured. This section examines a variety of self-help groups to determine how such groups form and develop. Alternative hypotheses considered are: forces in society that may have been instrumental in the development of such organizations; inadequacy of services provided by traditional helping resources in society; new forms that provide service in alternative modes. This section also addresses the factors that facilitate the spread of such movements and examines these developments historically. Case histories of several self-help organizations are presented: Mended Hearts, a medical self-help group for individuals who have had open-heart surgery; women's consciousness-raising groups; Compassionate Friends, a self-help group for parents who have lost children; and Naim, a self-help group for the widowed. Chapter One places self-help groups in the context of voluntary associations and examines self-help as a specific form of voluntary association. It also provides a historical context for examining the current growth and development of a variety of self-help organizations with a focus on the nature of professional involvement. Chapter Two examines the history and current functioning of Mended Hearts and looks at the factors that enabled it to grow into a highly organized national movement. Chapter Three reviews the twenty-year history of Naim, with particular emphasis on the transformation of this organization from a support group directed towards bereaved widows and widowers to a social linkage system. Chapter Four presents a case history of the development of Compassionate Friends in the United States, showing how the organization grew, in a relatively brief period of time, from several unrelated local chapters into a structured national organization. Chapter Five then examines the evolution of women's consciousness-raising groups with an eye to the transformation of group purpose, as in the case of Naim. The evolution of consciousness raising shows the relatively rapid transformation of purpose, and the responses by the women's movement to such changes. In all four of the groups studied, changes in function and structure are examined as well as the role of national or regional organizations in the growth and development of self-help groups. Of particular importance in each study of group development is an examination of the role of the mass media, the mechanisms developed by each of these systems for including new members, and the sources of legitimization for their acceptance in society.

Part Two: Who Participates in Self-Help Groups. This section asks why people enter self-help groups and examines the procedures through which the individuals locate and are attracted to and maintained in such organizations. Chapter Six provides a comparative framework for examining self-help groups in a context of help utilization in our society—kith and kin as well as professional helpers. Self-help groups and other helping resources are compared by means of an ongoing transition study (by Morton Lieberman) in which the use of social networks and professional helping resources by a large probability sample of adults was examined in relation to a variety of crises, transitions, and role problems. Various self-help organizations are also compared with two professional helping systems. Chapters Seven through Nine examine specific self-help systems by studying the individuals who use them. Chapter Seven provides findings from a large-scale survey of 1,700 women who were participants in consciousness-raising groups. Chapter Eight examines the complex process by which members with medical afflictions are recruited and maintained in medical self-help groups. Issues of access and legitimization and a variety of motivational hypotheses are explored through an analysis of 779 heart surgery patients. Chapter Nine looks at informal support networks, a heretofore ignored area in understanding why people join self-help groups. A pilot study of participants and matched controls is used to examine the hypothesis that failures in social network relationships during bereavement and subsequent periods of widowhood are critical to understanding motivations for joining self-help groups.

Part Three: How Self-Help Groups Work. This sections concerns itself with the characteristics of self-help groups that provide relief and change. In short, what helps in self-help groups? The four chapters in this section collectively provide two alternative, theoretical perspectives. One, stemming from a social-psychological position, examines certain events or experiences that occur within such settings as are assumed to be associated with positive change. The other position examines the role of ideology as a cognitive antidote specifically addressed to particular afflictions, which is seen as the major source of help in self-help groups. Chapter Ten examines the social-psychological perspective on change by comparing a variety of self-help and professional helping systems, using participants' perceptions of what events or experiences were helpful to them. Chapter Eleven provides a comparative analysis of a variety of self-help groups. Chapter Twelve develops a theory on the role of ideology of self-help groups and their specific relationship to particular afflictions by comparing three self-help groups directed toward behavioral change: Alcoholics Anonymous, Recovery, Inc., and Synanon. Chapter Thirteen utilizes the ideological theoretical perspective and applies it to Compassionate Friends, a major self-help group that deals with the crisis of losing a child rather than with behavioral reorganization.

Part Four: Evaluating the Impact of Self-Help Groups. Chapter Fourteen addresses three basic questions: What to measure? When to measure? And whom to measure? A number of alternative solutions to dilemmas facing self-help researchers are examined and discussed. Chapters Fifteen through Seventeen demonstrate some of the specific strategies outlined in Chapter Fourteen. Chapter Fifteen presents a study of consciousness-raising groups in a classic "pre-post design" and illustrates the impact of such groups on women with particular regard to the specificity of change. It also shows the utility of a normative comparison group when "ordinary control groups are unavailable." Chapter Sixteen, using large-scale survey data, examines the impact of Mended Hearts on its members. It illustrates both the strengths and pitfalls of a one-time measurement strategy in assessing self-help impact. This chapter also illustrates a major problem confronting researchers in their efforts to understand the outcome of participation in self-help groups. The fact that many of the "afflictions" forming the membership basis for self-help groups show a natural history of change—much more so than would be expected in the similar setting for neurotic patients assessed in classical psychotherapy research—dominates the findings. Chapter Seventeen introduces a new group to the reader, SAGE, a modified self-help group for the elderly. This particular program offers a unique opportunity for utilizing classical psychotherapy research models on self-help groups: a delayed control condition, random assignment, and a pre-post design. This chapter demonstrates the relative strength of such designs, yet points out that this particular program offers a unique research opportunity that cannot, at this point, be replicated in other self-help systems. The final chapter reexamines the common perceptions of self-help groups in light of our findings and considers their policy implications.

CHAPTER 1

Characteristics of Development and Growth

Leonard D. Borman

Typological Considerations

Any effort to deal with the genesis of self-help groups and their subsequent development, diffusion, or demise must address the issue of typologies. How shall we classify self-help groups? A review of the various efforts at classifying and interpreting self-help groups, such as that presented by Killilea (1976), resembles the pattern found when relatives or friends meet one's offspring for the first time. They seem to note a striking resemblance to the side of the family they know best. Or the reverse—they may see no resemblances at all.

So has it been with scholars who have written about self-help groups. They have usually noticed the resemblance of these groups to the forms of organizations or activities with which they are most familiar. And just as children are often viewed in terms of what they will be like when they grow up, so too are self-support groups. Killilea has characterized most of these per-

spectives, ranging from natural support systems and social movements to kinds of subcultures, organizations of deviants, and
forms of psychotherapy. The variety of groups is matched only
by the great variation in interpretations and characteristics, all
of which complicate the attempt to understand their genesis
and development. At the same time, this complexity offers
some clues to the nature of self-help phenomena.

Many of the typologies of contemporary groups have
been constructed from a helping, healing, and therapeutic perspective. Gussow and Tracy (1976), for example, have focused
on the nature of the problem or affliction and have identified
self-help groups in fifteen of the seventeen World Health Organization disease categories. Katz and Bender (1976a, 1976b) have
classified groups according to their primary purposes: self-
development, social advocacy, creation of alternative patterns
for living, personal protection, and so forth. Levy (1976) has
focused on finer nuances of purpose, as in groups formed around
behavioral control that are distinct from those focused on coping with stress (see Chapter Eleven).

This process of inquiry on the part of scholars and professionals tells us something special about the nature of these
self-help groups. The fact that they are of considerable and
growing interest to a variety of professionals drawn from diverse
disciplines casts these groups in a different light from other
forms of social organization that they closely resemble—for they
represent uncommon forms of helping distressed populations.

What are these forms? How shall we array self-help groups
as modes of social organization? It is clear from the growing
literature that has developed, including information on the
groups reported in this volume, that self-help groups, at least in
their early stages, belong to the class of common interest groups
or voluntary associations. In an earlier general description that
needs to be qualified, I characterized self-help groups in this
way:

> Their membership consists of those who share
> a common condition, situation, heritage, symptom,
> or experience. They are largely self-governing and

self-regulating, emphasizing peer solidarity rather
than hierarchical governance. As such, they prefer
controls built upon consensus rather than coercion.
They tend to disregard in their own organization
the usual institutional distinctions between consumers, professionals, and Boards of Directors,
combining and exchanging such functions among
each other. They advocate self-reliance and require
equally intense commitment and responsibility to
other members, actual or potential. They often
provide an identifiable code of precepts, beliefs,
and practices that includes rules for conducting
group meetings, entrance requirements for new
members, and techniques for dealing with "back-
sliders." They minimize referrals to professionals
or agencies since, in most cases, no appropriate
help exists. Where it does, they tend to cooperate
with professionals. They generally offer a face-to-
face, or phone-to-phone fellowship network usually available and accessible without charge. Groups
tend to be self-supporting, occur mostly outside
the aegis of institutions or agencies, and thrive
largely on donations from members and friends
rather than government or foundation grants or
fees from the public [Borman, 1975, p. vi].

It becomes necessary, first of all, to distinguish this class
of phenomena, seen as common interst groups or voluntary associations, from two other senses in which self-help is commonly used. One sense is in the notion of individual self-help or self-
reliance. Most book stores that devote shelves to self-help focus
on this dimension. Here is the classic notion of individualism in
American society, including stories and cases of famous self-
made men who worked their way up to the heights of success
through the principles of individual self-reliance. The works of
Dale Carnegie (1936), W. Clement Stone (1962), and Napoleon
Hill (1972) epitomize this literature. Self-help seen solely as
self-reliance also includes the "do-it-yourself schemes" that focus on how individuals can rely on their own resources, whether
it be in assertiveness training or repairing plumbing. In many re-

spects, this conception of self-help is the antithesis of self-help seen in common interest groups, where members become means to the ends of one another. This interdependence is ignored among these writers, who emphasize instead how you are your own means to your own ends. There may be some connection with this individual notion of self-help seen as self-reliance and self-help groups. Many groups, for example, stress the use of one's own resources, character, and hard work. But it is beyond our efforts in this chapter to elucidate these connections.

The second sense in which self-help is commonly used in the literature is connected to the notion that mutual aid and cooperation is a quality underlying social and community life. This dimension has been discussed by Katz and Bender (1976b), citing the earlier work of Kroptkin (1914) who emphasized the role of mutual aid and protection in the development of all animal species, including mankind. Kroptkin was responding to the Darwinian notion that species survive through a competitive and ruthless struggle for existence. He argued that the surviving forms of life, including mankind, owed their success primarily to mutual aid and social cooperation, which were key elements in the formation and continuity of the family, the tribe, the village, and eventually the state. This mutual aid dimension, which characterizes many small, primary groups, has been contrasted to individual self-centeredness as well as to the large, impersonal hierarchical systems that have developed as bureaucratic forms that can be highly coercive. Yet these large systems, or what MacIver (1931) has called "great associations", are derived from small, face-to-face groups in which, for many, common interest and mutual aid were central. What happens to such small groups over the course of time? How do they begin to change their size, form, and function? Many small families or tribal groups that maintain historical continuity over several generations often project a splintering or factionalism with mutual hostility frequently replacing mutual aid between the factions (see Borman, 1979b). These are some of the issues that need to be understood more fully as we analyze development and growth. Although mutual aid is central to self-help groups, it is still necessary to understand how this reciprocal form of assistance arises as it does with particular groups and how to account for the changes that occur over time. As self-help groups develop, this central ability of mutual aid and interdependence is often minimized as the group becomes a more formal organization.

Common Interest Groups and Voluntary Associations

Viewing self-help groups as common interest groups or voluntary associations may help us to understand some of these issues in the light of comparative social organization. Historically, these forms seem to have an ancient history. Anderson's (1971) review finds associations developing minimally in the Mesolithic (the hunting, gathering period), elaborating and becoming widespread during the Neolithic (agricultural villages), and reaching a crest of development in the modern urban-industrial period. He employs a broad definition for associations, seen as formally constituted volunteer groups based on shared ties and common interests rather than on kinship or coresidence. In these earlier historical periods, the primary forms of social organization revolved around kinship and territorial groupings. Yet both our historical and cross-cultural knowledge indicates that a variety of kinds of common interest groups were formed even in the small, isolated societies. Lowie's (1947) early review of associations cross-culturally found that many were based on age and matrimonial status, so that bachelors, those who were married, and those who were widowed or elderly were arrayed in distinct forms of social clubs or secret societies that crisscrossed the bonds of family, clan, and village. Each shared the common characteristics in excluding nonmembers. Smith and Freedman (1972) note that the empirical investigations conducted by anthropologists following World War II questioned the basic assumptions of earlier sociologists such as Louis Wirth, who saw the development of voluntary associations as concomitants of modern life. They arise, according to this view, when the primary bonds of kinship, neighborhood, family, and religion are weakened. The anthropological studies seem to indicate that although this may account for the development of some modern-day associations, the essential forms they take can be identified very early and in most societies of the world, ruling out any single cause. Associations formed and thrived even when the primary support systems were quite strong.

Common interest associations not only appear at most points in the history of human society but are also found both at times of rapid change in complex societies and in slowly developing pre-industrial nations, as in Rome and medieval Europe (Kerri, 1976). Moreover, associations are found among the tribes of the American plains, Oceania, parts of Africa, and along the Pacific coast of native North America (Anderson, 1971).

As a principle of social grouping, associations seem to have disparate functions. Banton (1968, p. 358) suggests that a general pattern can be discerned: "Among relatively small and technologically primitive groups, associations tend to be organized for recreation and the expression of distinctions of rank; in larger tribal societies they may exercise important governmental functions, and with an increasing division of labor they tend to be founded for the pursuit or defense of economic interests." In describing age sets in Africa, Bohannan (1963) indicates the difficulty in generalizing on their functions everywhere. Some are named and are usually involved in initiation ceremonies. They may mark the transition of their members through particular life stages. When members are young, age sets play an important educational, training, and socializing function. They may constitute a military organization or take on political functions, as a center for decision making and power. They may emerge as an arm of the local government. When its members consist of elders who have retired, the association may take on a religious function. Some are formed as work or labor groups and may become the basis for a residential grouping. Many sponsor feasts and entertainment and are marked by various degrees of formal organization. Little (1949) concludes that associations in Africa that take the form of secret societies provide the primary sanctions on behavior in nearly every sphere of community life.

This brief review of associations would suggest that modern-day self-help groups, viewed in this class of phenomena, have a long history as forms of groupings in practically every known society. They do not represent a unique development in our own. They often exist side by side with other forms of organization, or they may indeed assume functions of an eroded family or displaced tribe. Casting self-help groups in this larger comparative, even puzzling, perspective may help us examine dimensions of contemporary groups that currently we only dimly perceive.

One insight that emerges in this view of associations is their frequently transitory nature. Whereas kinship and territorial groups exhibit a more or less persistent and enduring structure, having continuity over time in spite of changes in membership and leadership, associations are more ephemeral. This may also account for their relative neglect in the study of social organizations, since most students in this field have been preoccupied with groups that have more predictable social structures. Many associations, moreover, have been concerned with relatively marginal, nonutilitarian aspects of society, which may also account for their neglect by social scientists. But if one's interest is in the dynamic aspects of societies, the processes involved in their changing forms and functions, associations take on a greater importance.

Anderson (1971) supports this view and suggests that the key role of such associations is best understood in the part they play in social and cultural change, and indeed in the evolution of society. This would apply as well to special populations or subsystems in a complex society. Simmel noted that associations, especially secret societies, emerge everywhere as a suitable social form for ideas in their infancy (Wolff, 1950). MacIver (1931, p. 201) elaborated more fully when he noted that associations "have a flexibility, an initiative, a capacity for experiment, a liberation from the heavier responsibilities of taking risks which the state rarely, if ever, possesses. They can foster the nascent interests of the groups, and encourage enterprise, social and economic, at the growing points of a society."

The literature on voluntary organizations is more voluminous for those groups concerned with the growing or changing aspects of governmental, educational, religious, and economic

functions than for those formed around health or related conditions. MacIver (1931, p. 193) articulates the positions taken
by other social theorists, that none of the "great associations,"
such as the state, economic corporations, or religious institutions, is ever all-sufficing; each is subjected to forces that cause
conflict, tensions, and strain. This would apply as well to primary groups mentioned earlier. Small groups, then, that we
identify as common interest or voluntary associations, form continually. In the economic sphere, they may be consumer groups
or partnerships or new budding corporations concerned with
issues of livelihood, including the early craft guilds and labor
unions. In the governmental arena, they may be new groups
concerned with legislative, even revolutionary actions, governmental services, or areas of justice. In the religious domain, they
may be formations of new sects, representing distinct interpretations of traditions, or splinter groups formed around new religious symbols or charismatic leaders. Indeed, Hunt (1966) suggests that the key role of voluntary associations in history can
be gleaned from an interpretation of the Bible as a narrative on
the fate of associations. God is seen as "active in history, choosing his people, forming the community, liberating it from bond-
age, holding it under judgment, and promising it fulfillment" (p.
362). Smith's (1966) analysis of formal voluntary organizations
(which he contrasts to formal work organizations), notes what
de Tocqueville discovered in the nineteenth century—that their
numbers in our society fill volumes. He also notes that such voluntary associations provide an important mode of organization
for advances in religion, science, sociability, recreation, and art.
These are the vanguard, the forerunner, and the gadfly in almost
every field of endeavor.

It should not be surprising, then, that similar forms of
organizations should develop around self-help groups in the
health and medical arena. As this volume indicates, many professionals have taken a special interest in these groups (see Borman, 1976b). Health associations—whether they be the more
formal hospitals, mental health clinics, or professional services
or the more informal social groupings—are also not all-sufficing.
It is more surprising that self-help health and related common
interest groups have not formed earlier and in larger numbers.

From this vantage point, a perspective emerges that I would like to pursue in considering genesis and development of contemporary self-help groups. Since these groups have emerged relatively recently, information about their origins, early development, and especially about their key founders or supporters is readily available. In viewing a number of groups, some discussed in this volume as well as others, I have found it instructive, moreover, to consider their formation in relation to the larger, great associations that are concerned with the same afflictions or ailments. Specifically, I have identified one or more key professionals who have played an essential role in the development of self-help groups and shall point out a number of ways in which these professionals, often collaborating closely with those afflicted or bearing the condition, have moved beyond the conventional practices of their disciplines. Then I shall consider some developmental aspects of these groups, looking at the diverse transitional forms many of them have taken in the course of their growth, including such dimensions as changes in size, structure, membership, and leadership. This will lead, finally, to a consideration of some issues concerning their adaptive functions in society and the forms they take for continuity and further development.

Characteristics of Founders and Supporters

Table 1 identifies ten groups, their focal concerns, and their founders and early supporters drawn from the great (formal) health, social service, or religiously oriented associations or disciplines. Just as with groups formed in the economic or political sphere, support and encouragment are often derived from critical or disenchanted members of these larger associations. In the case of self-help health groups, one can often find, either in the forefront or behind the scenes, helpful health, social service, or religious professionals who see the limits of their disciplines' conventional domain. In the groups identified in Table 1, all have benefited from support and encouragement of such professionals. With six of the groups, moreover, a professional played a key role in founding the organization or in giving it a major early boost (Recovery, Integrity Groups, GROW, Com-

Table 1. Characteristics of Founders and Supporters

Group	Year Formed	Founders		Supporters
		Laymen	Professionals	
Alcoholics Anonymous	1935	Bill Wilson	Robert Smith, M.D.	William Silkworth, M.D. Harry Tiebout, M.D. (psychiatry) Carl Jung, M.D. (psychiatry)
Recovery, Inc.	1937		Abraham Low, M.D. (psychiatry)	
Integrity Groups	1945		O. Hobart Mowrer, Ph.D. (psychology) Anthony Vattano, Ph.D. (social work)	
Mended Hearts	1951	Doris Silliman	Dwight Harken, M.D. (cardiology)	
NAIM	1956	William & Jean Delaney		Msgr. John Egan (clergy) Father Timothy Sullivan (clergy)

	Year		
GROW	1957		Father Con Keogh (clergy) Albert Lacey, Ph.D. (law)
Synanon	1958	Chuck Dederich	Daniel Casriel, M.D. (psychiatry) Lewis Yablonsky, Ph.D. (sociology)
Compassionate Friends	1969	Arnold & Paula Shamres (U.S., 1972)	The Rev. Simon Stephens (clergy) Elizabeth Kübler-Ross, M.D. (psychiatry)
Parents Anonymous	1971	Jolly K.	Leonard Lieber (social work)
Epilepsy Self-Help	1975		Lawrence Schlesinger, Ph.D. (social psychology) Doris Haar (nursing)

passionate Friends, Parents Anonymous, and Epilepsy Self-Help). With the four others, professionals played an instrumental role at various stages of the organization's development.

One dimension that characterizes all of these founders or supporters of self-help groups is that they did not adhere rigidly to the conventional theories or practices of their disciplines. I have identified at least nine ways in which some of these professionals have gone beyond such conventional restraints, leading them to found or support specific self-help groups. These ways may not be mutually exclusive but they at least serve to highlight some expressed disenchantment or limitation that helped provide the rationale and impetus for the involvement of these professionals with a particular self-help group.

Beyond Conventional Theories. First of all, some professionals clearly took issue with theories in their field. Both Abraham Low and O. Hobart Mowrer were avowedly disenchanted with prevailing theories of psychotherapy, especially psychoanalysis. For Low, the fundamental contrast between theory underlying psychoanalysis and his own development of Recovery was his recognition that "adult life is not driven by instincts but guided by will" (Low, 1950, p. 12; see Chapter Twelve in this volume). Mowrer, whose critiques of psychotherapy are rather extensive (1961, 1964, 1978b), writes: "Integrity Groups evolved from a reconceptualization of the causes and treatment of so-called 'neuroses.' The hypotheses of Freud and of Wolpe, relating such disorders of personality, respectively, to an overstrict conscience or false fear, are replaced by an alternative view. . . . We have found that a remedy for such persons is to enter a group of six to ten persons similarly struggling to *recover their integrity and enhance their sense of identity* (sometimes called 'ego strength')" (Mowrer and Vattano, 1976, pp. 419–420; italics in original). Both Harry Tiebout and Carl Jung, psychiatrists who treated original founders or members of Alcoholics Anonymous, found theoretical justification for the principles being developed by AA. Tiebout (1944) published an early paper on AA's therapeutic mechanisms (see also, Holton, in press) and was regarded by cofounder Bill Wilson as "AA's first friend in the profession of psychiatry" (Alcoholics Anonymous, 1957, p. 235). He also served for fifteen years on AA's governing conference. In discussing contemporary psychiatry, Tiebout (in Alcoholics Anonymous, 1957, p. 318) noted: "It is. presumed that, as the blocking emotions are uncovered and freed through analysis, positive, synthetic ones will appear instead. It is just as logical, though, to change emotions and then, after the change has been brought about, to bring the mind and intellect into play to anchor the new set of emotions into the structure of the personality. In a sense, this is what occurs in Alcoholics Anonymous; religion plays upon the narcissism and neutralizes it to produce a feeling of synthesis." Jung (1933), in contrast to Freud and Adler, also recognized the therapeutic value of a religious experience, which became a key tenet in AA. Bill Wilson (1968, p. 19) writes in a letter to Jung: "As you will now clearly see, this astonishing chain of events actually started long ago in your consulting room, and it was directly founded upon your own humility and deep perception."

Psychoanalysis was not the only psychiatric approach criticized by some of these professionals, as can be seen in this statement on shock treatment by Low (1943a, p. 4): "It is common practice in the field of medicine to disqualify a therapeutic measure if extensive tests have demonstrated conclusively that the dangers inherent in its use are not generously overbalanced by beneficial results. On the strength of this generally accepted rule the shock treatments ought to be relegated by now to the rubbish heap of discarded procedures."

Broader Definition of Afflictions. The second way, related closely to theory, in which many of these professionals were not bound by their disciplines was in their tendency to alter the usual specifications of a condition or affliction. The earlier quote from Mowrer and Vattano (1976) would apply here. Dr. William Silkworth, one of the physicians who treated Bill Wilson a year before AA was founded, did not accept the prevailing view of other physicians and of the American Medical Association in the thirties that alcoholism was due to a character defect, a moral weakness, and was not to be regarded as a medical problem (Thomsen, 1975, p. 194). "Silky," as he was known to thousand of alcoholics whom he treated, saw the

problems of alcoholics as due to a combination of mental ob-
session and physical allergy. The founders of AA adopted Silkworth's view among the basic tenets of the organization (Alcoholics Anonymous, 1957). Simon Stephens (1972), founder of
Compassionate Friends, attacked the "conspiracy of silence"
about death that pervaded conventional institutions, the professional community, and the community at large, depriving the
bereaved of an opportunity to be heard. In his early Recovery
groups, Low (1938, p. 4) discovered that the essential definitions of mental illness that needed to be addressed were the dis-
graceful, stigmatizing views held by the community: "The organization which we have formed has precisely this purpose: to
eliminate the prejudice and superstition of the community
against mental disease."

Expansion of Skills and Techniques. A third dimension
characteristic of these professionals was their effort to recognize
a broader repertoire of skills and techniques than was conven-
tionally utilized in their fields (Borman, 1979a). As supporters
of Synanon, Casriel (1963) and Yablonsky (1965) saw the value
of "attack therapy" (among other innovations) as it was employed in the game developed by Dederich, the founder of Synanon (see Chapter Twelve). Leonard Lieber, cofounder of Parents Anonymous, was convinced that Jolly K. could help other
abusive parents and encouraged her to advertise in a local newspaper (a most unconventional approach in social work) as
a means of contacting others suffering as she was. In a paper
presented at the first biennial conference of the Society for
Clinical Social Work, Lieber (1971, p. 5) described their early
efforts in this way: "Jolly, as she is now widely known, foresaw
a voluntary coming together of abusers, a sort of 'mothers
anonymous' group where venting of inner and outer horrors
could be shared together under the watchful eye of an agency
that directly or indirectly ran the show. We did not knowingly
use an already established treatment model with which to form-
ulate ideas. Rather, our respective backgrounds converged on
a mutual goal—to reach the abuser and stop, or reduce, child
abuse." In describing the importance of the group and community for GROW, Father Keogh (1978b, p. 21) points out: "Actual

experience of rehabilitation work among mental sufferers, alcoholics, drug addicts, and so on, reveals that spiritual conversion, however vital in itself and sincere in the particular individual, is not enough. Commonly, the rehabilitee who has reached only an unstable equilibrium has to remain close within the sheltering environment of his fellow believers who keep him reminded, prompted, and almost controlled from the outside. If he is to get a lasting recovery, one that is viable in the world at large, he has to get the strong consolidation of insights, habits, and health relationships that have grown out of natural experience and reason." Tiebout (in Alcoholics Anonymous, 1957, p. 309) identified in AA what has come to be known as the "helper-therapy principle" (Riessman, 1965) when he noted: "Helping others is a two-way situation since it not only assists the beginner in his first efforts but also aids the helper, who derives from his efforts something which is essential for his continued sobriety." Silkworth (in Alcoholics Anonymous, 1957, p. 302) described this approach even earlier when AA was in its infancy with only 100 members: "The beginning and subsequent development of a new approach to the problem of permanent recovery for the chronic alcoholic has already produced remarkable results and promises much for the future. . . . The central idea is that of a fellowship of ex-alcoholic men and women banded together for mutual help. Each member feels duty bound to assist alcoholic newcomers to get up on their feet. These in turn work with still others, in an endless chain. Hence there is a large growth possibility." Mowrer (1975) viewed AA's central recognition of the fellowship as stemming from the early Jewish and Christian communes where exomologesis was practiced, involving complete openness about one's life in the presence of a small, meaningful group or congregation. This was adopted as a basic technique in the development of Integrity Groups.

Focus on Neglected Stages of Conditions. A fourth dimension that characterizes most of these professionals is their concern with a stage of the affliction or condition normally overlooked by their professional colleagues. The problems of rehabilitation and after-care, following treatment for acute conditions, were a major focus of these professionals and many of the self-help groups with which they were identified. Low was concerned, as was Keogh, with what could be done to help mental patients after formal treatment. Low focused primarily on family and community receptivity to discharged mental patients. This led him to develop a finely honed set of procedures, including a specialized language, to control the consequences of tempers in everyday life (Low, 1943b). Silkworth and Tiebout were more than usually concerned with the problem of relapses in the treatment of alcoholics (Holton, in press). Keogh (1975), influenced by AA, was originally concerned with the quality of after-care for patients leaving mental hospitals in Australia but eventually began to shift his focus to prevention as well. Elizabeth Kübler-Ross (1969) was one of the early psychiatrists to focus on terminal illness, including the psychological problems faced by surviving relatives. She wrote the introduction to Stephens' (1972) book and was invited by Compassionate Friends to be the keynoter at their first convention (see Chapter Four).

   Concern for Neglected Populations. A fifth dimension is concern for a population normally neglected by conventional service delivery, or even by religious systems. Lieber (1971, p. 3) writes: "I was involved with hundreds of young victims whose destiny was always cloudy, but more often than not, they were legally removed from their parents' custody because the home situation was found unfit for a variety of reasons. Some form of psychiatric treatment, even if it was a healthier milieu in foster care, was usually available to the children. But even if strongly advised by the authorities, treatment for the parent has been consistently hard to come by." What was true of abusive parents was also true of drug addicts, alcoholics, formerly hospitalized mental patients, widows, and persons coping with the personal and social consequences of epilepsy. One might note here that many of the other self-help groups that have been formed consist of people suffering from certain conditions or afflictions for which there is little effective conventional help, among them ex-offenders, schizophrenics, stutterers, and parents whose children suffer from a variety of conditions from terminal illness to Down's syndrome. (See Evans, 1979, for the most extensive roster of self-help groups to date.)

Altered Professional Roles. A sixth dimension in which the professionals viewed here diverge from the conventional is in their view of the role of the professional. (For a further discussion of this topic, see Borman 1966, 1978.) In most cases, it moves from a principal and solo role to a collaborative one. Even in the case of Dr. Low, whose books and recorded tapes continue to be used in Recovery meetings throughout the world, leadership of the organization is vested in the volunteer leaders and members, and professionals are excluded from group leadership positions. In many groups, the professionals may indeed be very active, giving advice, becoming spokesmen and interpreters for their groups or for the self-help movement—but their involvement is quite different from that of their conventional colleagues. In some cases, as with Schlesinger, the professionals played an important part in the initial launching of the movement and then withdrew. In a similar way, Stephens wrote the key book and launched the organization that began Compassionate Friends around the world and then moved into a peripheral, supportive position, including presentations in the public media. Stephens (1972) recommends that professionals stay in the background: "Originally when we started the self-help groups, we invited a psychiatrist who felt that before the beginning of each group he should talk, and he talked for about a half hour about psychoanalysis. This is no good. The parents feel that the only person who can help them is somebody who has watched their own child die, who has buried their own child, and who has come through it. The psychiatrist had to take a back seat and the same with the clergy. In all our groups we do our very best to match all the parents up . . . parents of children who die in road accidents could only best be helped by parents who had been through that situation." Monsignor Egan took an unconventional position and approved the movement to aid the widowed that Naim launched in the Chicago area. He gave it his blessing, appointed a spiritual advisor, and made referrals to the developing organization (see Chapter Three).

New Group Auspices. A seventh way in which these professionals have gone beyond the conventional boundaries of their disciplines is in the development of new auspices under which these groups can form. Not bound by the hospital, clinic, or church, they have formed in homes, libraries, or any settings that would allow small groups to gather. Integrity groups were among the few formed as part of an interdisciplinary practicum for graduate students in social work, psychology, and other human service departments at the University of Illinois, Urbana-Champaign. There was little concern with issues of legal liability, professional prerogatives, or accountability and reporting requirements. Most groups eventually formed into nonprofit corporations for tax purposes.

Some of the cautions and concerns of conventional auspices are revealed in this excerpt from the early *Guidelines* (1977, p. 3) of Compassionate Friends: "After the initial organizational meetings which may take place in a home, and after the membership becomes too large for a home get-together, a meeting place needs to be found . . . neutral and nonoffending. It would certainly not be appropriate to meet in a hospital conference room, or in a medical facility, or a funeral director's building. Such places would regenerate bad memories. Community centers are better, as are meeting rooms in banks, or savings-and-loan associations, or the Y. Meetings in church facilities are satisfactory provided it is stressed that the Society is nondenominational and not related to the particular creed of the meeting place."

Recruitment Innovations. An eighth dimension is seen in the matter of recruitment. Most frequently, members were obtained through word of mouth or through media publicity. Naim recruited its early new members through personal contact by the founders and initiators. Parents Anonymous used newspaper ads. Compassionate Friends contacted mortuaries and coroner's offices and eventually was inundated with inquiries as a result of publicity in the media. The media also provided the major boost in AA membership in its early years. The first members of some epilepsy groups were literally obtained through door-to-door canvasses. There were indeed variations, and many of the recruitment procedures for some of these groups changed over time. However, with the exception of Mended Hearts, which worked closely with cardiologists and nurses, there was little reliance on conventional referral and screening procedures by professionals.

Fees Minimized. Finally, but significantly, these professionals and the groups they formed and supported were rarely concerned with fees. Menninger (1975) suggests that the issues concerning compensation may make for the essential differences between self-help and professional help. Mowrer (1975, p. 475), however, notes the large number of salaried mental health professionals employed by community-supported programs "which are entirely compatible with the development of Integrity Groups." Most of the professionals who have participated in the development of self-help groups have done so without concern for remuneration for themselves. More frequently, they have invested their own funds, in addition to their time, in the early and continuing efforts. The groups have varied, moreover, on issues of financial support. Some, such as AA and Recovery, refused government grants and sought to be self-supporting through contributions from members and the eventual sale of literature. Others, such as Parents Anonymous, Synanon, and Epilepsy Self-Help Groups, were not averse to receiving funds from any source.

Self-Help Group Development

Once launched, the self-help groups described here followed divergent courses. Many of these courses were determined to a considerable extent by the disciplinary backgrounds of the professional founders or early supporters. But as with other voluntary associations, self-help groups change over time. It is this developmental dimension that I would like to explore, citing findings in part from some of the chapters to follow.

There is an early zig-zag process of groping, trying out various approaches, dropping some, and developing new ones. Changes occur on a number of fronts, and they may be grouped, for purposes of analysis, into seven general headings: (1) organizational size; (2) organizational structure; (3) program focus; (4) nature of membership; (5) nature of leadership; (6) articulation with professionals and agencies; and (7) sources of financial support.

Organizational Size. Each of the groups identified in Table 1, except for Integrity Groups, has either maintained or sur-

passed the rate of growth, based on 3 percent per year, computed by Gussow and Tracy (1976) in their analysis of growth
trends of self-help groups. In tabulating the number of functioning chapters in six self-help groups over a thirty-year period,
1942 to 1972, they found a total increase of sixty-seven chapters
formed each year since the mid 1950s. These growth data were
based on information from the following organizations: International Laryngectomee Association; Recovery, Inc.; International Parents Organization; United Ostomy Clubs; Gam-Anon;
and Parents Anonymous. The number of chapters of these six
groups combined has reached 2,022 by 1972. Alcoholics Anonymous, although much larger, exhibited a similar growth rate.
By 1972, the number of functioning chapters of AA had reached
18,612. By 1978, AA identified over 30,000 chapters in 92
countries, revealing a growth of over 50 percent in six years.
Gussow and Tracy (1976, p. 409) admit that their figures reflect only the tip of the iceberg, "since we are continually being
informed of new groups for which no data are available or
which are completely local in character. The situation is open
and viable and current indications point to more groups forming
around other focus conditions and to an increase in the number
of chapters and established organizations." Indeed, this is the
case with three groups discussed here: Compassionate Friends,
Parents Anonymous, and Epilepsy Self-Help Groups. As Chapter Four indicates, Compassionate Friends, which did not exist
in the United States until the fall of 1972, had reached almost
126 chapters by 1979. Parents Anonymous has exhibited a phe-
nomenal growth since 1972, when it had 40 chapters, and currently has 1,000 groups in the United States. (*Parents Anonymous Frontiers*, 1979, p. 4). Epilepsy Self-Help Groups were
formed simultaneously in fifteen cities in 1975 and reveal efforts at persistence and expansion in at least ten of those localities. GROW claims to have formed nearly 400 groups in Australia by 1978 and, in its early efforts to "transplant" the program to the United States, organized 10 groups in October 1978
in the Champaign–Urbana, Illinois, area alone. This development
in Illinois and in the rest of the United States was boosted considerably by the cooperation of the founders and some members
of Integrity Groups. Mended Hearts has tripled the number of

its chapters since 1969 and currently recognizes 88 (see Chapter Two).

Organizational Structure. The structural lines of development of self-help groups seem to take diverse forms. Comparing Naim (Chapter Three) with Compassionate Friends (Chapter Four), one can see that even two groups founded or assisted by religious functionaries can diverge considerably in their structural development. Naim is a Catholic program for the widowed, conducted primarily within the archdiocese of Chicago. Priests assigned as spiritual advisors have assumed important functions in recruitment, the dissemination of information, and the conducting of conferences for the newly widowed. The priest who recently resigned from this position after ten years admitted that he received inquiries from other localities regarding interest in widow groups but ignored most of them since Naim operated only in the Chicago area. Compassionate Friends, however, is becoming international in scope, and the rapidly growing U.S. program has little formal relationship to the founder in England. Moreover, since 1978, Compassionate Friends has formed its own national board of directors. Mended Hearts modified its organizational structure in 1975 by hiring its first part-time paid national secretary and establishing a national board of directors made up of regional leaders and past presidents. In 1972, Recovery appointed its first nonmember professional administrator, who administers the national office in Chicago but is accountable to the board of directors that consists of members of Recovery. In the two-year development of Epilepsy Self-Help Groups in fifteen cities, from 1975 to 1977, a centralized reporting arrangement prevailed, with a program director in the Washington, D.C., office. At the termination of the program, however, when the contract funds were exhausted, the individual groups were on their own and no national effort at coordination was continued. In only one locality thus far, West Palm Beach, Florida, Epilepsy Concern has formed as an autonomous organization developing the structure of a national self-help council with groups chartered in other areas.

Program Focus. Synanon began around frivolity, fun, and bull sessions that evolved to focus on "attack therapy," then developed into a community-based program with the operation of schools, and currently emphasizes Item Six of the Articles of Incorporation: "To operate a church for religious purposes and to establish, maintain, operate, and promote institutions of the Synanon religion." In contrast, Naim began as a bereavement-focused discussion group and now focuses on sociability and fun. The women's consciousness-raising groups (see Chapter Five) were originally formed to enlist women into active, feminist causes. They rapidly evolved to focus on providing personal help for members rather than enlisting them in social action efforts and never sought a national formal organization. More recently they have been absorbed by the National Organization of Women, which is attempting to shift the groups' primary focus from mutual aid and self-interest to social influence and action.

Alcoholics Anonymous (1953, p. 11) formulated its position, ten years after its initial development, into Tradition 5: "Each group has but one primary purpose—to carry its message to the alcoholic who still suffers," and Tradition 6: "An AA group ought never endorse, finance, or lend the AA name to any related facility or outside enterprise, lest problems of money, property, and prestige divert us from our primary purpose." Mended Hearts has followed a similar, though implicit, policy in not becoming embroiled in the controversy over the advisability of coronary bypass surgery. Most groups that develop a national program do, however, begin to concern themselves with problems of recruitment, organizational maintenance, chapter development, and public education. This diversion from the original small-group focus can result in a major transformation of the organization, as Katz (1970) has indicated in his study of groups for the handicapped. These evolved into groups eventually administered and controlled by professionals, with a resulting change in the groups' primary focus. Fund raising, relations to professionals, and legislative interests became major concerns as professional experts replaced members with the affliction or concerned parents in the key organizational positions. These potential threats to a group's initial primary focus have been met in various ways. The Twelve Traditions of AA, for example, were published in 1946, eleven years after AA was formed, to deal with the organization's growing pains. "Everywhere there arose threatening questions of membership, money, personal relations, management of groups, clubs, and scores of other perplexities" (Alcoholics Anonymous, 1953, p. 18). Just as the Twelve Steps were developed as a group of principles to be followed by individual alcoholics, the Twelve Traditions were developed so as to allow the organization to sustain its primary techniques and mission.

Nature of Membership. Many self-help groups are faced with changes resulting from some shift in the nature of their original membership. Naim was significantly affected by a shift from the younger, newly widowed to the older, less recently widowed. Bereavement concerns seemed to be replaced by more pressing social linkage and friendship needs, and the discussion handbook that had been formulated to deal with the issues of bereavement fell into disuse. Mended Hearts was originally organized in 1951 by founding women who had had valve replacements, but its major growth came in the late 1960s with men who had had bypass surgery. Since hospital visitation is the key program of Mended Hearts, matching patients with appropriate visitors is of central concern. The rift between the valve and bypass groups has not resulted in a splintering of the organization, but some differences continue to exist. GROW changed its name from Recovery in 1960 (no relationship to Recovery in the United States) as a result of an influx of new members throughout Australia who were concerned with their own personal growth and maturity and who had not been former mental patients. There is little indication, however, that this shift to members concerned with prevention has resulted in a change of the group's format or philosophy, which was based on an adaptation of AA's Twelve Steps (Keogh, 1975). The original Recovery groups, established by Dr. Low, were formed by patients at the University of Illinois Psychiatric Institute who apparently had recovered from their mental illness as a result of the new use of electroshock treatment, which, as reported earlier in this volume, was eventually viewed by Low as dangerous (1938). As indicated in Chapter Twelve, although Recovery has become international in scope, membership does not include the full spectrum of mental disorders but primarily those with recurrent depressive, psychosomatic, or anxiety disorders. Those in the general population who might feel a sense of alienation, and are attracted by GROW, are not the major membership of Recovery.

Synanon, although it focused originally on drug addicts, described its service as "a community which provides a lifestyle for former drug addicts, juvenile delinquents, alcoholics, and other criminal delinquents. Approximately two thirds of Synanon's population are people with character disorders and their dependents. The population varies in terms of racial, ethnic, religious, socioeconomic, and regional backgrounds. More than a therapeutic community, Synanon offers an alternative lifestyle to those who seek its help" (*Synanon Fact Sheet*, 1976). Although Integrity Groups originally focused on neurotics and psychotics, "it soon became obvious that with the highlighting of relationships and openness it could have a clear application to marriage counseling. In one particular marriage counseling center the results have been so good that all the activities of the center have been directed towards this group approach" (Drakeford, 1969, p. 116). Alcoholics Anonymous has steadfastly concentrated on the problems of alcoholics only but has encouraged the formation of Al-Anon/Alateen, which, since 1954, has formed as a separate organization to serve the families of alcoholics. By 1976, Al-Anon Family Groups claimed over 12,000 groups in over fifty countries (*Al-Anon/Alateen Fact Sheet*, 1976).

Nature of Leadership. The relationship of founders to collaborators, "disciples," and new members has taken diverse directions with different groups. With Epilepsy Self-Help Groups, Schlesinger formulated the proposal, administered the development of groups in fifteen cities for a two-year period, and then had little to do with the ongoing program. He was aided considerably in these early efforts by the support of Doris Haar, a key professional in the federal Office of Vocational Disabilities, which funded the project. In contrast, Chuck Dederich, founder of Synanon, continues to be its central persona to this day. In the case of Alcoholics Anonymous, cofounder Bill Wilson describes AA's "coming of age" in 1955 (twenty years after its founding) when the General Service Conference of Alcoholics

Anonymous was named as successor to the founders, assuming custody of the Twelve Traditions and guardianship of AA's world services. This conference included seventy-five delegates from the United States and Canada, trustees of the General Service Board, and directors and secretarial staffs of AA's World Services in New York (Alcoholics Anonymous, 1957).

Articulation with Professionals and Agencies. This is a critical area and deserves special focus. If one considers the disciplinary backgrounds of some of the early founders and supporters, one can discern some distinct institutional arenas around which self-help groups develop special relationships. In the case of Alcoholics Anonymous, on the one hand, hospitals, detoxification centers, and mental health clinics recognize the valuable service of AA groups where they refer their alcoholic patients for follow-up, complementary, or alternative care. The gradual recognition of the important role of AA in the treatment of alcoholics has presented a special problem to the organization, namely, members who may attempt to profit from their AA association by pursuing professional counseling careers. AA's Tradition Eight discouraged such professionalism: "Freely ye have received, freely give" (Alcoholics Anonymous, 1953). Recovery, on the other hand, has received little comparable recognition on the part of mental health professionals and agencies. In its early years, it was supported enthusiastically and publicly by key professionals (Douglas Singer and Major Worthington) of the University of Illinois Psychiatric Institute. But until recently, with the interest of the President's Commission on Mental Health, professional support has generally been indifferent if not hostile. Integrity Groups have been even more "studiously avoided" by most mental health professionals. Mowrer (personal communication, 1976) conjectures on the reasons for this:

> We've some idea why IG hasn't been widely adopted and perpetuated, but they are very tentative. People who have had IG experience are afraid to try to start new groups elsewhere. Alcoholics who wanted to become contentedly sober weren't

afraid they would get into trouble for violating the "Medical Practices Act," nor have persons who have gone into Recovery, Inc. Dr. Low provided a medical coverage, and he taught them to speak of "recovery training," not treatment, diagnosis, or analysis. Thus theirs was a self and mutual education enterprise, not a psychiatric one. Members are admonished to have their own "doctor," if they want one, and to cooperative fully with him or her. But our people are pretty much on their own, and everyone has been warned by psychiatrists that "mental illness" is a very mysterious and dangerous condition, which laymen should not attempt to deal with. . . . Because we have recognized a moral (ethical, contractual, interpersonal) aspect of much psychopathology we have been castigated as "moralistic" by our fellow psychologists, even some emancipated clergymen.

In recent years, however, this picture appears to be changing. In a progress report, one of the founders of GROW comments on his initial efforts to develop GROW groups in central Illinois (Keogh, 1978a, p. 5):

During the past few weeks, we seem to have met, either in private interviews or in special gatherings set up at the Mowrer home, most of the people in Champaign-Urbana who are closest to the work we are doing and the kind of people GROW can help. I can only summarize these by designating the different categories of people who have been involved. They are: key ministers of religion representing the main churches; academics (especially psychologists) and professionals in counseling services; and last but not least, the authorities and staff in the mental health system (both voluntary and state run). With some of them we have been able to expound and discuss GROW and community mental health during long sessions lasting up to two hours or more. Almost invariably the interest has been of a kind to assure us that GROW is very

relevant and opportune; the response has been generally favorable and even enthusiastic; and in
a number of cases there have been practical invitations to follow through and start a GROW group
under the auspices of the person or agency concerned.

Mended Hearts has not met with the kind of resistance
over the years that the mental health groups report. Moreover,
their essential visitation program could never have developed
without the support of cardiologists, nurses, and hospital administrators. Harken (1975, p. 9), an early supporter, saw
Mended Hearts as strengthening the patient-surgeon bond and
potentially diminishing the malpractice crisis which "adversely
affects the quality, distribution, and cost of health care." As
for women's consciousness-raising groups, special group therapeutic programs for women began to be offered by more mental health professionals. In this case, professionals developed
treatment programs to meet the needs of a neglected population.
Accordingly, groups may collapse if their functions are appro-
priated by others. Parents Anonymous represents a different
kind of articulation with professionals. In drawing attention to
the special needs of child abusers, PA played a part in the development of the National Committee for the Prevention of Child
Abuse, as well as in stimulating the formation of the National
Center on Child Abuse and Neglect in Washington, D.C. As federal and state funds became available, parental stress services
were provided, and Parents Anonymous became one of the
sources of referral for identified abusers.

Mention should also be made of "spin-offs," connected
ideologically to the original groups but not organizationally
affiliated. Alcoholics Anonymous (1953, p. 16) anticipated the
development that has since occurred with overeaters, gamblers,
neurotics, potential suiciders, and others, in the foreword to
Twelve Steps and Twelve Traditions: "Many people, nonalco-
holics, report that as a result of the practice of AA's Twelve
Steps, they have been able to meet other difficulties of life.
They think that the Twelve Steps can mean more than sobriety
for problem drinkers." Synanon, as well, has become father to

the idea of "therapeutic communities" for drug addicts that began with the federally funded Daytop Village in New York in 1964, with comparable programs developed in cities "from one end of the country to the other" (Bassin, 1973, p. 333).

Sources of Financial Support. There is no consensus among self-help groups as to the basis of their support, nor have their policies in this matter been consistent over the years. Alcoholics Anonymous, for example, was not always bent on its path of self-sufficiency. An early grant of $5,000 contributed by John D. Rockefeller, Jr., with a warning, "I am afraid that money will spoil the thing," seemed to have played a decisive part in AA's philosophy to operate on a shoestring and support itself from its own membership and the sale of literature (Alcoholics Anonymous, 1957, p. 150). By 1945, AA began to decline all outside contributions. Synanon has placed no restrictions on its funding sources and has developed into a multimillion-dollar enterprise. Recovery derives its support from collections at group meetings (there are no membership dues), donations, and the sale of literature, but eschews government or public funds. Following a small foundation grant, Parents Anonymous has received the bulk of its grants (totaling over a million dollars) from federal sources. Naim and Mended Hearts derive their essential support from membership dues, whereas Compassionate Friends merely solicits contributions and has no dues structure. GROW was given a considerable boost in the development of its program in Australia through the availability of government support. These grants paid for the cost of secretaries and coordinators throughout the country. GROW is also considering the possibility of government support in its developing programs in the United States, which have been supported initially by a foundation grant. Epilepsy groups, which were initiated by a two-year federal grant, are finding diverse sources of funding in their separate localities. Most continue to be associated with chapters of the Epilepsy Foundation, and their coordinators are often paid staff members. The groups formed in the Chicago area have diverse relations with local chapters, and most are led by unpaid volunteer group leaders.

Frequently, financial barriers have kept the formal, voluntary associations concerned with the same affliction, such as the

Heart and Mental Health Associations, from being more helpful to the related self-help groups. In 1975, the Heart Association acknowledged a "mutually satisfying" relationship with Mended Hearts, including its recognition that the self-help group "does not conduct a fund drive for its own organization" (*Pro-Time*, 1975, p. 2). The Mental Health Associations of Illinois and Hawaii have provided important auspices for the development of GROW in the United States by serving as the recipient organization for initial fund raising. Frequently, members of self-help groups spearhead fund-raising campaigns for the voluntary associations, as with epilepsy and heart groups.

    Conclusion: Some Adaptive Considerations. A look at the capacity of self-help groups to sustain themselves, or spread in society, reveals a diverse pattern not unlike the overview of associations presented in the first part of this chapter. None of the ten groups discussed here has followed the path of the handicapped groups described in an early work by Katz (1970)—that is to say, they did not evolve into professionally run associations with founding members being relieved of most responsibilities. In a later publication, Katz (1976b, p. 122) also found that the latter stages of his original model—the emergence of leadership, the beginnings of formal organization, and the beginnings of professionalism—do not universally occur among self-help groups.

    One explanation for the aversion to this professionally run model is simply that founding and supporting professionals of the groups described in this chapter were apparently a new breed, not succumbing to traditional professional models. They may be representing a "paradigm shift" for many human service professionals. Although these groups have not become professionally run associations, neither have they become social movements—with the exception of Alcoholics Anonymous. Perhaps as groups sharing some common goals and tactics, they may together be coalescing into a social movement, as suggested by Bach and Taylor (1976, p. 300). But this general movement is not as yet discernible.

    Most groups seem to array themselves somewhere between these two models, adapting in diverse ways to their changing or expanding membership and to the specific institutional arenas in which they find themselves. We have considered some of these previously, including the articulation of Naim with the Catholic archdiocese of Chicago, Mended Hearts with hospitals conducting heart surgery, Parents Anonymous with parental stress services, and Integrity Groups as part of the psychology and social work curricula on a variety of college campuses. This diversity of relationship and affiliation would seem to follow the very nature of common interest groups and voluntary associations. They have been historically and cross-culturally ubiquitous, and there seems no reason why that would change. The rest of society, however, organized in more powerful and professional forms, might be more attentive to the nascent interests of these small groups, for they may provide the minute variations in forms, format, norms, and beliefs that may be vital for selection and retention, insuring the survival of the whole of our society (see Campbell, 1975).

CHAPTER 2

Growth of a Medical Self-Help Group

*Gary R. Bond, Leonard D. Borman,
Elizabeth A. Bankoff, Steven Daiter,
Morton A. Lieberman &
Lynn M. Videka*

The recent increase in the number of medical self-help groups has been linked to the increase in chronic conditions (such as heart disease, stroke, epilepsy, and cancer) that have no known cure but permit patients to maintain a modified life-style (Tracy and Gussow, 1976). Despite the widespread impact of these chronic illnesses on many Americans and their families, medical treatment in the United States is oriented toward acute illnesses, which have declined with the development of cures and vaccinations for most infectious diseases. The prognosis has also improved dramatically for many conditions previously considered hopeless. However, programs devoted to helping patients adapt

Note: Portions of this chapter are reproduced by special permission from *Social Policy*, "Mended Hearts: A Self-Help Case Study," by this chapter's authors, January/February 1979, *9* (4).

psychologically to their physical illness have not kept pace with these medical advances. In this time of rising health care costs, are medical professionals most appropriately employed in day-to-day care and rehabilitation? These factors have encouraged the development of alternative community support networks.

Self-help groups are one such nonprofessional support system organized for the chronically ill. A medical self-help group is a network of persons suffering from the same affliction or condition, who meet together or otherwise contact each other regularly to exchange information and share common experiences. Some groups have programs in which experienced members visit people just coming to terms with the condition or those who have not received adequate help from other resources. The organizations are sustained by the members themselves, though often they are initiated with the help of health care professionals.

This chapter examines the growth of Mended Hearts, a national organization for heart surgery patients and their families. We were interested in Mended Hearts particularly because of its long history and sustained growth. Through an examination of its organization and activities, we hoped to gain insight into factors that have contributed to its development.

Four Mended Hearts chapters representing different regions of the country were chosen for study. The first chapter observed was located in the Midwest and was chosen for its proximity to Chicago. The Midwest (MW) chapter, chartered in 1974 and with approximately 140 dues-paying members, was the youngest and smallest of the chapters studied. The remaining three chapters were in the Southwestern (SW), Western (W), and Southeastern (SE) regions, and were chartered in 1966, 1972, and 1972, respectively. The organization designates members who have had surgery as "active" members, whereas spouses and professionals are eligible to become "associate" members. The SW chapter had 328 members (209) active, the W chapter approximately 350 members (236 active), and the SE chapter 236 members (169 active). All four chapters were continually increasing membership roles at the time of the survey. The latter three had been recommended as exemplary chapters on the

basis of an annual award given out during each national convention.

A team of four observers made an initial field trip to the NW chapter in the summer of 1976 after preliminary contacts with the newly forming Chicago chapter. Observers went to a chapter meeting, interviewed the president and members of Mended Hearts, physicians, hospital administrators, and nursing staff. As a result of these observations, the "visitation program" (to be described later) was identified as a key activity of the organization. Chapter visitation programs became the focus of attention in field trips in 1977 to the other three chapters. These later trips included attendance at chapter meetings, interviewing, and observation of accredited visitors on their hospital rounds. Following the field trips a mail survey was conducted (reported in Chapters Eight and Sixteen).

Organizational Growth

Mended Hearts was founded by four patients who met while recovering from surgery in a Boston hospital. They began sharing "their new feelings of well being, their plans and hopes for the future, and with renewed happiness they spoke of 'their mended hearts.' From their conversations together, they realized how wonderful it would be to help others facing the same experience" (*Pro-time*, 1975). With the help of a heart surgeon, Dr. Dwight Harken, they formed the first group in 1951. Their adopted slogan, "It's great to be alive and to help others," was indicative of an optimistic attitude toward initially experimental surgical techniques on the heart. In 1955, Mended Hearts was formally incorporated and adopted a constitution and bylaws.

Until the mid 1960s, development of new chapters was guided primarily by the founders and original chapters in Massachusetts and New York. As hospitals in other regions of the country started performing heart surgery, the organization spread to other cities. The Texas Heart Institute, for example, became a well-known center for heart surgery, particularly because of the reputations of Drs. Michael DeBakey and Denton Cooley. These surgeons are revered by the organization and frequent reference is made to them in recounting the history of the organization.

The early years concentrated on developing a hospital visitation program, and on building close, working relationships with professionals, hospitals, and many local chapters of the National Heart Associations. A minimal dues structure was established from the start. (This continues to be the major source of income. The current budget anticipated $69,000 from members' dues.) Both active and associate members (mainly spouses) have held major offices in the organization throughout its history. In the early years there was no paid staff, and it was not until 1975 that the first salaried position of part-time secretary was added to the national office in Boston. As chapters proliferated, the nation was divided into six regions, and regional chairmen were appointed by the president and included on the board of directors. These regional chairmen were primarily responsible for conducting the visitor training program.

By 1966, Mended Hearts had chapters in twenty-six cities. Starting in 1971, the number of chapters mushroomed. Mended Hearts now has eighty-eight chapters with approximately 10,000 members. The number of chapters has tripled since 1969, with an average increase of nine new chapters in each of the last eight years. Thirteen chapters disbanded during this time, among them two nominal chapters in Argentina and Puerto Rico.

Two facts about heart surgery help explain the increase in new chapters after 1970. First, the number of heart surgeries performed in the United States has increased dramatically. By 1977, over 70,000 coronary bypasses were being performed yearly. Secondly, heart surgery requires the assembly of surgical teams with specialized skills and equipment. These conditions have led to centralization of surgery in hospitals having these resources. Guidelines of the U.S. Department of Health, Education, and Welfare recommend that hospitals performing coronary bypass surgery do at least 200 per year in order to maintain the proficiency of the surgical team. Hospitals that are centers for heart surgery have become informal settings in which patients having surgery can meet one another.

In several instances, the spread to new cities grew from positive experiences of out-of-town patients having surgery in one of the early centers. Among the founding members of the MW, SE, and SW chapters were patients who first made contact with Mended Hearts at the Texas Heart Institute. Relocation of physicians supportive of Mended Hearts has also been instrumental in the formation of new chapters. In some cases, a relocated member of one chapter has formed a group in a new area. In another instance, a chapter was formed by someone whose first contact with Mended Hearts was through the mass media. The chapter founders interviewed all shared a strong moral commitment and altruistic attitude toward those undergoing surgery. They linked their sense of mission to their own experiences with surgery, and often to their gratitude toward those who had helped them during surgery. Because Mended Hearts was already a well-established organization more than a decade before coronary bypass surgery first became widespread, it was prepared for the expansion of chapters into new geographic areas. The model for national and local chapter organization was already established. Lacking these unique historical circumstances, other medical self-help groups have not evolved so smoothly, since they have been faced with the problems of organizational development at the same time that their prospective membership has been rapidly growing. We now examine the organizational structures and activities of Mended Hearts that have permitted the organization to absorb this chapter growth.

Current Organizatonal Structure

National Board. The formation of a national board to guide the organization has been a vital step in its growth and consolidation. Without a national board, the transmission of the organzation from city to city would be difficult. The fact that there is a central body that maintains the traditions of the group distinguishes Mended Hearts from support groups for heart patients that have not evolved beyond local settings. The chapter charters, bylaws, national newsletters, and other written forms of guidance provided by the national board offer initial structure and support to fledgling chapters. And established chapters offer moral support and role models for development to new chapters.

Regional chairmen visit regularly and maintain communication with chapters in their jurisdiction. A past national president during her two-year administration personally visited nearly all the active chapters nationwide. Another officer on his own initiative planned his summer vacation around visits to chapters in another part of the country. These visits bolster the enthusiasm of local chapter leaders and assure the adherence of local groups to the values of the organization. Dormant chapters have their charters revoked, assuring that existing chapters are more than nominal organizations.

Local Chapters. Local chapter officers typically include a president, several vice-presidents, a treasurer, recording secretary, and visitation chairmen. Some chapters have as many as thirty-seven officers and committee chairmen, including visitation coordinators for specific hospitals. Typically, about 25 percent of the active members are involved as "accredited visitors."

The conduct of the monthly chapter meetings was similar for the four chapters studied. Meetings were held in the hospitals where heart surgeries were performed. The meeting room is typically arranged with rows of folding chairs facing a podium. Often the hospital auditorium or classrooms are used. A typical meeting will present a physician or medical expert speaking on some aspect of heart disease, surgery, and the recovery process. Presentations are often followed by a question-and-answer period and the serving of light refreshments. Other topics and speakers are covered as well, including issues of social security, nutrition, exercise, insurance, and employment. These meetings are large and formal, with chapter business covered before the presentations.

The meetings are open to heart patients, their spouses, and professionals, and although the meetings are usually well attended, only a fraction of the dues-paying membership is involved. Twenty-eight percent of those surveyed had attended

five or more meetings in the last year; 36 percent attended between one and four while 34 percent had attended none. The
average number of meetings attended by a spouse was two; 10
percent had attended five or more meetings.

The local chapter also sends out monthly newsletters containing inspirational material, lists of new members, "surgiver-
saries" (anniversaries of members' heart surgeries), news stories
about research in heart surgery, and announcements of general
activities of the local and national organizations.

Visitation Program. Each local chapter has a visitation
program, in which "accredited" visitors make hospitals rounds
to offer information, support, and encouragement to patients,
both before they go into surgery and afterward while they are
recuperating at the hospital. According to its records, Mended
Hearts visited an estimated 47,000 patients in 1976 and 1977,
some indication of the scope of these programs. The visitation
program involves training and coordination with hospitals as
well as actual visiting. Each of these activities has significance
for the morale and reputation of the chapters and their continued existence.

Training Program. Visitors are required to attend a series
of seminars consisting of lectures, role playing, and discussion
of visitor guidelines. There are approximately eight to ten hours
of training, followed by a test on knowledge of the functions of
the heart, various heart problems, and their corresponding cor-
rections.

The guidelines, which have evolved on a trial-and-error
basis over a twenty-five year history, deal with the pragmatics
of both the patient's circumstances ("don't visit when he or she
is asleep") and the hospital regulations ("don't go into the intensive care unit"; "don't visit late at night"). They offer concrete recommendations for avoiding situations that have led to
difficulties in prior visitation programs, including recommendations to circumvent discussions of such topics as religion,
finances, or specifics of the surgery. The guidelines stress a positive optimistic outlook ("bring cheer") rather than sympathy.
Significantly, the guidelines suggest a studied avoidance of issues
under the jurisdiction of professionals: doctors ("never give

Table 1. Instructions for Mended Hearts Visitors

Do

1. Plan your visit for the afternoon or evenings; never before 11 a.m. and never late at night.

2. Identify yourself at the nurses' station and ask permission to visit. Explain the Mended Hearts organization and that you have the permission of the physician and the hospital administration.

3. Enter the patient's room as quietly as possible.

4. Introduce yourself and the organization to the patient, and offer your help.

5. If the patient has other visitors, introduce yourself and offer to come back another time. Never visit when there is a large group in the room.

6. Delay your visit if a doctor or nurse is in the room.

7. Be considerate of the patient's condition. Speak softly and keep your visit short to avoid overtiring the patient.

8. Be enthusiastic about hospital care, particularly the attention the patient receives *after* the operation.

9. Answer all questions honestly but tactfully.

10. Urge the patient to do exactly as his doctor advises.

11. Provide the family with information on housing, restaurants, shopping and best methods of transportation if needed.

12. Remember . . . it is important to bring cheer . . . not fear! You are there to be helpful and encouraging.

---

medical advice"): nurses ("delay visit if nurse is in room"); and chaplains ("never discuss religion"). This theme of respect and sensitivity for the physicians, nurses, and other medical specialists, embodied in the guidelines, plays an important role in the acceptance of this organization within a hospital setting. Recent training programs also stress that the visitor refrain from the implication that successful surgery is merely a matter of fate. Visitors are warned, for example, never to say "good luck." A recent compilation of guidelines for visitors by the national organization, shown in Table 1, illustrates these points.

Before visiting by themselves, prospective visitors accompany accredited visitors on their rounds; the organization has learned to be cautious about the qualifications of visitors. We

Table 1. Instructions for Mended Hearts Visitors (continued)

Don't

1. Do not awaken a patient to make a visit. If you find the patient sleeping, leave a calling card, or return later.

2. Never visit if there is a cold or virus in your family, or if you generally feel under par.

3. Do not visit a patient the first few days after sugery, unless by special request of the doctor in charge.

4. Do not overdress and do not use heavy perfume.

5. Do not, under any circumstances, go into the ICU or CCU, unless asked by a doctor or nurse. Visit with the family if they are there, outside the unit.

6. Never give medical advice. Do not try to do the job of the doctor.

7. Never smoke in the patient's room.

8. Never discuss finances or religion; and do not offer prayer.

9. Do not tell the patient what to expect in the rate of improvement. You can't possibly know.

10. Do not discuss your operation . . . or other problems. Take a positive attitude. Describe your improvements, then compare them to your past limitations. Avoid unnecessary detail.

11. Never show your incision, or even discuss it! It the patient brings up the subject be as tactful as possible in answering.

12. Do not use sympathy, for sympathy can make the individual feel sorry for himself. Take a positive approach, instill the feeling of well-being and happiness that can be looked forward to.

were told that one or two visitors can "wreck" a visitation program, and some chapters have experienced such difficulty. Worse yet, the conduct of people unconnected with Mended Hearts has made entry into some hospitals difficult. Thus, our informants impressed on us that prospective visitors are screened before they are accredited. The prevailing concern is that visitors are "ready"—that they have achieved sufficient psychological distance from their own surgery and coupled it with a positive and future-oriented outlook. Patients who dwell on their surgery are not good candidates for visitation. "Those of us who still get an emotional satisfaction in dwelling on the past do not make good visitors. The urge to do this is a characteristic of many people who have undergone any kind of surgery. For us, we put it this way: If you still want to go into the details of your own illness and operation, you are still mending. If you do not need to do so, you are a real Mended Heart" (*Pro-time*, 1975, p. 4).

The training program and a philosophy of visitation that emphasizes an important but nonintrusive role for the visitor have probably been critical for the entry and acceptance of Mended Hearts in many hospitals.

Hospital Visitation

Coordination with Hospitals. The establishment of visitation programs requires negotiation at several levels—with the administration, physicians, nursing staff, volunteer services, and social services. Entry is not always easily accomplished. As our field notes record; a former visitation chairman recalled his initial difficulties in establishing a program in a Western hospital: "After my sales pitch, in which I tried to convince the professional staff of the need for a visitation program, the head cardiologists said, 'Thanks, but no thanks. This is a very complicated surgical procedure, and our professional staff can do the job.' I said, 'I am well aware of their skill and stand before you as a successful case. But I've got something none of your professionals have—I've been there and they ain't!' Shortly afterwards, I was able to set up a most effective visiting program, and the cardiologist who questioned my plan is now one of our leading supporters." Positive publicity about Mended Hearts spread by world of mouth and by the media has facilitated entry into new hospitals. Also, Mended Hearts has been involved in public relations through the compilation of letters from professionals commenting on the work of Mended Hearts in their hospitals. The most recent compilation contained over forty letters lauding their work (*Pro-time*, 1975).

Receptiveness to Mended Hearts in new locations has varied. In one instance, a Mended Hearts chapter president was consulted by the administration of a hospital in a neighboring city on how to set up a visitation program, even before the hospital began performing heart surgery! In contrast, Mended Hearts has not yet been recognized in many of the large city hospitals. In Chicago, for example, where 4,000 heart surgeries were performed in 1977, the local chapter has not yet gained hospital entry despite the active interest of about twenty patients who have completed the training program. The directory of Mended Hearts chapters (and of visitation programs) reflects a concentration in small cities and surburban areas. The few chapters located in large cities generally do not have active visitation programs. It is not clear at this point why coordination with large city hospitals is more difficult, but the observation that it is so is well documented.

Beyond gaining initial entry, Mended Hearts requires ongoing liaisons with hospitals in which it has visitation programs. In some hospitals, we found that Mended Hearts had an official, legitimized status, with a room designated for its visitors to use. Visitors were treated almost as if they were part of the staff and were routinely called upon by nurses and physicians. In these hospitals, Mended Hearts had developed arrangements that gave it blanket permission to visit all cardiac patients. Other hospitals viewed Mended Hearts visits as an imposition and added responsibility for the staff. Control over Mended Hearts was sometimes maintained by coordinating visits through an office of volunteer services or a social service department. In still other hospitals, visitation required permission of the physician in charge, on a case-by-case basis.

Mended Hearts frequently plays an important role in facilitating communication between staff and patients. Some nurses noted that Mended Hearts visitors provide a critical lay perspective that no hospital professional or paraprofessional role could supplant. An example from the SE chapter illustrates this educational role and its impact on professionals. Visitors were routinely telling "pre-ops" that after surgery they would have a "tube" down their throats that would prevent them from talking. An anesthesiologist, fearing this would upset patients, asked the visitors to stop giving this information. They did, but later the anesthesiologist discovered that informing the patients

of the procedure prior to surgery proved helpful and subsequently requested that the Mended Hearts personnel again include the
information in their visits.

Mended Hearts visitors also provide feedback to physicians. They learn about patients' problems and hear suggestions
and complaints that carry greater impact than concerns voiced
by single individuals. Through their involvement with Mended
Hearts, some physicians take a more knowledgeable and active
part in advocating effective rehabilitation programs for heart
surgery patients. In talking with us, one cardiologist emphasized
the feedback function of Mended Hearts: "For me Mended
Hearts is an epi-center. It is the first effort I know that brings
people together who have survived heart surgery, managed
through day-to-day crises, and come back to tell us how they
dealt with their problems. They get there by going through
a surgical process we know something about. But from that
point on, they are going through other processes that we need
to learn about. What medicine works? What stress can they
undergo? What is the impact of the surgical procedure? And
simple, but important things, like how do you make love to
your spouse six weeks after surgery?"

Concomitantly, Mended Hearts encourages doctors to
spend more time talking with their patients and answering their
medical questions in a careful manner, recognizing that the patients are frightened and consequently that their powers of attention may not be up to par.

Self-help groups are sometimes portrayed as antiprofes-
sional, but this stereotype clearly does not fit Mended Hearts.
Since the visitation program requires coordination with medical
personnel, it is not surprising that the organization is strongly
proprofessional. Thirty professional advisors are listed on the
national stationery. Heart patients, regardless of affiliations, had
high positive regard for their physicians. Eighty-eight percent of
the survey respondents felt that their doctors "answered all my
important questions about heart surgery," 78 percent felt they
were "easy to talk to," 86 percent felt they "treated me like an
individual," and 66 percent said they "gave emotional support."

Impact on Patients. Perhaps the best way to convey the nature of the visits is through the field report of an observer who accompanied "Mr. A" on his rounds.

Mr. A and I arrived at the beginning of visiting hours on Sunday afternoon, which was his regular time to visit each week. We went immediately to the space allocated for Mended Hearts at a desk in the lobby. Records of visits were kept there. Mr. A prepared his props—a badge designating him as an official Mended Hearts visitor attached to his coat, and a clipboard with the names of patients we were visiting. Later I was to learn of an additional prop for visitors to children, an "autograph hound," a small stuffed dog, which was given after surgery and signed by nurses and doctors.

We visited 14 patients during the next 3 hours. We began with four "pre-ops." All had their families with then when we arrived, and were apprehensive and serious in anticipation of the ordeal. Mr. A gave a standard introduction, "Hello, I'm ____and I'm a member of an organization called Mended Hearts that you may have heard about. I've had the same surgery as you, and this is what you're going to look like when you get out. (Gestures to himself.) The doctor asked me to stop by to visit you. Do you have any questions?"

His approach was not unlike a salesman who was selling a product he believed in fervently, and he gave a strong endorsement of the hospital and staff. His manner was aggressive but polite. While his main attention was to the patient, he acknowledged the family as well, and answered their questions. He would tell the wife, "Mrs.____, this time two months from now you won't be able to keep up with your husband." Then he would make reference to "Mr.____, whom I talked to this morning, is out playing tennis right now, as he does every Sunday. He wasn't able to do that before the surgery." He encouraged the family to return home while the patient was in surgery, explaining that they would be more comfortable and therefore more refreshed to respond when the patient came out of surgery, and that they would actually be more accessible to the staff than if they remained at the hospital. Some of the patients had heard of Mended Hearts, others had not. They asked questions about hospital procedure and about the surgery. Mr. A answered the questions forthrightly, giving more general answers when the questions were of a medical nature. For some questions he referred them to the doctor. On occasion he would pull out a diagram of the heart and explain their surgery. If patients asked us to sit down, Mr. A would refuse, saying that "we didn't want to get too comfortable."

In one of the pre-ops, the patients and his wife were in a state of panic because a neighbor had had a traumatic experience with similar surgery. We spent the most time with this couple— they probably needed it the most. The visitor's approach was to suggest that "most people have a tendency to dramatize their surgery" and he stressed the positive, hopeful aspects of the surgery. He was skillful in shifting the mood of the family from depression and fear, to hopefulness and focus on the future.

The post-op visits were generally brief. Mr. A entered every room, even those which had "DO NOT DISTURB" signs. Nearly all of the patients seemed genuinely glad to see us. A few asked questions. (Mr. A had told me that some patients may not take the visitor into their confidence until the third or fourth visit.) Others simply chatted with us cheerfully.

The face-to-face contact of the hospital visitation creates a favorable impression of Mended Hearts as a group of dedicated, selfless volunteers. Patients whose future critically depends on heart surgery must be encouraged by the strong belief in its value that the visitors convey. Although the purpose of the visitation is not to recruit new members, Mended Hearts visitors believe, with some justification, that a good visitation program is the best way to attract new members. In the SW, SE, and W chapters between 1975 and 1976, visitors saw over 2,000 patients. Of those, approximately 15 percent were members by the end of 1977.

Importance to Chapters. A successful visitation program is crucial to a chapter's continued existence. This factor makes the initial stage of chapter formation the most problematic, since new chapters require several years to establish an optimal visitation program. Historically, Mended Hearts chapters without visitation programs have had difficulty surviving. Virtually all of the existing chapters maintain visitation programs, and it is generally a Mended Hearts policy to refuse to charter a new chapter unless it has contact with a hospital where heart surgery is performed. An interview with a former national visitation chairwoman is illustrative:

> Ms. G. related the demise of her local chapter to difficulties in their visitation program. Although the chapter had the usual monthly meetings with a variety of lecture topics, it was primarily built around the visitation program. In fact, Ms. G. was quite explicit in stating that visitation was the "primary aim" of the Mended Hearts organization. This chapter ran into trouble when a key cardiac surgeon in the area stopped referring his patients for Mended Hearts visitation. After a few years of irregular referrals, during which the chapter floundered, visitation under the auspices of Mended Hearts completely ceased due to the lack of referrals. Ms. G. reported that this chapter could no longer recruit members because their visitation program, which she saw as their major recruitment mechanism, was no longer functional. The core members continued to meet for a time, but without the recruitment of new members and the sanction of the cardiac surgeon, enthusiasm and interest in Mended Hearts dwindled, even on the part of

these formerly highly committed members, and
meetings ceased. Despite a second attempt to re-
organize, this chapter has been unable to successfully reinstitute its visitation program and has returned its charter to the national organization.

Thus the visitation program helps maintain chapters by
providing them with a mission and central focus. An ongoing
monthly lecture format in the absence of the service orientation is not sufficient to sustain the interest and enthusiasm of
members.

Impact on Visitors. The visitation program, which provides the major mechanism for publicity, also provides the major
source of satisfaction for members of the organization. A range
of survey questions explored the impact of visitation on the visitor. Visitors rated Mended Hearts more highly than nonvisitors
on relevance, enjoyment, and helpfulness. (There were no differences on ratings of informativeness.) Whereas 46 percent of
the visitors reported talking to other members at least weekly,
only 9 percent of the nonvisitors reported such frequent contact; 75 percent of the visitors reported "thinking of" Mended
Hearts weekly or more often, compared with 44 percent of the
nonvisitors.

Field observations and interviews supported the finding
that visitors derived satisfaction from their role. One, for example, described the "sense of communion" he felt with the
hundreds of heart patients with whom he had spoken over the
years. As one of the first people in his community to have heart
surgery, he had received calls from people hundreds of miles
away. Another visitor described vividly the "energizing" effects
of visitation even after a hard day's work. A visitation chairman
confided that he gave the responsibility for visiting to a man to
help him "come out of his depression." Several informants mentioned the fact that retirees are often asked to be visitors because "it gives them something to do with their time." Visitors
also achieve status and a sense of importance in their quasi-
official role within the hospital. Here is an example from our
field observations:

Sam, a retired lumberjack, visits virtually all the heart patients in one of the ten area hospitals that the W chapter services. A researcher accompanying him on an afternoon of visits realized that Sam was known to all levels of hospital personnel. He first stopped for a cup of coffee in the hospital cafeteria and was greeted by name by attending physicians and cafeteria workers. The ward nurse knew Sam personally and joked with him easily. Hospital staff freely shared with Sam the status and situation of each heart surgery patient. Sam had invested increasingly more time and energy into visiting as he became personally known by the hospital staff. He noted that visiting heart patients had become a daily routine for him and that it gave him a personal sense of accomplishment and meaningfulness. Because of the level of trust and rapport between Sam and the hospital staff, all patients were referred for Mended Hearts visitation. Nurses and doctors alike were enthusiastic about Sam's visiting and freely sought him out to visit "problem patients."

As self-help groups become large organizations, it is more difficult for new individuals to become personally involved in the group's core activities. The large formal meetings lead most participants to view themselves as an audience. For members who are not involved in a help-giving capacity (that is, non-visitors), perceived benefits of group membership are minimal, and their peripheral involvement in the organization is underscored.

Implications for Other Self-Help Groups

We have identified a number of factors that have contributed to the growth of Mended Hearts: *critical mass, common setting, publicity, corporate structure, legitimacy, recruitment,* and *involvement*.

By *critical mass* we mean a sufficient number of heart patients in a given area to form a group.

The *common setting* is the hospital, and we have suggested that the intricate nature of the heart operation promotes bringing patients together in the limited number of hospitals in which open-heart surgery is performed.

Publicity makes the public, medical personnel, and heart patients aware of the organization, and ultimately affects the degree of acceptance by the community. Mended Hearts utilizes media coverage, newsletters, and face-to-face contact to publicize its program.

Corporate structure refers to the national board, which provides the basis for nurturing early development of chapter interest through information, guidelines, training programs, and the creation of opportunities for contacts with more established chapters. The corporate structure also provides public relations information, organizes workshops, and conducts the national convention, providing broader opportunities for all members to become involved in the large-scale development of the organization.

Legitimacy is a crucial concern for Mended Hearts, and the group has worked hard to receive the active support of physicians and other professionals.

The *recruitment process* in Mended Hearts is inherent in its visitation program. It would appear that face-to-face contact concerning the critical life event of major surgery has a great impact in recruitment of new members.

Finally, the *involvement* of members around a central activity that gives the group a purpose and sustains the psychological investment of the members is crucial to the maintenance of the group.

In spite of the uniqueness of Mended Hearts and the specific crisis it addresses, we shall attempt to extend our speculations to other self-help groups, using our conceptualization of factors that contribute to organizational growth.

The lack of a critical mass inhibits the formation of self-help groups for rare diseases, or at least refocuses the energies of the group on finding members. The Committee to Combat Huntington's Disease is an example of such a group in which the rarity of the disease limits organizational growth. However,

merely publicizing a "rare" disease often uncovers a wider incidence in the population than was previously thought. Some self-
help groups have solved the critical mass problem by broadening
their focus to include people with different diseases but who
share similar life circumstances. Make Today Count, for example, invites all those who have "life threatening" diseases,
regardless of the specific illness, and the Committee to Combat Huntington's Disease has spearheaded a national effort
to focus attention on hundreds of rare genetic and neuro-
logical disorders.

The existence of a critical mass of people suffering from
the same problem is not sufficient for the formation of a group.
Hypertension and diabetes are examples of widespread medical
conditions around which no groups comparable to Mended
Hearts have yet formed, even though the characteristics of these
two conditions would suggest that support groups could be
beneficial.

A common setting for those suffering from the same affliction is an important but overlooked factor in the coalescence
and maintenance of a group. The common setting is a familiar
environment where informal communication on the common
problem is likely to begin. Hospitals are an important meeting
ground for people with physical problems. We have found
churches and parishes to be likely meeting places for groups
formed around the death of a spouse or child. Perhaps the failure of Mended Hearts to form chapters in most large urban
cities is related to the difficulty in dealing with impersonal bureaucratic structures. In smaller communities, hospitals probably have closer ties with other community activities and services and may be perceived as being more integrated into the
community.

Publicity has played a major role in the growth of self-
help groups. Make Today Count has received considerable public attention through the distribution of a book by the same
title written by the group's founder, Orville Kelly. Compassionate Friends, a self-help group for bereaved parents, increased its
number of chapters from fourteen to twenty-six in the six
months following the broadcast of a nationally televised talk

show that focused on the problems of bereavement and on Compassionate Friends.

Publicity alone is not sufficient to build a national organization. In some instances, publicity has led to more inquiries from prospective members than a fledgling organization has been able to assimilate. Especially when the organization is initially a single founder who is operating out of the proverbial shoebox, the initial period of expansion is prone to be haphazard and not entirely under the control of the founder. Until they develop a corporate structure, such organizations may encounter such problems as a lack of coordination between chapters, the emergence of splinter groups, and rapid turnover of membership. The superhuman efforts of an energetic founder, such as Orville Kelly, may be necessary to bridge the gap between the initial period and a subsequent period when a viable national network is established. The expansion of Make Today Count, in which the development of organizational guidelines occurred at the same time as the rapid proliferation of chapters, is probably more typical of the development of a national self-help organization than the more orderly evolution of Mended Hearts during the past decade. The existence of a corporate structure with explicit guidelines for local chapters has been a major difference.

Professionals whose expertise is relevant to the affliction often lend legitimacy to the self-help group through their support. They enhance the credibility of the group and its activities in the eyes of both members and outsiders. In Mended Hearts, physicians and medical staff serve this function. In Naim, a priest has served as an advisor to the organization and as a liaison to other priests in identifying newly widowed persons. Several chapters of Compassionate Friends have been developed through the efforts of professionals (social workers, funeral directors, and clergymen) who are either bereaved parents themselves or who have extended their services to the organization. Other possible sources of legitimation are the social action organizations directed toward basic research and lobbying for a medical condition. In the past, however, such organizations have seldom coexisted with self-help/mutual aid groups like

Mended Hearts for the same medical condition (Tracy and Gussow, 1976). The role of the National Heart Association during the formative years of Mended Hearts is a case in point. The National Heart Association did not officially endorse Mended Hearts during its formative years when its leaders were actively seeking such support. Only recently, after Mended Hearts achieved a national reputation among heart surgery patients, has the NHA been openly supportive of the group.

The face-to-face contact of Mended Hearts visitors with heart surgery patients is an effective recruiting mechanism. The neutrality of the hospital setting and urgency of the patient's circumstances contribute to positive reception of visitors. A home visitation program would be more difficult to implement, as the abandonment of early attempts by Compassionate Friends and Naim would seem to indicate. The recruitment or attraction process appears to be fundamentally different for groups organizing around behavioral problems than for groups whose concern is a stressful life event. It may be that persons suffering from addictions such as alcohol, drugs, and compulsive gambling need to reach a point of readiness before self-help groups and other forms of assistance will benefit them. Alcoholics Anonymous has long believed that the only time an alcoholic is ready for help is when he hits bottom. Only then does he have the motivation to follow their Twelve Steps program.

The involvement of group members in a central activity is critical to its sustained existence. As Antze's analysis suggests (Chapter Twelve), the kind of involvement must tie in with the needs of the members. In one case study of a Make Today Count chapter on the verge of collapse, suggestion that the group refocus its energy from endless debates on organization problems to an agenda of mutual sharing of feelings was a critical turning point (Wollert, 1978). The outreach program of visitation appears to be suited to the needs of heart surgery patients.

Conclusions

Despite the widespread growth of Mended Hearts, it did not follow the path of other self-help groups that have aban-

doned their original priority of mutual aid for individuals suffering from disease and have become bureaucratic organizations,
with full-time paid staff and major interests in legislation, basic
research, public education, and fund raising. Katz's 1970 model
for the growth and development of self-help groups postulates
this evolution toward paid staff workers and professionalization,
though Katz and Bender (1976a, p. 281) note the attempt of
some organizations, such as the United Cerebral Palsy Association and the National Association for Retarded Citizens to "restore (self-help) participation, at a new and higher stage than
occurred in their early development." Similarly, Tracy and
Gussow (1976) observed the evolution of the Committee to
Combat Huntington's Disease from a "Type I" organization
(that is, a self-help/mutual aid group) to a "Type II" (that is,
a large foundation directed toward research and lobbying).
Mended Hearts, in contrast, has a minimal bureaucratic structure and has maintained a low profile on social policy. For example, Mended Hearts National has chosen not to enter or
even comment on the recent controversy over the advisability
of coronary bypass surgery. In this sense, it has followed the example set by Alcoholics Anonymous in remaining outside political, legislative, or scientific questions surrounding its focal interest. As with AA, members who choose to become active in such
public issues must do so under auspices other than their self-help
group. Just as many AA members participate in the National
Council on Alcoholism, which engages in policy issues and receives support from government and other sources, many
members of Mended Hearts actively participate in their local
Heart Associations and often spearhead fund-raising and other
programs. At its 1971 convention in San Diego, Mended Hearts
adopted a "resolution of cooperation" with the American Heart
Association which recognized that their members "spend thousands of hours annually working for the heart fund and cause
without any formal guidance from the National Heart Association." Although seeking close cooperation with the Heart Association, Mended Hearts follows a distinctive and autonomous
path.

Mended Hearts' visitation programs are also quite distinct from visitation programs conducted by other medical outreach programs. For example, Reach-to-Recovery, conducted by the American Cancer Society, provides a program of one-to-one visitation for women who have had mastectomies. These are all postsurgical contacts, since with current mastectomy procedures the surgery may be performed during the same operation in which the diagnosis is made. There has been little opportunity for a woman about to have breast surgery to meet and talk with someone who has already experienced the surgery. Accordingly, the Reach-to-Recovery volunteer will most often conduct her visit in the hospital following surgery.

Another critical contrast to Mended Hearts is the fact that the Reach-to-Recovery program functions directly under the American Cancer Society. Moreover, the attending physician must request a visitor. This means that the society screens, selects, and supervises the volunteers as an arm of its program. The volunteer is under strict instructions from the society and brings materials, pamphlets, and prosthetic equipment provided by the society. Reach-to-Recovery volunteers rarely meet in face-to-face groups. And they do not launch the development of their own activities independently of the society, as does Mended Hearts. The failure of one professionally directed visitation program for cancer patients was attributed to the professionals' excessive control of the volunteers (Kleiman, 1976).

A visitation program resembling that described in this chapter has been sponsored by the United Ostomy Association, a self-help group for persons who have lost the normal functions of their bowels or bladder. Most hospitals that perform this type of surgery automatically call upon the Ostomates to visit with both patients and family members. The American Cancer Society also makes referrals to the United Ostomy Association.

One may ask how Mended Hearts compares to some of the newer programs in hospitals that have focused increased concern on patient and consumer rights, services, benefits, and personal treatment. Many of these hospitals have staff positions for consumer advocates and ombudsmen in the social services, vol-

unteer, or other hospital departments. Several contrasts are
readily apparent. The advocacy programs are staffed by full-time
hospital functionaries, with some voluntary assistance. They are
"generalists," as many kinds of problems fall into their net.
Their purview does not reach beyond their particular hospital
or community. They are not part of an outside organization or
community program that sustains their efforts. They obviously
do not duplicate the unique service function provided by
a Mended Hearts volunteer.

In comparison with the more circumscribed focus of hospitals, agencies, and professional service programs, Mended
Hearts follows more of a public health model combined with
a missionary zeal. Its target is to reach all, or nearly all, of those
patients about to have heart surgery. A typical newsletter will
report on the total number of patients visited in comparison to
the number of heart surgeries performed. Not bound by a fee
for service structure, Mended Hearts can proliferate widely
through the efforts of unpaid volunteers. Compare this to the
typical careful but cumbersome efforts of professional programs,
which move from a needs assessment to a proposal development
to funding review, hiring of staff, securing of space, and finally
to provision of services through an intake procedure. Mended
Hearts, as a widely dispersed community support system, may
have much to teach us all on the development of services of
persons with debilitating diseases or chronic conditions.

CHAPTER 3

Transformation of a Group for the Widowed

Mark Steinberg & Carrie Miles

One special characteristic of self-help groups is the drawing together of participants who have a specific common affliction or need. The common condition or affliction that draws members together does not encompass a single need but is rather a broad category of distress that may affect many aspects of an individual's life. For example, alcoholism may have far-reaching impact on the individual's social, work, and financial status as well as on his or her emotional and physical well-being. Widowhood also encompasses a range of complex and changing emotional and social needs.

What consequences does the multifaceted and changing nature of widowhood have for the self-help groups that offer service to the widowed? The Naim Conference of Chicago provided an opportunity to explore this issue with a self-help organization that has served a Catholic widowhood population for over twenty years. The changing needs of the widowed have played an important role in the transformation of Naim from an organization with an emphasis on bereavement problems of the newly widowed to a current orientation toward social activities for the older, longer-widowed person. As indicated in Chapter One, many self-help groups have undergone major shifts in focus as they developed. The history of the Naim Conference illustrates one such shift that may have implications for other self-help groups for the widowed as well as for other transitional or crisis-oriented self-help groups.

The Naim Conference is a Catholic organization for widowed Catholics or spouses of deceased Catholics. Currently part of the Family Life Bureau of the Chicago Archdiocese, its development by widowed lay people and concerned clergy was seen to fill a void in the church's ministry. Its founders, William and Jean Delaney, were motivated by their belief that the needs of the widowed were being neglected by the church. The Delaneys had both been widowed prior to their marriage and, as widowed people, found that the church had not provided help in dealing with psychological, social, and spiritual problems they faced. They wanted to create a group for the widowed modeled after the Cana Conference, an outgrowth of the Catholic Family Life Movement, which utilized group discussions to allow its married couple participants to examine problems of marriage and family life. Early in 1956, Jean Delaney approached an official of the Chicago Archdiocese with this idea. He was receptive but believed the group should be exclusively for women, contending that if men were included they would use the group solely as a means of finding new mates. Mrs. Delaney rejected this alternative and subsequently contacted Monsignor John Egan, Director of the Cana Conference. His response to the Delaney's proposal to extend the approach of the Cana Conference to the widowed was positive. With his sponsorship, their idea received support from the Archdiocese.

Monsignor Egan provided the names of other widowed persons, and the first meeting was held at the Delaney's home late in 1956, with the Delaneys, four widows, and four widowers in attendance. The first meeting was intended to be organizational but became a "rap session" around the experience of losing a spouse. For the second meeting a month later, the

Delaneys formulated a series of questions concerning widow-hood which they hoped would serve as a basis for discussion. This meeting drew twenty-five people.

As founders, the Delaneys hoped to establish lasting patterns for the new organization. Priority was given to group discussion of questions related to the problems of widowhood that would allow the widowed to express their feelings and seek solutions to common problems. This discussion approach was an adaptation of methods employed by the Cana Conference. In choosing a name for the new organization, Cana's choice of a scripturally significant name was also imitated. The name was taken from that of a village where Jesus performed a miracle for the sake of a widow: "And it came to pass soon afterwards, that he went to a town called Naim . . . and as he drew near the gate of the town, a dead man was being carried out, the only son of his mother, and she was a widow. And the Lord seeing her, had compassion on her and said to her, 'Do not weep' " (Luke 7:11–13). The miracle Jesus performed there was bringing the woman's only son back from the dead.

In addition to group discussion, Naim also stressed personal contact with the newly bereaved. Each month, members were required to visit one bereaved individual as soon after the death of his or her spouse as possible. This was seen both as a service to the newly widowed and as Naim's primary recruitment mechanism. In addition, in order to identify Naim more clearly as a church-affiliated organization, Naim obtained a priest to serve as its chaplain.

For the first two years, the membership of Naim averaged about forty, now the size of a typical chapter. The first meetings were not widely publicized and one-to-one contact was the primary mechanism for recruiting new members. Typically, friends or relatives would pass the name of a newly widowed individual to a Naim member who would then visit that individual and extend an invitation to attend a Naim meeting. This system of outreach did not generate large numbers of new members but, at the time, a membership of forty was seen as a good size for the group and there was no impetus to expand. Care was exercised to keep the membership evenly divided between men and women in order to maintain a social environment in which members could interact comfortably. In addition, forty was accepted as the group's age limit. By setting an upper age limit, Naim clearly hoped to limit its membership to those widows and widowers who had families to raise and to focus on the needs of the "untimely widowed," those who had been widowed relatively early in life. Older widows and widowers were purposely excluded.

From its inception, what the Delaneys called "research" was a central purpose of the Naim Conference. Since Jean Delaney had found little sociological literature that addressed problems of widowhood, the Naim group attempted to generate its own findings. This research was undertaken by means of interviews, questionnaires, and, most prominently, group discussions. At each meeting, the group was divided into smaller subgroups that discussed a selected question and met together later to report their conclusions. Eventually, when there were several Naim chapters, each one was asked to keep notes of discussions and to send these to headquarters periodically so that findings of the various chapters could be shared.

Most importantly, Naim's emphasis on group discussion had a cathartic and supportive objective. The discussion format recognized the need of the newly widowed to, as one former member told an interviewer, "get out of the circumstances of [their spouses'] death and about [their own] life after the death" as a part of an ongoing process of adjustment. Widows and widowers often found that their nonwidowed friends were unable to provide the understanding and support they needed, particularly the need to talk about their loss. Naim attempted to meet this need. An early Naim member described the process: "After a reasonable discussion period we would call for reports from these various people as to what was happening. And we made notes on it, sort of minutes, so that we knew the consensus of thinking that we could anticipate. You know what people are going to say. And they're thinking that they're saying it for the first time which is good for them. But they now know themselves a little better and most of all they know that they are not unique. There are other people having the same thoughts and concerns. And what gives you heart is the fact that someone else has probably greater problems than you and has coped with them. There's encouragement in that."

There was considerable conflict in Naim's early years over providing social activities in addition to the group discussions. Even though Naim's first chaplain wrote that one of the three main purposes of the organization was "to provide some kind of Catholic social outlet for the members of the Conference" (Sullivan, 1964), the fears of the first priest contacted by Jean Delaney were echoed by others. These fears reflected ambiguity about the place of remarriage in a church holding "the higher ideals of celibacy and chaste widowhood" (Sullivan, 1964). As an early member noted, many priests feared that Naim was "creating occasions of sin." However, a particularly distressing problem many widowed people face is the loss of their social support network. No longer part of a couple, the widowed often lose an entire network of relationships built upon an identity as a married person. Both the widowed and their married friends may begin to feel uncomfortable with each other and eventually become more distant. Naim's social activities were accordingly justified as meeting the needs of the widowed for a new social support network within a safe, church-sanctioned context. However, it was clear that Naim's social support role was a secondary function.

Providing social activities for the widowed was, to some degree, an original part of Jean Delaney's plan for the group and reflected her recognition that the widowed are faced with social isolation as well as spiritual and psychological needs. She often stated that "some young widows did not even have a friend with whom they could take their children to the zoo." Social needs were also reflected in the makeup of the original group, which consisted of equal numbers of men and women. It is interesting to note that of the eight original Naim members, six married within the group. For these members, meeting with other widowed people led to marriage and the meeting of social needs. In an effort to maintain a balance between focusing on bereavement and social needs, a basic format of one business meeting, including a discussion program, and one social meeting a month gradually became accepted and served as a model for new chapters. But maintaining such a balance proved difficult as the organization began to grow.

In 1958, two years after its formation, the Naim Conference sponsored a "forum" for widows that drew an unexpectedly large turnout. This event, often referred to as "Naim Sunday," consisted of a religious service and a progam on widowhood presented by Naim members. The forum was preceded by an active effort to contact parish priests, and Naim members were assigned to visit approximately 40 to 50 Chicago parishes to encourage priests to help Naim reach the widowed in their parishes. Notices also appeared in parish bulletins and neighborhood newspapers announcing the upcoming forum. This new effort at outreach complemented the one-to-one contact program as Naim sought to recruit up to 100 new members. However, a metropolitan daily newspaper article describing Naim and announcing the upcoming forum resulted in a totally unanticipated response. Nearly 700 people attended the forum, filling the cathedral to overflowing. Although Naim had hoped to reach more widowed people, the organization was not prepared to deal with the hundreds of widowed people now seeking membership. Since only one chapter then existed, a plan to form additional chapters was adopted. In the year following the forum, three new Naim chapters were formed. Initial meetings of the new chapters were led by members of the original Naim chapter, who gradually turned leadership over to chapter members.

By this time, the chaplain had assumed a major role in directing the Naim Conference, become actively involved in the chapter expansion program, and eventually assumed the title "Reverend Father Director." In 1960, Naim secured office space with the Cana Conference, providing the chaplain with additional prerogatives in coordinating the office and directing the part-time secretary. By 1961, the chaplain was also holding weekly "indoctrination classes" for prospective Naim members in a downtown Chicago location. These classes were intended to be an introduction to the Naim Conference as well as to provide some basic guidance about widowhood. They combined lecture and discussion and covered "the psychology of widowhood," including "how to understand themselves, the adoption of a new life plan, and proper Christian attitudes toward remarriage." Those invited to these indoctrination classes were identified from lists of people who had attended the original Naim Forum and subsequent annual forums. In addition, Naim solicited names of the widowed from parish priests. Each class consisted of approximately 50 widowed people. After attending four such classes, the widowed were invited to join an existing Naim chapter or to form a new one. This activity produced such extraordinary growth in the Naim Conference that by 1963 there were 25 chapters with a membership of 800.

The influx of new members created unanticipated problems for the Naim Conference. Whereas the original chapter of Naim was composed of the "untimely widowed"—people under forty with children still at home—those attracted by the forum and classes were over forty, widowed for many years, with no children at home. Naim's open invitation to the widowed attracted a group more typical for the widowed population than the original Naim members: those less recently widowed, older, and without dependent children. Within a short time, over 50 percent of Naim's membership was over fifty years of age. This shift in the demographic characteristics of the membership had a lasting impact on the organization, for the needs of these two age groups seemed different. The older widowed, who tended to have been widowed longer, were dissatisfied with the content of Naim meetings that focused on the problems of the newly widowed. They found discussions of the problems of widowhood repetitious and tiring. "We've heard all this before," they said, "and we don't need to go over it again and again." The chaplain responded to this dissatisfaction by suggesting that the widowed be divided into two groups: those under forty-five with dependent children, and those over forty-five. This disparity of needs as well as the growing size of Naim were further impetus for the formation of new chapters. Some new chapters were formed with the needs of the older or younger widowed specifically in mind.

The dilemma facing Naim was compounded by other factors as well. Although the founders expected Naim to be a transitional group, there was no mechanism or incentive to encourage members to leave. The one built-in device to keep members from remaining indefinitely, the age limit, was never enforced. When the original members, for example, approached the age of forty-five, the upper age limit was moved to fifty. Eventually the age limit was dropped, except for chapters designated for the widowed with dependent children. Even in these chapters, age limits have been difficult to maintain. All of this has resulted in a membership that has matured and remained within the organization. Whereas there had always been an underlying tension between those who wanted the Naim Conference to become more socially oriented and those who wanted to focus on the grief needs of the newly widowed, the influx of new members tilted the organization toward social goals. The group discussion format began to disappear from Naim meetings, and distinctions between the monthly business and social meetings blurred. Consequently, the business meetings became more social. These changes, moreover, were occurring subtly, with little formal recognition that the needs of an older population were taking precedence over those of the newly widowed.

By 1964, with the expansion of Naim to twenty-five chapters, functions needed to be standardized and communicated to the new chapters. Accordingly, a handbook formulated by a program committee was published. In addition to providing organizational and procedural guidelines, the twenty-six-page handbook included twelve pages devoted to the discussion program and a section entitled the "Art of Leading Group Discussions," indicating the procedure to be carried out as part of each monthly business meeting. The longest section was entitled "Selective Program for Discussion" and included sixteen topics related to widowhood for discussion, with questions to be used by group leaders. It was projected that these topics would provide the basis for a year's discussion program in every Naim chapter. By the time the discussion program was formalized and the handbook published, this format no longer reflected the needs of the majority of Naim's members and fell into disuse.

Another development that contributed to the demise of the chapter discussion program, and with it a large part of Naim's commitment to the newly widowed, was the handbook's proposal to conduct Naim-sponsored "conferences." This program was initiated by Naim's first chaplain and expanded by Naim's third chaplain in 1967. These conferences succeeded the "Indoctrination Classes" or "Education for Widowhood" classes held earlier. As this program evolved, newly widowed Catholics were invited to conferences sponsored monthly by various Naim chapters in different parts of the Chicago Archdiocese. A team of speakers consisting of a priest and several widowed lay people made presentations and guided group discussions among the newly widowed participants. This development was seen as a new way to spread the message of Naim and increase the opportunity for people to join chpaters or form new ones.

The development of the conference program is crucial to an understanding of Naim's transformation from a bereavement-oriented group to one that is socially oriented, since such development encapsulated Naim's commitment to the newly bereaved and freed the chapters to function primarily as social groups. The members could feel their original commitment was not abandoned but shifted to a new place within the Naim organization. This shift was the result of concurrent but coincidental events. On the one hand, the chaplain saw appropriate use of his services in working with the psychological and spiritual needs of the newly bereaved within the conference format. On the other hand, the majority of Naim's members concerned with their own social needs were willing to limit their formal responsibility for the newly widowed to the conferences. By this time, the membership was far less interested in the discussion format for chapter meetings and, in some cases, actively opposed to its use. Accordingly, this delegation of functions seemed congenial to all sides. At present, there is some variation among chapters as a few smaller chapters sometimes hold face-to-face meetings devoted to problems of widowhood. However, the formal program of discussion, derived from the handbook and established by the founders, is not evident in any of the existing Naim chapters.

Support for those having difficulties, whether newly or long-term widowed, is available but only informally through friendships rather than formally through group discussion as it once was. Instead, the tone of most group meetings is decidedly upbeat, with attention given primarily to planning and enjoying a year-round schedule of social activities. This emphasis reflects the wishes of the membership who, according to the findings from our pilot survey (see Chapter Nine), now join Naim primarily to meet their social needs.

As Naim grew to an organization with 26 chapters and over 1,000 members, responsibility for coordination of the organization's activities was assumed by a "council of presidents," composed of the presidents of each chapter, which forms the central governing body of Naim. Although each chapter functions independently, planning its own activities and meetings, the council coordinates conferences for the newly widowed, interchapter activities such as yearly dinner dances, family activities, and special religious services. It also publishes a monthly newsletter.

The most important and regular activities of Naim are the monthly "business" meetings held by each chapter. These meetings combine planning for future activities with socializing and a program. Most meetings open with a discussion of activities sponsored by the chapter. These may include social events, such as dances, excursions, house parties, activities for members and their children, and religious observances, as well as plans for future chapter meetings. Activities sponsored by other chapters are announced so that members may join in these also. Following the business portion of the meeting, some special program is usually presented. In larger Naim chapters, this is likely to be an invited speaker presenting an educational or entertaining talk. Some groups try to alternate programs dealing with serious subjects with entertaining programs. One month a talk may be on coping with stress, whereas the next month's program may feature lessons in disco dancing or handwriting analysis. Problems of widowhood are rarely topics for these programs. Smaller chapters of Naim may offer other activities following the business meeting, such as card playing or party games. In all chapters, an informal coffee hour (which may include dancing in the chapters with sufficient numbers of men) follows the activity and may last well into the night.

The following excerpt of notes by a field observer conveys the flavor of a typical Naim chapter meeting:

The meeting was scheduled to begin at 8:30, but they told me on the phone that that is just when they set up the bar. They usually socialize for about 45 minutes before they begin the meeting. And sure enough, the meeting did not begin until 9:35.

The president of the chapter opened [the] formal meeting. As part of the meeting, guests and new members were introduced. As each person was introduced, the chapter members applauded and the atmosphere was very friendly. I had the sense that each guest and new member were made to feel very welcome at the meeting. Another impressive part of the meeting was a reading of a letter of thanks from a member who had been in the hospital. In this letter the woman expressed her thanks for the visits by the various members, and I believe for a mass that had been offered. . . . They were planning a tenth anniversary dinner and dance as well as a trip to Lincolnshire where they would have a brunch and see a play. The weekend before they all had been to a German restaurant and to see a local amateur version of "Cabaret." Other activities were in the planning stage.

At this point the speaker was announced. This is a woman from the Parents Effectiveness Training Program. Today this woman is speaking about being effective as a single person. After she finishes she invites those with questions to talk to her privately because no one in the group seemed to have questions just then. She also mentioned that the person who had contacted her had told her that they were mostly interested in socializing so she doesn't want to take up any more time than she has to.

At the close of the presentation the man next to me, upon learning that I had to leave right away, urged me to stay and have coffee and cake. . . . At

this time they had put the dance music on, and
[the president] was spreading dancing wax all over
the floor. . . . Two couples were dancing when I left.

Naim's shift in program priorities over the years is reflected in its population change as well. Those who now belong to Naim have been widowed an average of 6.5 years and
their average age is 54.5, according to data from our pilot survey. The newly widowed and the younger widowed have been
replaced by an older and long-term widowed population, most
of whom tend to remain active in Naim for many years. In addition, while the proportion of men and women varies, there is
no chapter whose membership is more than one-third male and
most chapters can count only a handful of men as members.
This contrasts sharply with the nearly equal number of men and
women the first chapter sought to maintain and is more reflec-
tive of the proportion of widows to widowers in general (about
four to one).
      This change in the constitution of its membership from
the relatively younger newly widowed to the older longer-
widowed played a large part in the shift of Naim's goals. The
original plan for a transitional group that would emphasize
bereavement over social needs was reordered and revised over
time. This shift of the group's original emphasis can be explained not only by its changing population but also by the
many-sided needs presented by widowhood itself, moving from
initial bereavement and grief to social isolation. Moreover, as
Naim articulated more closely with the church, bereavement-
oriented functions were assumed by the chaplain through the
conferences, with the assistance of the president's council and
specific members.
      One issue raised in this history of Naim is whether self-
help groups that focus on transitory afflictions or conditions
can maintain their original focus. Two other organizations currently being reviewed by our research team—THEOS (They
Help Each Other Spiritually) and CCWS, (Coordinating Council
of Widowed Person Services of Southeast Michigan)—are likewise directed to the needs of widows. Both groups discourage

social activities so that they may focus on bereavement issues. Accordingly, those widowed for a longer time are inclined to leave these focused groups once bereavement needs are met.

Yet, as with Naim, these groups often are faced with pressure by some of their widowed participants to address social needs. Chapters of THEOS and member groups of CCWS have resisted these pressures to change with varying degrees of success. Some widowed leaders of these groups are ambivalent about remaining so singly focused on bereavement. They often identify with the need for social activity and, as leaders, are concerned about growth and increase in membership. So far they have succeeded in encouraging time-limited participation of newly widowed, especially those who have lost a spouse within the year. CCWS, moreover, encourages "graduation" by repeating its program of workshops and discussions on an annual basis. Longer-widowed people, however, are welcome to join, which suggests the potentialities of a shift to social events if this possibility is not carefully guarded against.

It seems clear that although both bereavement and social needs are equally important and troublesome dimensions of widowhood, each may require a distinct approach. Naim has succeeded in drawing the Catholic Church's attention to a neglected population. Indeed, the pioneering efforts of the founders and others involved may have helped to develop techniques and approaches that can be utilized by priests and other professionals in helping this special population. Professionals can be more focused than those who share the condition and, accordingly, may be especially useful around transitional afflictions. And if this focus and selected emphasis leads over time to a professional astigmatism, then small groups may again arise, led by other "Delaneys," to call attention to the neglected needs of special populations.

CHAPTER 4

Development of a Bereaved Parents Group

Harriet Davidson

The growth and development of Compassionate Friends can be viewed within the heuristic frame provided by Katz's (1970) work on the evolution of self-help groups. In his study of groups of parents of handicapped children, Katz discerned a "natural history" of five stages or phases in the growth and development of these organizations: (1) origin; (2) informal organization; (3) emergence of leadership; (4) beginnings of formal organization; and (5) paid staff workers and professionals. It is useful to view the beginnings of Compassionate Friends in terms of this framework.

Phase 1: Origin. Compassionate Friends was founded in England in 1969 by the Reverend Simon Stephens, a young Anglican chaplain working in a hospital for terminally ill children. The concept of the organization grew out of his work with families in Coventry and is described in Stephens' (1972) book, *Death Comes Home*, which recounts the case study of a family with whom he had worked. Stephens described the problems of many bereaved parents: the gradual withdrawal of the family's social network, which had been active and helpful in the initial period of bereavement, during the long coping and readjustment period; the "conspiracy of silence" surrounding death in contemporary society; the denial of grief and isolation of the bereaved by friends and relatives; a lack of training and sensitivity on the part of professionals who deal with grieving people; and the unavailability of "specialists" and "volunteers" to help the bereaved. His book has become a significant inspirational and cognitive tool for Compassionate Friends and provides its ideological stimulus, for it demonstrates the need for a "ministry of compassion" for parents who are, themselves, working through their mourning in the context of a peer support system.

The first meeting of the Society of Compassionate Friends occurred in Coventry, England, on January 28, 1969, with six members attending. The aims stated at that time were: "To offer friendship and understanding to any person, irrespective of color and creed, who finds himself or herself heartbroken and socially isolated by the death of a child" (Stephens, 1972, p. 76). The group was restricted to bereaved parents from its beginning. One year later, the society had become a national organization with chapters throughout England.

Although Stephens can be identified as the founder of Compassionate Friends, he did not play a central role in the organizational activities of the group. In this sense, he did not become the charismatic leader who served as a central focus of the organization. Although he had lost his own parents in a traffic accident as a youth, he was not a bereaved parent himself. As founder, he performed an essential task—he saw the need and articulated the idea of a society of Compassionate Friends. Although he set up "coffee clinics" that met weekly at hospitals and became the prototype for most of the forty chapters in the British Isles, his primary function was symbolic, inspiring the establishment of the organization through his book, speeches, and media appearances. These evoked a powerful response. Following his appearance on a British broadcast in 1970, he received over 4,000 letters from bereaved parents from every part of the

United Kingdom: "From a duchess whose son had committed suicide, . . . from a farmer's wife in the far highlands of Scotland whose two sons had died of cancer, and they both said the same thing: 'We need help.' " Stephens saw that the problems of bereaved parents transcended differences among people and he worked to bring them together for their mutual advantage.

His contribution to the growth of Compassionate Friends in the United States has been important over the years, as will be seen. Once the American group began, however, his centrality diminished, and others began to take a greater part in its development and expansion.

Phase 2: Informal Organization. In the spring of 1971, an article on Simon Stephens and his work in England appeared in *Time* magazine. In response, Arnold and Paula Shamres, whose daughter had died two years earlier in a train accident, began a correspondence with Stephens which led to his visit to the United States in October of 1972.

The *Time* article and subsequent publicity on the "Today Show" during Stephens' visit in 1972 were significant in the development of the organization in the United States. Just as his ideas had struck a responsive chord in England, so they did in America. Thousands of people from all over the country wrote to Stephens in England.

The first U.S. chapter had begun to hold meetings in a community room in the Miami area. In the fall of 1972, the new American organization of Compassionate Friends published a brochure and guidelines, obtained a post office box, and began to serve as a clearinghouse. Stephens began to refer American correspondence to their headquarters in Hialeah, Florida. Other local chapters were begun by people who wrote or called and said that they wanted to begin a group in their area. With few criteria and no restrictions, a chapter could be started by anyone who expressed a desire to do so. Membership was unrestricted, with no dues or membership fees. A 1975 statement on "Operations" reported: "The branches of the society meet monthly or bi-weekly on an informal basis. Newly bereaved parents are contacted (generally four to six weeks after the death of the child) and invited to come to a meeting. Each branch has a chairperson, and officers and directors who are responsible for keeping minutes and records, and for planning future programs" (Shamres, 1975, p. 9).

The developing national organization in Florida was primarily a two-person organization, staffed by the Shamres who spent most of their spare time answering correspondence and making long-distance phone calls. In the early 1970s, guidelines and substantive advice to local groups from the national office were scant, communication between local regions and the national headquarters was informal, and coordination was loose. Since chapters began with few directives, they developed a great range in format, size, and tone—with varying degrees of stability and success. The leadership and composition of local chapters became important factors in individual group survival.

In some regions, new chapters spun off from established ones in neighboring areas. Typically, parents would travel to meetings for a period of time and then seek to organize a chapter closer to home. Partly because of the convenience of proximity, partly because someone had seen the model and learned the mechanics of holding meetings and sustaining a group, and partly because some parents had arrived at a point where they could help others and wanted to participate in the expansion of the organization, this pattern of "spin-off" became a major mechanism of expansion.

Prior to the first national convention in April of 1978, the University of Chicago Self-Help Project conducted a survey. Forty organized chapters in nineteen states, Canada, and the District of Columbia responded and the growth pattern of the organization to that point was documented. Between October 1972 and November 1976, only seven chapters had been formed (Hialeah, Florida, 1972; Detroit, Michigan, 1973; Hinsdale, Illinois, 1974; Lansing, Michigan, and Tampa, Florida, 1974; Ann Arbor, Michigan, 1975; and Commack, New York, 1976). In 1977 twenty-three additional chapters formed, and in the first four months of 1978 ten more were organized. The slow growth of the first four years accelerated rapidly in 1977.

Many factors contributed to the increased expansion in 1977, including the publication of Harriet Schiff's (1977) book,

The Bereaved Parent, a discussion of the issues and problems faced by a family in which a child has died. Its publication brought a number of public appearances by the author. Perhaps most significant to the development of Compassionate Friends was an appearance by Schiff on the Phil Donahue television show on July 7, 1977. This nationally broadcast "talk show" uses the format of a featured guest and an audience of individuals interested in the topic of the program, who participate in a dialogue with the speaker. Schiff, a former member of Compassionate Friends in Detroit, contacted the Hinsdale, Illinois, chapter and invited them to be a part of the audience on the Chicago-based show. Following this program, Compassionate Friends headquarters in Florida received more than 1,000 letters and calls. Approximately fourteen chapters had existed prior to the July 1977 broadcast, but twenty-six new chapters were started in the nine months following this publicity. Additional significant media attention occurred early in 1978 when Ann Landers published a letter from a member of Compassionate Friends describing the organization and how it had helped her. Again, an outpouring of letters from parents wanting to join an existing chapter or start a new one arrived at the national headquarters.

Thus, the organizational phase of Compassionate Friends in the United States began with loosely coordinated activity on the local level, the establishment of a small functioning national organization, and publicity in the national media. Yet that national organization, with little financial and manpower resources, had difficulty responding to the deluge of requests for new chapters. It required more than motivation, good intentions, and publicity, for it involved making personal contacts, securing meeting places, developing programs, recruiting speakers, publishing newsletters, and manning phone lines by a local core group. It soon became apparent that the national organization needed a greater capacity to respond to the growing requests from bereaved parents.

In sum, the early 1970s saw a tremendous growth in the number of chapters formed and the number of people involved in Compassionate Friends. Nationwide publicity provided exposure for the group and lent legitimacy to its stated goals. Furthermore, there was, during this period, growing receptivity to lifting the taboo that surounded death and dying. This change was evidenced by the steady increase in publications, workshops, and training sessions for professionals and lay persons, the work of Kübler-Ross, widespread acceptance of Schiff's book, the establishment of professional journals, and interest in research on the subject of death and dying. Another factor contributing to the expansion of Compassionate Friends from 1972 to 1978 was the phenomenon of "spin-off," mentioned earlier, where parents participated in groups and then formed their own. Finally, it has become a widely noted phenomenon that many self-help groups were growing at a rapid rate during this period, that in fact the self-help movement as a whole was in a phase of expansion in the United States. As this growth was taking place, the chapters of Compassionate Friends were increasingly finding the need to develop a different structure in order to cope more effectively with the growing complexity of their organization.

Phase 3: Emergence of Leadership. Although the Florida headquarters assumed major responsibilities for organization, members of chapters throughout the country were emerging with skills and experience to meet the changing needs of the organization. A significant development occurred in the 1970s with chapter formation in the Chicago suburb of Hinsdale. Following Simon Stephens' visit to the United States in May 1977, when he met with leaders of the Chicago area chapters, he suggeted that a first national convention be held in the Chicago area to be hosted by the local chapters. The events involved in the convention planning and its aftermath crystallized the emergence of new national leadership.

Since the members of the Hinsdale chapter played a central role in the convention and eventually in the expansion of Compassionate Friends, it is instructive to look closely at the development of this chapter and the leadership that evolved there. The chapter of Compassionate Friends in Hinsdale, as was true of many chapters, began with a few people with a shared experience and a common need. The influence of Simon Stephens was clearly felt. How they took the ideas of the founder and the groundwork that had been laid during the early phases and developed it further is a critical aspect of the history of Compassionate Friends in the United States.

The Hinsdale chapter began in March 1973 when the Reverend Donald Balster, a local clergyman, and his wife experienced the sudden death of their young son. As leaders of their church for fifteen years, they had a strong social network of friends and parishioners who offered support and comfort. The strong visibility and existing relationships of a minister who had been active and involved in the community provided a circle of friends and professionals who helped to "cushion the shock" for them, but left them with a concern and question about how others found the resources to deal with a similar situation.

Although the Balsters had the support of the community, they had other strengths as well. They had dealt with death and loss on an almost daily basis in their joint work in the ministry and in Mrs. Balster's job as nurse in an oncology unit of a local hospital. They were familiar with the existing literature on death and dying since it was germane to their professional lives. On a personal level, they had each experienced the early loss of a parent, had grown up in a rural atmosphere where, as they noted, "we were aquainted with dealing with death . . . as a normal part of life." Although no amount of familiarity with death could minimize the impact of the loss of their child, the foundation of strength and appreciation of the example of others who had endured and survived a loss were a significant resource to them. They had come from a tradition where everyone in the community came to the support of a grieving person and, in the sharing, eased the difficulty. The Reverend Balster viewed the isolation of urban life as contributing to the hardship of coping with grief, so that the notion of a self-help group, a specially formed community, came as a natural response when he saw others struggling with their grief in the absence of the support he had known.

One of the people who had responded to the Balsters at the time of their son's death was Marge Longo, a bereaved parent herself. Although she did not know the Balsters personally, she sent a contribution to the memorial fund for their dead child.

Particularly touched by a gift from someone not known to them, Mrs. Balster responded with a note and a call. Telephone calls were exchanged and gradually an acquaintance formed. Soon it became clear that the shared experience of losing a child and the need for a "listener" with experiential expertise was to be an underpinning of an emerging relationship. The phone calls developed into visits. Discussions, listening, support continued. As Marge Longo told an interviewer: "I invited her over for some coffee and from that a friendship was formed. We went out to lunch once and in the meantime Marian had read Stephens' book, *Death Comes Home*. She brought it over and asked me to read it and I read it and she asked to start a group, and I said, 'Sure, why not?' " They wrote to the Florida headquarters whose address was listed in the back.

In the meantime, the momentum in Hinsdale had started. Two other mothers who had lost a child joined Marian Balster and Marge Longo, and the four began to meet more frequently to discuss books on grief and grieving and how their own experiences related to what they read. While they waited for official guidelines from the Compassionate Friends offices, they developed the procedure of visiting any newly bereaved parent they could and delivering a plant as a token of support. As their work became known, a chaplain who was acquainted with the Balsters called with a referral. Another parent was contacted and recruited through a newspaper article. The coffee groups began to meet on a regular basis. When a new mother would arrive, it was discovered that she "needed a listener," and that each of them could "be a listener." In fact, it was "really very comfortable" to offer that support.

In February of 1974, the small Hinsdale group received guidelines from Florida national headquarters. In April, they met to discuss them, and in May of that year eight to ten people from different parts of the area attended the first "sharing" group meeting of Compassionate Friends in the Reverend Balster's Hinsdale church. The meeting began with the participants taking turns introducing themselves and sharing the death that had brought them there. They then took Granger Westberg's (1962) *Good Grief* and, using it as a stimulus for discussion of the issues they faced, began to go through the book's chapters, talking of their rage at the death, the "shock and denial" they knew, the anger at medical errors, and the difficulties of coping with siblings of the lost child. The early tone was set.

The Reverend and Mrs. Balster and Anthony and Marge Longo, with the help of the others who had joined them, had set in motion a peer support system. By the time the national guidelines were received, the local Hinsdale chapter had a brochure of its own, a logo, and a commitment to forming a self-help group for bereaved parents. When the Hinsdale group received the material from Florida, they decided to join the national effort of Compassionate Friends as a local branch. They became an affiliate in the spring of 1974. Whereas in Florida it was basically one family attempting to start a local chapter, establish a national structure, and sustain a strong publicity effort simultaneously, in Hinsdale a number of people were involved in these activities. The Hinsdale group developed slowly and deliberately. Various group processes and techniques were tried, evaluated, and refined, step by step, and the chapter was a going concern by the time mass publicity brought an influx of new members.

The Balsters and the Longos came from very different backgrounds and made very different contributions to the founding of their group. The Balsters provided the facilities of the church, skills in organizing and leading the meetings, and the stability and position of a clergyman's family. The Longos contributed the seed money to get the group started and served as a sounding board for the day-to-day workers in the tasks necessary to keep the group functioning and growing. Neither couple felt that they could have carried on without help of the other.

When the group began to meet formally, Reverend Balster was able to utilize his training and experience in group process. This led him naturally to the role of "group facilitator" of the sharing meetings. This became important in helping bereaved parents express their anger and rage at religion, their doubts and fears of losing or having lost faith, and ideas and attitudes that might be antagonistic to his own. Often his most important contribution was that of being a "silent model" to a grief-stricken parent who needed a representation of a bereaved parent successfully reinvesting his energies in life.

Anthony Longo was a successful small businessman, father of fourteen, whose official role was chairman of the board of the Hinsdale chapter. He has provided much of the day-to-day practical work in administration of the group. Both Longos had been involved in "one group or another" for many years, and it was Mr. Longo's experience with church, community, and other self-help groups that led him to see the possibilities of the newly forming chapter of Compassionate Friends. The complementarity between the Longos and the Balsters undoubtedly was an important factor in the successful beginning of the Hinsdale chapter. As other parents joined, new hands and skills were added. It was decided quite early in the chapter's formation that the regular "sharing" meeting of Compassionate Friends should be devoted entirely to "grief work" of the bereaved period, whereas all administrative work, program organization, and policy planning would be done at board meetings. Consequently, the board meetings were as businesslike as the sharing meetings were emotional. The division, administration and service, resembles the organization of the church itself, in which the organizing component is important but kept separate from the spiritual service work. At present, the ten local board members are all people who have been active in Compassionate Friends for several years. They joined the group, became involved and interested, and were identified as "leadership people who had basically worked through their own grief."

Thus, the local Chicago area Compassionate Friends progressed slowly from a group of eight to ten people at the first meeting to a sizable force of six chapters in the Chicago region in 1978. From 1974, when the first group started, until 1977, the Hinsdale Compassionate Friends continued with anywhere from fifteen to thirty people attending each meeting. Bereaved parents heard about the group and came to the Hinsdale suburb from many parts of the area. As the group solidified, the need for other, more conveniently located chapters was felt. By 1978, five new chapters had begun in the Chicago area.

A period of expansion was occurring in the Hinsdale region with some success, but at the national level the organization was having difficulty coping with its growing complexity.
The Detroit chapter that had spawned the book, *The Bereaved
Parent*, was in the midst of dissolving; the Florida leadership,
which had begun the national effort, had not been able to keep
together the wide diversity of the regional branches and support
all of the needs of an expanding organization at the same time.
It appeared that the leadership qualities necessary to *develop*
and sustain the system as a nationwide self-help group were different from those compatible with the *founding* of a society in
the United States. In Katz's terms, the phases of the Origins and
Informal Organization embodied different tasks and required
different talents from those of subsequent phases.

In suggesting a national convention, the Reverend Stephens saw the opportunity to encourage the national unifica-
tion and leadership that Compassionate Friends needed. The
Florida headquarters and five other key chapter leaders agreed
to hold the convention in the Chicago area. Many months were
spent in the planning. The Florida and Hinsdale leaders met to
establish basic ground rules. Telephone calls and letters went
back and forth across the country. Finally, the leaders from
New York, Florida, Michigan, Illinois, and Indiana met in Hinsdale to formalize the planning of the convention program. When
the fifty-seven chapter delegates gathered for the convention on
April 28, 1978, they had two major goals. The first was practical: to set up a regionally based board of nine members to guide
the policies and operations of Compassionate Friends. The second was educational and inspirational: to bring together bereaved
parents, delegates, and guests from all over the country in order
to share experiences and build a symbolic structure of identification with Compassionate Friends as an organization and a commitment to work on self-help for bereaved parents in their local
areas.

The convention began with a reception for Simon Stephens, followed by an introduction by Arnold Shamres for the
opening address. On the second day, the morning was spent on
the work agenda of the convention. A report was given by the

United States founder, Arnold Shamres; bylaws were ratified; elections were held; and a national newsletter committee formed. The open meeting allowed a discussion of policy, issues, and membership criteria. Following considerable discussion, the delegates agreed that being a bereaved parent was a crucial requirement for membership on the national board. The national newsletter, a connective link between members of Compassionate Friends in different parts of the country, and an auxiliary communication to people who live in areas too far from existing chapters, was recognized as an important element in building the new national structure. The afternoon sessions run by bereaved parents were devoted to two sets of workshops on such topics as "Coping with Grief," "Marriage and Grief," "Siblings and Grief," "Relationships with Professionals," "Library and Publications," "New Chapter Development," and "Chapter Programs and Leadership Training." In the evening, there was a banquet at which Dr. Elizabeth Kübler-Ross spoke to a large group of members and guests about the work she was doing and the importance of the work of Compassionate Friends.

On Sunday morning, an ecumenical memorial service was led by the Reverend Stephens, the Reverend Balster, and Mr. Shamres. Formal meetings were brought to a close with discussion of funding and budget for the coming year and with the announcement that the Reverend Donald Balster of Hinsdale had been elected president of the new national board of directors of Compassionate Friends. At the close of this convention, Compassionate Friends could be said to have reached the next phase in its development.

Phase 4: Beginnings of Formal Organization. Within days after the convention ended, central national offices were opened in Oak Brook, Illinois. A mailing address was obtained, a schedule of volunteers to staff the office daily from 1:00 to 3:00 P.M. was set up, and a switchboard service to answer calls at all other times was secured. The main task of the office volunteers is to handle correspondence that comes to Compassionate Friends. There are two major functions of the national office. One is to receive letters from bereaved parents and interested professionals from all over the country, sort them into categories for response, and answer each letter as quickly as possible. A great deal of emphasis is put on the rapidity with which the letter is answered, because it is believed that when people write to Compassionate Friends they are in need of an immediate reply. The second major function is to coordinate the system of local chapters. This involves developing new chapters, facilitating communication between the national office and new chapters in the early formulative stages, providing program planning information and advice, and supplying chapters with names of interested individuals who have contacted the national office.

The office staff of parent volunteer members of Compassionate Friends is organized, trained, and efficient. High levels of these qualities are maintained through monthly staff meetings for discussion of problems, methods of operations, and refinements of techniques. The office staff has established procedures for handling correspondence. If a letter is from a bereaved parent requesting advice on ways of coping with grief, there are several possible responses. Where a chapter exists in the area, the parent is directed to it. Where there is no chapter but people are preparing to start one, they are informed of the interested parent, and the correspondent is given the contact's name. In either case, a supportive letter, often containing the name of some helpful books on bereavement, is sent. The staff also coordinates Compassionate Friends contacts and members through extensive record keeping. New chapter development is a crucial part of the business of the national office. At the close of the convention, there was a roster of over 100 names of chapter leaders. Since it appeared that many of these were contacts who had never actually organized a group, the first order of business was to sort out which branches were actually established chapters. A mail survey, conducted by the national office immediately after the convention, indicated that there were sixty functioning chapters as of May, 1978.

Since that time, many new chapters have been formed. When bereaved parents contact national headquarters stating that they want to start a chapter, they are sent information in two phases. First, they are given the national bylaws and general guidelines and asked to write back for a request form for organizing a chapter. If they decide to follow through, they are sent the duties and functions of the national office, a sample newsletter, and a sample news release. They also receive guidelines for volunteers who are contacting newly bereaved persons, an introductory letter to a new parent, and a "library list." After receiving this packet, they are sent a third mailing of legal forms, including those required by the Internal Revenue Service, a letter of permission to use the logo, and Articles of Association. They then formally become an affiliate of Compassionate Friends.

An important factor in the post-convention development of Compassionate Friends was that the opening of the national office in Oak Brook in the Spring of 1978 coincided with repeated broadcasts in cities across the United States of the Phil Donahue Show featuring Compassionate Friends. As a result, during the first summer of operation, letters arrived at the national office at the rate of more than 100 a week. Following this, a "Dear Abby" column on the work of Compassionate Friends appeared in newspapers across the nation, and the volume of people wanting information or assistance, or volunteering to set up a chapter, continued. As of this writing, more than 3,000 letters have been received from bereaved parents, chapter leaders, and others interested in the work of the organization. There are presently 126 chapters meeting formally on a regular basis, and several more are in the process of forming.

The coordinating services of the national structure to chapters include: distributing up-to-date membership rosters to each branch; receiving local newsletters, meeting announcements, and other printed material; and compiling year-end financial reports of the individual affiliates. The second issue of the national newsletter is in the process of being completed, and Certificates of Association are being sent to each chapter indicating its formal affiliation.

It appears that, at this phase of the development of Compassionate Friends, the national system has been solidified into a firmly organized base for expansion in three ways. First, services provided to bereaved parents all over the country have been unified and refined, and new methods by which bereaved parents may help each other can be more easily disseminated.

Second, the content of what is offered, the cognitive information on living with grief and "sharing" with one another, which is the basis of Compassionate Friends, can be improved through communication in a strong national structure. Finally, the organization is able to reach more people and help create more stable local groups by the carefully planned efforts of the national office.

Phase 5: Paid Staff Workers and Professionals. As of this writing, Compassionate Friends is well into the formal organizational phase in its development and shows no signs of moving toward the phase of paid staff workers and professionals. This may indeed not be an inevitable direction for Compassionate Friends. Bereaved parents from all over the United States have invested great amounts of time and energy in the organization and have expended much personal effort in providing help to other bereaved parents. Through their efforts, they have created a strong national self-help system.

CHAPTER 5

Changing Goals in Women's Consciousness Raising

Gary R. Bond & Janet Reibstein

Women's consciousness-raising (CR) groups differ in origin, membership, group structure, and recruitment mechanisms from the other types of self-help groups whose patterns of growth and change have been discussed in this section. Spurred by the intense political climate of the civil rights and antiwar movements in the late 1960s, CR groups were one manifestation of the growing interest of women in the women's movement. As small, autonomous, face-to-face support groups often only loosely affiliated with the larger feminist mass movement, CR groups have never developed their own national organization, although recently the National Organization for Women (NOW) has begun coordinating the formation of such groups nationwide.

The phrase *consciousness raising*, used to describe a change in women's awareness of and interpretation of their problems, started appearing in speeches and pamphlets around 1968. At

a mass ceremony billed as "The Burial of Traditional Womanhood" held by radical women in Arlington, Virigina, during the
height of an antiwar demonstration, feminist leader Kathie
Amatniek articulated the basic notion behind consciousness
raising, that her "sisters . . . really do have a problem as women
in America . . . that their problem is social, not merely personal."
Groups that feminist leaders started forming were called consciousness-raising groups because feminists hoped that through
sharing personal experiences women would reinterpret what
they formerly felt were personal inadequacies as consequences
of the structure of American society. For example, women experiencing difficulty advancing in their careers might realize
that job discrimination, not competence, was at issue.

A decade has passed since the phrase *consciousness raising* was first used to describe these activities. We now have some
perspective on the evolution of CR groups; thus, we can begin
to describe the history of this part of the feminist movement
and to distinguish between actual events and the original hopes
of its proponents. We divide the development of CR into three
phases.

The *first phase* covers the early political beginnings of
CR, when the conception of a new type of group was taking
form. We will describe the context in which the first groups
formed and discuss the originators' intentions—that is, that CR
groups be "relatively short-lived groups [providing] a constant
supply of recruits to the movement's social activist core" (Carden, 1974, p. 73). Many later distinctive features of CR groups
—such as the emphasis on a distinctive *process* rather than on
a particular organization, the loose structure and ambiguity of
CR groups goals, the deliberate avoidance of discussing traditional political issues, and the desire to involve all women, regardless of personal motivations or political consciousness—were
foreshadowed in this early phase. Our documentation for the
pre-1970 period was derived mainly from three articulate accounts by feminist historians (Hole and Levine, 1971; Freeman,
1973; Carden, 1974).

In the early 1970s, CR groups proliferated across the
country. During this *second phase*, CR groups were typically

nonpolitical support groups attracting women whose primary interest was to understand themselves and who often had little desire to become involved in political activities. A national survey in 1974–1975 of 1,669 CR participants (Lieberman and Bond, 1976; see Chapter Seven for a description of the survey), provided a basis for delineating trends during this period. These trends included the ways in which CR spread, the increased use of organizational sponsorship, and the shift in CR groups away from their close association with New Left politics toward becoming a broader-based movement.

By 1976, when we conducted an intensive follow-up study of CR groups sponsored by two suburban New York women's centers (see Chapter Fifteen), the loosely formed, supportive types of CR groups, as represented both in the survey and in the 1976 study, were declining in number. Although we cannot pinpoint the beginning of this *third phase*, currently we can find little evidence of newly forming CR groups of the early 1970s type. In their place are highly structured, time-limited "feminist CR groups." These groups seem to be recapturing the intentions of the early feminists to politicize women.

This chapter traces the evolution of CR groups and attempts to identify the factors explaining both their spread and the changes that have occurred in sponsorship of groups by centers and organizations, in the kinds of women attracted, and in the form and structure of the groups themselves.

Origins

Feminist historians (Hole and Levine, 1971; Freeman, 1973; Carden, 1974) distinguished between the women's rights and women's liberation factions within the women's movement. Organizations devoted to women's rights, such as NOW, were viewed as part of a more conservative, reformist wing of the movement, devoted to legislative changes such as abortion laws and legal reforms. Women's liberation groups, however, had a different history, objectives, and strategies for effecting change. Women involved in these latter groups were generally younger and more radical.

Women's liberation groups were originally formed by women active in the antiwar, civil rights movements and in New Left politics, who found these various male-dominated political bodies unsympathetic to emerging feminist ideas. Jo Freeman in Chicago and Shulamith Firestone in New York, whom Hole and Levine (1971) identify as founders of the original women's liberation groups in these two cities, began groups only after concluding that feminists would not find a forum within extant New Left groups. These groups, formed in 1967, were precursors of the so-called consciousness-raising groups. In 1968, during an antiwar demonstration in Washington, D.C., 500 women from a coalition of women's peace groups split off from the main protests to dramatize the unique goals of the emerging women's movement. Other events similar to these, described by Hole and Levine (1971) and Carden (1974), suggest that the original women's liberation groups grew out of other protest groups, often during the drama and excitement of significant historical events. Other locations for early women's liberation groups included such geographically dispersed cities as Detroit, Seattle, Toronto, and Gainesville, Florida (Freeman, 1973). University campuses were also sites for feminist groups (Carden, 1974).

In this early phase, there was no national organizaton for CR groups. On Thanksgiving weekend in 1968, a national convention on women's liberation held in Chicago attracted 200 women from 37 states. Some represented organized groups, whereas others belonged to no formal group. This conference generated considerable enthusiasm but did not lead to the formation of a single national organization, which in other self-help organizations has served to crystallize the formation of these groups and to focus efforts. In contrast, this conference emphasized the diversity of opinions and goals that has characterized the women's movement, and participants decided against forming closer ties betwen groups in different cities. Apparently, no subsequent national convention of these groups was ever held, although various regional conferences were conducted (Freeman, 1973).

Almost from the beginning, the concept of "consciousness raising" was being used in women's liberation groups. Sometimes the term was used to depict a general process of attitude change, regardless of the specific context. In other cases, the term was used more or less synonymously with the women's liberation groups themselves. The most widespread use of the term referred to a particular *kind* of group with a specific type of format. These were small face-to-face groups in which women shared personal experiences as women. The discussions were directed toward a loosely defined set of "women's issues." The initial inspiration for this particular format derived from numerous sources. The groups were not intended to imitate political study groups. Although many members had experience in political organizations, they were often reacting against the hierarchical structures and abstract rhetoric they had encountered in such groups. One of the early women's liberation groups, the New York Radical Women, provided an early model for CR. According to one account (Brownmiller, 1970), the technique of personal testimony used frequently in their meetings was inspired by the experiences of Carol Hanisch and Kathie Amatniek, two prominent members of the group, who had been impressed by the revival-like mass meetings of civil rights workers in Mississippi. The two women discovered that outraged testimonials by blacks in the equal rights struggle constituted an effective technique for mobilizing blacks to action in the South. The CR format was beginning to take shape.

At the 1968 Thanksgiving conference, Kathie Sarachild, a leader of the New York Radical Women, presented a model for women's liberation group meetings. In her presentation, "A Program for Feminist 'Consciousness-Raising' " (Sarachild, 1970), she outlined an approach to group discussions that legitimized personal experience as a valid and essential method for discovering political truths. Her paper was a response to criticisms within the women's movement by political ideologues who felt that rap groups devoted to personal experiences were unproductive and that these groups should instead discuss the philosophical and sociological underpinnings of feminism. CR, she felt, should not be based on political philosophies. She suggested: "In our groups, let's share our feelings and pool them. Let's let our feelings go and see where our feelings lead us. Our feelings will lead us to ideas and then to action. Our feelings will lead us to our theory." (1970, p. 78).

From other accounts we know that the primacy of feelings over political abstraction did, indeed, become a dominant motif in CR, although probably with different consequences from those intended by Sarachild and others agreeing with her. Feelings did not lead to action in most groups, nor was an articulate theory or ideology forthcoming, leading some women to criticize the structurelessness of CR (Payne, 1973; Joreen, 1973).

Allen's (1970) personal account of her experiences in "Sudsofloppen," a San Francisco group, provided the first published, detailed description of a CR group. Like Sarachild, she described the initial stages of CR as involving the sharing of personal experiences, followed ultimately by a stage of "abstraction" in which a feminist ideology would become apparent after an analysis of personal experiences.

Along these same lines, the "Redstockings" in New York, formed in 1969 by women involved in antiwar protests, changed their original commitment to activism to a commitment to form CR groups. The *Redstockings Manifesto* (1970), detailed an explicitly ideological, persuasive model of consciousness raising in which various topics were discussed within a feminist framework. Shortly thereafter another group formed, called the New York Radical Feminists. This group was perhaps the first to make explicit a new function for CR groups—recruiting women into women's liberation groups. They established a three-stage procedure for inducting new members into their organization. The first stage was an introductory CR group of five to fifteen women meeting over a three-month period. During this period, women would study women's literature. The plan was that these groups, upon completing the CR experience, would continue as an activist cell within the organization.

In this early period of experimentaton with the CR group format, organizers made decisions that influenced the evolution of CR. The fact that CR groups became closely affiliated with women's liberation and not women's rights helped account for the lack of a national organization for CR, since these women's liberation groups prided themselves on their local autonomy. The fact that the founders of the original cells of women's liberation were reacting against abstract political ideology that had, in their view, blinded others to seeing the validity of the feminist viewpoint, helps explain the strong insistence that women speak from personal experience. Perhaps the most important development at this time was the growing identification of the term *consciousness raising* with a particular group format having a distinctive way of discussing personal issues, and not with specific groups themselves. CR became more identified with a *process* than with specific women's liberation coalitions or organizations like the Redstockings or Sudsofloppen. Furthermore, CR groups were viewed, in theory at least, as being more appropriate for women becoming involved in the women's movement than for those already involved. The intention was to create a mass movement with wide appeal. As will be seen, CR did consequently attract women with motivations different from those of the women in the earliest groups.

The central focus of CR as a process suggested a different model of self-help from that used by Mended Hearts, Naim, or Alcoholics Anonymous, all of which institutionalized the local organizational unit, the *chapter*, as the central focus of the organization. In contrast, CR groups were not generally conceived of as organizational entities. Instead, groups were supposed to meet for a finite, but unspecified time, the amount of time necessary to introduce women to then novel ideas about their role in society and to mobilize them for activism within the women's movement. In practice, the groups became ends in themselves, dissociated in large part from the political goals of the women's movement. CR groups actually often continued over a period of years. In the survey, for example, 31 percent of the respondents had been in their current group for a year or more.

Spread of CR Groups

CR groups increased in numbers in the early 1970s. Actual national estimates of women involved in CR were hard to obtain, given the fragmented nature of the movement. Carden (1974) reported that the number of groups in San Francisco increased from six to thirty-five between 1969 and 1970, while in Cleveland the number jumped from one to ten, and in New Haven the number of participants increased from twenty to eighty during the same period. She also cited reports that in 1970 there were fifty CR groups in New York, thirty in Chicago, and twenty-five in Boston. It seems fair to conclude that in the period from 1969 to 1970 or 1971, the number of CR groups expanded rapidly.

How did CR spread? In Chapter Two we identified several factors instrumental in the growth of Mended Hearts, centering on its visitation program. CR groups, unlike Mended Hearts, do not emphasize formal organization, and thus the history of their diffusion offers an interesting contrast. For CR, factors contributing to the spread of groups included the *mass media*, individual *proselytizing* for groups, widespread *availability* of newly forming groups, and the eventual *sponsorship* of CR groups by various women's organizations and women's centers.

The spread of CR groups was facilitated by the popularization of the women's movement through television and newspaper coverage of "media events," such as the protest of the 1968 Miss America pageant (Carden, 1974). Deliberate attempts by feminists to gain public attention often accomplished this end but also led to frivolous stereotypes of feminists ("bra burners," for example), which were also gaining currency in the media. Thus, attention-getting tactics led to both favorable and unfavorable images of feminism. Moreover, the coverage of the women's movement in the general media was not the primary way of reaching women who would later join groups. In the national survey, we asked women to indicate "the three most important sources by which you learned of CR." Women's movement publications, with 46 percent of the respondents indicating this source, were more important than newspapers and magazines (40 percent) or television and radio (16 percent). A further indication of the role of feminist newsletters and magazines in the spread of CR was the manner in which the growth of these publications mirrored the growth of the CR movement. Carden (1974) found eighty-three different feminist periodicals published between 1968 and 1973, with the number of new periodicals greatest in 1971 and declining thereafter.

Freeman (1973) has suggested that the emergence of women's liberation was made possible by the "cooptation" of an existing information network within the New Left, but the survey findings suggest only a marginal role of political networks in direct recruitment. Only 6 percent of the survey respondents indicated that they learned of CR "as a member of a political organization." Women's organizations, however, were a factor in the dissemination of information about CR; 34 percent of the respondents learned about CR from women's organizations to which they belonged, and 28 percent found out through activities sponsored by women's groups.

Personal contacts were more important than mass media and women's organizations as sources for learning of CR: 68 percent of the women surveyed indicated that they learned of CR in this fashion. A majority of the respondents (77 percent) also reported that they had encouraged others to join. The spread of CR seems to have been helped by the enthusiastic response of participants, who would tell others about their positive experiences in groups. More than half of the respondents had joined a CR group after one of their friends had had a positive CR experience.

The widespread availability of groups, once they began to be formed on a broad scale, made it relatively easy for women to become involved. Ninety-seven percent knew personally of at least one group prior to joining. Since CR groups were not joined in a formal organization, women wanting to be in a group could simply form one. In the early 1970s, many groups were formed in this grass-roots fashion: 43 percent of the survey respondents who joined their first group in 1971 or earlier said that their group began among a set of friends. The percentage joining groups formed in this way dropped progressively in the years that followed, going from 33 percent in 1972 to 24 percent in 1973 and to 18 percent in 1974–1975. As another indication of the ease women had in finding or forming a group, we note that 58 percent of the survey respondents were either invited by women about to form a group or were themselves involved in its formation. Most of the remaining 42 percent had little difficulty finding a group. Only 10 percent reported any difficulty.

We can contrast the spread of CR groups with that of self-help organizations with chapter structures (such as Mended Hearts and Naim). Whereas such organizations focus their energies on strengthening their chapters, CR groups did not: Only 12 percent of the CR respondents were invited into an existing group. Thus, CR's membership did not increase through the growth of existing groups but by formation of new groups. The recruitment process of CR was also far less formal than that of such organizations as Naim and Mended Hearts. These organizations specifically identify potential members and then formally invite them to join chapters. Instead, CR groups, formed in a grass-roots fashion, depended on voluntary personal efforts for their spread.

Another contrast between CR and formal self-help organizations concerns the degree of encouragement and support of members' friends and families for the decision to join a group. Not surprisingly, CR participants often felt disapproval from these sources. For example, only half of the CR respondents' closest male friends (or husbands) approved their decision to join a group, compared with encouragement from 87 percent of the spouses of Mended Hearts survey respondents. We can only speculate as to whether this disapproval by persons holding traditional attitudes may have limited the spread in formation of new CR groups.

Increasingly over the years, however, women's organizations played a major role in the formation of groups. Among women joining groups in 1971 or earlier, 40 percent joined groups sponsored by a women's organization or center. The percentage of women joining organizationally sponsored groups grew to 53 percent in 1972, then to 69 percent in 1973, and finally to 73 percent in 1974–1975. During this period, there was no single women's organization that performed this function exclusively, although local chapters of the National Organization for Women or local women's centers appear to have been major organizers. Carden (1974) reported that fifty-five women's centers had been formed nationwide by 1972. These centers, located in homes, YMCAs, churches, and university buildings, served both as meeting places and as communication centers. Some of the centers produced newsletters and some organized CR groups on a regular basis. (See Chapter Fifteen for a description of the role of two such centers in the formation of CR groups.)

The increasing importance of women's centers and national organizations in the formation of CR groups, and the concomitant decline in grass-roots groups, suggest what seems to be an important component in the spread of self-help systems. We propose that such volunteer associations may encounter difficulty in sustaining themselves for any length of time if they depend solely on spontaneous recruitment by members, and thus they require a formal organization to provide coherence and continuity to the volunteers' efforts. We suspect that the enthusiasm for a particular phenomenon—in this case, CR—is often greatest when the ideas are new and possibilities seem unlimited. Whatever the reason, the survey indicated that the numbers of CR participants who were encouraging others to join did, indeed, decline during the 1970s. Over half of those joining in 1971 or earlier said that they had encouraged others to join. Of those joining in 1973, only 37 percent had done so, and among the most recent CR group joiners, only 25 percent had encouraged others. The decline in individual efforts to proselytize for CR also may reflect the growing tendency for women's centers and organizations to assume the responsibilities of publicizing and recruiting new members, responsibilities formerly taken by individual participants. In fact, as we examined the history of other self-help organizations, such as Naim and Compassionate Friends, we found that in their earliest stages the groups' original proponents acted as individuals and reached out to others on a personal basis. Later the responsibility for such outreach typically was taken over by a committee. In the cases of both Naim and Compassionate Friends, these committees used fewer personal modes of contact, instead using letters and notices in church bulletins. Although individual members continued to make some contacts, the major responsibility had shifted.

It seems that as groups began to be formed by women's centers and organizations, they also became more tightly struc-

Table 1. Initial Group Activities by Method of Group Formation

Activity[a]	Method of Group Formation			Total	X^2 (2 d.f.)
	Women's Organization (N=917)	Friends (N=380)	Spin-Off from Another Group (N=155)	(N=1443)[b]	
Members talked about their lives	68.6	66.3	62.6	67.4	2.4
Scheduled general topics for each meeting	68.3	44.4	45.2	59.6	32.4[c]
Talked about whatever members wanted to bring up	49.4	63.4	63.9	54.6	27.3[c]
Person with experience in CR group came to get the group started	67.8	19.7	28.4	51.0	284.2[c]
Scheduled specific personal issues to discuss each meeting	40.6	25.8	25.8	35.1	78.1[c]
Discussed reading on women's issues	22.0	28.4	25.8	24.1	6.3
Debated whether the focus should be personal or political	18.6	26.3	22.6	21.1	9.7

Note: Entries in table are percentage of repondents.
a "What did your group do in the first month or two?"
b The remaining 226 either had not yet joined a group or listed some other specific method of group formation.
c p < .001

tured in their format, as indicated by the "initial group activities" shown in Table 1. The most important change employed by the women's organizations and centers was the use of "starters." These were women already experienced in CR who would attend the first few sessions of a CR group and help direct the group. Often they helped to train women according to a set of guidelines which suggested such things as setting a topic and having each woman speak on that topic from personal experience for a set, short, uninterrupted period of time. Two thirds of the survey respondents in groups formed by women's organizations reported that they had such an outside leader. This seldom happened in grass-roots groups. Groups formed by women's organizations or centers stressed the assignment of topics for each meeting, whereas women in groups formed through friendship networks were more likely to have free-floating discussions on whatever the members themselves wanted to bring up. This growing insistence on greater focus, we believe, stemmed from the antagonism of women's centers toward the use of CR groups for psychotherapeutic purposes. But even in groups formed by women's centers, members often used the groups in this fashion. (See Chapter Fifteen.)

Thus, despite the increasing feminist focus brought by the growing role of women's organizations, CR groups were continuing to diverge from their original purposes. Perhaps this can be explained in part by the fact that the kinds of women attracted to CR changed during the 1970s. When we examined women's motives for joining, using the dimensions described in Chapter Seven, we found a sharp decline in political activation as a motive (see Table 2). And, although help seeking did not increase during this period, more recent joiners reported greater psychological distress prior to starting groups than those starting earlier. Using the Hopkins Symptom Checklist (see Chapter Seven), the level of distress by year of joining was as follows: 1.58 (1970 and earlier), 1.64 (1971), 1.68 (1972), 1.73 (1973), 1.76 (1974), and 1.96 (1975) (linear trend significant at .001 level). The typical woman joining CR in 1975 was very different from the one joining in 1970. She was less attracted to the political goals of CR and more psychologically distressed. There-

Table 2. Motives of CR Participants by Year of Initial Involvement

Motive	Year						1976 outcome sample	Total survey	Trend analysis (Survey data only)	
	Pre 1971	1971	1972	1973	1974	1975			Linear F	Nonlinear F
Interest in women's issues	1.52	1.54	1.54	1.54	1.55	1.52	(1.56)	1.54	<1	<1
Help seeking	2.54	2.52	2.41	2.44	2.44	2.22	(2.43)	2.44	1.8	<1
Social needs	2.61	2.57	2.60	2.46	2.60	2.36	(2.77)	2.56	<1	2.2
Political activation	2.23	2.54	2.63	2.72	2.77	2.72	(3.22)	2.68	31.9[a]	1.6
Sexual awareness	2.95	2.96	3.03	2.95	2.87	2.80	(2.92)	2.93	4.0	<1
Curiosity	3.06	3.06	3.18	3.16	3.05	3.28	(3.04)	3.10	<1	1.7
N	89	113	217	357	593	29	41	1398		

Note: See Chapter Seven for a description of these factors. Scores are mean ratings for items loading on each factor: 1=very important, 2=important, 3=somewhat important, 4=not important.
[a] $p < .001$

fore, the typical woman was more likely to use her CR group for a psychotherapeutic experience.

Later Trends Within CR

Although our information on current trends within CR is scanty, it appears that women's liberation groups, as separate organizations from women's rights groups, have declined in number since the mid 1970s. There has been a consolidation of groups within the women's movement, so that the split is much less pronounced that five years ago (Libbee, 1978). NOW has incorporated some of what were previously "controversial" stances (on abortion and lesbians, for instance) within its official policy, although passage of ERA has recently been its top priority. Women's liberation, as that term was understood in 1970, is receiving little mass media attention. From interviews with feminists living in Chicago, Los Angeles, New York City, and Boston, we have discovered no active effort to form CR groups in the fashion of the early 1970s. College campuses apparently have fewer feminist organizations sponsoring CR groups. Admittedly, it is difficult to estimate the extent of grass-roots activity, and CR groups may still be widespread in some areas. There is some evidence that the mental health professions, which previously assimilated many of the ideas generated by the Human Potential Movement, are responding similarly to the concept of CR in their groups for women only. For example, at the 1978 meeting of the American Psychological Association, a demonstration of CR by mental health professionals generated considerable enthusiasm among forty to fifty participants in attendance (McGrath, 1978).

Groups of the CR type have been used in outpatient clinics (Reibstein and others, forthcoming) and in an evaluation study for a widowed population (Barrett, 1978).

Since the split between rights and liberation groups has, by and large, mended, and since the trend has been for CR groups to come under the wing of women's organizations, we turned to NOW as the most public feminist organization to find out what it now offers, if anything, under the rubric of consciousness raising. In 1974, NOW established a National CR Task Force. Subsequently, NOW has been active in the formation of "feminist" CR groups. The guidelines developed for these groups by the Los Angeles chapter (Perl and Abarbanell, 1976) sharply distinguish "feminist" CR groups from the autonomous CR groups that predominated in the early 1970s.

Specifically, the groups are structured by NOW to counteract tendencies that led earlier CR groups toward psychotherapeutic goals, and to promote feminist "political activation" goals. In contrast to CR's earlier days, when groups had no organizational affiliation, NOW can and does exert control over groups and their format. The primary differences between NOW-led groups and the types of CR groups that preceded them are:

1. NOW groups have a designated, trained leader who guides the group along the lines of feminist issues.
2. NOW groups are time limited. The groups meet for a span of ten weeks, after which they are disbanded. Formerly, CR groups, which often met indefinitely, would, over a period of time, become diverted from a topic orientation to a general discussion of life problems. Long-term groups, in the view of NOW organizers, implicitly if not explicitly encouraged the use of a sympathetic group to absorb whatever anger, frustration, or determination the sessions evoked, rather than mobilizing members for action in their personal lives. The short-term groups were conceived to counteract this tendency, and to generate a degree of personal dissatisfaction which would then be directed toward tangible goals.
3. Topics for group discussion are defined more precisely in feminist terms. For example, while the use of guidelines was widespread among the former type of CR groups, the suggested topics would often be more general (for example, "Mothers and Fathers") than the topic formulation in the NOW manual (for example, "When/how were you first aware of your mother as a woman and wife instead of only a mother? To your knowledge, was your mother ever rebellious or unhappy as a woman/wife?").

Workshops for NOW CR groups have been held in various cities around the country, and Harriet Perl, the national NOW coordinator of CR, has indicated to us in a telephone conversation that "thousands" of copies of the guidelines have been requested and distributed nationwide over the past three years, suggesting widespread interest in this model of CR. Four regional chairpersons of the CR Task Force have been appointed. These women supply manuals to NOW chapters requesting them, schedule CR training workshops, and coordinate other CR-related meetings. In telephone conversations with two of these chairpersons, we learned that CR groups are currently forming, although the chairpersons indicated that the requirement that leaders be trained has led to there being fewer groups available at any one time than the number of women interested in them.

Conversations with key women in the women's centers that participated in the outcome study described in Chapter Fifteen revealed that, in response to the findings of this study, one of these centers disbanded and formed chapters of NOW; these chapters have adopted the NOW model of CR. This occurred because the organizers were dissatisfied with the fact that their CR groups had evolved into personal support groups, which the study documented. In the second center, there was a similar response, and their guidelines have been reshaped to include focused feminist discussion at the end of each session. Although these groups remain leaderless, there are "connection" meetings every other month in which ongoing groups or representatives of them join at the center to conduct a joint CR session, thereby increasing the training in and encouraging the use of the focused discussion segment of the CR session.

The question arises whether or not these new "feminist" CR groups actually promote political activism, as their antecedents did not. Organizers reported that participation in NOW CR groups was closely linked to recruitment into other NOW activities. As a rough indicator of whether these feminist CR groups indeed have been feminist, four women with personal experience (either through leading or participating in, or by starting and remaining in regular touch through "connection" meetings) of twenty-seven groups over the past two years were asked whether participants were becoming members of the organizations' various issues- and activities-oriented task forces. In roughly half the cases, on the average, women who had completed the ten CR sessions had joined such task forces. In the case of one feminist CR group, all the women signed up for a NOW task force. In others just less than half did so, but in most cases just over half did sign up for further activities.

In summary, it would appear that a new type of CR— "feminist" CR—is emerging and being promoted by NOW. It is too early to tell whether this development is a temporary phase, or even whether these groups will become further institutionalized within the NOW structure. Although NOW organizers are optimistic about their feminist CR groups, it is difficult to predict the future character of CR groups.

Conclusions

The evolution of CR has involved the resolution of a number of core issues critical to the stability and growth of any self-help organization or movement. Some of the same themes that have been important in the history of CR groups may be discerned in the development of Mended Hearts, Naim, and other self-help groups, though the actual resolution has varied.

One issue has been how to transmit the self-help group founders' ideas to succeeding "generations" of new members. A system may evolve in quite different directions from that which its originators intended, as the histories of CR and Naim suggest. In part, the different needs and motivations of succeeding generations contribute to these divergences. Founders may "misread" the needs and goals of those who will in actuality seek out their group.

In CR, as in other groups, this issue has emerged most acutely in *the competing needs of old and new members*. The problem facing the early women's liberation groups was the dramatic influx of women interested in the women's movement but whose "consciousness" was much different from that of the early organizers. One solution, which did not prove manageable, was to organize these women into their own CR groups on the assumption that, as cohorts, these new "cells" of women would move toward a more activist stance. One problem with this strategy was that it failed to create bonds between old and new members, making assimilation into the organization difficult.

This same problem, the competing needs of old and new members, was found in the widows' groups described in Chapter Three. For widowed persons, the solution may be to form entirely separate organizations. In other groups, such as Mended Hearts, the older members assumed the express function of reaching out to those who have recently experienced the loss or trauma. In such groups, old and new members are given complementary roles, which, Riessman (1965) has suggested, benefit both helper and helpee. In groups that treat addictions, such as Alcoholics Anonymous, the ethos that one is never cured reduces the status distinction between members.

The place where the evolution of CR has departed most radically from the development of other self-help groups has been in the relationship between the groups themselves and some national organization. It is interesting to speculate what would have happened had the 1968 Thanksgiving Conference coalesced the incipient women's liberation movement into a formal organization. The current NOW sponsorship of CR groups represents a vast change in the relationship between CR groups and superordinate organizations. From a deliberate "nonrelationship" between them to a rather loose sponsorship (for example, organizations started groups and provided suggested guidelines), there is now great organizational control over CR groups. NOW indeed sponsors groups as an ancillary activity to its major goals of legal and economic reforms. The relationship of NOW to CR groups might be likened to the American Cancer Society's sponsorship of Reach-to-Recovery volunteers. In both cases the main mission of the parent organization is directed toward social policies, not to providing direct service to members. In such an arrangement the commitment of resources by the parent organization is not guaranteed. It remains to be seen whether CR groups will flourish under these circumstances.

Nonetheless, the changes toward highly structured CR introduced by NOW represent solutions to vulnerabilities such as loose structure, loose goals, and shaky recruitment and publicity procedures previously faced by newly formed CR groups. Other self-help groups face such issues too. The very fact that NOW apparently has become the major organizer of CR groups can be linked to the need for a source of *legitimation* for newly formed groups, as has been discussed in Chapter Two. The vacuum in goals, for instance, found in grass-roots groups, which led them to become therapeutic rather than political groups, has been counteracted both through imposing well-defined guidelines and introducing leaders who are clearly feminist into CR groups to help control their content and format. The imposition of a time limit—ten weeks—also inhibits the possible discovery of potentially fundamental differences among women on, for instance, the basis of age, marital status, degree of psychological need, or occupation. This is important since there is evidence that this variety can undercut the discovery of commonality in CR groups. In interviews with women who participated in the outcome study (Chapter Fifteen), we found that some women were bothered by the *lack* of commonalities among their group members. The time limitation introduced in NOW "feminist" CR groups, by decreasing the likelihood that important differences will emerge over time, probably helps to cement the bond of assumed similarity in CR groups.

Another issue faced by self-help groups is how to prevent the emergence of topics that do not focus directly on the problem the group is meant to address. For CR groups, the question was how to ensure that topics explicitly relate to feminism. How can this be done if groups are essentially unstructured? Divergence from a central focus seems to be a likely outcome when members share personal experiences around general topics. The decision by NOW organizers to promote highly structured groups helps to ensure that the "right" teachings are transmitted to the members. It is at this point that the distinction Libbee (1978) made between *persuasion* and *education* becomes relevant. Persuasion is the process of converting someone to a specific set of beliefs, for example, an ideology. As Antze (Chapter Twelve) points out, persuasion is the goal in Alcoholics Anonymous, Synanon, and Recovery. The purpose of education is to discover personal truths through an examination of ideas and facts—which was precisely the modus operandi of the nonideological CR groups. The organizers of the early CR groups had the conviction that the educative—or consciousness-raising—process would lead, presumably without persuasion, to a feminist ideology. NOW groups, by moving toward an explicit ideology, have transformed the structure of CR groups so that they more closely resemble the "persuasive" type of self-help group, since in NOW groups there currently is an explicit feminist ideology with group leaders focusing discussions to *persuade* women toward the feminist view.

CHAPTER **6**

Help Seeking
and Self-Help Groups

Morton A. Lieberman

A central concern of our self-help studies has been to understand why individuals in our society utilize self-help groups
rather than other societal resources when confronted with crises
in their lives. We have examined characteristics of the people as
well as the social surrounds of self-help group users. We have
also looked at certain self-help groups' characteristics that may
offer users, given alternative helping resources, a unique setting
or type of service leading to their choice of self-help groups.
The results of such examinations could aid in our understanding
of the role and place of self-help groups in the total range of
societal helping resources.

Some Hypotheses

In setting out to examine this issue, our studies have been
guided by several general hypotheses about why people seek out
self-help groups. One common explanation, which has historically been used to explain both the rise of self-help groups in
our society and the motivation for seeking out such institutions,

rests upon the notion that self-help groups arise to fulfill services not being currently met in society by other systems. On an individual level, we asked whether, given a particular affliction, people sought out a specific self-help group because they perceived the world they lived in as not containing appropriate resources for their particular dilemma. In brief, we designed our studies to test, from the individual's perspective, the lack of resource hypothesis.

An alternative hypothesis about the pathways through which individuals reach particular helping resources in our society involves a chain of attempts by individuals to find suitable service. This "disappointment hypothesis" is based upon the oft-noted observation that many individuals use a multiple series of helping resources (those that they previously used were "disappointing to them") and that one of the factors causing individuals to find their way to the doorstep of self-help groups is that they are individuals who did not receive the kinds of help they wanted from other societal resources.

Yet another perspective on help seeking is embedded in exchange theory. For those seeking help as well as those offering help, the exchange of tangible and intangible resources provides a framework for examining the helping process as well as the pathways through which individuals locate necessary resources. Individuals may seek out self-help groups not because they are disappointed users of other societal resources nor because other resources are unavailable, but rather because self-help groups require the least expenditure of resources, the least effort in order to locate a needed resource for themselves.

Another alternative for understanding why individuals seek out self-help groups is offered by a view regarding the specification of service. Here the issue centers on the particular form or kind of service a helping resource in our society can offer. Those in need of help may perceive the self-help group as being the best fit between their needs and its particular characteristics of service delivery. The perception of the clients is that among alternative institutions within our society, they judge a particular helping resource to maximize the fit between their needs and what that system can offer.

Of course, these four views are not mutually exclusive or contradictory. They do, however, serve to organize our investigations and channel them into appropriate directions of inquiry with regard to the motivations of individuals who have sought out self-help groups.

Most investigators of helping resources have divided the turf into the study of either the individual's social network or professional systems. Those interested in informal helpers have asked questions about the utility and frequency and the characteristics of the person and the social system that lead individuals to utilize significant others in solving life's dilemmas. Other investigators have turned their attention to a wide variety of professional systems that are perceived as resources: physicians, psychotherapists, clergy, lawyers, police, teachers, and social agencies. This division of, on the one hand, informal social network and, on the other hand, professional helping systems does not provide a useful structure for examining self-help groups; they are formal systems usually composed of similarly afflicted strangers. Self-help groups have a structure and a set of boundaries distinguishing them from what has been commonly described as informal networks. In this sense, they share some important characteristics of professional resources. However, they rarely possess the societal legitimation so characteristic of formal helping-giving professions, nor do they require the type of exchange characteristic of professional helping resources. In this sense they resemble informal resources.

Despite such differences between self-help groups and formal service providers, the decision by an individual to join a self-help group involves many of the same processes. Since self-help groups are not readily available, seeking them out requires expenditure of effort and energy comparable to that expended in seeking out professional systems. Self-help groups are bounded systems usually composed of strangers not in the immediate social network of the individual. As with professional help, people must cope with their "resistance" in obtaining help from self-help groups.

A comparison between help-seekers who use their kith and kin when faced with distress and those who rely primarily on professional systems in similar circumstances provides a starting point for examining the pathways to self-help groups. Are the factors that influence use of professionals similar to the ones that influence the choice of self-help groups? Or, do such groups possess characteristics that resemble more the conditions found in a person's own social network?

Empirical Findings on Help Seeking

Prior to examining some of the findings from our studies on self-help groups, we will briefly review the state of knowledge from empirical studies on who seeks help. The review is based upon the work of Nancy Gourash and was reported in its fuller version in the *American Journal of Community Psychology* (Gourash, 1978).

Epidemiological studies have established that the majority of people who report experiencing troublesome life events do seek help for their problems (Gurin, Veroff, and Feld, 1960; Lowenthal, Thurnher, and Chiriboga, 1975). The key factors that differentiate those who do and do not seek help are age and race. Help seeking has been shown to decline consistently with age (Gurin, Veroff, and Feld, 1960) and to be more prevalent among whites than blacks (Baker, 1977; Gurin, Veroff, and Feld, 1960; Rosenblatt and Mayer, 1972).

People who solicit help are usually looking for comfort, reassurance, and advice (Gurin, Veroff, and Feld, 1960; Weiss, 1973; Zimbardo and Formica, 1963). They tend initially to turn to family and friends and contact relief agencies or professional service organizations only as a last resort (Booth and Babchuk, 1972; Croog, Lipson, and Levine, 1972; Litman, 1974; Quarentelli, 1960). The sole use of professional services occurs much less frequently than either exclusive reliance on family and friends or help seeking from both the social network and professional sources (Rosenblatt and Mayer, 1972).

Although people who seek help within their social network appear to represent a cross section of the general population, those who eventually go to human service agencies are readily identified by a common core of characteristics. Investigators of discretionary medical and dental care, mental health, social service, and legal facilities, and self-help groups have found repeatedly that users tend to be young, white, educated, middle-class, and female (Beck, 1961; Hollingshead and Redlich, 1958; Kadushin, 1969; Kammeyer and Bolton, 1968; Katz and Bender, 1976a; Kravits, 1972; Srole and others, 1962; Sue and others, 1974). More recent investigations, however, suggest that social class may no longer differentiate those who do and do not use professional services. In studies of people experiencing emotional distress, education and income were not found to correlate with the use of mental health facilities (Baker, 1977; Tischler and others, 1975). These authors suggest that the success of efforts to link public services and lower-class consumers accounts for the lack of association between socioeconomic variables and help-seeking behavior.

No one type of problem invariably precipitates the search for assistance, but there appear to be some common linkages between certain types of problems and sources of help. The social network is the primary resource for general worries and unhappiness, with spouses being the focal helpers for worries and friends the major resource for unhappy emotions (Gurin, Verhoff, and Feld, 1960). Family, friends, and neighbors are the predominant source of aid in national (Quarentelli, 1960) and family crises (Boswell, 1969). Within the middle and working classes, the social network is a major provider of economic assistance (Burchinal, 1959; Sussman, 1960). Professional help is sought for problems ranging from severe emotional distress (Gurin, Verhoff, and Feld, 1960; Kadushin, 1969) to discrete strains suffered under the press of work or family roles (Beck, 1961; Kammeyer and Bolton, 1968; Levine and Preston, 1970; Lurie, 1974)—strains that frequently arise from problems with network members.

Studies attempting to link help-seeking patterns to various network characteristics have yielded inconsistent findings. Size and proximity (Baker, 1977; Horowitz, 1977; Kammeyer and Bolton, 1968; Martinez, 1977), relative amounts of contact with friends as opposed to family (Horowitz, 1977; McKinlay, 1973), centrality with regard to provision of economic and emotional support (Hammer, 1963; McKinlay, 1973), and the number of reciprocal relationships (Ferber and others, 1967; Tolsdorf, 1976) were found to predict both use and nonuse of professional services. As a consequence, subsequent investigations considered the functions of networks in attempts to account for whether and from whom help is sought. It has been hypothesized that members of the social networks can affect help seeking in a number of ways: (1) by buffering the experience of stress, which obviates the need for help; (2) by precluding the necessity for professional assistance through the provision of instrumental and affective support; (3) by acting as screening and referral agents to professional services; and (4) by transmitting attitudes, values, and norms about help seeking.

First, the social network appears to serve as a natural support system that counteracts the effects of stressful life events. The proportion of network members providing emotional support and the frequency of contact with network members were found to be inversely related to psychological distress among college students (Liem and Liem, 1976) and residents of low-income housing (Hessler, and others, 1971). Among women who experienced multiple life changes prior to and during their first pregnancy, only those with minimal social resources developed serious medical complications (Nuckolls, Cassel, and Kaplan, 1972).

Second, most people perceive their social network as a major source of help (Litwak and Szelenyi, 1969; Wellman, 1973, 1976). Empirical evidence suggests that these perceptions are generally accurate (Croog, Lipson, and Levine, 1972; Quarentelli, 1960). In many instances, people turn to professional agencies only when assistance is not available within the network (Kasl, Gore, and Cobb, 1975; Quarentelli, 1960).

Third, a parallel body of research has demonstrated the central role of the social network in decision making and referral to formal services. Investigations in which respondents named the people who influenced their decision to seek health care from a new medical facility (Booth and Babchuk, 1972), to request treatment at a psychiatric hospital (Liberman, 1965), and to have an illegal abortion (Lee, 1969) revealed that family members, friends, or co-workers made up at least 75 percent of the people named as influential. In addition, these same individuals were reported to be instrumental referral agents once the decision to seek professional assistance had been made. In a study of information community care givers Leutz (1976) reported that one of the most frequent forms of assistance supplied to help seekers was referral to human service agencies.

The fourth function of social networks is the transmission of values and norms that facilitate or discourage the use of professional services. Freidson (1969) suggests that many people (accountants, lawyers, teachers) participate in a network characterized by values and norms congruent with those of people who deliver services. Such people may subsequently use professional services regardless of the availability of a supportive social network. This mechanism of network influence, however, has received scant empirical attention. Kadushin (1969) found that urban adults entered psychoanalysis by meeting people actively involved with psychotherapy or by making contact with local "sophisticated" cultural circles. In an epidemiological study of psychological well-being, Gurin, Veroff, and Feld (1960) found that the elderly composed the one subgroup of the general population most likely to prescribe to norms of self-reliance. In addition, they were a group that tended not to seek assistance for their problems.

Some investigators see the help-obtaining behavior of adults in our society as a sequential series of approximations in which, in the ordinary course of events, individuals utilize their social networks for some forms of help but more frequently as a means of locating appropriate professional helping sources. A critical role of the social network is its channelization and focusing function in influencing the form of help individuals will receive from professional systems. Social networks function as gatekeepers and channelers. Where does self-help lie in this sequence? Is it one of the alternative series of settings on a par, from this perspective, with systems staffed by professionals?

Yet another perspective would be that the chain runs from informal sources that channel into professional systems, and that professional systems serve to channel individuals into self-help groups. Or are sources of help used serially, with individuals migrating from one to another depending on their actual experience in each? From this viewpoint, individuals initially seek out their social networks, find that the help they desire or need is not forthcoming, then seek out other professional systems, are disappointed, and, perhaps then, utilize self-help groups. An understanding of the role and function of self-help groups in our society would be appreciably aided if we were able to describe which of these alternative pathways best fit. It would make a difference in understanding the rapid spread and expansion of self-help groups if participants entered such groups because of failures of other helping systems—for example, if the self-help groups were preferred to alternative helping resources because of some of their unique characteristics, such as an emphasis on egalitarianism.

In order to understand better the characteristics of those who seek out self-help groups for aid, we need to step back and examine, in general, individuals who seek both formal and informal sources of help when faced with distressing life circumstances—be they problems of everyday living, problems created by particular crises within individuals or their families, or radical changes in their lives associated with particular transitions across the adult life span. To place help seeking in context, we have drawn upon an ongoing study, the Transitions Study (by Morton Lieberman), to put in perspective the utilizers of self-help groups.

The Transitions Study: A Model for Predicting
Help-Seeking Behavior

This study examines the process by which people, who, for the most part, adapt successfully to changes in their lives, utilize the helping resources within their environments for such adaptation. We were interested in identifying these resources, both formal agencies specifically structured to provide help and the informal social networks that may play a crucial role in adaptation. The study was designed to analyze the major events and changes in the lives of adults that require coping effort. Inquiry into help seeking involved the identification of relevant institutions in our society, both formal and informal, that are contacted by persons seeking assistance in coping with stressful life situations. Our research also involved the isolation of personal factors associated with effective resource utilization, such as the person's place and role in society. Other major considerations involved the differences between people who are able effectively to use society's resources for coping and those who cannot, and the characteristics of resource systems that enable them to provide effective services for various groups in our society.

This project has been underway since 1972. In that year, scheduled interviews were conducted with 2,300 people representative of the adult population of the census-defined urbanized area of Chicago. In 1976–1977, 1,106 respondents were reinterviewed.

The survey interview schedules for both Time 1 and Time 2 studies share three major focuses. First, the interviews were designed to assess a wide range of problems and hardships that people experience as workers and breadwinners, husbands and wives, and as parents. A second focus involved the identification of resources and reactions people use in coping with life strains. The third focus was on enumeration of symptoms indicative of emotional stress and psychological disturbance. The 1976–1977 follow-up was enlarged to include both the life-cycle transitions through which people had passed and the crises they had confronted in the four years following the first interview, as well as the processes of obtaining help that they had employed in their efforts to cope with these events.

Chapter One of this volume demonstrated the rapid growth of self-help groups. Studies reported in Chapters Two through Five of specific self-help groups—Mended Hearts, Naim, women's consciousness-raising groups, and Compassionate Friends—document their growth pattern. These studies do not, of course, address the rates of utilization within society. No good epidemiological data exist with which to assess such rates in contrast to other sources of aid in our society—both informal (social networks) and professional systems. However, some information from the Chicago probability sample of adults, the Transitions Study, provides an overview of a variety of problems people encounter over the adult life cycle and the frequency with which they use various helping resources, including self-help groups. (See Table 1.)

Overall, approximately 5 percent of our sample, in turning to some resource for help, used self-help groups. At best, this is a crude approximation; detailed inquiry and definition of what constituted a self-help group in the minds of our respondents were not available. What the information contained in Table 1 does show is that, given a set of life problems that occurred within a four-year period, a small but meaningful number of adults turned to self-help groups for aid.

Given a particular life dilemma, what are the characteristics of individuals and their social content that influence them to seek help? Do those general factors of help-seeking help us to understand the seeking out of self-help groups for such aid? To begin, we will draw from the previously mentioned Transitions Study and from the work of Brown (1978), who has developed a model for examining influences on help-seeking behavior. What follows is a synopsis of Brown's findings using the Transitions Study data.

The framework developed by Brown attempted to link the nature of particular life crises or life conditions with individuals' responses in seeking resources external to themselves, that is, in seeking help. A variety of intervening conditions were postulated to affect whether or not an individual would seek help. Explored was the degree to which a particular event or crisis thought to generate help-seeking behavior was, in fact, perceived by an individual as distressful. Aside from the particular characteristics of a specific life crisis, the overall amount of life strain that the individual was experiencing was thought to be a potential source leading him or her to seek out help. Help seeking was viewed in a framework of one of a variety of alternative coping strategies, and it was thought that individuals who had considerable coping resources or personal resources might be less likely to utilize help. Brown assessed three types of coping resources. The first was self-esteem. The second was adequa-

Table 1. Help Seeking and Self-Help Groups

Condition	Sample	Percentage having event who sought help	Type of Help Used		
			Social network	Professional	Self-Help
Problems at work	29	22	79	23	1
Being unemployed	1	62	10	60	30
Being retired	2	40	38	62	
Problems being homemaker	1	54	71	29	
Problems with child 0–5	0	100	50	50	
Problems with child 6–15	3	55	29	64	6
Problems with older child	9	44	43	53	5
Problems with marriage	9	27	69	27	4
Problems being separated	2	50	44	55	
Problems being single	3	34	50	50	
Problems with parent(s)	38	27	55	42	3
Respondent had health problem	30	47	5	94	1
Spouse had health problem	27	39	12	88	
Child had health problem	28	47	15	84	1

Event				
Start (back to) work	8	21	83	17
Having a child	15	15	50	42	8
Child starting school	18	8	44	56
Child becoming teen	22	10	56	34
Child leaving home	14	15	45	55
Child getting married	7	9	29	72
Becoming widowed	2	62	31	61	8
Becoming separated or divorced	4	51	28	68	4
Temporarily unemployed	8	26	46	56
Being demoted	2	48	50	50
Changing standard of living	54	7	62	38
Death of someone close	47	20	66	34

Note: Entries in table are percentage of respondents.

cy of coping in the major role areas of life—parent and marital relations, economic, and occupational—for which he developed a coping scale based upon empirical study of the relationship between strain in each of the four areas and reduction of perceived stress by types of coping strategies. The last coping resource was a measure of personal mastery, a phenomenological sense of the individual's efficiency or sense of mastery. These three dimensions reflect psychological resources. In a similar fashion, social resources were seen as possible factors influencing whether an individual utilized external resources—help— in order to cope with a particular life crisis. Aside from the person's role and status in society, social class, age, and race, two other measures were assessed on the utility of the individual's informal social network: quantity, which included the variety of individuals within the person's world that he or she saw as a resource, and the amount of interaction the individual had with these resources. A qualitative dimension of the social resources was also assessed, which included an index of intimacy and an index of dependability. As in the case of psychological resources, it was thought that to the degree that an individual possessed usable social resources, the need for certain forms of help would be mitigated. Finally, because help-seeking behavior requires an expenditure of effort and energy, certain potential barriers to seeking such help were examined. Included was an attitudinal set regarding help seeking—the individual's reluctance to use others—as well as an index of trust—the degree to which an individual could rely on others. This framework—beginning with the particular kind of life crisis or dilemma confronting the individual, the degree of stress involved for him or her in a particular life condition, the resources both social and personal, and the barriers—formed the model for examining in a large probability sample who it was that sought help.

As expected, different life events differed in their magnitude of disruptiveness. Of the twenty-six events or life conditions listed in Table 1, the magnitude of stress perceived by the individuals varied from a low of 10 percent for an event such as a child starting school to over 90 percent for events such as unemployment and widowhood. However, when the number of individuals distressed by any particular event was examined, the rate of seeking help for those who were distressed did not differ —in other words, the particular kind of circumstances creating distress was not a factor in accounting for the frequency of help seeking. Whether individuals used their social network for help or used formal structures within society did depend on the particular type of life event (a time-limited event, such as death) or life condition that was creating the distress. Overall, 48 percent of those who sought help used the social network as a sole source of aid, 12 percent used formal systems as their sole source, and 40 percent utilized both. If we examine those in the sample studied who, at any point, used formal helping systems, we find the following situations: health problems of respondent, spouse, or child; marriage of a child; separation and divorce; problems with school-age children; retirement; unemployment; and widowhood. Such events or life conditions were associated with high usage of professional help. At the other end of the continuum, events and life conditions such as starting back to work, problems at work, problems in a homemaker role, problems with the day-to-day issues of marriage, children's care of elderly parents, entrance of children into teenage, changes in standard of living, and death of someone close were situations in which individuals relied solely on the social network for the major source of help.

Overall, it was found that both personal resources and social resources did not have a major influence on whether or not an individual sought help. However, the reason for the relative lack of influence of such parameters on help seeking soon become apparent in the study. Those who did not seek help appeared to form two relatively distinct groups: Some individuals did not seek help because they believed that the problems they were encountering were ones they could handle themselves. Others did not seek help because of a variety of reasons—they felt that no one was available, that they could not locate helping sources, or that seeking help would require too much effort or engender too much shame. When these two non-help-seeking groups were divided—the former termed the self-reliant, the latter reluctant—it was found that those who were self-reliant nonseekers of help were, on the average, individuals who possessed the most social and psychological resources. In contrast, those who were classified as reluctant nonseekers of help had poorer personal and social resources. Those who sought help were individuals who fell in between these two extremes. There was some tendency for individuals with more resources in the social arena to be the ones who more often used their social network for help rather than relying solely on professional systems. Barriers to help seeking, particularly in the attitudinal set toward help, were found, as might be expected, among those who were reluctant nonseekers as well as those who sought out only formal or professional systems rather than relying on their social network.

Findings from the Transitions Study provide a context for examining the specific conditions leading individuals to utilize self-help groups.

Implications of the Model for Self-Help Groups. What are some of the implications of Brown's (1978) findings for our studies of the factors that influence the use of self-help groups? Foremost, despite a complex model for determining help-seeking behavior, relatively low predictability was achieved in ferreting out those conditions or attributes of individuals, given similar crises, that indicated whether the person would or would not seek help. The lack of general predictability suggested that it would be difficult to answer the more specific question regarding the selection of a particular kind of helping resource—self-help groups. The findings also suggested that the majority of individuals are multiple help seekers; when they do make a decision to look beyond themselves for resources, they frequently turn to a variety of kith and kin as well as a variety of professional help resources. The pattern of multiple use, as will be seen in the next three chapters, proved to be the rule rather than the exception for the one affliction and two status conditions studied: heart surgery, womanhood, and widowhood. The findings from the Transitions Study further suggest that help seeking is the rule rather than the exception, and that most individuals faced with high levels of distress do seek out others for aid. Thus it is unlikely, except for a minority of any sample studied, that we would find individuals who had no resources other than the self-help group for aid.

The simple hypothesis that individuals seek out resources external to themselves when their own coping strategies fail was certainly not borne out by Brown's (1978) data. He did not find that individuals low in personal and social resources were more likely to seek out help than those well endowed with psychological and social resources. What his study did show was that those who did not seek out help represented two rather distinct populations: a group labeled self-reliant who were well endowed with resources, both psychological and social, and a group labeled reluctant, who had few resources. The existence of these two distinct populations should alert us, in our study of self-help users, to the problem of utilizing appropriate contrast groups for comparison with those individuals who seek out self-help groups. As will be seen in our study of the widowed self-help groups as well as in heart surgery groups, this issue becomes particularly relevant in attempting to understand what characterizes those who choose to utilize self-help.

Studies of Self-Help Groups and Help Seeking. The three chapters that follow examine some of the characteristics of individuals and their social surrounds that influence individuals to join and participate in self-help groups. A variety of hypotheses were explored about why some individuals sharing a common affliction use self-help groups whereas others do not. The first study, based on a large-scale national survey of 1,669 women, presents findings about women who participated in consciousness-raising groups. It looks at "reasons for joining" within a framework that views consciousness raising as an alternative to psychotherapy. The second study reports on Mended Hearts, a medical self-help group. As previously described, one central characteristic of this organization is its vigorous and successful recruitment program. The success of its recruitment—as well as the opportunity for a total sample of afflicted, including nonmembers who were recipients of the recruiting efforts—made this an ideal sample for examining a series of alternative hypotheses about users of self-help groups by comparing them to those who chose not to join. The last study in this section reports on a pilot sample of Naim, a Chicago-based self-help group for widows and widowers. It focuses on the role of informal social networks and the influence on users and nonusers of self-help.

Before turning to these three specific studies, let us examine the findings from data gathered on the reasons given by individuals for joining self-help groups. To provide a context for comparison, findings from studies we conducted on psychotherapy and on growth centers, both formal professional systems, are also reported. Although the growth centers have a high degree of professional input, they are not classically seen as sources of aid for individuals who are troubled. The growth center, a relatively new institution in our society, developed outside of traditional professional structures to provide participants with certain kinds of experience.

Reasons for Joining Self-Help Groups

For each of the five self-help systems—women's consciousness raising, Compassionate Friends, mothers' groups, Naim, and Mended Hearts—as well as the two professional systems—group therapy and growth centers—participants were provided a list of items and asked to indicate on a scale (three or four points, depending on the particular study) how appropriate or inappropriate to them was each of a list of reasons for joining or participating in the various settings. The specific wording and the number of items differ from study to study. They can conveniently be grouped under three major headings: (1) goals referring to endstate or type of change desired; (2) process goals—experiences that individuals would like to have as a consequence of their participation; and (3) social hedonistic goals. Each of the first two goal areas was further subdivided into a variety of desired endstates and specific experiences.

Endstate Goals. Among those assessed here were *mental health* goals, which involved issues of relief from distress as well as certain kinds of inner change. Items included were: "to deal with current life problems," "to bring some change in myself," "to solve some long-term personal hangup," "to obtain relief in the things I do or feelings I have that trouble me," "to obtain help," and "to work on some personal problems." A different type of goal was expressed in terms of the individual's desire for *awareness*: for example, "to increase self-awareness," "to expand political awareness," and "to increase my understanding of how I feel about my body." A third goal area assessed *existential issues*: "to seek increased meaning in life." A fourth indexed *interpersonal relationship goals*: "to improve or change my relationships with women," "with men," "with my children," "I wanted help for my marital problems," "to help my baby." A fifth involved the *political-social arena*: "to become more active in the women's movement," "to work for stronger laws to prevent crime and suffering," "I wanted to get involved with a group concerned with discrimination against heart patients." And finally, some goals were expressed in terms of *change of life-style*: "to find an alternative life-style."

Not all of these goal dimensions were indexed for each of the professional and self-help systems studied. Asking psychotherapy patients, for example, their political or social goals within psychotherapy would certainly be considered by most as inappropriate; asking members of the mothers' groups about existential goals would likely not engender a believable response from the surveyed participants. In other words, our attempt in indexing goals required that they not be dissonant with the participant's view of why he or she was in a particular system. This "believability" criterian does, however, present us with the difficulty of comparing systems.

Process Goals. Individuals select out specific helping systems not only for the extrinsic aid they may provide but also for some of the intrinsic experiences that a particular self-help or professional system may offer. Such intrinsic experiences are perhaps most clearly seen in a previous study contrasting psychotherapy with growth centers (Lieberman and Gardner, 1976). In that study, we found that individuals who sought out growth centers were similar in their extrinsic motivations to populations who sought out psychotherapy. However, the settings differed in the type of experiences expected and sought. Lieberman and Gardner suggested that certain experiences or events unique to each of these two settings were, of themselves, motivating goals and not halfway stations to a desired end-state. The fact that participants enter helping systems with specific change goals does not necessarily preclude their seeking certain types of experiences they may or may not directly tie to the intrinsic goal that brought them to the setting. For example, we believe that the encounter group represents a setting appealing to troubled individuals who are seeking relief from distress but, at the same time, attracting those motivated by a need to find community, a certain kind of experience that may or may not be related to the aid they seek for relief from distress. In a similar fashion, a variety of experiences or events or types of helping processes represented by certain self-help groups are relevant, in and of themselves, to the participant's reasons for seeking out such groups.

A variety of events and processes appeared to be sought after by those who participated in the self-help groups. We divided these into six subcategories, beginning with what we considered to be the core experience sought after by self-help participants—the finding of the similarly afflicted.

The *similarity-communion* goal is represented by such items as "to share thoughts and feelings of being a woman," "to be with people I could feel comfortable with," "to share thoughts and feelings about being a widow," "wanted to talk over my surgery with others who had the same experience," "to find community."

Both professionally conducted helping groups as well as self-help groups emphasize a wide variety of *cognitive-informational* processes. The range of these processes is quite broad (for further discussion see Chapter Ten). In terms of participant goals, we asked about a variety of informational-cognitive processes: "to learn about women and their experience," "to obtain political information," "to get advice," "to learn from professionals who have studied grief," "to get information about widowhood," "I wanted more information about my medical condition," "to learn how other women feel about me (feedback)."

The group setting in both professionally led and self-help groups offers a particular kind of cognitive learning, *modeling*, that resembles finding individuals that are similar to oneself and being able to identify with and use them as examples for change: "to learn how other widows had coped with their problems," "to learn how other bereaved parents cope with their problem."

A simple, yet apparently important attraction of all groups is the *emotional support* they offer their members. Somewhat similar to support is the *abreactive-cathartic* dimension of help-ing groups. This area, stressed most clearly in group psycho-therapy and encounter groups, may also play a role in some of the self-help groups we studied. Items used to examine this area included: "to have an emotionally intense experience," "to learn to express anger," "to grieve without fear of others' reac-tion," "to have a chance to grieve with others who understand my feelings."

Another process that was apparent in some of the self-help groups studied was the use of a group setting as an oppor-tunity to find *linkages with others* who could be called upon for support outside of the group setting: "to make contact with someone I could call on to talk about the death."

The psychology of affliction and extreme personal crises, such as those found with the loss of a child or the possibility of facing one's own death, appears to focus goals towards *altruistic* endeavors. For example, we found that one of the motivations for seeking out groups is to help others: "I looked at life dif-ferently after surgery and I want to spend more time helping others." Such experiences have been pointed out previously in the group psychotherapy literature, in which altruism has been cited by numerous authors as an important mechanism for help. In that literature it has been referred to as a process, counter-acting some of the more self-oriented, neurotic dilemmas, and the experience of being genuinely helpful to others is seen by many professionals as an important "curative factor" in group psychotherapy. However, as a motivation for joining, it rarely would appear in the minds of those who enter psychotherapy. But because of the possibility that it plays a role in self-help groups, not only in the actual experiences of what is important as members participate in the organization but also as a specific attraction to such organizations, we studied altruistic motives for joining in several of the groups.

Social-Hedonistic Goals. Despite the fact that most of those who seek out self-help groups do so because of personal crises, distress, or involvement in a meaningful life dilemma, some of the motivation for joining touches other aspects of individuals' lives that are less somber, deliberate, or painful. Cer-tainly, in our studies of growth centers, in which we were able to demonstrate that the predominant motivation for joining in such activities did involve help seeking and that it was instrumental for individuals looking for a setting to relieve their distress, some were attracted to such settings for their lighter, more playful aspects. A similar theme is apparent in many of the self-help groups studied, and we set out to measure this social-hedonistic goal by including such items as: "to do something different," "to get out of the house," "to make friends," "to have fun," "to get away from my problems," "to meet someone I might date."

We are now ready to examine what the individuals who sought out and participated in the five self-help groups and the two professional systems studied said about their reasons for joining, and to compare across these systems to determine what they share and what was unique to each. Because the number of items used to elicit participant's goals varied from system to system, Table 2 divides each of the set of items used for a particular system into quartiles, as well as providing the percentage of individuals who saw these as important goals for their seeking out and joining such groups or professional systems.

Comparisons Between Professional Helping Groups and Self-Help Groups

An examination of Table 2 suggests that there are some striking differences among professionally led groups and the five self-help systems studied. It is no surprise that individuals who enter group psychotherapy emphasize mental health goals. Participants were given a choice of sixteen reasons for entering psychotherapy—twelve had to do with endstates or types of change desired, one with process goals, and three with social-hedonistic items. The first six rank items focus specifically on mental health goals: working on personal problems, dealing with current life problems, getting help, and so forth. The remaining two of the top 50 percent of the ranked items were a desire for increased awareness and a wish to improve relationships with people. The social-hedonistic goals were ranked low, as was the one process goal included in this list. Unfortunately, the lack of process goal items vitiated comparisons between types of changes desired and types of experiences wished for. However, an examination of the professionally led encounter groups does permit such a comparison. We found a striking similarity to psychotherapy patients. Of the twenty-seven goal items provided to the encounter participants, fifteen represented change goals, six process goals, and six social-hedonistic ones. In the top 50 percent of the ranked items, all but one of the items represented change goals; six out of a possible eight mental health items were chosen, with *awareness* and *relationship with people* being the remaining goal areas seen as highly important.

There appear to be a specific set of expectations and needs of those entering professional helping systems that are highly instrumental and help oriented, no matter what the particular ideology surrounding the professional system. In short, individuals come with an expectation that they will take away a change in self that will create a "problem-free existence." This is particularly striking with regard to encounter groups, whose ideological perspective would lead one to expect that participants would emphasize process experiences as well as more pleasure-oriented pursuits. The fact that these two professional systems differ in their ideology and yet produce relatively similar sets of findings suggests that the critical element is not the particular belief system of the group but the images surrounding professional helping systems. Individuals enter such systems with sets of expectations of what are appropriate and inappropriate goals. It is almost as if participants who enter professional change systems, whether for reparative psychotherapy or for growth and change, construe what is appropriate and inappropriate, and their reasons for entering appear in terms of their implicit images of the nature of the professional relationship. They "must come" in order to rectify problems and not for certain events or experiences felt to be useful and/or pleasurable. For example, despite the fact that individuals value certain experiences in encounter groups—as will be seen in Chapter Ten where we explore the events or experiences that individuals found useful to them—such as getting information from others about their behavior or having peak experiences, such goals are not rated high prior to the person's entrance into the system.

Table 2. Participants' Stated Goals

First Quarter   *N=425*

Group Psychotherapy

Rank	Item	%
1.	To work on personal problems A1	88
2.	To deal with current life problems A1	83
3.	To get help A1	83
4.	Relief from troubling feelings and things A1	80

Encounter Groups

Rank	Item	%
1.	To change self A1	72
2.	Self-awareness A2	70
3.	To expand consciousness A2	54
4.	New person A1	53
5.	Body awareness A2	52
6.	To increase meaning in life A3	48

Consciousness Raising

Rank	Item	%
1.	To share thoughts and feelings about being a woman B1	71
2.	To increase self-awareness A2	59
3.	To learn about other women and their experiences B2	55
4.	For emotional support B4	50
5.	To examine problems women have with their traditional roles (mother, wife) B2	48
6.	To bring about some change in myself A1	43
7.	To deal with current life problems A1	33
8.	To seek increased meaning in life A3	31

Compassionate Friends

Rank	Item	%
1.	Wanted to talk with others who had the same experience B1	77
2.	To learn how other bereaved parents coped with their problems B3	76
3.	To share thoughts and feelings about the loss of my child B1	71
4.	To get relief from things or feelings troubling me A1	57

First Quarter

Mothers

Rank	Item	%
1.	To meet people C	89
2.	To share my feelings about being a mother B1	73
3.	To get out of the house C	69

Naim

Rank	Item	%
1.	To make friends C	68
2.	To be with people I could feel comfortable with B4	65
3.	To learn how other widowed persons cope with their problems B3	58
4.	To become more active A6	53
5.	To get involved in social activities C	53
6.	To have fun C	57
7.	To share thoughts and feelings about being widowed B1	50

Mended Hearts

Rank	Item	%*
1.	Felt that Mended Hearts stood for something I believed in B7	54
2.	I looked at life differently after surgery and I wanted to spend more time helping others B7	40
3.	Wanted more information about my medical condition B2	42

Table 2. Participants' Stated Goals (continued)

Second Quarter   *N=425*

Group Psychotherapy

Rank	Item	%
5.	To solve long-term personal hangups A1	79
6.	To bring about some change in myself A1	74
7.	To increase self-awareness A2	54
8.	To improve relationships with people A4	49

Encounter Groups

Rank	Item	%
7.	To solve long-term hangups A1	45
8.	To deal with current life problems A1	45
9.	To work out personal problems A1	40
10.	To improve relations with people A4	39
11.	New approach working with people B2	33
12.	To change how I relate A4	29
13.	To obtain relief from troubling feelings A1	29

Consciousness Raising

Rank	Item	%
9.	To examine problems women encounter in academic and work settings B2	25
10.	To find community B4	26
11.	To improve or change my relationships with women A4	25
12.	To get relief from things or feelings troubling me A1	25
13.	To solve personal problems A1	22
14.	To be more active in the women's movement A5	23
15.	To make friends C	23
16.	To expand political awareness A2	22

Compassionate Friends

Rank	Item	%
5.	To make contact with someone I could call on to talk about the death B6	48
6.	To learn from professionals who have studied grief B2	38
7.	To grieve without fear of others' reactions B5	38

Second Quarter

Mothers

Rank	Item	%
4.	To help my baby A4	52
5.	To discuss my pregnancy and birth experiences B1	52

Naim

Rank	Item	%
8.	To deal with current life problems A1	46
9.	To bring about some change in myself A1	46
10.	To get information about widowhood B2	42
11.	To discuss my feelings with others B1	48
12.	To do something different C	42
13.	To get out of my shell A6	44

Mended Hearts

Rank	Item	%
4.	Appreciation for the help I got from the Mended Hearts visitor B7	39
5.	Wanted to talk over my surgery with others who had the same experience B1	25
6.	To keep me active A6	17

Table 2. Participants' Stated Goals (continued)

Third Quarter   *N=425*

Group Psychotherapy

Rank	Item	%
9.	To seek increased meaning in life A3	38
10.	To change how I relate to people A4	35
11.	To move toward becoming a new person A6	23
12.	Loneliness C	23

Encounter Groups

Rank	Item	%
14.	Feedback on how others feel about me B2	26
15.	Professional training A5	24
16.	To get help A1	21
17.	To do something different C	18
18.	To have a "peak" experience B5	17
19.	To find a community B1	17
20.	To find a new life-style A1	16

Consciousness Raising

Rank	Item	%
17.	To learn about some change in myself A1	26
18.	To explore my sexual feelings toward men A4	18
19.	To learn how other women feel about me B2	14
20.	To solve long-term problems A1	14
21.	To improve or change my relationships with men A4	14
22.	To increase my understanding of how I feel about my body A2	11
23.	To have an emotionally intense experience B5	12
24.	Loneliness C	14

Compassionate Friends

Rank	Item	%
8.	To get advice B2	34
9.	Spiritual guidance B2	16
10.	Wanted help for parental problems A4	13

Third Quarter

	Mothers	
Rank	*Item*	*%*
6.	To help myself A1	51
7.	To become more active socially A4	49

	Naim	
Rank	*Item*	*%*
14.	To get relief from things or feelings troubling me A1	42
15.	To get involved in a Catholic organization C	39
16.	To get advice B2	33
17.	To make contact with someone I could call on B6	31
18.	To get away from my problems C	33
19.	To learn from professionals (priests, lawyers, and so on) B2	35

	Mended Hearts	
Rank	*Item*	*%*
7.	To make friends C	14
8.	To bring about some change in myself A1	11
9.	Wanted to get involved in a group concerned with discrimination against heart patients A5	14

Table 2. Participants' Stated Goals (continued)

Fourth Quarter   *N=425*

Group Psychotherapy

Rank	Item	%
13.	To learn how people feel about me B2	20
14.	To find a new life-style A6	19
15.	To do something different C	15
16.	Curiosity C	

Encounter Groups

Rank	Item	%
21.	To turn on B5	14
22.	To meet people C	13
23.	Curiosity C	10
24.	To get away C	9
25.	Loneliness C	8
26.	Vacation C	7
27.	To find new sexual experiences B5	5

Consciousness Raising

Rank	Item	%
25.	Curiosity C	11
26.	To learn to express anger B5	12
27.	To get help A1	10
28.	To obtain political information B2	7
29.	To find an alternative life-style A6	8
30.	To explore my sexual feelings toward women A4	7
31.	To do something different C	6
32.	To get out of the house C	6
33.	To change my relationship with my children A4	6

Compassionate Friends

Rank	Item	%
11.	To work for stronger laws to prevent crime and suffering A5	12
12.	To get psychological help A1	10
13.	Wanted help for marital problems A4	7

Fourth Quarter

	Mothers	
Rank	*Item*	*%*
8.	To learn more about childrearing B2	41
9.	To become involved in a service organization A5	25

	Naim	
Rank	*Item*	*%*
20.	Curiosity C	21
21.	Spiritual guidance B2	21
22.	To meet someone I might date C	22
23.	To solve personal problems A1	17
24.	Had a chance to grieve with others who understood my feelings B5	24
25.	To get psychological help A1	8
26.	To find a new spouse C	4

	Mended Hearts	
Rank	*Item*	*%*
10.	Wanted to talk over other problems besides surgery (such as family, finances) B1	5
11.	To get out of the house C	3

Key

A. *Endstate Goals*
1. Mental Health
2. Awareness
3. Existential
4. Interpersonal
5. Social-Political
6. Life-Style

B. *Process Goals*
1. Similarity-Communion
2. Cognitive-Informational
3. Modeling
4. Support
5. Abreactive-Cathartic
6. Linkage
7. Altruism

C. *Social-Hedonistic Goals*

An instructive contrast to participants' perceptions of what are legitimate and illegitimate reasons for entering professional systems can be found in the items members of women's consciousness-raising groups ranked in order of importance. Consciousness raising (CR) offers a meaningful contrast because it provides a control for the "affliction." As will be seen in Chapter Seven, women who enter consciousness-raising groups are drawn from the same populations as those who enter psychotherapy or encounter; in all three systems, the basic motivation was relief from distressing personal problems. This conclusion is based upon the level of distress measured by symptoms and life strain of the three populations, their utilization of psychotherapy simultaneously or serially with their being a participant in one of the other systems, and, to some extent, their stated goals for entering.

Table 2 shows the reasons given for entering consciousness-raising groups, based upon thirty-three possible reasons, nineteen of which represented change goals, nine process goals, and five social-hedonistic goals. We found that six of the top-ranked (top 50 percent) items were process goals—a sharp contrast to encounter group findings. We see both an emphasis on process goals and on mental health and changing awareness goals. These CR goals findings in a sample whose basic motivations are similar to those entering psychotherapy and encounter groups suggest that the key element is that the latter are professionally directed systems, whereas CR is a self-help group. The explanation of the difference in goals, however, does not rest on the fact that individuals in our society perceive only systems that contain professionals as being able to provide the ultimate relief from troublesome life problems. Rather, it appears as if how one arrives at the desired endstate is to be left in the hands of professionals and not anticipated by the participant. Perhaps these findings reflect what we see as one of the essential features of self-help as opposed to professional helping systems: a sense of control in the shaping of one's own destiny induced by being able to consider not only what one wants to take away from a change-induction setting but also how one wants to arrive at such an endstate. This distinction remains, despite some profound changes over the years in attitudes toward professional help, particularly regarding psychotherapeutic interactions. Since the 1960s, there has been an alteration in attitudes about professional help received from psychotherapists expressed in terms of patient's demand for greater transparencies of the therapist and for more control of what occurs—an attitudinal shift perhaps that in part expresses a greater coequal relationship. Despite this general shift in societal expectations away from seeing psychotherapists as performing priestly functions, it is clear from the findings that a large gap remains between images of the help-providing functions of professional systems and self-help systems.

The two professional systems and one self-help group we have discussed so far are similar in that they appeal to those with generalized distress and do not have the focused affiliation or circumstances characteristic of most other self-help groups. If we turn to these other groups, we see even more clearly that individuals who join them have distinct sets of expectations not only about what they want to take away from such groups (their endstate goals) but also about how they want to participate (the process), as well as about some of the social and pleasurable potential that such groups can offer.

In Compassionate Friends, where thirteen goal statements were provided to the participants, five of which represented endstates and eight process goals, we found that six of the seven top-ranked (first 50 percent) items were process goals. Individuals had an image of what kinds of events or experiences they desired in order to obtain some mastery over and relief from the devastating impact of losing a child. They wished to share their experiences with others who had been through the same event; they wanted to learn from others how to cope; they wanted to make contact with other bereaved parents who could become resources outside of the group setting; and they wanted to express their profound grief without fear of negative sanctions. The desire for these highly articulated experiences expresses perhaps most clearly the desire of these individuals to see themselves, despite the devastation of the loss, as attempting to control what would be helpful to them.

The other three self-help groups studied showed goal patterns similar to Compassionate Friends. The mothers' self-help group was provided nine goals, four of which were endstate goals, three process, and two social-hedonistic. The reason for the existence of the mothers' self-help group is clearly expressed in their goal statement; social-pleasurable experiences are emphasized as well as processes that have to do with the mothering role. This is clearly perceived by the participants as a support group with highly limited objectives, and self, as an object of change, is not perceived as part of the reason individuals enter such systems. Focus is on motherhood and the child, not on psychotherapeutic objectives and self-improvement unrelated to the specifics of motherhood, as found in the other all-women self-help group.

The participants who joined Naim were offered a list of twenty-four goal statements, seven having to do with desired change, eight with processes, and nine with social-pleasurable reasons for joining. The social-pleasurable aspects of involvement in the widowed groups were stressed by the participants. Naim's current mission, as described in Chapter Three, is clearly reflected in the individuals who enter it. They desire an interactive setting with similarly afflicted individuals in which social activities can be provided in a safe and legitimized fashion; they desire to be with individuals who can accept their status and to whom they can express some of their feelings about widowhood. Clearly, the participants anticipate Naim as meeting their needs as a social and support system.

Mended Hearts has a distinctive characteristic: Service goals predominate. Chapter Ten examines comparative helping processes, what participants see as being helpful to them, and reasons for the altruistic character of Mended Hearts. To briefly anticipate, we see Mended Hearts as a self-help system that provides a resolution through altruism to the psychological dilemma created by the affliction.

As might be expected in our study of individuals who were members of these groups or about to become members, there is a high degree of match in the self-help groups between participants' stated goals for entering and the specific characteristics of the group culture. Clearly, such a match makes sense, and we would anticipate that individuals whose need systems, expressed through the goals, do not relate to the group would either not become members or would leave the group. As we are still in the process of completing some of these studies, we do not have sufficient findings at this juncture to reflect on those who terminate their participation in such groups.

CHAPTER 7

Women's Consciousness Raising as an Alternative to Psychotherapy

Morton A. Lieberman &
Gary R. Bond

The study of consciousness-raising groups was our first attempt to examine self-help systems from the perspective of their membership. Here, as in subsequent studies, we sought to understand the forces within persons and society that propel individuals to coalesce into small face-to-face groups based upon a similar affliction or perceived deviant situation. The findings reported in this chapter are based upon a study of 1,669 current or former members of women's consciousness-raising groups.

Note: Portions of this chapter are reproduced by special permission from *The Journal of Applied Behavioral Science*, "The Problem of Being a Woman: A Survey of 1,700 Women in Consciousness-Raising Groups," by this chapter's authors, 1976, *12* (3), 363–380.

Simply put, this was a study to determine why women join consciousness-raising groups. The survey focused on a central hypothesis that women at the time of our survey (1974–1975) were using consciousness raising for the same purposes as those who avail themselves of psychotherapy.

Given the political origins of consciousness raising, it may seem strange at first glance to examine them from this perspective. However, our belief, based upon our previous examinations of consciousness raising and on Lieberman and Gardner's (1976) study on growth centers, is that many institutions in our society attract individuals whose goal is the relief of personal distress. The growth centers study found that settings developed in the 1960s to offer growth and personal development experiences to individuals were, in fact, utilized by the majority of clients for therapeutic purposes. In setting out, our study emphasized this simple hypothesis, contrasting it to alternative possibilities that consciousness-raising groups were primarily politicizing and that they functioned in society to energize the feminists or women's movement. The findings reported in this chapter, like others that follow in this section, reflect a method of studying the role and function of specific institutions by examining both the social and psychological characteristics of those they attract as well as their perceived goals. Who comes to these groups? Why do they come? And what do they hope to gain from their participation?

Survey

A twenty-six-page questionnaire was developed for distribution to women actively involved in CR groups, former members, and women planning to join. The first section of the questionnaire concerned personal stresses and social circumstances of the respondents; the second concerned the nature of the groups themselves; and the third section asked for demographic information. A national sample was developed using the grassroots network of the women's movement for distribution.

During 1974, we obtained 1,669 completed questionnaires from women in forty-one states. It was difficult to determine return rates accurately since organizations often requested more questionnaires than were actually distributed. A conservative estimate is that at least 40 percent of women who actually received a questionnaire participated in this research.

A method of publicizing the research may account for the sizable proportion of respondents from groups sponsored by large women's organizations (55 percent). However, women from groups started by friends (22 percent) were also represented. The remainder of the sample came from groups growing out of other settings, such as classrooms or unions. In such a survey, we were most likely to reach women who had continued in their CR group and/or had remained within the women's movement; we were unlikely to reach the women who had been most dissatisfied.

In our sample of 1,669 women, 66 percent were current, 31 percent former, and 4 percent prospective members of CR groups. The amount of time spent in CR was substantial: 17 percent had been involved for over two years, 25 percent between one and two years, 28 percent between six and twelve months, and 30 percent less than six months. About one third had been in more than one group. Seven percent of the sample joined before 1971; 8 percent during 1971; 16 percent during 1972; 26 percent during 1973; and 43 percent during 1974. The sample, then, consisted of women at varying stages of involvement.

Most respondents were from urban (41 percent) or suburban (50 percent) areas, and all regions of the country were represented: Northeast (35 percent), Midwest (26 percent), West (25 percent), and South (14 percent). Ninety-nine percent were white. Age (median = thirty-one) was distributed among the twenties (41 percent), thirties (39 percent), and forties (12 percent), underrepresenting women in their fifties (6 percent) and essentially excluding women sixty or older (less than 1 percent). Two percent of the sample were teenaged. Over half of the respondents were married, 25 percent were single, and 20 percent divorced, separated or, widowed. Slightly over half had children.

The selectivity of this sample, despite efforts to locate working-class respondents, was most striking when we turned to occupational and educational characteristics: executive or major professional (11 percent), lesser professional (31 percent), administrative (20 percent), skilled, semiskilled, or unskilled (4 percent), unemployed (3 percent), housewife (14 percent), and student (16 percent). Among respondents giving husband's occupation, 48 percent indicated they were professionals or executives. In addition, the respondents were well educated, 90 percent having attended college and two thirds having received a bachelor's degree.

While the predominant political label was that of "liberal" (58 percent), there was a sizable segment of the sample who called themselves radicals (21 percent). The extent of political interest was further indicated by previous political affiliations: civil rights movement (19 percent), antiwar movement (27 percent), a "politically radical" Women's Liberation organization (7 percent), professional women's organizations (10 percent), League of Women Voters (11 percent), and women's political organizations, such as NOW (25 percent). Altogether, four out of ten women were affiliated with a women's political group prior to joining CR.

Survey Findings

Who, then, was attending CR groups at the time of the survey? The demographic characteristics have already given a distinctive shape to this client system. They were predominantly white, liberal, educated, upper-middle-class women, a socioeconomic segment of the population that has been reported as most likely to seek out formal institutions for help in times of personal crisis and distress. Gurin, Veroff, and Feld (1960) found that in a representative national sample, 32 percent of men and women with college educations and above-median incomes had seen a psychiatrist for personal problems, compared with only 4 percent of the least educated and below-median income subgroup.

In order to determine both the amount of psychological stress and distress, we used a measure of stress based on life crises—forty-one items from the Life Events Stress Index, (Paykel, Prusoff, and Uhlenhuth, 1971)—and a measure of self-reported symptoms—thirty-five items from the Hopkins Symptom Checklist, (Derogatis and others, 1974). The first scale measured objective events commonly leading to physical or mental distress, whereas the other measured subjective distress and discomfort. Both measures have been found by other investigators to be related to help seeking for physical and psychological problems.

We were interested in comparing women in CR with comparable groups of women not involved in CR. We used two comparison samples of women from Lieberman and Gardner's (1976) study: those entering personal growth center groups or starting psychotherapy. Lieberman and Gardner found that clients in all systems were seeking help for personal problems. Both comparison samples were similar to the CR sample in demographic characteristics, especially social class. We also selected from the Oakland probability sample developed by Uhlenhuth and others (1974)—all white women between the ages of twenty and forty-nine—as a third comparison group.

Stress and symptom scores for all samples are reported in Table 1.

The psychotherapy sample, as expected, was significantly higher in stress than the normative sample, replicating the well-known finding that the accumulation of life events associated with stress correlates with seeking psychotherapy. The CR sample, however, did not differ from the normative sample in stress. Thus there is no evidence that women joined CR because of an unusually frequent number of recent stressful life events.

The CR participants had a significantly higher level of symptoms, notably depression and anxiety, than the normative, though still significantly lower than the psychotherapy sample. Since the level of personal dissatisfaction and dysphoria expressed in the symptom checklist are just the feelings that lead people to enter therapy, it is not unreasonable to assume that the same explanation may hold for women entering CR. In other words, the findings indicated that some women may enter CR because they are depressed and anxious. This higher level of dysphoria was also consistent with the view that

Table 1. Comparison Between CR Sample and Other Women on Stress and Symptoms

	CR sample (N=1,669)	Growth center (N=219)	Psycho-therapy (N=57)	Normative sample (N=126)	F-Value	Significant comparisons (Duncan's test)
Stress	35.7 (30.9)	36.5 (28.3)	54.2 (36.8)	33.3 (32.9)	5.3[a]	PT>CR, GC, Norm
Symptoms	23.9 (15.0)	24.8 (13.4)	40.3 (14.4)	13.2 (9.9)	36.0[a]	PT>CR, GC CR, GC>Norm

[a] p < .001

women, at the time they were entering CR, were experiencing a "consciousness-raising" in the sense of experiencing greater personal dissatisfaction in their lives. However, other findings suggested that symptoms were part of a long-standing pattern for many of the respondents, and not merely a result of their emerging feminist awareness.

Fifty-four percent of the CR participants had been in therapy during the past five years, including 17 percent in psychotherapy. One third had been in an encounter group. These proportions were considerably higher than those reported by Gurin, Veroff, and Feld (1960) and highlighted the fact that women in CR were users of multiple "helping" systems.

Direct evidence about the expressed reasons for joining CR was assessed by an instrument developed by Lieberman and Gardner (1976). Women's self-perceived motives for joining CR groups were indexed by an instrument consisting of thirty-three items rated on a 4-point scale of importance (1 = very important, 2 = important, 3 = somewhat important, 4 = not important). To reduce redundancies in the items, they were factor-analyzed using principal factor analysis with Varimax rotations. Six motivational factors emerged, as shown in Table 2.

We were especially interested in three of these factors:

Interest in women's issues consisted of three items representing instrumental goals: desire "to share thoughts about being a women," "to learn about other women," and "to examine problems women have with roles." Its apparent intent is to render change in one's own life situation. Unlike the help-seeking factor, which emphasized intrapsychic change, the emphasis in this factor was on change in the context of one's role as a woman.

Help seeking contained six items which, with a common-sense notion of problems, would lead people to seek out therapy or professional help. Lieberman and Gardner (1976), who had derived a factor with the identical six items, found that patients in psychotherapy almost always reported this motive as the major one for seeking therapy.

Political activation represented a motive to engage in discussion of feminist issues and ultimately to become involved in the women's movement. Women with previous experience in

Table 2. Motivational Factors

Factors	Overall Means, S.D.[a] N=1,668
Interest in Women's Issues To share thoughts and feelings about being a woman To learn about other women and their experiences To examine problems women have with their traditional roles (mother, wife)	1.54 (.55)
Help Seeking To get relief from things or feelings troubling me To solve personal problems To get help To deal with current life problems To solve long-term problems To bring about some change in myself	2.41 (.76)
Social Needs To make friends Loneliness To find community	2.56 (.82)
Political Activation To expand political awareness To obtain political information To be more active in the women's movement	2.66 (.85)
Sexual Awareness To explore my sexual feelings toward men To explore my sexual feelings toward women To increase my understanding of how I feel about my body	2.90 (.79)
Curiosity To do something different Curiosity	3.12 (.82)

Note: Items are listed in the order of loading on each factor. All loadings are .59 or greater.
[a] 1 = very important; 2 = important; 3 = somewhat important; 4 = not important.

women's political organizations scored significantly higher, suggesting that it was truly a political factor. This factor, along with *interest in women's issues*, most closely resembled the kinds of motivations that feminists believe to be served by a CR group. "Expanding political awareness," one of the items loading on *political activation*, closely matches one explicit function of consciousness raising.

The relative importance of the six motives was indicated by the proportion of women whose mean score on each factor showed that motive to be "important" or "very important": *interest in women's issues* (98 percent), *help seeking* (74 percent), *social needs* (59 percent), *interest in sexual issues* (44 percent), and *curiosity* (28 percent). The common denominator for all participants was their desire to explore what it was to be a woman. Help seeking was also an important motive.

The relative lack of importance of *political activation* and the universal *interest in women's issues* offers an important clue to understanding the appeal of CR groups. Purely political motivations were much less important in a CR group than were motivations to explore what it was to be a woman. Reinforcing the idea that women join CR for the enhancement of their personal lives were other major reasons for joining not included in the six factors listed above: notably, "to increase self-awareness" (90 percent, "very important" or "important") and "to seek increased meaning in life" (62 percent). A basic conservatism to fundamental changes was indicated by the low salience of the desire "to find an alternative life-style" (22 percent).

Help seeking in this sample was a less important motive than in the comparison samples. One hundred percent of the women in psychotherapy, 69 percent of the women in growth centers, and 48 percent of the CR participants rated help seeking as at least moderately important.

Let us step back for a minute to examine these motives more closely. We started with the hypothesis that it was the press toward solving personal problems that brought women to CR. We found, in addition, that strong political motivations did not characterize women joining CR. Help seeking, conceptualized as relief for personal problems, was relatively important—but not so important as we might have thought, given the degree of reported anxiety and depression.

To return to our original question, Why was it that women came to CR? Why CR and not some other helping system, especially psychotherapy? Based on the evidence presented so far, we asked whether women were seeking out CR groups because their psychotherapy experiences were not helpful.

Of the 909 women with therapy experience, 49 percent reported the experience was "very helpful," 22 percent reported that it was "somewhat helpful," 18 percent gave a "mixed response," and 11 percent said it was "not helpful." In other words, over two thirds found therapy to be worthwhile. These figures were comparable to those reported by Gurin, Veroff, and Feld (1960) for a random national sample. (Sixty-six percent of those responding reported a "good" experience with a psychotherapist.) The proportion of women with favorable therapy experiences was also similar to that in the Lieberman and Gardner (1976) study. Of the women in their study who had seen a therapist, 70 percent found that experience "helpful." Thus many women in CR were satisfied users of multiple systems, and a motivation to join based on previous dissatisfaction could not be supported.

If they were not dissatisfied users of traditional helping systems, perhaps women who entered CR groups saw themselves as possessing specific personal or situational characteristics that "fit" the CR group. It should be noted that the "affliction" that CR addresses—namely, sexism—ostensibly pervades all areas of one's life. Thus aside from the basic attributes of femaleness, membership criteria are undefined. The appeal to women may be universal. In this regard, CR differs from most other self-help groups, all of which limit the domain of their clientele. We sought the opinions of women in the survey on the particular attribute that would prevent obtaining benefit from a CR group. Forty-four percent of the sample estimated that "all" women they knew would benefit; another 32 percent believed that "three quarters" would benefit, and less than 8 percent thought "few" women would benefit. Successful careers, happy marriages, lack of political awareness, satisfaction with personal life—none of these characteristics was a roadblock to joining. Such a view differs markedly from the one experienced in therapy, where the "ticket of admission" is an acknowledgment that one is suffering and less than competent in at least one salient area of life. However, women experiencing conflicts with men in their lives ("unstable marriages," "sexual conflicts," "have husbands who disapprove of women's movement") were more often perceived as most likely to benefit from CR.

This study sought to determine the role and function of a new institution in our society, women's consciousness-raising groups. Our strategy for studying such institutions was to make inquiries of their participants. We asked who sought out such groups and what were their goals? We began with a simple hypothesis—that women's consciousness-raising groups serve as an alternative institution for those seeking solace from psychological distress. In other words, we asked whether such institutions were alternative structures to the more traditional institutions that currently exist in society for delivery of mental health services. The basis of the simple hypothesis is located in a former study by Lieberman and Gardner (1976) on growth centers—institutions that sponsor various activities such as encounter groups, meditation, sensory awareness, and a variety of transcendental experiences. In that study, the evidence clearly pointed out that the vast majority of the participants were individuals in distress seeking help akin to that which they would seek in formal psychotherapy. Although the historical roots of the humanistic psychology movement that spawned these growth centers and the women's consciousness-raising groups are disparate, both caught the public fancy and media about the same time and both appealed primarily to middle- and upper-class, well-educated individuals.

From the data we have presented so far in this chapter we would suggest that perhaps half of the women who seek out women's consciousness-raising groups do so for help-seeking motives, much like those who seek out psychotherapy. Many of these participants are currently experiencing emotional distress in their lives and perceive women's consciousness-raising groups as viable institutions for providing help.

The parallel between those who utilize growth centers and those who utilize consciousness-raising groups was underscored by our finding that in both studies, a significant majority of the participants sought out traditional mental help services either currently or in the past. Although the growth center study did not have information on the number of women who

participated in consciousness-raising groups, our study of consciousness raising found that over one third of the participants
had been members of encounter groups, the most visible form
of activity offered by growth centers. The similarity of the two
institutions was further found in the negation of a hypothesis
that those who seek out alternative institutions do so because
they are dissatisfied with the consequences of their participation in traditional institutional settings. Both in the growth
center study and in the current study of consciousness-raising
groups, respondents' perceptions of their current or former
psychotherapy experiences were highly positive, and one could
not explain the seeking out of alternatives on the basis of rejection of traditional forms.

What have we learned from this exploration of consciousness raising as an institution through the eyes of its participants?
Clearly there is a discrepancy between the view of the institution derived from current ideology of the women's movement
and historical antecedents, and the view held by participants.
Many come for psychological help, and the unique characteristic of women's consciousness-raising groups from their inception—an emphasis on a personal analysis of women's role and
place in society—is of relatively little interest to participants. We
have described elsewhere in this book the evolution of consciousness-raising groups, their changing characteristics and decreasing political emphasis over the years. We have also learned
that the total number of activists created by these groups is
small. A total of 42 percent of the sample were politically active
prior to joining CR groups; after joining, 55 percent of the sample were active. (Twenty percent of those who were politically
active pre-CR groups dropped their activity; 38 percent of those
not active pre-CR became so.)

A study subsequent to the survey of 1,669 women reported in Chapter Fifteen further underscored the psychotherapeutic appeal as well as the therapeutic effects of women's
consciousness-raising groups. Using interview data as well as
questionnaires in this later study, we found that the problems
that motivate women to join consciousness-raising groups are
"problems in living," in existential anxiety associated with ex-

pectable transitions of the life cycle. Lack of a clear identity, low self-esteem, loneliness, and nonassertiveness—these are the major issues mentioned by women who entered consciousness-raising groups.

Utilizing such findings, we can, with some confidence, locate the consciousness-raising groups as a new institution in our society which, in general, appeals to somewhat emotionally distressed women who are seeking help. And in that sense they represent "psychotherapeutic systems." What we have been unable to isolate in our study with any degree of certainty are the specific needs that such groups serve, in contrast to the variety of other institutions existing in our society for similar needs.

Conclusions

In this chapter, our focus has been on the institution through the eyes of its participants. The transformation of an institution such as women's consciouness-raising groups from political activism and a highly ideological setting to a relatively amorphous help-providing support system is addressed in Chapter Five. As described there, the dilemma faced by such institutions in using personal experience in a relatively unfocused, ambiguous, face-to-face, intensive interaction is, in all likelihood, a condition for the transformation from political activity to psychotherapeutic system.

In closing, it is appropriate to draw on the major explanation we offered in understanding the development of growth centers and their wide appeal to the educated middle class in our society (Lieberman and Gardner, 1976). There we observed that those who participated in such centers displayed a chronic involvement in the wide variety of institutional forms of help providing. Perhaps roughly 50 percent of the women we observed who participated in women's consciousness-raising groups represent the same stratum, a group of special seekers who are after a sort of therapeutic, problem-solving, changing process and seek it wherever they can find it. It is almost as if, in this view, the institutions themselves—their images, how they work, and what they can accomplish—are irrelevant. What is, perhaps, unique about these populations is not their commitment to growth or change but their propensity to seek out formal institution psychotherapy, growth centers, and women's consciousness-raising groups for this process. The propensity of a segment of our population to place high value on growth and change and to seek out institutions to provide it may be at heart the basis of understanding that brings many women to consciousness-raising groups. It is not the specifics of the activity but rather another setting in a long line of settings used for similar purposes. In understanding such institutions, therefore, we need to understand not so much the specific characteristics of the institution but rather the condition in our society that has brought forth this segment of our population who appear to utilize almost all forms of institutions society provides that can be adopted for personal change.

CHAPTER 8

Participation in Medical Self-Help Groups

Gary R. Bond & Steven Daiter

The pathways to participation in self-help groups, or the processes by which persons learn about, join, and become active members of self-help groups, consist of a series of events and conditions related to the nature and timing of the organizational contact, access to meetings, and other external factors; in addition to individual motivation, all of these factors may influence decisions by individuals to become more active. How likely is it that a prospective member will learn of the existence of a group that focuses on his or her special concern? What is the nature of the initial contact with the group? Does the geographic location of the group make participation possible? What influence do professionals, family, and friends exert on participation? How critical is it that the individual seek out the organization on his or her own initiative? What part do one's motivations, needs, and self-concept play in participation? What role does the group's offerings play in encouraging some people to join but not others?

In this chapter, we attempt to trace the chronology of prospective members of Mended Hearts from the time of surgery forward and to identify the events and conditions that serve to screen heart surgery patients in or out of the organization. In contrast to preceding chapters, which have focused on individual motivations and needs that lead to self-selection into self-help, this chapter will consider such external factors as organization efforts in outreach and the opinions of significant others as they influence participation in the group.

As described in Chapter Two, Mended Hearts is very active in attracting new members and, therefore, it is quite appropriate to examine the selection issue in the broader context. In addition, the nature of the Mended Hearts visitation program, which routinizes contact by the organization at the time of heart surgery, permits a more detailed examination of the pathways model than is possible in the other systems studied. Despite the growth of Mended Hearts, only about 15 percent of the heart patients visited in the hospital by Mended Hearts visitors actually join the organization. Accordingly, we modify the preceding line of inquiry—why do people join?—and ask, Why do people choose not to join? What are the forces acting against their involvement? The exclusionary factors do not exactly coincide with those leading to involvement.

Survey

In a 1976–1977 national survey of 779 heart patients, we sought to explore the differences among Mended Hearts visitors, nonvisitor members, and nonmembers at various stages in the pathways to participation. Our reference to participation in self-help, rather than simply "joining," is to anticipate the distinction in Mended Hearts, as well as in other self-help groups, between active and nominal membership. Our interest was in identifying not only the factors that explain initial attraction to self-help but also those that account for sustained involvement in the organization. Our criterion for active involvement in Mended Hearts was that the member be an "accredited visitor" (see Chapter Two).

Sample. A mail survey of heart patients in four geographic regions of the country—Southwest (SW), Southeast (SE), West (W), and Midwest (MW)—was conducted after obtaining rosters of active members in four Mended Hearts chapters and names of heart surgery patients living in that area who had not joined. In each chapter, the entire roster of members who had had heart surgery, and a stratified random sample of nonmembers, were mailed the questionnaire. In the MW chapter, all nonmembers were mailed surveys. The nonmember rosters came from records maintained by Mended Hearts in hospitals in which they had active visitation programs.

The survey was sent to 1,293 heart patients but 75 questionnaires were returned with insufficient addresses; 779 returned completed questionnaires (64 percent). Overall, 473 of 689 members (69 percent) and 306 of 529 nonmembers (58 percent) receiving questionnaires returned them. Among the members, 118 were visitors and 309 were nonvisitor members. Forty-six of the members described themselves as "former members" and were eliminated from the major analyses. As members who were attracted to the organization but eventually left, they provide a basis for comparison around the issue of sustained involvement in the organization, as we shall report on these differences later in this chapter.

Visitors had a much greater participation rate in the organization than either nonvisitor members or former members. For example, 46 percent of the visitors had attended nine or more meetings in the previous year, compared with 5 percent of the nonvisitor members and 2 percent of the former members. Forty-four percent of the visitors had held a chapter office in addition to being a visitor, compared with 4 percent of the nonvisitor members and 4 percent of the former members. (Thirteen percent of the former members had been accredited visitors.) The distinctions in membership status are well delineated.

The mean age of respondents was 56.6, with 91 percent over age 45 and 40 percent over 60. Seventy-eight percent of the sample were men, reflecting the higher incidence of heart surgery among men. Eighty-nine percent were married, 3 percent single, and 8 percent separated, divorced, or widowed. Most respondents had discovered their heart problems within the previous five years, shortly before their surgery; 16 percent had surgery prior to 1974, 12 percent in 1974, 26 percent in 1975, 32 percent in 1976, and 14 percent in 1977. Ninety-two percent had only one surgery; 81 percent coronary bypass, 13 percent cardiac valve replacement, and the remainder (6 percent) had other types of heart surgery. Sixty-seven percent were employed prior to surgery; after surgery, the percentage of the respondents employed full or part time dropped to 56 percent. This drop in employment was accounted for by respondents who retired after their surgeries (28 percent as compared to the 12 percent who were retired before surgery). Of those who retired, 75 percent related retirement to their heart problems. Twenty-four percent of the respondents had received a bachelor's degree, another 51 percent were high school graduates, and the remaining 21 percent had not finished high school.

Survey Instrument. A thirty-six-page survey instrument was used to assess pathways to participation, psychological adaptation to surgery, and member experiences in the group. The major questionnaires of concern in this chapter included the following: *visitation experience*, a one-page checklist describing the heart patient's perceptions of visitation by Mended Hearts at the time of surgery; *reasons for not participating*, a fifteen-item checklist consisting of six kinds of reasons—familiarity with the organization, contact with the organization, logistics of attending meetings, responsibility of membership, physical illness, and alternative sources of help; *attitudes of significant others*, a checklist of attitudes of physicians, spouse, friends, and other heart patients toward Mended Hearts. *Reasons for joining* were assessed by a checklist described in Chapter Six. A modification of Leary's (1957) personality inventory was used to assess two dimensions of interpersonal style: *love* ("I want everyone to like me," "I am a friendly person" are illustrative items) and *dominance* ("I enjoy being in charge of things," "Generally, I can be counted on to help others" are examples). *Affiliations* with other volunteer organizations were assessed with five survey items.

Survey Findings

Awareness of the Group. Large numbers of eligible people never join self-help groups because they are unaware of the existence of the organizations. For example, perhaps one third of the Catholic widowed population of Chicago are unfamiliar with the citywide Naim network of chapters. Although we have no solid epidemiological information on the extent to which self-help groups are known in their communities, we speculate that the low percentage of people undergoing stressful life events who turn to self-help groups is partly a result of ignorance of such groups' existence.

For Mended Hearts, however, ignorance is not a major explanation of why heart patients do not join, at least for those having surgery at hospitals represented in the survey. (We should note that some hospitals in the cities surveyed did not have visitation programs, but these were not major sites for heart surgery.) Only 6 percent of the nonmembers in the survey sample were not aware of the existence of Mended Hearts. Admittedly, a majority of these names were generated from a list of people visited by Mended Hearts in the Hospital. Even so, among those not visited, 59 percent also knew about Mended Hearts. Furthermore, only 17 percent of the nonmembers gave as the reason for not becoming more involved that they "knew little about Mended Hearts."

Favorable Initial Contact. Four fifths of both the members and the nonmembers were visited by Mended Hearts visitors in the hospital at the time of surgery. As shown in Table 1, heart patients were ordinarily visited between one and three times. The lack of differences in frequency of visits suggests that the amount of attention provided by Mended Hearts was not a factor in determining who joined. In Table 1 we report differences in their experiences in what was for most of them their first contact with the organization. (Only 14 percent of the respondents had heard of Mended Hearts prior to entering the hospital.) Since this visit occurs at a time when prospective members are likely to be highly receptive to an organization concerned with heart surgery, such contact may be instrumental in predisposing heart patients to join the group.

The fact that members remembered the visits as generally more helpful than nonmembers suggests the possibility that a favorable initial impression of the organization may influence heart patients to investigate Mended Hearts after surgery. Sixty-eight percent of the current members, compared with 46 percent of the nonmembers, found the visits "extremely helpful." Of more importance, perhaps, is the fact that 16 percent of the nonmembers remembered it as "minimally helpful," a figure more than twice that for members. Thus initial unfavorable contact with Mended Hearts may discourage further participation.

Additional evidence that members found the visits more worthwhile is given by the findings that significantly more reported that the visits made them "feel more optimistic" and that they deemed it important that they "saw how well someone else was doing who had had the surgery." Interestingly, significant differences were found for the discussion of "visitor's surgery" and "joining Mended Hearts," both topics that visitors are discouraged from discussing. Possibly some nonmembers resented such intrusions by an outsider at a time of personal crisis. However, even if we accept at face value the retrospective reports about being visited (an event that occurred several years prior to the survey for most respondents), they at best account for but a fraction of those who chose not to join the group.

Finally, as Table 2 suggests, very few nonmembers gave as a reason for nonparticipation any indication that Mended Hearts suffered from a poor image. Only 3 percent of the nonmembers were "turned off by Mended Hearts." Eleven percent said that they "don't see how Mended Hearts can help." In general, then, members and nonmembers were sympathetic to the goals of the organization, regardless of their level of involvement. For most people, the initial contact was positive.

Geographic Accessibility. Does geographical location of chapters play a part in the pathways to participation? Table 2 suggests that the location of chapter meetings posed a problem for 32 percent of the nonmembers and 25 percent of the non-visitor members, compared with only 8 percent of the visitors. If we take this finding at face value, we might conclude that a major mechanism for screening out prospective members con-

Table 1. Patients' Experiences with Mended Hearts Visitation

	Participation Status			
	Visitor (N=86)	Nonvisitor Member (N=260)	Nonmember (N=234)	Significance
How many times did a Mended Hearts visitor see you at the hospital?				
1	22	24	30	
2	38	35	31	NS
3	40	41	39	
What did you talk about at that time?				
Information about Mended Hearts	66	64	69	NS
What the visitor's life was like after surgery	56	69	65	NS
Visitor's own surgery	46	65	69	.003
Facts about heart surgery	61	62	63	NS
What to expect after surgery	60	59	63	NS
Everyday things	46	42	39	NS
Joining Mended Hearts	35	36	48	.03
What was important to you about the visit?				
Saw how well someone else was doing who had had the operation	87	85	77	.02
Realized others go through the same ordeal	76	82	79	NS
Got useful information	60	62	53	NS
Made me feel more optimistic	62	62	48	.005
Shared some of my fears and anxieties	44	45	39	NS

Did a Mended Hearts member talk to your family?

	78	69	70	NS

Overall, how did you feel about the Mended Hearts visits?

				.001
Extremely helpful	68	68	46	
Somewhat helpful	24	26	38	
Minimally/not helpful	9	5	16	

When you came home from the hospital, what was the next contact with Mended Hearts?

				.001
None	0	15	47	
Mended Hearts contacted me	20	33	35	
Spouse contacted Mended Hearts	1	1	0	
Self-Initiated contact	78	52	18	

Note: Entries in table are percentage of respondents.

cerns decisions about where chapter meetings are held or, more generally, where chapters are formed.

For a Mended Hearts chapter to receive formal charter from the national office, its leaders must demonstrate that they can develop a viable visitation program. By setting these conditions, the organization excludes those who live any distance from major medical centers where heart surgery is performed. These centers are the sites of both the major function of the organization (to visit heart patients) and of chapter meetings. In terms of the major organizational goal, there is no reason to attract new members and form new chapters in areas lacking medical centers.

Another important goal of Mended Hearts is to provide information for those recovering from heart surgery, partly to compensate for a lack of access to medical personnel. Yet the very people who live the greatest distance from major medical centers, and may therefore have least access to medical personnel, are also most likely to find distance to Mended Hearts chapter meetings an impediment to their further participation. The national policy of Mended Hearts concerning chapter locations effectively screens out people who might benefit from such chapter activities.

Encouragement to Others. Do professionals, family members, and friends influence whether an individual joins Mended Hearts? The influence of physicians is suggested by findings concerning perceptions of the attitudes held by cardiac surgeons and family doctors toward Mended Hearts. Seventy-nine percent of the members (visitors as well as nonvisitors) perceived their cardiac surgeons as having favorable opinions, which was significantly higher than the corresponding figure of 64 percent of nonmembers. Similarly, 67 percent of members felt their family doctors had favorable attitudes, compared with 55 percent of the nonmembers. The major difference lay in the higher proportion of "no opinion" responses from nonmembers rather than the perception of unfavorable attitudes by their doctors. Our field visits suggested several ways in which physicians influenced membership. The most noteworthy instance was given by a surgeon who actually paid membership dues for one year

Table 2. Reasons for Not Participating

	Visitor	Nonvisitor Member	Nonmember	Significance
Familiarity with organization				
Know little about Mended Hearts	2	4	17	.01
Contact with organization				
Turned off by Mended Hearts contact	3	2	3	NS
Don't see how Mended Hearts can help	1	4	11	.01
Bored by meetings	8	6	4	NS
Logistics of attending meetings				
Never invited	0	1	7	.01
No one to go to meetings with	2	9	7	.01
Meeting place too far away	8	25	32	.01
Meeting time inconvenient	11	18	14	NS
No transportation	2	3	3	NS
No meeting since surgery	0	0	2	.04
Responsibility of membership				
Don't want obligations of belonging	0	4	14	.01
No reason to be reminded of surgery	0	4	10	.01
Don't think I can help others	0	5	6	.05
Physical health				
Too ill	2	2	5	NS
Alternative sources of help				
Get all the help I need elsewhere	3	2	10	.01

Note: Entries in table are percentage of respondents.

in Mended Hearts for all patients in his charge. Other physicians did actively encourage their patients to attend Mended Hearts meetings, according to our interviews.

More members than nonmembers also viewed spouses (85 percent for members; 75 percent for nonmembers) and other heart surgery patients (82 percent for members, 72 percent for nonmembers) as having favorable attitudes toward Mended Hearts. No differences were found with respect to friends.

These findings do not permit us to pinpoint the role of others in influencing members to join the group. We do not know, for example, how often physicians actually referred their patients to Mended Hearts, but only that they were favorably disposed. One conceivable route to membership that did not occur was an active role taken by the spouse in contacting the Mended Hearts visitor after surgery. Less than one percent of members and nonmembers alike indicated that this occurred. We conclude that favorable attitudes by important others may play some part in routing people into the organization, though this influence is probably not decisive in the majority of cases.

Self-initiated Contact. How important is it that the individual seek out the organization on his or her own initiative, rather than simply respond to invitations from members? As shown in Table 1, among those visited, those who later became visitors were much more likely to initiate posthospitalization contact with Mended Hearts than were others. Seventy-eight percent of the visitors reported having gone to meetings or contacted members on their own initiative, compared with 52 percent of the nonvisitor members and only 18 percent of the nonmembers—self-motivation appears to be a critical factor for participation. The organization can only go so far in making prospective members welcome. The lack of participation by nonmembers cannot be attributed to a lack of organizational response. One third of the nonmembers were extended special invitations by members subsequent to hospitalization yet chose not to join. In fact, only 7 percent of the nonmembers visited in the hospital indicated that they did not become involved because they were not invited. Thus even with face-to-face contact and invitations to attend meetings, most heart patients chose not to become involved. Self-selection, and not selective recruitment, was the decisive factor in their nonparticipation.

Nonetheless, note that 16 percent of the nonmembers did attend at least one chapter meeting. For this subgroup, the most frequently given reasons for not becoming more involved were as follows: "too far away" (25 percent), "time inconvenient" (19 percent), "know little about Mended Hearts" (15 percent), "bored by meetings" (13 percent), "don't see how Mended Hearts can help" (13 percent), "don't want obligations of belonging" (13 percent). No single reason stands out as an explanation for their lack of further involvement.

Thirty-five percent of the nonvisitor members had never attended a meeting. Undoubtedly, some members paid their membership dues in the spirit of contributing to a worthwhile organization. This financial support may often have been motivated by the gratitude they felt for the hospital visitation and may have also been intended as a way of endorsing the goals of the organization short of active participation (see Table 3). As with nonmembers who attended one meeting and never returned, it appears that the organization did make an impact on these nominal members, but they were simply not self-motivated to become more active participants.

Match Between Individual Characteristics and Organizational Goals. The external factors considered thus far have failed to uncover any outstanding differences among visitors, nonvisitors, and nonmembers. We consider now the match between individual characteristics and the goals of the organization. As Chapter Two indicates, Mended Hearts is a service organization. This is expressed very clearly in its motto: "It's great to be alive and to help others." At each stage in the pathways to participation, individuals make judgments about how well they fit with the organizational objectives and choose accordingly. We shall introduce into our discussion at this point the former members, since their decision to disaffiliate is germane to a "mismatch" hypothesis. (Evidence for this perceived mismatch is given by the finding that former members had significantly lower ratings on testimony items, such as "Mended Hearts met my goals.")

Reasons for joining Mended Hearts are given in Table 3. The altruism expressed in the visitors' most frequently given reason ("look at life differently and wanted to help others") is obviously compatible with the organizational goals. Further, visitors felt a congruence between their values and the organizational goals, as indicated by the fact that 92 percent "felt Mended Hearts stood for something (they) believe in." In both instances, significant differences were found among the three groups of members, with visitors having the highest ratings. A desire for more medical information was an important motive, shared by visitors, nonvisitors, members, and former members alike. Since medical information is the single most important reason for joining given by former members but is ranked fourth for visitors, we might speculate that this motive may be instrumental in attracting someone to the group but is not sufficient to sustain their involvement.

A self-screening process is also indicated by the reasons for not joining (Table 2), where significantly more of the nonmembers indicated that they did not want the obligations of belonging, did not want to be reminded of surgery, or did not see how Mended Hearts could help. All these reasons indicate a perception of the organization that was not suited to their needs or self-concept.

An examination of demographic characteristics suggests that education and occupational status were significantly associated with participation in Mended Hearts. Visitors were the best educated, and more held white-collar jobs. For example, 32 percent of the visitors, 27 percent of the nonvisitor members, 18 percent of the former members, and 16 percent of the nonmembers had received bachelor's degrees. The results for those working prior to surgery who held administrative or professional positions parallel those for education. A higher percentage of visitors (58 percent) and nonvisitor members (52 percent) held such positions than either nonmembers (30 percent) or former members (35 percent). The explanation may be that more educated people see themselves as compatible with the purposes of the group. Since chapter meetings often consist of speakers on topics such as the physiology of the heart, medical aspects of

Table 3. Reasons for Joining Mended Hearts

	Visitor (N=117)	Nonvisitor Member (N=305)	Former Member (N=35)	Significance
1. Look at life differently and wanted to help others	93	85	70	.000
2. Felt Mended Hearts stood for something I believed in	92	65	68	.002
3. Appreciation for help from Mended, Hearts	74	73	65	NS
4. More medical information	64	72	74	NS
5. Keep active	59	39	47	.02
6. Talk over surgery with others who had it	49	52	57	NS
7. Make friends	41	34	28	NS
8. Bring about some change in self	39	30	32	NS
9. Concern with discrimination against heart patients	35	26	19	NS
10. Talk over other problems	22	13	17	NS
11. Get out of house	11	4	16	.04

Note: Entries in table are percentage of respondents indicating reason was "very important" or "important."

surgery, and postsurgical case, it would make sense that more educated people would be inclined to attend meetings. In addition, those who are more financially secure may be more responsive to an ethic of social responsibility and altruism which the group promotes.

Another demographic variable differentiating members and nonmembers was the number of surgeries. A significantly higher proportion of members (10 percent) than nonmembers (5 percent) had had more than one surgery. A simple explanation would be that when a person has more than one heart surgery, the surgery becomes more central to the self-concept and an organization devoted to heart surgery becomes more salient.

Significant differences were found in the tendency to affiliate with volunteer organizations. More visitors and nonvisitor members belonged to church groups, community groups, service organizations, professional organizations, and social groups than did nonmembers or former members. For example, among visitors, 70 percent belonged to a church group, 79 percent to a community group, 69 percent to a service organization, 60 percent to a professional organization, and 67 percent to a social group. The comparable figures for nonmembers were: 50 percent, 28 percent, 31 percent, 36 percent, and 47 percent. Supporting evidence of the greater affiliative orientation of visitors came from the Leary (1957) personality inventory. On the *love* dimension, visitors had a significantly higher mean score (5.5) than any of the other groups: nonvisitor members, 1.9; former members, 2.0; nonmembers, 1.7.

Visitors are more gregarious and friendly and have a history of seeking out volunteer organizations to a greater degree than nonvisitor members, former members, or nonmembers. This suggests that a match between this view of themselves and the organizational goals at visitation leads to their self-selection.

On the other dimension of the Leary inventory, visitors were also significantly higher than the other three groups. The *dominance* dimension reflects a leadership orientation and a sense of responsibility toward others. Mean scores on this scale were: visitors, 8.7; nonvisitor members, 5.6; former members, 3.8; and nonmembers, 4.8. It is apparent that these qualities are highly compatible with the visitor role.

Conclusions

We have examined three levels of pathways to participation: the organizational efforts to attract members, or what we could call *selective recruitment*; influence of professionals and informal networks in encouraging people to join, or *selective referral*; and *self-selection* by individuals as to the congruence or match between their own motivations and what the organization stands for.

Selective recruitment, or the biases in the manner in which the organization attracts new members, is suggested by unequal access to the group by segments of the target populations. In Mended Hearts, any bias in the amount of initial contact is minimized by the fact that visitation programs assure that essentially all those undergoing surgery have contact with the Mended Hearts visitors. In most other self-help groups, however, the contact with prospective members is unequal and may be a function of the degree of enthusiasm of those members charged with this function. Nonetheless, even with pervasive publicity of a self-help group, and easy accessibility, only a small percentage of prospective members actually participate.

For some self-help groups, selective referral is probably more crucial than selective recruitment in attracting members to groups. The encouragement of spouse and physicians was statistically associated with participation in Mended Hearts. The impact of the opinions of others may be even greater for groups in which the individual ordinarily lacks firsthand contact with a member of the group.

The key to understanding participation in Mended Hearts, however, is to recognize its service orientation. As such, it attracts people whose self-image is compatible with service objectives. Membership is viewed as an obligation to help others by those who become actively involved. The selection factors are, accordingly, quite distinct from other self-help groups where the primary goal is to provide help to current members.

A matching hypothesis is useful, for example, in interpreting the reversed findings regarding educational level in Mended Hearts, compared with that for members and invited nonmembers in Naim, in which members were less educated.

As suggested in Chapter Three, the social camaraderie of Naim may appeal more to a working-class membership than to a more highly educated population of higher socioeconomic status. Mended Hearts, which stresses service and medical information, understandably would attract people comfortable with this format.

One implication for self-help groups directed toward service is that their active members will tend to be people who serve as volunteers in other organizations as well. Thus active members will generally seek out Mended Hearts not because they lack community, but precisely because they have the social skills and prior experiences that makes it easier for them to become visitors. The question remains whether Mended Hearts and other such groups essentially screen out those who are most in need of alternative support networks.

Our findings suggest that the process of selection does not occur at a single decisive point but can occur at any of a number of junctures from the point of the stressful life event forward. Membership and sustained involvement requires the confluence of the opportunity to join, as given by the knowledge of the group and accessibility to it, and a felt readiness to become involved. The readiness or motivation derives from a perceived match between the organizational goals and individual needs and self-concept.

CHAPTER 9

Widow Groups as an Alternative to Informal Social Support

Elizabeth A. Bankoff

One hypothesis advanced to explain people's attraction to self-help groups is that the professional help givers in our society have not met the needs of people suffering from specific traumatic life crises (for example, widowhood). In this view, self-help groups are alternative mental health resources that respond to the unique needs of their target population. In a study of one kind of self-help group, however, Lieberman and Bond (Chapter Seven) found that women joining consciousness-raising groups were, in fact, more frequent users of psychotherapy than the general population. Moreover, these women's experiences with therapy were usually positive, indicating that dissatisfaction with existing services was not necessarily a major determinant of participation in consciousness-raising groups. In general, there is little evidence documenting whether or not people join self-help groups because of perceived inadequacies in existing professional resources.

There is, however, an alternative hypothesis for why certain people join self-help groups. A number of studies have shown that a person's immediate social network (friends, family, and neighbors) is his or her primary source of help when facing difficult transitions or unexpected crises (Brown, 1978; Croog, Lipson, and Levine, 1972; Quarentelli, 1960). Perhaps if individuals' social networks have been inadequate in helping them through a crisis or a difficult transition, they will then turn to a self-help group for help. In this view, rather than being alternatives to professional helpers, self-help groups function as alternative social support and social linkage systems. Although some investigators have, indeed, suggested that people seek help from professionals when their network resources are inadequate (Kadushin, 1969; Kasl, Gore, and Cobb, 1975; Mayer and Timms, 1970; Quarentelli, 1960), there has been no investigation into the possible relationship between the adequacy of people's networks and their use of self-help groups.

This chapter examines the relationship between membership in Naim, a Chicago-based self-help organization for Catholic widows and widowers, and the availability and adequacy of both their professional helping and social network resources. Survey and ethnographic data were used to explore the question: Is Naim attracting widows and widowers whose informal social networks have proven inadequate in helping them with the problems of widowhood, and/or is Naim attracting widowed people who have found professional help to be either inadequate or unavailable?

Naim, founded in 1956, with a current membership of over 1,000 Catholic widows and widowers, is perhaps this country's oldest self-help group for people who have lost a spouse. As this organization focuses on long-term adaptation to an irreversible life crisis, it stands somewhat distinct from more publicized self-help groups such as Alcoholics Anonymous, Parents Anonymous, or Synanon, which are geared toward the control and modification of problems in their members' behaviors. Despite these differences, Naim is a self-help group. It is an organization limited to people with a common set of problems who congregate to help each other. Moreover, the twenty-six chapters of Naim in the Chicago area function with a minimum of professional intervention. (See Chapter Three for details.)

Survey

In the spring of 1978, following several months of intensive field investigations, we selected the founding chapter of Naim for a pilot survey. This chapter had a membership of 134 widows and widowers drawn from the greater Chicago area. A nonmember control group was incorporated into the research design for the purpose of comparing the availability and adequacy of professional and informal network resources of members and widowed people who had not joined Naim. The controls were drawn from two sources. First, we asked the Naim Council to provide us with records of people who had been referred to Naim and subsequently invited to attend a "get-acquainted with Naim" conference. From 9,000 persons contacted by Naim during the preceding several years, we randomly chose for study 120 women and 30 men. In addition, we contacted priests of nine Chicago parishes, all of whom agreed to provide us with names of widowed people in their parishes. One hundred sixty-five people were identified in this fashion, with known members of Naim excluded.

Sample. Questionnaires were mailed to the total membership of the Naim chapter and to the two control samples. Sixty-seven percent of the Naim members, 20 percent of the conference sample, and 37 percent of the parish sample returned questionnaires. From these returns, two groups were identified for the present study. The control sample (N = 52) consisted of widowed people who had not joined Naim, although they knew of Naim, had been invited to a Naim conference, or had attended a Naim function. Analyses were performed which contrasted those nonmembers who had been invited to and/or attended a Naim function with those who knew of Naim but had neither been invited to nor had attended a Naim function. Because these two groups did not significantly differ on any of the selection indices, they were combined into one control sample. The member sample (N = 72) consisted of members of the chapter who had not remarried. (Remarried respondents were not considered in this study, since Naim is oriented toward single persons.) Since only widowed people aware of the group's existence can select into the system, nonmembers who were not certain they had heard of Naim (N = 29) were dropped from further analyses in this study.

Members and nonmembers did not differ measurably from each other in terms of sex ratio, percentage who were parents, percentage who worked, income level, or age distribution. Eighty-one percent of our sample were females, 92 percent were parents, and 79 percent were employed at least part time. The median yearly income for the respondents was $10,500, and the mean age was 54.9 years. Despite these basic similarities, there were a number of important differences. Nonmembers were more educated than members (35 percent of the nonmembers had a bachelor's degree, compared with 9 percent of the members) and were of a slightly higher socioeconomic status (SES). Furthermore, Naim members had been widowed, on the average, a little more than 6.5 years, whereas the nonmembers had been widowed, on the average, only a little more than 2 years. This difference in length of widowhood might confound simple comparisons between members and nonmembers (for example, the amount of time since the spouse's death might affect the frequency of contact with relatives). Therefore, in the following analyses, length of widowhood was statistically controlled by the use of analysis of covariance.

Survey Instrument. All respondents completed a twenty-four page questionnaire which had been designed as part of a larger research project to examine issues bearing on both selection into Naim and the impact of the group on the individual. Members also answered additional questions about their reasons for joining Naim and their subsequent experiences in the organization. The following measures allowed us to assess the adequacy, availability, and use of both professional and informal helping resources.

Extensiveness of use of professional help was measured by asking the respondents how many professional helpgivers (for example, "priest or clergy, counselor, doctor") they had consulted about problems related to widowhood. Intensity of use of professional help was measured by asking how many of these professionals they had used for help at least four times. Perceived adequacy of professional help was indicated by how much satisfaction respondents had experienced with the professionals' response to them.

The extensiveness, activity, intimacy, and dependability of the respondents' social network were determined by scales developed by Brown (1979). The extensiveness scale assessed the breadth of the informal social network. The activity scale indicated the amount of contact respondents had with their friends, family, and neighbors. The intimacy scale determined the frequency with which respondents discussed their personal problems with their network associates. And the dependability scale measured the confidence respondents had that their fellow network members would help them in an emergency. In order to get a more complete picture of the respondents' social linkages, we asked if they had made new friends since their spouse's death and if they were seeing their old friends and relatives more or less frequently than before they were widowed. We also determined how adequate and available was the help provided by friends, family, and neighbors for two of the most compelling problems faced by widowed people: grief ("How helpful were others to you in handling your grief?"), and an unfulfilling social life ("How frequently do you have a chance to have fun? Go out for recreation or entertainment? Have difficulty in finding a companion for your entertainment activities?" and "How satisfied are you with your social life?")

Survey Findings

Members and nonmembers differed in their use of professional help-giving resources (see Table 1). The nonmembers were less likely to have sought professional help for problems of widowhood: 89 percent of the members reported that they had talked with at least one professional, compared with 71 percent of the nonmembers. Moreover, the nonmembers who had sought such help consulted fewer professionals and returned for continued help less frequently than did members. Those members and nonmembers who had seen a professional on a continuing basis did not differ in their evaluation of the help they had received: both were positive. Only 2 percent of the fifty-one members and none of the twenty nonmembers who had seen a professional at least four times indicated that their interactions had been negative.

Overall, these two groups were quite similar with regard to their informal social networks. Although more members reported having made new friends, they had been widowed several years longer, as earlier noted, and thus had had more time in which to make friends. Moreover, since Naim members often consider each other to be friends, this finding may simply reflect the fact that members had joined Naim. However, members did indicate that their informal networks had been less adequate than those of nonmembers in their times of grief and that they had less confidence that their friends, relatives, and neighbors could be depended upon for help in an emergency.

A common assumption held by many researchers of self-help groups is that people turn to such groups because of deficiencies in the quantity and quality of contacts with professional help givers in our society. In our investigation of Naim, however, we found no evidence to support this assumption. The data clearly suggest that Naim members are not involved with Naim in order to compensate for inadequate experiences with professional helpgivers. Not only do Naim members tend to be frequent and consistent professional help seekers, they also give highly favorable reports of the help they have received. Further support for the conclusion that membership in Naim is *not* the result of professional help-giving inadequacies is found in the reasons given by members for joining Naim (see Table 2). If members joined Naim to compensate for inadequate professional help, it would be reasonable to expect that their motivations for joining Naim would coincide with those for seeking psychotherapy. However, members did not turn to Naim for the type of help typically associated with going to professionals ("to get psychological help," "to solve personal problems"). Instead,

Table 1. Comparison Between Naim Members and Widowed
Nonmembers on Selection Factors

Selection Dimension	Membership Status		Significance[a]	
	Naim member (N=72)	Non-member (N=52)	Member vs. Nonmember	Covariate (length of widowhood)
I. Demographic Characteristics				
Age (years)	54.1	56.1	NS	NS
Length of widowhood (months)	80.7	26.9	.000	–
Parent	94%	86%	NS[b]	
Female	76%	87%	NS[b]	
Employed	83%	75%	NS[b]	
Retired,	7%	12%	NS[b]	
SES	44.5	49.5	.04	NS
Education	12.6	13.8	.02	NS
Income	3.5	4.0	NS	NS
II. Professional Resources				
Sought professional help	89%	71%	.03[b]	
Extensiveness of use	2.6	1.7	.001	NS
Intensity of use	1.2	0.6	.002	NS
Satisfaction with help	1.8(N=51)	1.6(N=20)	NS	NS
III. Informal Network Resources				
Extensiveness of network	0.5	0.4	NS	NS
Activity of network	13.4	13.3	NS	NS
Intimacy of network	10.2	9.8	NS	NS
Dependability of network	10.5	12.4	.02	NS
Made new friends	97%	59%	.000[b]	
See old friends	1.3	1.5	NS	.004
See relatives	1.9	1.8	NS	NS
Helpfulness with grief	2.2	2.5	.05	.01
Chance to have fun	2.0	2.1	NS	NS
Frequency go out for entertainment	4.0	3.6	NS	NS
Entertainment companion	2.1	2.2	NS	NS
Satisfaction with social life	2.1	2.3	NS	NS

[a] Unless otherwise indicated, all statistical analyses are calculated by analysis of covariance between member and nonmember means, with length of widowhood introduced as a covariate. (Adjusted means are entered in table if the covariate was significant.)
[b] Fisher's Exact Test.

Naim members joined "to make friends," "to be with people I could feel comfortable with," "to have fun," and "to get involved in social activities." In short, they turned to Naim not

Table 2. Initial Reasons for Going to Naim

	Percent Responding "Very Important"
Make friends	68
Be with people I could be comfortable with	65
Learn how other widowed people cope with their problems	58
Have fun	57
Get involved in social activities	53
Become more active	53
Share thoughts and feelings about being widowed	50
Bring about some change in myself	46
Deal with current life problems	46
Get out of my shell	44
Do something different	42
Get relief from things or feelings troubling me	42
Get information about widowhood	42
Discuss my feelings with others	40
Get involved in a Catholic organization	39
Learn from professionals (priests, lawyers, etc.)	35
Get advice	33
Get away from my problems	33
Make contact with someone I could call on	31
Have a chance to grieve with others who understand my feelings	24
Meet someone I might date	22
Spiritual guidance	21
Curiosity	21
Solve personal problems	17
Get psychological help	8
Find a new spouse	4

as an alternative professional mental health resource but as a social linkage system and social life resource.

This brings us to the question of whether or not joining Naim is related to deficiencies within members' immediate social networks. Members and nonmembers depicted their social networks as being, in general, equally extensive, active, and intimate—suggesting that, on a normal day-to-day basis, the two networks function equally well. However, when the respondents were asked to evaluate how well their friends, family, and neighbors responded during times of pain or crisis, the similarities disappeared. For, in comparison to the nonmembers, members not only considered their friends, family, and neighbors to be less dependable sources of help in any emergency but also indicated that these people had been much less helpful to them when they were undergoing the trial perhaps most pertinent to widowhood—their grief. These findings suggest that joining Naim is related to functional inadequacies in widowed peoples's informal social networks during particularly difficult times for them.

Joining Naim is perhaps also related to the adequacy of the widowed person's existing social network in dealing with yet another major problem typically faced by widowed people— a disrupted and unfulfilling social life. Although we have no direct survey data on the quality of members' social lives prior to their involvement in Naim, our field investigators were repeatedly told by members that "Naim made all the difference in the world for their social lives." Many members indicated that they had found that being widowed seemed to "scare away" old friends. Consequently, their social lives were suffering. Others reported that they had tried to maintain their old social relationships for a while but, because they felt conspicuous as the only single person on outings with a crowd of couples, they eventually pulled away, the end result for them being the loss of social companionship and an inactive social life. These observations are consistent with our survey finding that members joined in search of friends, to be with people with whom they could feel comfortable, and to have fun and become more active. In combination, these data suggest that members considered the quality of their social lives to be inadequate after the death of their spouses but prior to their involvement in Naim, and thus they turned to Naim. Concomitantly, we found that even without the linkages and active social life provided by Naim, the nonmembers had friends, companions for entertainment and outings, numerous opportunities to have a good time and, in general, as active and satisfying a social life as those who had the services of Naim. This suggests that widowed people whose companionship and social activity needs are being met elsewhere will not become Naim members.

Discussion

In sum, then, our social network data indicate that when facing crises and dealing with major problems specific to widowhood, members may have received less assistance from their friends, family, and neighbors than they expected or desired. Thus, perhaps widowed people do turn to Naim as an alternative social support and social linkage system to compensate for inadequacies in their existing informal social network.

At this point we might ask, "Why would Naim attract people whose existing social networks provided unsatisfactory assistance for problems they are experiencing as widowed people?" Perhaps the explanation can be found, in part, at the interface between the problems of widowhood and the nature of the self-help group. Loss of companionship, loss of social life, feelings of abandonment and grief are well-documented problems experienced by the widowed (Glick, Weiss, and Parkes, 1974; Lopata, 1973; Parkes, 1972). Naim offers a group of people who claim to care and who assert that they can be "counted on" when others "drop you like a hot potato." The group provides structured companionship and numerous built-in opportunities to socialize with people in the same life circumstances. Moreover, although Naim does not cater to its members' grief per se, it does represent itself as an organization filled with people who are "all in the same boat" and thus able to understand each others' grief. Indeed, many long-standing members explained their continued attraction to Naim in terms of the "familylike" relationships that existed between themselves and fellow members. As one member reported: "Leave Naim? Never. These people are my family now. They care. They understand. They are there when I need them. Why would I want to give that up?" Thus it seems reasonable that widowed people who feel their existing social network is unsatisfactory in terms of its dependability, its grief support, and its attention to their companionship and social life needs might be attracted to Naim as an alternative source of help.

Although not a focus of the present study, the lower educational and SES levels of members compared to nonmembers might also be factors influencing selection into Naim. In other words, social-class differences may help determine who would be attracted to Naim. Perhaps those ranked in a higher social stratum may not be inclined to mix socially with those in a somewhat lower stratum. An alternative interpretation is suggested by one major study of widowhood. Lopata's (1973) investigations indicate that more highly educated middle-class widows have more of the necessary skills and resources to enjoy their lives without societal help. The education and SES differences between members and nonmembers might reflect that the latter group, with four times as many college graduates, were more capable of reconstructing old social relationships and initiating new ones on their own, thereby being less in need of the ready-made linkage system provided by the Naim community.

In general, our findings should be viewed in the light of the strategic and technical problems which this study faced. Because self-help organizations comprise ongoing and *in vivo* groups, it is extremely difficult in a relatively short term investigation such as ours to incorporate into the research design a measurement of a sufficiently large sample of members before they joined Naim. Consequently, with no direct measurement of members prior to their involvement in Naim, it is impossible to clearly distinguish selection factors from possible effects of membership. For example, we cannot ascertain whether Naim members have come to see their former networks in a more negative fashion since their involvement in Naim. A second concern is the low return rate for the control samples, for with an average return rate of only 29 percent for both control samples (in other words, the Naim Conference sample and the Parish sample) the representativeness of our nonmember controls is questionable.

The limitations of this study notwithstanding, a number of important implications for our understanding of self-help groups have emerged. The original goal of self-help groups may have been to reach needy and isolated populations previously not reached by society's professional help-giving systems (Katz and Bender, 1976a). However, our findings, corroborated by the study of women's consciousness-raising groups (see Chapter

Seven), indicate that people who use self-help groups are people who also use more traditional modes of help. In short, self-help groups do not appear to serve a different clientele from that served by professionals. This implies perhaps that the originally targeted population for self-help groups—people who have not been reached by the traditional help-giving systems—are also not being reached by self-help groups.

Self-help groups and professionals may serve an overlapping population, but our study suggests that, at least in some cases, they may serve distinct functions. Naim members, at least, do not appear to be joining their self-help group to compensate for the unavailability or poor performance of professional help givers. Instead, it appears that they have turned to Naim as a source for new social linkages in compensation for inadequate support and assistance from their existing informal network associates. As such, Naim's function may be more akin to that of an informal social network than that of a professional treatment system. Instead of helping people to restructure their personalities, it seems that Naim's function is to allow people with much in common to congregate in order to restructure their informal social networks, forming an alternative or at least supplemental active and supportive social linkage system.

Now, perhaps such a social linkage function is peculiar to a self-help group that serves people whose social relationships, often built upon years of couple-oriented activities, tend to become strained and to deteriorate once they become single (Lopata, 1973; Parkes, 1972). However, such a function may also be viable among those self-help groups that serve people with even more stigmatized "afflictions," which also tend to be accompanied by deterioration of existing social relationships. From this perspective, self-help groups for the divorced, the alcoholic, and the homosexual, for example, may similarly function more as a replacement for inadequate social linkage and support systems than as a substitute for inadequate professional help.

At the very least, it would appear that some theorists have too quickly equated self-help groups with professional treatment systems. They have assumed that these groups function as alternatives to defective professional help-giving systems. In the meantime, they have overlooked the possibility that, at least in some cases, self-help groups act as remedies to social networks that have failed to provide adequate support and assistance for dealing with difficult life events.

CHAPTER 10

Analyzing
Change Mechanisms
in Groups

Morton A. Lieberman

This section explores how self-help groups aid their members. Two distinct perspectives on how such groups work are offered. One view, reflected in this chapter and by Levy in the following chapter, provides a framework on the change induction processes of self-help groups stemming from the generally credited mechanisms that have grown out of small group social psychology and psychotherapeutic models of change. Both share a goal of determining the general mechanisms of help providing in self-help groups and comparing these mechanisms to other change-induction groups.

Antze in Chapter Twelve offers a contrasting perspective, seeing highly specific cognitive restructuring unique to self-help groups as the prime mechanism of change. He explores in detail the role of ideology, the "teachings" characteristic of each of the self-help systems he has studied. Fundamental to this view is that each self-help group develops a belief system, a cognitive restructuring relevant to specific details of the affliction that brings the members together, and that change induction can be best understood in self-help groups through examining the value transformation—the alteration of belief systems being at the heart of such help.

Although I in this chapter and Levy in the following share a similar perspective, the studies differ in important ways. Aside from major differences in sample size and in many of the self-help groups studied, this chapter begins by providing a comparative framework between self-help groups and change-induction groups conducted by professionals. Although Levy's perspective resembles some of the categories of change process in the framework, it is based upon a grounded theory approach, in which mechanisms of change are extracted from a series of intensive observations of self-help groups rather than an "imported" model. The final chapter in this section uses the role of ideology framework to explore self-help groups directed toward coping with life crises rather than the behavioral reorganizational groups considered by Antze.

Examples of the capacity of small face-to-face groups to render change in the attitudes, beliefs, and behavior of their members are legion. It appears to make little difference in how that influence is rendered whether the impetus for joining such small groups is based upon sharing some condition or affliction, identification with some transcendental symbol, or sharing a similar goal, be it political or personal. Our study of change processes was illuminated by a perspective that emphasized potential similarity across a diversity of such groups. We were interested in change-induction processes common to a host of diverse settings.

Change Mechanism

The method of exploration was based upon a research tradition developed by psychotherapy investigators. For over thirty years, psychotherapy researchers have theorized about and studied the transactions associated with patient change. A number of events and experiences are thought to be directly associated with such change. These events or experiences are cast in a variety of conceptual terms. One recent statement of this approach, which gave rise to much of the work reported in this chapter, stems from the work of Yalom (1975) and Lieberman, Yalom, and Miles (1973). Both studies collated and collected a variety of "curative mechanisms"—specific experiences that were central in effecting change in group therapy patients and encounter group participants. We have followed these leads in developing both the conceptual framework and measurement procedures in pursuing our goal of describing, from the perspective of the participants, what events and experiences they found useful in self-help groups. Our approach is frankly phenomenological; we have viewed self-help groups through the eyes of the participants by asking them to recall experiences they believed to be helpful.

We thus began with a rather broad framework, borrowing heavily from the extensive theoretical and empirical works of psychotherapy regarding mechanisms of change. As our study on self-help groups progressed, we began to enlarge and embellish this framework, omitting events and experiences that seemed irrelevant to the self-help context and adding some that heretofore had not been given prominence by psychotherapists. Table 1 shows the general framework of change mechanisms adapted from psychotherapy and encounter research.

This list of "change mechanisms" needs elaboration, particularly when considering cognitive factors in change. Traditional psychotherapy sees cognitive factors as a major change mechanism. For dynamically oriented theories, a particular type of cognitive learning is stressed. There are, however, a variety of other cognitive factors, both in traditional psychotherapy and in the newer "therapies," which originated with the humanistic psychology movement. In addition to the traditional cognitive mechanisms of insight and understanding, we emphasized other processes, including the simple transmission of information, the perspective alteration in which small groups offer alternative belief systems about source, cause, and cure of the affliction or problem, the cognitive restructuring that may take place when individuals are exposed to approaches used by other group

Table 1. Change Mechanism Dimensions

Change Mechanism	Examples of Patient Statements
Altruism	Helping others has given me more self-respect. Giving part of myself to others.
Group Cohesiveness	Belonging to and being accepted by a group. Feeling alone no longer.
Universality	Learning I'm not the only one with my type of problem; "We're all in the same boat." Seeing that I was just as well off as others.
Interpersonal Learning "Input"	Learning how I come across to others. Other members honestly telling me what they think of me.
Interpersonal Learning "Output"	Feeling more trustful of groups and of other people. Learning about the way I related to the other group members.
Guidance	Group members suggesting or advising something for me to do. Group members telling me what to do.
Catharsis	Getting things off my chest. Learning how to express my feelings.
Identification	Admiring and behaving like my therapist. Finding someone in the group I could pattern myself after.
Family Reenactment	Being in the group somehow helped me to understand how I grew up in my family.
Self-Understanding	Learning why I think and feel the way I do (that is, learning some of the causes and sources of my problems). Discovering and accepting previously unknown or unacceptable parts of myself.
Instillation of Hope	Seeing others getting better was inspiring to me. Seeing that others had solved problems similar to mine.
Existential Factors	Recognizing that life is at times unfair and unjust. Recognizing that no matter how close I get to other people, I must still face life alone.

Source: Yalom; 1975.

members to a common dilemma, and a cognitive mechanism familiar in social psychology, feedback, in which information is imparted to the recipient about his or her behavior within the social setting of the group.

The following cognitive items were used to study several of the groups reported on in this chapter. For traditional psychotherapy groups, the items included "getting insight into the causes and sources of my problems," "examining the way society shapes my behavior and attitudes," "getting ideas about how I can approach problems by seeing how others do it," "learning the impact that I have on others," "learning that my experience in growing up influenced my current problems." Similar items in the consciousness-raising study were "seeing undesirable or unacceptable things about myself," "getting insight into the causes and sources of my problems," "examining problems of discrimination," "examining problems women have with traditional roles," "seeing how others approach problems gave me ideas of how I could," "the group helped me understand the impact I have on others," "examining political issues." The Compassionate Friends study indexed cognitive mechanisms such as "getting practical advice," "getting insight into the causes and sources of my problems," "seeing the difference in reaction between men and women helped me better understand my spouse's reaction," "getting feedback from other members." In the Mothers groups, items included "getting help from more experienced mothers," "getting feedback from other group members," "gaining a new perspective on my role as a mother," "getting practical hints," "becoming aware of why I behave as I do," "seeing the variety of reactions to childrearing made me more tolerant of differences," " recognizing that raising a child is often a frustrating and arduous task."

Whether the cognitive learnings reflect the group's ideology, are arrived at out of comparative judgments, or are the result of directed information volunteered by other members, all such events highlight the groups' effect on altering the perspective from which a particular problem or issue is examined. Most of the scales used to assess comparative mechanisms are similar for all groups studied; a few unique items reflect each particular group setting. A complete list of all the items appears in Table 2.

In setting out to compare the helping processes used by the various self-help groups described in this volume, we began with an examination of participants' perception of what was helpful to them. In order to use such data effectively, we needed to address the possible errors in such perceptual data. We began by examining the factors that could influence participants' experience as well as their perception of what it was about the experience that was helpful. We needed to distinguish between the events that occur in a group which are linked by participants to the group's utility from the group's belief system about what helps. Although they are conceptually distinct, it is obviously difficult to determine empirically whether the respondents' statements were based upon a generalized belief system or were a phenomenological report based on actual experiences.

We have elsewhere, in a study on encounter groups (Lieberman, Yalom, and Miles, 1973), attempted to examine this very issue by studying the perceptions of participants in encounter groups and organizing these perceptions of what was useful in their learning by comparing those who learned and those who did not. Such a strategy, which did provide some distinctions between learners and nonlearners, proved to be marginally useful in isolating events perceived as useful from the groups' belief systems about how people change.

In psychotherapy studies, the effects of the therapists' beliefs or value systems bear great weight on the clients' belief about what it was that helped them. The beliefs or values of the therapist must, to some extent, be accepted by the client; otherwise considerable dissonance exists, making it nearly impossible to participate in a change-induction setting. The mutual beliefs in psychoanalytically oriented psychotherapy that certain kinds of understanding of one's past (insight) are a crucial condition for change offers one such example. The likelihood that "insights" will occur is enhanced if the therapist generates the information required to explore this area. Professionals who have over their careers changed their intellectual or ideological orientation to change induction can readily attest to the fact that, upon changing their beliefs, clients were more likely to talk about the particular kinds of data that were appropriate to the specific ideology—whether it was early childhood experiences, discrepant self-images, or existential issues. This simple fact of influence, reinforcement, and dissonance reduction be-

clouds and makes it empirically difficult to examine phenomenological information in a change-induction study and distinguish
it from the inculcation of a specified belief system that is not
necessarily a true reflection of the client's experience.

Thus, in approaching our task of comparing respondents'
perceptions of what members of self-help groups found useful,
we must, of necessity, view this as flawed data. Our attempt to
fractionate the sources of influence on these perceptions will be
discussed later. Following is a brief description of the change
mechanisms for the self-help systems studied in this volume.

Change Mechanisms—Comparisons Among Self-Help Groups

Table 2 shows the rank order of participants' perceptions
of the events and experiences they found helpful in their self-
help groups. For each item, the percentage of people seeing the
item as important is also shown.

Women's Consciousness-Raising Groups. An examination
of Table 2 reveals that the central experience for women in consciousness-raising groups focuses around three elements. The
first element is the normalizing function of the group as expressed through sharing thoughts and feelings about being
a woman and learning that their problems are not unique. Universality is a central process in consciousness-raising groups. It
addresses a deep-felt need by women to recast their own personal experiences in terms of a generalized status, making the private and previously felt unique dilemmas part of a process shared
by others. The second major element in consciousness-raising
groups is the provision of support and acceptance; the simple
yet extremely impactful experience of finding acceptance from
a group of peers is an oft-noted experience in almost all small
face-to-face groups. Both the normalizing and acceptance aspects of consciousness-raising groups are certainly not unique
to such settings—they occur in almost all change-induction settings. Significant is the fact that they are the elements perceived
by participants as the most important change-producing ingredients of their experience. Consciousness-raising participants emphasize cognitive mechanisms as the third element: increasing

understanding, putting women's roles into perspective, and providing insight into personal problems.

What events or experiences did the women see as unhelpful? An examination of Table 2 indicates that the expression or experience of negative or aggressive affects was not viewed as being helpful. It is likely that the emphasis on support and similarity as a core experience mitigated or at least limited the perceived utility of such experiences. Unlike the ideology of encounter groups, for example, which emphasizes the expression and experience of aggression and confrontation, it appears that for women in consciousness-raising groups, such events may detract from the support-universality emphasis and thus are ranked as unhelpful. Also not valued are the cognitive mechanism of advice, and the examination of political issues. Advice, so highly valued in other group settings such as encounter groups, is negatively perceived in consciousness-raising groups, probably because it partakes of a particular form of intrusion interfering with the egalitarian norms of consciousness-raising groups. Political analysis, despite the ideological emphasis in consciousness-raising groups, is not perceived as important because it does not meet the personal needs of the individuals who actually join such groups (see Chapter Seven).

Compassionate Friends. This self-help system offers an instructive contrast to consciousness-raising groups. If we look again at Table 2, in the top-ranked items we again see the normalizing emphasis in finding individuals who are in similar predicaments, as well as the support and understanding that we found characteristic of consciousness-raising groups. However, several other mechanisms are seen as crucial to participants in Compassionate Friends. Foremost is the inculcation of hope and acceptance of the ultimate loss. Perhaps because of the particular nature of the affliction—losing one's child—and the confrontation with death and loss of personal future that the death of a child implies, existential issues come to the fore. The single most important aspect perceived by members of Compassionate Friends was the fact that seeing what others in similar distress had endured provided a salient help for them. An important belief in Compassionate Friends is the notion that one can become

Table 2. Perceptions of Important Change Mechanisms

First Quarter

Group Psychotherapy

Rank	Item	%
1.	Being an involved group member	66
2.	Getting insight into the causes and sources of my problems	59
3.	Learning that my problems are not unique	52
4.	Being supported, approved of	52
5.	Learning the impact I have on others	52
6.	Sharing common experiences	50

Encounter Groups

Rank	Item	%
1.	Impact I have on others	49
2.	I learned that "we're all in the same boat"—not unique	37
3.	Express feelings	34
4.	Advice or suggestions about how to deal with some life problems	31

Consciousness Raising

Rank	Item	%
1.	Sharing thoughts and feelings about being a woman	76
2.	Being supported, approved of	68
3.	Learning more about my positive strengths	63
4.	Learning that my problems are not unique	63
5.	Examining problems women have with traditional roles	51
6.	Getting insight into the causes and sources of my problems	52

Compassionate Friends

Rank	Item	%
1.	Hope from others' endurance	80
2.	Helping others; feel worthwhile	74
3.	Find there are others, too	74
4.	Helping others lessens my pain	66
5.	Empathy from other bereaved parents	66
6.	Feedback	65

First Quarter

Mothers

Rank	Item	%
1.	The experiences other mothers speak about are strikingly similar to my own	84
2.	Learning that I'm not the only one who finds child-rearing difficult	72
3.	Getting feedback from other group members	72
4.	Having fun	70
5.	Getting practical hints	66
6.	Recognizing that raising a child is often a frustrating and arduous task	62

Naim

Rank	Item	%
1.	Realizing my problems are not unique	66
2.	I don't feel different	66
3.	I don't feel like a "fifth wheel"	66
4.	Gives me hope—see others who are coping	62
5.	I feel understood	59

Mended Hearts

Rank	Item	%
1.	Learned what medical science knows about the heart	47
2.	Learned that I am responsible for my well-being	37
3.	Realized that surgery does not make me any less a person	37
4.	Helpful to others facing a similar situation	36
5.	Realized my problems are not unique	36
6.	Received advice	36

Table 2. Perceptions of Important Change Mechanisms (continued)

Second Quarter

Group Psychotherapy

Rank	Item	%
7.	Experiencing and expressing negative feelings	50
8.	Getting some things off my chest	48
9.	Revealing things about myself	48
10.	Helping others	46
11.	Receiving advice	43
12.	Experimenting in the group	43

Encounter Groups

Rank	Item	%
5.	Experiment with new forms of behavior	29
6.	Understanding why I think and feel the way I do	27
7.	Being an involved member of a group	26

Consciousness Raising

Rank	Item	%
7.	Seeing how others approach problems; how I could	49
8.	Being an involved group member	48
9.	Experiencing feelings of excitement and joy	45
10.	The group gave me hope	45
11.	Helping others	40

Compassionate Friends

Rank	Item	%
7.	Being able to talk—not hold it in	62
8.	Free to talk about my grief	56
9.	When down, I can call another	53
10.	Understand spouse	51
11.	Accept death	51

Second Quarter

	Mothers	
Rank	*Item*	*%*
7.	Having a chance to share fears and anxieties	63
8.	Learning more about my positive strengths	58
9.	Expressing my feelings openly	57
10.	Feeling accepted by other mothers	55
11.	Knowing that I have people to turn to for help	52

	Naim	
Rank	*Item*	*%*
6.	Places to go for fun	59
7.	If I feel down I know I can call another member	57
8.	Have Catholicism in common	55
9.	Upbeat, uplifting	55
10.	Trust the people	53

	Mended Hearts	
Rank	*Item*	*%*
7.	Was supported	33
8.	Inspired and uplifted	31
9.	Others serve as examples	30
10.	Learned about my positive strengths	29
11.	I feel accepted by other members	29
12.	Share fears and anxieties	27

Table 2. Perceptions of Important Change Mechanisms (continued)

Third Quarter

Group Psychotherapy

Rank	Item	%
13.	Being confronted and challenged	43
14.	Examining the way society shapes my behavior	43
15.	Finding I am pretty much like other people	43
16.	Learning that my childhood experiences influence current problems	41
17.	Seeing undesirable things about myself	41
18.	Getting ideas about my problems by seeing others do so	39

Encounter Groups

Rank	Item	%
8.	Helping others	24
9.	Use others as models	23
10.	Take ultimate responsibility for the way I live	20

Consciousness Raising

Rank	Item	%
12.	Experimenting in the group	45
13.	Seeing undesirable things about myself	38
14.	Discussing sexuality	37
15.	Revealing things about myself	39
16.	Understanding the impact I have on others	34
17.	Examining problems of discrimination	28

Compassionate Friends

Rank	Item	%
12.	Practical advice	49
13.	Insight	49
14.	Freer to cry	39
15.	First constructive step	43
16.	Seeing others worse off lessens my depression	35

Third Quarter

Mothers

Rank	Item	%
12.	Getting help from more experienced mothers	51
13.	Gaining new perspective on my role as a mother	51
14.	Seeing variety of reactions to childrearing made me more tolerant of differences	42
15.	Feeling that I am giving useful suggestions to others	42
16.	Being an involved member of a group	36

Naim

Rank	Item	%
11.	Source of inspiration	50
12.	It gets me out of the house	50
13.	Help others	50
14.	I can forget my troubles	36
15.	Other members give me ideas how to tackle problems	31

Mended Hearts

Rank	Item	%
13.	Others gave me hope	24
14.	Understood the causes of my behavior and feelings	22
15.	Felt involved	22
16.	New way to think about my problems	21
17.	Felt needed by the organization	21

Table 2. Perceptions of Important Change Mechanisms (continued)

Fourth Quarter

Group Psychotherapy

Rank	Item	%
19.	Learning about my positive strengths	36
20.	Discussing sexuality	34
21.	Experiencing feelings of excitement and joy	32
22.	Examining problems with traditional sex roles	27
23.	Examining the way society shapes my behaviors	25

Encounter Groups

Rank	Item	%
11.	Insight into the causes and sources of my hangups	19
12.	Revealing and still being accepted	16
13.	Gave me hope	15
14.	The group was like my family; able to understand old hangups	14

Consciousness Raising

Rank	Item	%
18.	Experiencing and expressing negative feelings	30
19.	Receiving advice or suggestions	27
20.	Being confronted and challenged	25
21.	Examining political issues	14
22.	Becoming anxious or depressed	12

Compassionate Friends

Rank	Item	%
17.	Freer to be angry	42
18.	Feeling accepted	32
19.	Trustful	33
20.	Recognize life is unjust	12
21.	Find a model	8

Fourth Quarter

Mothers

Rank	Item	%
17.	Meetings give me some-place to go	36
18.	Other members in the group give me hope	27
19.	Becoming aware of why I behave as I do	24
20.	Being with other women I want to be like	24
21.	Hearing others speak stirs up strong feelings in me	16
22.	Revealing personal things about myself which I don't ordinarily tell others	7

Naim

Rank	Item	%
16.	I call on Naim member to go out	29
17.	Meet people I might date	28
18.	My friends are members	24
19.	Speakers give important information	22
20.	Help me in raising my family	22

Mended Hearts

Rank	Item	%
18.	Meetings kept me active	14
19.	Express feelings of depression	12
20.	Examined discrimination against heart patients	8
21.	Others laid it on the line about what I was doing	7
22.	Tried out new ways of thinking or acting	3

whole again by helping others. Altruism is a mechanism, as reflected in two of the top six items ranked by members of Compassionate Friends.

Despite their ideology, cognitive and rational aspects of
what they have to offer bereaved parents are not perceived by
the participants as being central to their experience of help.
Looking again at Table 2, we find that the affective expressive
experiences—being able to talk and express their grief—are high
in centrality compared to the more cognitive mechanisms which
only appear in the third quartile of ranked items. This lack of
emphasis on cognitive restructuring is made all the more striking
by the fact that the structure of Compassionate Friends—the
use of speakers—and their emphasis on a lending library around
the issues on grief are seen as cornerstones of the group. Yet
from the point of view of the participants themselves, it is the
similarity, support, the touching of their inner selves with regard to existential issues, and the ability, above all, to make
oneself whole by reaching out to others that characterizes this
self-help group.

Mothers' Self-Help Groups. The key element in this self-
help system is the experience of universality, the normalizing
function such groups appear to play in the lives of women who
participate in them. It appears from the items listed that a fundamental dilemma for many of the mothers participating in
such groups is their ambivalence toward motherhood. Three of
the six top-ranked items suggest that the ability to share this
inner anxiety in a supportive setting is the key factor in the aid
that such groups offer their participants. Unlike the other all-
women group, consciousness raising, the mothers' groups, although attracting a demographically similar population are
highly focused on the specific experience of motherhood and
do not seem to ge beyond the boundaries of that issue. Unlike
CR, mothers' groups are emphatically not a psychotherapy alternative. They are highly focused and whatever cognitive learning
is important to these women concerns the role of motherhood.
Of all the groups we have studied, the mothers' self-help groups
represent the purest form of a support-sharing group in which
the reason for being is a normalizing function of the group.

Their boundaries are tightly drawn, not by the organizational structure but by members' views of what is important and appropriate. For example, the lowest-ranked item—revealing personal things about oneself (self-disclosure), a frequent accompaniment of psychotherapy change—provides a clue to the singular emphasis of this group.

Naim. Unlike most of the other self-help systems and professional groups discussed in this chapter, Naim is not a small face-to-face interactive self-help group. It is, as we have described in previous sections, a social linkage system, a context in which groups of widowers and widows are able to socialize in a setting that emphasizes their similarity not only by affliction but also with regard to their place in society—Catholicism, social class, and age. An examination of Table 2 indicates that the normalizing function of this group is the singular aspect that the members perceive as useful to them. Of the top-ranked five items, the first three speak directly to this issue. Unlike many small face-to-face interactive groups where this finding of similarity between oneself and others in the group is emphasized directly, because of Naim's format, similarity is "assumed" rather than a direct process of interaction. Despite this difference, the normalizing function of not feeling like an outsider, not feeling different, finding out that one's problems are not unique, and experiencing understanding in a supportive environment are central to this system. Another critical aspect of Naim is the inculcation of hope; the perception that others who are similarly afflicted are able to reintegrate their lives despite the loss is an important element of the impact of this group. Cognitive restructuring, whether it be advice, insight, or an altered perspective, is not central to Naim. If we look at the second quartile of ranked items, we note the social aspects of the group as well as the linkage elements, the ability when one is in distress to find another human being from the self-help group to call upon. Of note is the fact that although both loss groups, Compassionate Friends and Naim, have widely different formats and, of course, different sources of loss, mastery through cognitive restructuring appears not to be central in either, despite the fact that Compassionate Friends sees itself as providing such a function. What distinguishes these two loss groups is the emphasis in Compassionate Friends on altruisim as a central mechanism for change and the absence of this in the widowhood groups.

Mended Hearts. Mended Hearts, similar to Naim and dissimilar to such self-help groups as consciousness raising, mothers' groups, and Compassionate Friends, is not primarily a face-to-face interactive group. Looking once again at Table 2, we note that the single most important element from the point of view of the participants is the cognitive input—information about the affliction—and that of the top-ranked six items, two reflect cognitive input at an informational level. As in most of the other self-help groups we have studied, universality is again stressed. Two other central elements in this self-help group are the emphasis on altruism and the confrontations with existential problems, a theme we have seen in Compassionate Friends. The life crises common to both Compassionate Friends and Mended Hearts elicit survival and integrity concerns. It appears that such concerns are associated with existential preoccupations.

This brief overview of the events or experiences emphasized by the participants in the various self-help systems we studied pointed to some important commonalities among groups—for example, universality—as well as some important differences, such as the role of cognitive elements. The following section examines some aspects of influence on the participants' view of what was helpful to them.

Sources of Influence on Participants' Perceptions

There are several important sources of influence on a person's response to the question, "What event or experiences in the group were helpful to you?" They are: (1) the professional leader; (2) the system or group ideology; (3) the unique characteristics of small face-to-face groups; (4) the nature of the affliction; and (5) general societal beliefs about what helps.

Leader Influence. A reading of any standard text in group psychotherapy readily reveals a set of change mechanisms that usually represent the core theory of what needs to occur to patients in groups in order for them to change. The standards in the field are perhaps best expressed by Yalom (1975), who lists ten mechanisms: installation of hope, universality, information, altruism, the corrective recapitulation of the primary family group, development of socializing techniques, imitative behavior, interpersonal learning, group cohesiveness, catharsis, and existential factors.

This relatively inclusive list reflects an amalgam of specific theories of group therapy as well as the sensitivity of the observer of therapy groups to what actually takes place. In other words, it reflects both psychotherapists' theory and their appreciation of helpful factors intrinsic to small face-to-face groups. For the purposes of our analysis, it is useful to distinguish these "curative dimensions" that are essential to the belief system of professionals from those that are part of "clinical" lore, that is, intrinsic to any small face-to-face group.

Central to most theories of psychotherapy, whether they involve treatment in the dyad, the group, or the family, are those specific conditions more or less under the control of and centrally contributed to by the therapists themselves. It is axiomatic for a theory of therapy to stress both those conditions that are directly controllable by the therapist and those conditions that do not ordinarily occur in a person's day-to-day life. Most theories of therapeutic change emphasize unique events or experiences that are relevant to the fundamental assumptions the theorist makes about the nature of emotional distress or mental illness. The emphasis, for example, by psychoanalytically oriented therapists on a specific kind of cognitive learning, insight, reflects the model of psychopathology, the relative rarity of this kind of cognitive learning in everyday life, and the fact that it is an experience that can occur because of the presence of a trained professional who can influence, if not control, such happenings. All theories of psychotherapy stress particular types of cognitive learning. Some emphasize such cognitive learning about the early life events that shape current pathology; others emphasize interpersonal learning, with the group serving as a setting to provide an opportunity for patients to gather alternative information. Some theories express this latter focus in terms of "feedback," a particular kind of information exchange that provides patients a new source of information about themselves not ordinarily available within their life experiences.

In addition to the cognitive elements in therapeutic theories, most also emphasize specific, affectively tinged behavior that they believe is critical for patients to experience if they are to change. For example, entire schools of psychotherapy are based on the notion that the need is for a certain kind of revelation experience, described technically as self-disclosure. This again is a form of behavior that is seen as occurring with low frequency in the ordinary lives of individuals who come to psychotherapy. It is a behavior that directly addresses the belief about the source of the problem and is within the control of or highly influenced by the therapist. Other views stress affective expression, believing that high levels of emotional expression and experience within the group setting are necessary to change. Again the belief here is that such experiences are not generally available to the client who enters psychotherapy. High levels of emotional expression address what such theorists think is central to the source of pathology and again they are factors influenced readily by the therapist.

In general, I believe that the core of any professional system for change is made up of events or experiences controllable by the therapist. If they are uncontrollable, they usually are not emphasized within the theoretical system. For example, altruism, that factor unique to group settings in which a person can experience the fact that he or she has helped another human being, is certainly discussed in the therapy literature but nowhere at a "level of importance" of, for example, self-disclosure. In part, the reason for this relative low emphasis on such a "change mechanism" is that it is less controllable by the therapist. I would suggest that such issues as modeling, although discussed in the psychotherapeutic literature, are less emphasized except by behaviorists because, in the ordinary group setting, they are less specifically controllable by the therapist than are other kinds of experiences. Another class of change mechanisms has, in recent years, come to be highlighted. The primary one would be the experience of belongingness or, as it is usually expressed in the literature, cohesion. Such conditions are intrinsic to small face-to-face groups and, although somewhat under the influence of the therapists, are rarely at the core of therapeutic theory.

With this in mind, let us reexamine Table 2. The first column shows the rank order of judgments by group psychotherapy patients of what experiences and events encountered in their groups were useful to them. Looking at the first and second quartile of ranks (the top 50 percent), we find that of the twelve items listed, half could reasonably be attributed to the specific belief system of the therapist about what is important. All these experiences or events are controllable, to a greater or lesser extent, by the behavior of the therapist. They are, in order of appearance: insight, feedback, the expression and experiencing of strong affects, self-disclosure, and experimentation. If we accept the premise that those elements in a group that are more readily influenced by a therapist form their core theory, we are left with six change events that patients perceive as important. They are, in order of their rank: cohesiveness from an experiential point of view, the sense of belongingness and involvement in a small face-to-face group that takes on some primary group characteristics; universalities, the experience that one's problems are not unique; another item stressing similarities, namely, sharing common values and beliefs, altruism, the experience of helping others; and receiving advice from others, a cognitive mechanism stressed in most psychotherapy 'heories.

It is important to underline once again that most therapists would, at this juncture in the history of psychotherapy, see all twelve events perceived by patients as important in their change as being compatible with their psychotherapy mode. But not all of the events stem directly from the theory that energized psychotherapy. Rather they reflect both theory and the consequences of putting individuals in small face-to-face groups.

The question of which characteristic of the professional belief system influenced patients' perceptions of what was important can perhaps best be answered by contrasting patients in group psychotherapy with participants in another professionally conducted change system—encounter groups. Although many, if not most, encounter groups are led by professionals possessing mental health backgrounds, the belief system around encounter groups, the influencing factors, and the mythology about the motives of participants suggest that other forces might influence the particular professional belief system and be transmitted to the clients of the encounter group. (It is worth noting that we have elsewhere demonstrated [Lieberman and Gardner, 1976] that from a client's point of view, the need systems of those entering encounter groups and those in group psychotherapy are identical. And although these are two specific, distinct systems of offering change experiences for participants, from the point of view of participants they may be more alike than not.) If we look at the second column in Table 2, we find that many of the same mechanisms emphasized by group therapy patients appear in the top-ranked items, but that they clearly have a different relative rank. Feedback, a specific kind of cognitive learning, is central. Insight, although important for the psychotherapy patient, is perceived as much more important than feedback. In encounter groups, insight is not seen as important. The two systems stress distinctive kinds of cognitive learning, which is reflected in their participants' attributions of what was important to them in their group. In contrast, the expression of strong feeling, catharsis, is similar in both. The relative weight given to particular kinds of cognitive learning distinguishes the two professional systems. Both, of course, share the basic characteristics of the small face-to-face groups whose purpose is to offer opportunity for change. Thus we see that in both groups, feelings of similarity and a sense of belongingness become important.

There are certain similarities across all groups whether professionally conducted or not and whether or not they have an articulate ideology. Some of the elements stressed by participants in professionally led systems which we have hypothesized to be under the relative control of the therapist or leader are rarely seen as important in self-help groups. These differences underscore what we believe to be a fundamental distinction between professionally led systems and self-help groups.

But these differences may also reflect the simple and direct influence of being a participant in a system where an individual with high degrees of power and perceived resources has a fundamental belief system about what is important. Whether, in fact, these events occur with more frequency in one system than the other cannot, obviously, be answered by these kinds of data. Some of the change mechanisms are unobservable. For example, one can observe the insight-producing behavior of a therapist, but insight as an event or an experience is something that occurs within the person and does not necessarily have direct consequences in the transactions within the group. We can only learn of this experience by asking the patient. And when we ask, our information is, of necessity, colored by the belief system of the most powerful person in the setting, the therapist.

Role of Ideology. Most of the self-help groups we have studied do not have highly visible or consistent leadership patterns. They do not have a leader in the same sense that a psychotherapy group or encounter group has a professional who possesses the resource or legitimization for conducting the change experience. However, there is a parallel in self-help groups, mainly expressed through ideology. These are standard belief systems, often highly articulated, which provide a pathway for participants in self-help groups akin to the pathway offered by the professional therapist as to how change can occur and what about the affliction needs to be redefined. The role of ideology in self-help groups will be described in detail in a following chapter. Here our concern will be the potential influence of ideology on respondents' perception of what in the experience of the self-help groups helped them to change, grow, or learn. Unfortunately for the purposes of this analysis, the particular set of self-help groups that we studied—consciousness raising, Compassionate Friends, Mended Hearts, Naim, and mothers' groups—are at the low end of the articulate ideology continuum when compared with the groups described by Antze in Chapter Twelve—Alcoholics Anonymous, Recovery, Inc., and Synanon.

Of the systems we have studied, perhaps the most articulate ideologies can be found in Compassionate Friends and

Mended Hearts. As previously discussed, though the women's movement has a highly articulate ideology, the ideology in consciousness-raising groups is relatively ambiguous and unarticulate. Similarly, the mothers' groups do not espouse a particular belief system in regard to the source and cause of problems and the steps that individuals need to take, beyond a general belief that getting together and sharing will help. In contrast, Compassionate Friends has a view of the dilemmas that face parents who have lost a child, and to some extent Mended Hearts has a view of what heart surgery patients need to do in order to establish a life for themselves.

For the purpose of illustration, I have chosen the two self-help systems we have studied that have the most articulate ideologies. The first is Compassionate Friends, whose ideology Sherman details in the last chapter of this section. He analyzes the ideology in terms of the group's counteracting maladaptive responses to the loss of a child. These cognitive antidotes stress that aberrant feelings or behavior are not intrinsic but attributable to the external stress of grief. They counteract denial of the loss and intense feelings of anger, guilt, and consequent despair by encouraging reconceptualization of the loss and gradual reinvestment in social and educational activities—three elements central to the ideological focus of Compassionate Friends. When we turned to the participants' perception of experiences they found useful in the group, however, we found that there was little reference to cognitive factors in general and that, as described, the core experience from the participants' point of view was the normalizing function of the group (the experience of universality), the opportunity to help others (altruism), and existential factors. In short, we have not been able to develop evidence of a correspondence between the specific ideology of this self-help group and members' conceptions of what was important to them in their participation in the group.

How might we explain such a discrepancy? Should one expect perceptions of utility of the experience in a change-induction group to mirror the ideological belief system that energizes such a system. At face value, it seems a sensible and reasonable hypothesis, made more so by our analysis of professional systems which does suggest that the leader and his or her belief system about the nature of the dilemma and how one overcomes it certainly play a role in patients' perceptions of why or how the experience was important to them. Part of this lack of correspondence between ideology and perceived processes that were useful to members may be a product of the particular measurement procedures used; we did not, at the time the study was developed, emphasize ideological beliefs in the construction of our process measures. However, there may be a more fundamental reason for this lack of correspondence. Unlike articulate ideology groups such as Alcoholics Anonymous, where the Ideology is expressed directly in a codified fashion, self-help groups such as Compassionate Friends and others studied do not directly codify and constantly reinforce ideological beliefs; they are expressed much more subtly and indirectly. The fact that we can show professional leader influence on individuals' perception of what was helpful to them would again suggest that constant, repetitive deliverance of the message may be the critical element, and without that element, other influences on what individuals see as important may have preeminence. Thus, as will be elaborated, the nature of the affliction, as well as the characteristics of small face-to-face sharing groups, may have more influence on what individuals perceive as important than a general ideology that is not reinforced by the presence of a highly influential individual (a professional leader) or by a codified system such as Alcoholics Anonymous through which all interaction is funneled.

Mended Hearts, a self-help group that emphasizes service to others through its visitation program, does provide some small support for the relationship of ideology to individuals' perceptions of what was helpful to them. Here we see that altruism is perceived by most members as being important, and, in fact, when we analyzed the Mended Hearts system according to whether the individual was a peripheral or central member—that is, visited others—the distinction became sharper. Mended Hearts, which, unlike Compassionate Friends, does not have the compelling features of a face-to-face interactive group and thus the force and influence of a context in which people talk about their feelings and share with one another, may provide the key to understanding this distinction. The compelling features of any small face-to-face group, the nature of the affliction, general societal beliefs about what helps, and the specific belief system relevant to each self-help group that we have termed ideology—all are sources of influence. These sources of influence could, in some sense, be competing influences on a person's perception, and in a system where some are missing, other factors become dominant. In Compassionate Friends, the compelling influence of the interactive situation of a small face-to-face group and, we believe, the nature of the affliction are much more powerful factors working on perception than is a general ideology flowing from the self-help group itself. In Mended Hearts, which does not have the compelling force of the small face-to-face group, the specific belief system may have more influence on persons' perceptions of what was helpful to them.

Unique Properties of Small Face-To-Face Groups. No matter what the ideology, the influence of a professional and/ or charismatic leader, or the nature of the affliction, most self-help groups are small face-to-face interactive units. The fact that individuals enter such structures in a high state of personal need and are required to share with others topics and feelings that are often considered personal and private leads to some important consequences for the kinds of experiences they will encounter. They arrive at the self-help groups and find themselves faced with a number of strangers frequently dissimilar to themselves except for one critical characteristic, the shared affliction. No matter whether the group is a professionally led traditional psychotherapeutic one, one of the varied settings promulgated in the last decade for personal growth, or a collectivity of similarly afflicted—all such groups share some basic elements: the needs of the individuals joining them; the requirements, no matter how banal, to share something personal; and the real or perceived similarity in their suffering, whether it be behavior, roles, life crises, or the need for growth or change. These conditions and the structure of a small face-to-face interactive system have profound consequences for what will occur. These consequences, the specific properties of such groups that may influence the occurrence of certain events and experiences, are likely to be perceived by the participants as being relevant to the aid they so desperately seek in joining such groups.

Foremost is the capacity of such groups to generate a sense of belongingness among the participants, a shared sense of similar sufferers that creates a feeling technically referred to as cohesiveness. Cohesiveness has been well studied and is operationally defined as the attractiveness of the group to its participants. It provides the motivation for participants to remain in and work with the group. Cohesive groups offer their members almost unconditional acceptance and provide a supportive atmosphere for taking risks, which in most such groups involves the sharing of personal material and the expression of emotions that may, from the participants' perspective, be difficult to do in a group of strangers.

Another factor creating a high sense of belongingness, especially in self-help groups composed of the similarly afflicted, is the perception by the afflicted of their deviant status in society. The feeling of being stigmatized leads frequently, in small groups, to the creation of a feeling of "we-ness" and a sharp boundary line between them and us, the "us" usually referring to the rest of society.

The high level of cohesiveness, perceived similarity, and the perception that they are "different" from others outside of the "refuge" creates in many self-help groups a strong influence on the saliency of being a participant. In some ways, the self-help group takes on the characteristics of a primary group; it becomes "familylike" and does, in fact, serve as a new reference group for the participants. These interrelated properties of small groups are not a product of the particular ideology, affliction, or influence of leadership but are instrinsic conditions of small groups, made all the more pronounced in groups of similarly afflicted individuals by the state of need in which they enter such groups and the requirements for certain kinds of personal sharing and banding together against a perceived hostile external world. No wonder then that the members see such groups as aiding them through support, acceptance, and normalizing of their perceived affliction. It is almost axiomatic, given the instantaneous sense of comfort and acceptance found by most participants, that members would emphasize such helping processes.

The group's capacity to control behavior and to provide a system of rewards and punishments is closely associated with and dependent on the level of cohesiveness. As a microcosm of a larger society, small face-to-face groups develop their own cultures and depend on special rules or standards which they establish as they extend their lives. How much one talks, what one does or does not talk about, even "the way" one talks about certain things are aspects of behavior which the group influences. The group member is almost inevitably confronted with pressure from others to change behaviors and views. The need to be in step, to abide by the rules, is a powerful factor inducing conformity in the group. Disregard for the rules means possible punishment. The ultimate punishment available to the group is the power of exclusion, either psychological or physical. An additional strong force pulling members toward conformity is the group's most prized reward, the authenticating affirmation of one's peers. The experience of consensual validation (approval by other members who have become important) appears to be one of the most important and gratifying experiences available to members in the group.

Perhaps the most dramatic example of the reward and punishment capacity of small face-to-face groups can be found in Antze's chapter in this section where he describes the role of ideology in three self-help groups: Alcoholics Anonymous, Synanon, and Recovery, Inc. However, other examples from groups we have studied are abundant, such as the emphasis in consciousness-raising groups on issues centered around being women. The interest in women's issues as important change processes is in part understandable, not because of the intrinsic needs of the participants but because of the influence of the group toward a certain kind of conformity. As we have described in a previous chapter, the motivational system of women joining consciousness-raising groups appears to be an alternative to psychotherapy, and the needs are more directed toward personal learning. However, it is probably impossible to remain a participant in consciousness-raising groups without being influenced by their particular emphasis on women's issues. This is not to say that these explorations do not prove useful to the members of such groups, but rather to place such perceptions in context and see them not only as a product of ideological issues or the nature of the affliction but also as a product of the particular characteristics of all face-to-face groups.

Another important aspect of small face-to-face groups is their capacity to induce powerful affective states in the participants. Historically, emotional contagion was the first phenomenon to interest investigators of groups. LeBon (1960) and Freud (1940) pointed out that powerful primitive affects can be released in groups. Individuals may get carried away, experiencing feelings which they later believe are uncharacteristic of themselves, and act on feelings without displaying their typical controls. The group's potential to stimulate emotionality is an important characteristic which bears directly on the experiences members have in small face-to-face groups. This is particularly important in change-induction groups, where members arrive with high needs, frequently in states of vulnerability, and are required to share personal matters. This group property is likely to lead to certain expressions of affect. Most notable, in the groups that we have studied, are the emotional expressions of pain, anger, and profound sadness characteristic of participants in Compassionate Friends—especially the opening ritual of Compassionate Friends, in which members recite the loss of their child. New members, particularly, experience strong affects which soon become shared by all in attendance. This property of groups to induce intense affect expressions has been described as akin to contagion.

Another characteristic of groups that plays an important role in influencing their capacity to change individuals is the fact that they provide a context for social comparison. Because the group members are placed in a social context that expects, and often demands, that they talk about personal matters and needs relevant to the affliction that brought them to the group, this social comparative process is made all the more compelling in such change-induction groups. It is a natural outgrowth of such demands. Individuals compare their attitudes and feelings about things that matter, and such comparisons facilitate revision of the person's identity by suggesting new possibilities for feeling, perceiving, and behaving. The cognitive mechanism of modeling described earlier in this chapter, in which individuals are able to compare their own approach to particular problems with that of others and to gain new perspectives, is a prime example of this process. Another illustration is the emphasis in Compassionate Friends on the inculcation of hope through seeing others endure and comparison of one's own predicament. Because such groups focus around specific relevant issues in an emotionally charged setting, they provide their members with a wide variety of information about how others who are perceived as similar feel, think, believe, and behave. It is this context that maximizes the opportunity for productive social comparison—at times providing hope, cognitive restructuring, information about new approaches to coping with painful dilemmas, and solace through seeing that others may be in worse conditions.

Taken together, these characteristics especially prominent in small face-to-face groups, but also in part characteristic of most group systems, provide the commonness across self-help groups and professional change-induction groups that we have seen in an examination of Table 2. They are intrinsic properties of groups and are conditions that prevail no matter what the particular ideology, the affliction, or the belief system of a leader of such groups. They certainly influence what members perceive as important and, in fact, influence the actual kinds of experiences people are likely to have in such groups. They occur because individuals in high need have sought out such groups; they are not a product necessarily of the other influence factors that shape the specifics of change-induction groups, whether professionally led or self-help groups.

Effects of the Affliction. What is the effect of individuals' conditions or predicaments on their perceptions of what aided them in coping? At one level, the answer is obvious: The nature of the affliction should exert a profound influence on the helping processes. Whether they are traditional help-providing settings or self-help groups, both settings provide a definition not only of the affliction but of its cause(s) and cure. In professional systems, the cause and cure of the predicament are described and articulated in the theory surrounding "treatment"; in self-help systems, they are expressed in the ideology of the group. We explored in a previous section the effects of professional belief systems on participants' views of what aided them in their treatment. We have also touched upon the role of ideology but have left the detailed exploration to the chapter by Antze, who elaborates the role of ideology on the relationship between the cause and cure of affliction.

Although a match between theory or ideology and the causes and cure of a particular affliction would be expected and should be expressed by participants' perception of what helped them, identity between the two is, by no means, always demonstrable empirically. For example, an examination of Table 2 on professionally conducted encounter groups indicates that members perceive advice giving as an important factor that aided them in the groups. Almost all professional systems, and particularly those stemming from the humanistic psychology tradition, would take a position that advice is not a salient productive help-providing source. Despite this, participants rate advice as being highly significant in their group experience. What is also obvious is the fact that theories about the cause and cure of disease vary widely for the same affliction, and there is no reason to assume the accuracy of the fit between such belief systems and the phenomenological experience of help by the afflicted individual.

There is an alternative way of looking at the relationship between the affliction and the person's experience in a change-induction setting. Each affliction creates a range of psychological and social dilemmas for the individual, and it is that "reality" that may influence individuals' perceptions of what aided them. This view of the relationship between affliction and members' experience of helpfulness can be illustrated from several of the self-help groups we studied. Table 2 reveals that participants in Mended Hearts and Compassionate Friends saw altruism as playing an important role in help providing. Members of Mended

Hearts reported in their interviews that heart surgery was experienced as a court of last resort. Psychologically, a common experience was rebirth, a sense of returning from the dead or the near-dead. The outcome findings on Mended Hearts reported in Chapter Sixteen suggest that there is a near euphoria during the year following open-heart surgery. Surviving open-heart surgery patients are—and this is probably much too tame a word—grateful. There is a strong desire to pay back, perhaps at a deeper psychological level, to propitiate the forces that have brought them back from the dead. This psychological experience by Mended Hearts members of the importance of altruism, of helping one's fellow sufferers, is perhaps an expression of this feeling. Altruism may serve to relieve guilts often expressed in the interviews as: "Why me?" and "How was I spared?" This is a psychological burden on such individuals, and membership in Mended Hearts provides a mechanism for relieving this by helping others. Thus altruism stems directly from the psychological dilemmas created by the affliction.

Compassionate Friends provides another example of how the particular affliction shapes participants' views of the helping processes. One of the central helping processes for Compassionate Friends participants was existential considerations. Some background on existential processes as help providing will help place this in the context. A study of encounter groups (Lieberman, Yalom, and Miles, 1973) systematically examined a wide variety of orientations to change-induction groups. Despite the presence of several professional leaders who were committed to an existential position, participants in such groups rarely perceived such processes as being helpful to them. In contrast, Compassionate Friends participants saw existential issues as central. It does not seem too far-fetched to conjecture that such concerns are more a product of a particular affliction than they are of the theory around therapeutic processes. Parents who have lost a child do confront the fundamental pscyhological dilemmas of "Why us?" and the rage at God for letting this happen. The loss of a child confronts individuals with some basic and profound dilemmas regarding their own mortality and, perhaps more importantly, interferes with their ability to see their lifelines extended beyond their personal lives. No wonder then, given the psychological dilemma created by such a loss, that members of Compassionate Friends, no matter what the ideology or belief system of the group, would of necessity be required to cope with such fundamental human concerns expressed in terms of what we have called existential matters. This "helping process" is, in short, a product of the affliction.

Societal Norms on Helping Processes. Self-help participants do not enter as a tabular rasa. They bring with them prior experiences from a variety of helping situations and are embedded in a society that has developed expectations about what is helpful, from whom, and under what circumstances. Unfortunately, little research can be found that directly addresses social norms about helping processes. To aid in understanding the specific processes found to be central in the self-help groups, we have drawn on some findings from the Transitions Study. This study, a longitudinal analysis of a probability sample of Chicago metropolitan area adults aged twenty-two to seventy was described in Chapter Six. The study examined individuals' use of helping resources when they encountered role strain, eruptive crises, or life transitions. Respondents were asked to describe the helping interaction by indicating which of the following processes occurred; the helper listened, asked questions, made suggestions about who to see for the problem, provided a new perspective, took me to see someone who could be helpful, took some action, and suggested some action. The respondent was then asked to evaluate the helping relationship on a four-point scale from 1, feeling no better, to 4, feeling a great deal better as a consequence of the helping transaction.

Table 3 portrays the perceived value of various helping processes. Shown are the evaluations for each of the helping processes in the various segments of adult life: the work area, which includes such events as starting back to work, being demoted, job strain, and unemployment; the parental role, which contains a variety of events such as births, children starting school, entering the teens, leaving home, and marrying, as well as problems in the parental role; the marital role, which includes marital strain, separation, and divorce; the financial area, which includes changes in standard of living; and parent caring, which addresses issues of adults who feel burdened by the emotional, financial, psychological, and social concerns of their parents. Problems involving physical health are presented separately in Table 3.

The overall findings indicate, for the non-health-related problems, that helper action in response to the problem was seen as leading to the most relief. Second was cognitive help, where the helper offered new perspectives or information regarding the problem. Least helpful were passive responses such as listening or suggesting someone to see. A closer examination of Table 3, however, indicates considerable variation in helpfulness of particular processes that depend on the problem area. Thus, for example, losses of significant others were most relieved by the helper who listened and who offered understanding; problems in the marital area were most often relieved by helpers who provided individuals with a new conceptual way of looking at the problem.

Approaching helpers for health problems of oneself, one's spouse, or children provides further demonstration of the diversity of helping processes in relationship to particular dilemmas. Health problems overall are judged to be helped by referral and by the provision of cognitive restructuring. However, again, the diversity is clear. An active referral is judged to be the single most useful transaction when the health problem involves oneself or one's spouse; however, if children's health problems are involved, referral is useful but the helper who asks questions is equally useful.

Thus, the findings from the Transitions Study based on a range of life dilemmas indicate that a variety of helping processes are perceived to be helpful. The specific helping process depends on the particular set of circumstances requiring aid. The implications for our study of helping processes in self-help groups seem clear: The processes that individuals find useful are not a result of some societal abstraction but are more likely to be a product of particular life dilemmas. Although listening and sympathetic understanding may be irrelevant in many life areas, they are particularly relevant for some problems and those prob-

Table 3. Change Induction Chart
Perceived Value of Helping Resources in Random Sample of Adults Aged 22 to 70

	Listening	Asks questions	Passive referral	New perspective	Active referral	Active action	Passive action
Work area	1.31	3.18	2.00	2.67	—	2.84	3.20
Parental role	2.16	2.50	—	3.40	—	2.83	3.43
Marital role	2.31	—	—	3.67	—	—	1.50
Financial area	1.71	2.00	1.00	3.00	—	4.00	3.00
Loss of significant others	3.46	3.00	3.00	3.30	—	3.33	2.50
Parent caring	2.75	2.50	2.50	3.00	0.00	3.50	3.36
Overall	2.3	2.6	1.9	3.2	0.0	3.3	2.9
Health problems	1.85	2.00	2.67	3.43	4.00	3.00	2.77
Spouse's health	2.71	3.00	4.00	3.75	4.00	3.45	2.71
Child's health	3.12	4.00	4.00	3.71	2.60	3.80	3.58
Overall	2.6	3.0	3.6	3.6	3.5	3.4	3.0

Note: These figures are based on a scale of evaluation of helping process in which 1=felt no better and 4=felt a great deal better.

lems were frequently the ones addressed in the self-help groups we studied: the loss of significant others and issues regarding marital relationships. The most general positively perceived helping process across almost all problems is that of the provision of a new perspective, and this, in addition to sympathetic listening, is exactly what many self-help groups are constructed to offer.

Admittedly, this particular set of findings does not directly address societal norms, in the sense that individuals were not asked about their expectations for help. Rather our respondents were asked what transpired in the helping relationship and their evaluation of the helping relationship itself. The information reflects indirectly on social norms but it does provide some hints that valued helping processes may be more a product of particular life dilemmas than of societal expectations. Our findings from the Transitions Study are also severely limited regarding helping processes because, as previously indicated, any particular dilemma or "affliction" spans a wide variety of issues. In our analysis of the helping processes provided in this chapter and in subsequent ones in this section, the particular nature of the affliction and the specific dilemmas it presents the participant in the self-help group shape the helping process. Thus, for example, in trying to understand the processes involved in Mended Hearts, we suggested that they are closely associated with the psychological burden connected with radical "life saving" surgery. To classify this specific as a problem regarding one's own health, as we did in the Transitions Study, sacrifices specificity.

Conclusions

The helping process in a group setting, whether a professionally organized and conducted group or one of the multitude of self-help groups, occurs in a complex social microcosm. These groups create a special society with boundaries and rules of conduct that distinguish them from the remainder of society. Such helping groups, however, are not isolated from the larger society, with its cultural prescriptions and proscriptions about what problems are legitimized for aid, who is sanctioned to provide help, what are the appropriate procedures for obtaining the aid, and, to some extent, what procedures themselves are helpful.

Unfortunately, we have no direct evidence of how the larger social order shapes the specific helping processes that are obtained in the groups studied. We can, however, say with certainty that the afflicted who seek out self-help groups have needs that are not totally met by the larger society. Whatever the affliction, the kith, kin, and professional representatives of society do not provide all that is required for these individuals who migrate into self-help groups. Yet, as the studies presented in Part Two of this book amply demonstrate, participants in self-help groups are not primarily those in our society lacking in other resources for aid. In fact, more often than not they utilize, simultaneously, multiple helping resources. The use of many helpers, plus the obvious point that individuals who enter self-help groups carry with them societal norms about helping processes, suggest that it may be well nigh impossible to disentangle the specific processes in self-help groups that are helpful from all of the influences on such perceptions that we have considered. There are too many influences on a person's perception of helping processes to state with maximum certainty what particular processes are unique to a particular self-help system. That individuals experience such unique processes in self-help groups is, at least from a theoretical perspective, certain. For if what transpires in a self-help group or more traditional helping system did not contain unique events and experiences felt to be helpful by the participants, no help in fact would be forthcoming. If the processes were identical with those in the larger society and available from the ordinary interactions of the individual's social network, then the distress or maladaptive behavior experienced by those who seek out self-help groups either would be resolved by a person's transactions with other helpers or the problem would not exist. In other words, there could theoretically be no active and effective help providing in a self-help group if these processes were merely repetitions of the person's experiences in everyday life.

On the basis of such a perspective, we certainly would expect certain events or experiences to be critical in the group-helping situations, whether professional or self-help. The results of our comparative analyses across the various groups suggest that there are a number of potentially powerful influences on the person's perception of what helps. In our comparative framework, it appears as if what unifies all types of helping groups results from the simple procedure of individuals joining a group of fellow sufferers in high states of personal need, with a requirement that some aspects of their painful affliction be shared in public. In other words, what unifies all of the systems we have studied is a common setting and the properties of small groups that ensue from such a setting. The normalizing and support experiences judged to be so highly useful result from this characteristic. We have also been able to implicate the role of the theory and direct influence of the professional leader on those groups that contain such persons, but have not been able to show directly the role of ideology in shaping individual perception of what is helpful. As indicated, this lack of influence of ideology may be a result of the particular self-help groups we have studied rather than a general rule. The social and psychological dilemmas associated with particular afflictions also play a role in what participants value as helpful.

Of course, we have not addressed the bottom line: Do the events and experiences make any difference in help received? We have rather been addressing the question of whether the participants' perceptions are a reliable indicator of what actually occurs in the group and is experienced by the person: Are their reflections of helpfulness unbiased? Of course, it might reasonably be asked whether these distinctions are meaningfully related to the issue of help. If, in fact, these reports reflect, in some manner, the actual experiences of the person, are they not legitimate sources of information? Such perceptions could, on the one hand, represent nothing more than dissonance reduction and thus reflect a well-known psychological property of individuals in social systems, unrelated to the actual experiences that occur and to the person's accurate perceptions of what was helpful. On the other hand, these phenomenological reports could represent accurately the process by which the affliction and the distress associated with it is aided. No matter whether these perceptions are determined by the ideological proscriptions of self-help groups or based on professional belief systems, they may accurately reflect helpful processes. We do not as yet, in our studies of self-help, have direct evidence on the relationship between these curative processes and the help an individual receives. We do know from other research conducted both by ourselves and other investigators in group psychotherapy and the encounter field that some of these events and experiences do make a difference in how much a person benefits from the group. The relationship between such events and experiences and benefit is an answerable question in self-help and is currently being addressed, but has not yet been determined. Of the studies reported in this volume, we do have small indications that some of these processes make a difference. For example, the process we have termed altruism, important in the Mended Hearts self-help group, shows large distinctions between active visitors and nominal members. In Part Four of this volume, which deals with outcomes, we report a study of Mended Hearts that suggests that, under certain conditions, visitors receive more benefits; as visitors they are acting altruistically. When they were asked what was helpful, visitors pointed to altruism significantly more than did nonvisitor members of Mended Hearts. This is, of course, only a small indicator of the much larger and complex findings that are required to draw out the relationship between certain specified events and experiences and how members benefit.

CHAPTER 11

Processes
and Activities
in Groups

Leon H. Levy

Self-help groups may be one of the conceptually richest phenomena in all the social and behavioral sciences. As the history of
their development reveals, they are as much a political and sociological phenomenon as they are a psychological one. Not only
can they be seen as challenges to established institutions and attempts in many instances to redistribute power, but they can
also be viewed as responses to certain failures in the social order.
Indeed, it would not be too much of an exaggeration to propose
that were one interested in analyzing the effectiveness of a society in meeting the needs of its members, one might well look to

Note: The research upon which this chapter is based was supported
by National Institute of Mental Health Research Grant R01MH24961 while
the author was on the faculty of Indiana University. I wish to acknowledge
the help of Ronald Curry, Robert Durham, Cynthia Frame, Andrea Klein,
Bob Knight, Valerie Padgett, and Richard Wollert, who were members of
my research team and contributed materially to all aspects of the research.
A special acknowledgment is due Sandra Levy for her editorial and substantive contributions to this chapter.

those areas where self-help groups have developed as the points where it has failed in one or more of its functions. Thus, for example, just as Alcoholics Anonymous came into existence because of organized medicine's inability to provide adequate treatment for alcoholics, so the growth of welfare rights organizations and ex-convict organizations may be traced to failures in the functioning of other institutions in our society.

At the same time, as social entities in their own right, self-help groups invite our attention for the light they might shed upon how people come together to accomplish a common purpose. It is this latter perspective, more narrowly focusing on those self-help groups whose members are seeking to cope with problems that normally fall within the domain of the mental health professions, which informs the work to be discussed in this chapter. For it is our belief that such self-help groups may represent a potentially major mental health resource, the key to which rests in our understanding of how they function.

Although the ever-increasing popularity of self-help groups, and the recent growth of interest by the federal government in their role in dealing with mental health problems (President's Commission on Mental Health, 1978), suggests that questions concerning their effectiveness are of vital importance, this chapter will focus upon questions about how they function —that is, what activities their members engage in as they try to help each other, and what the psychological processes operating in these groups are that might account for their effectiveness, whatever it might be. For it seems possible that once these questions have been answered, we will be in a better position to address questions of effectiveness by examining how various patterns of activities and processes are related to different outcomes.

Such findings could contribute to a general theory of psychotherapeutic intervention that would transcend any particular helping modality and, at the same time, provide the basis for both evaluating and improving the effectiveness of particular self-help groups. This was the line of thinking that led to the research project upon which this chapter is based. It was designed to provide the data that would allow us to make inferences about the psychological processes operating in self-help groups and to describe the actual behaviors engaged in by self-help group members. Additionally, because of the self-help groups' generally pragmatic orientation (Katz, 1970) and the fact that they do not, for the most part, operate within any consistent professional or theoretical framework, we believed that their study might also provide us with insights into the essential nature of human care giving.

An Overview of the Study

This study was intended to provide a detailed description and analysis of the techniques used by self-help groups and to lead to a theoretical conceptualization of the psychological processes that are operative in these groups. Because we viewed self-help groups as an essentially new social phenomenon, somewhat amorphous and thus easily distorted by one's preconceptions, we decided to adopt an overall research strategy similar to that advocated by Glaser and Strauss (1967) for the development of grounded theory. This was a strategy in which, as much as possible, we adopted a generative rather than a verificatory approach, freely using qualitative data, in an attempt to derive our categories, concepts, and theory from the data rather than using the data as a means of testing already formulated theory. How this was realized in practice will become apparent as we describe the three phases of the study.

Although there has been no dearth of speculation about how self-help groups function and about their effectiveness (for example, Dean, 1971; Gartner and Riessman, 1977; Hansell, 1976; Hurvitz, 1974; Katz, 1970; Robinson and Henry, 1977; Trice and Roman, 1970; Wechsler, 1960), much of this literature is based upon anecdotal evidence and case studies, and tends to have a distinctly partisan flavor. Therefore, we attempted to study systematically as many different self-help groups in as many different communities as possible in the hope that our findings would have a reasonable degree of generality. The result was that twenty self-help groups were studied in one phase or another during the three-year period of this project, and they were distributed over two midwestern cities, one southern city, and two midwestern towns of moderate size. Where possible, we also attempted to study two chapters of the same group so we could get some idea of how much variability there was from one chapter to another within the same group. We were successful in achieving this goal in the cases of six groups: Alcoholics Anonymous, Overeaters Anonymous, Make Today Count, Parents Anonymous, Recovery, Inc., and Take Off Pounds Sensibly.

The study may be conveniently divided into three phases. The first consisted of immersion in the professional literature about self-help groups, in literature produced by self-help groups themselves (both those we were to study and those that did not exist within our geographical area), and informally attending meetings of several self-help groups that were readily accessible. Our objective during this phase was to familiarize ourselves as thoroughly as possible with the phenomena we were to be studying from a number of different perspectives. During this phase, we developed a working definition of a self-help group and a typology of self-help groups. We felt that the typology was essential in order to introduce some structure into what we found to be the very poorly defined domain of self-help groups so that we could have some basis for estimating how well we had sampled from this domain.

The second phase of the project involved both participant and nonparticipant observation of selected self-help groups and interviews with key members of these groups. Where possible, two observers attended meetings of each group as nonparticipants. In a few groups, such as a women's consciousness-raising group, the group insisted that the observer also participate. No notes or recordings were made at meetings since we learned during the first phase that these activities made many group members feel uneasy and that some groups would simply not allow them. Immediately following each meeting, the observers prepared a joint report which consisted of two parts: a narrative description of the meeting and a speculative analysis of the dynamics and processes operative during the meeting. Each group studied during this phase was observed for anywhere from two to eight meetings, depending upon how variable the group's meetings were from one session to the next. Weekly research team meetings consisting of discussions of the reports of group observations made during the previous week led to our postulation of eleven processes (Levy, 1976) which we believed we saw operating in these groups and which we believed could account for their effectiveness. During this phase, we also developed a set of descriptions of help-giving activities engaged in by group members which was to be used in the quantitative analysis conducted during the study's third phase.

The third phase of the study provided the basis for our description and quantitative analysis of the help-giving activities engaged in by self-help groups. Descriptions of twenty-eight help-giving activities that had been observed in one or more groups during the study's second phase were incorporated into an extensive questionnaire which also attempted to tap members' attitudes toward their groups, experiences in joining and as members of their groups, evaluations of their groups' effectiveness, and beliefs about the factors responsible for their effectiveness. Only the data on help-giving activities will be presented in this chapter. These data were generated by asking each member to rate how accurately each activity characterized what occurred in his or her group, where accuracy of characterization was defined in terms of frequency of occurrence.

Questionnaires were used during this phase of the study rather than structured interviews, as originally planned, because it became apparent that the time required to locate group members and conduct the interviews would so severely restrict the size of our sample that this would outweigh any benefits to be gained by face-to-face interviews. Additionally, we found that in a few instances in which we were testing the questionnaire by comparing it with a structured interview, the information obtained by the self-administered questionnaire was comparable to that obtained by interview.

In all cases, questionnaires were given to group leaders who were asked to distribute them to their members. The questionnaires were anonymous, with only the group being identified, and were returned directly to us by stamped, self-addressed envelopes, thereby assuring group members of the confidentiality of their replies. Finally, in order to encourage members to complete their questionnaires, each group was paid three dollars for each questionnaire received from its members.

Definition of a Self-Help Group. Self-help groups, also frequently referred to as mutual help groups (Caplan and Killilea, 1976), are just one segment of a vast array of alternative social arrangements by which people today are seeking to improve the quality of their lives without recourse to professional care givers. Ranging from communes to peer counseling to community crisis hotlines, and including proprietary organizations such as Smok-Enders and Weight Watchers, they all share some elements in common with self-help groups but are also sufficiently different that we felt it essential to delineate clearly the kinds of groups we intended to study. Thus, we decided that a group had to satisfy the following five conditions to be defined as a self-help group for our purposes:

1. *Purpose.* Its express, primary purpose is to provide help and support for its members in dealing with their problems and in improving their psychological functioning and effectiveness.

2. *Origin and sanction.* Its origin and sanction for existence rest with the members of the group themselves rather than with any external agency or authority. (This would not exclude, however, groups that were initiated by professionals—such as some chapters of Make Today Count—but which are then taken over by members themselves as the group becomes functional.)

3. *Source of help.* It relies upon its own members' efforts, skills, knowledge, and concern as its primary source of help, with the structure of the relationship between members being one of peers, so far as helpgiving and support are concerned. Helpers and recipients of help may change roles at any time. Where professionals do participate in the group's meetings—as, for example, in the case of Parents Anonymous—they do so at the pleasure of the group and are cast in an ancillary role.

4. *Composition.* It is generally composed of members who share a common core of life experiences and problems. A possible exception to this are personal growth groups, such as Mowrer's (1972) Integrity Groups, formed by individuals who hope that collectively they can improve the quality of their lives. But even

in these groups, there is a shared discontent with members' present circumstances and a common goal of improvement through mutual support.

5. *Control*. Its structure and mode of operation are under the control of members, although they may, in turn, draw upon professional guidance and various theoretical and philosophical frameworks.

Through the application of these criteria, we believed that we would be able to identify groups in which the successes and failures of the group, as well as the methods used in achieving its purposes, would be largely attributable to the activities and skills of the members themselves. If there was anything unique about how self-help groups operated as compared with other therapeutic modalities, professional and nonprofessional, we believed the groups that satisfied our definition would give us our best chance of discovering it.

A Typology of Self-Help Groups. As we continued to familiarize ourselves with self-help groups during the first phase of our study, we could not help but be impressed (and at times overwhelmed) by the diversity of groups that satisfied our definition of a self-help group. Thus it became apparent that some kind of differentiation between groups was needed if we were to arrive at any meaningful generalizations about them, and also if we were to be able to make some estimate at the end of our study of how well we had sampled from the domain of self-help groups.

Various classifications of self-help groups may be found in the literature. Hansell (1976), for example, distinguishes between *predicament groups*, made up of members who share a common predicament, *bridging groups*, in which he includes some telephone hotlines, which are intended as brief havens for persons in distress and which may provide them with support until they can become stabilized and/or enter an appropriate predicament group, and *professionally assisted groups*, composed of essentially isolated individuals who are brought together by the fact that they are all seeing the same professional or are being seen in the same agency. Hansell's predicament group seems too broad a classification, and his other two types of groups fail to satisfy our working definition of a self-help group.

A classification proposed by Katz and Bender (1976b, pp. 36–37) contains some elements included in the typology that we finally developed. They defined four types of groups on the basis of their primary focus: (1) groups primarily focused on self-fulfillment of personal growth; (2) groups primarily focused on social advocacy; (3) groups whose primary focus is to create alternative patterns for living; and (4) "outcast haven" or "rock bottom" groups. Katz and Bender's classification again seems to include too many different kinds of groups in its first type, and in our own observations of self-help groups and examination of their literature, we found so many instances of groups that Katz and Bender would characterize as attempting to create an alternative pattern for living that were also engaged in a substantial amount of social advocacy that we question the psychological meaningfulness of the distinction between their second and third types of groups.

Although the final test of any system of classification must be in its utility and in the empirical correlates of an element's belonging to one class rather than another in the system, it was doubts about existing typologies such as those cited above that led us to develop our own. In this system, we distinguish between four types of groups on the basis of their *composition* and *purposes*:

1. *Behavioral control* or *conduct reorganization* groups are composed of members who are in agreement in their desire to eliminate or control some problematic behavior. Frequently, this desire is the only requirement for membership. The activities of these groups have as their sole purpose helping their members control the problematic behavior common to them, and these groups often refuse to deal with any other concerns or problems of their members. Of the groups studied by us, Alcoholics Anonymous (AA), Gamblers Anonymous (GA), Overeaters Anonymous (OA), Parents Anonymous (PA), and Take Off Pounds Sensibly (TOPS) are examples of this type. Synanon

would also fit in this category, but our study was limited to nonresidential groups.

2. *Stress coping and support* groups are composed of members who share a common status or predicament that entails some degree of stress, and the aim of these groups is generally the amelioration of this stress through mutual support and the sharing of coping strategies and advice. There is no attempt to change their members' status; that is taken as more or less fixed, and the problem for members of these groups is how to carry on in spite of it. Groups representative of this type that were included in our study were Al-Anon, Emotions Anonymous (EA), Make Today Count (MTC), Parents without Partners (PWP), and Recovery, Inc.

3. *Survival oriented* groups are composed of people whom society has either labeled or discriminated against because of their life-style and values or on other grounds such as sex, sexual orientation, socioeconomic class, or race. These groups are concerned with helping their members maintain or enhance their self-esteem through mutual support and consciousness-raising activities, and with bettering their lot through educational and political activities aimed at gaining legitimacy for their style of life and eliminating the grounds on which they have been stigmatized and discriminated against. This type of group was represented in our study by a single consciousness-raising group sponsored by the National Organization for Women (NOW), but the gay activist groups and various racial and ethnic support groups such as the Black Students Association would also fall in this category.

4. *Personal growth and self-actualization* groups are made up of members who share the common goal of enhanced effectiveness in all aspects of their lives, particularly those involving their emotionality, sexuality, and capacity to relate to others. In contrast with other types of groups, there is no core problem that brings members of these groups together; instead, there is the shared belief that together they can help each other improve the quality of their lives. Examples of this type are Mowrer's (1972) Integrity Groups, as well as informal experientially oriented groups, which have borrowed in varying degrees from the

techniques of Gestalt therapy, T groups, and sensitivity groups. In our own study, this type was represented by two local women's support groups: a local chapter of La Leche League, and a mixed-sex support group.

   Methodological Problems. Some methodological problems must be borne in mind in considering our findings. We believe that they are essentially intrinsic to the study of self-help groups and that others who plan to study self-help groups or to read the literature on these groups should bear them in mind either in the design of their own research or in the degree of confidence they place in assertions made by writers about self-help groups, including those to be presented here.

   Generally, self-help groups do not lend themselves to the sophisticated data-acquisition methodology typically used in small-group research. In those groups we studied, we were not allowed to take notes or make tape recordings during the meetings, thus eliminating the application of any kind of interaction process analysis, but also more generally reducing, to some unknown degree, the accuracy with which it was possible to report on the contents of the meetings. It was for this reason that we adopted the strategy, during the second phase of our study, of having two observers attend group meetings and having them prepare joint reports immediately after each meeting in an attempt to reduce observer error and bias.

   Sampling bias (to an unknown extent) is also inherent in the study of self-help groups. This has been observed in the case of studies of Alcoholics Anonymous (Baekeland, Lundwall, and Kissin, 1975) and seems unavoidable, given the nature of these groups. The membership of most self-help groups is voluntary and made up of persons who are self-defined sufferers of the problem that constitutes the focus of each group. They generally do not keep records of either their current or past membership, so that it is impossible to determine what proportion of the total pool of afflicted (or eligible) persons in a given geographic area has tried a particular group as a source of help. For the same reason, it is also impossible to determine attrition rates, so that, in turn, there is no way of estimating what proportion of the total number of individuals who have entered a particular group over any given period of time is represented by its current membership. Although these problems may appear to be most critical for evaluative studies, they are of somewhat less consequence, we believe, for generative studies such as the present one, where the purpose is descriptive and aimed at the generation of theory.

In light of these problems, the choice seems to be either to forgo any attempt to study self-help groups or to make the attempt, tempering one's inferences about them by recognizing the possibilities of errors in observations and descriptions of the phenomenon of interest and bias in the sample giving rise to these phenomena. We have obviously opted for this latter alternative on the grounds that some empirical data are better than none and in our trust in the essentially self-correcting nature of science, since speculation about self-help groups will continue whether such data are available or not.

Processes Operating in Self-Help Groups

Focusing on their impact upon their members, rather than on such social system issues as how self-help groups are initiated, demarcated, supported, maintained, and changed, there are two ways of answering the question of how self-help groups work. One is by describing the overt activities of members as they interact with each other in the context of giving and receiving help; the other is by postulating the psychological processes that are subserved by these activities. Both approaches are legitimate and should lead to a greater understanding of how self-help groups function. To speak in terms of activities involves some degree of abstraction but requires considerably less in the way of inference than it does to focus on processes, which by their very nature are inferential and theoretical. Focusing on the techniques used by self-help groups is also consistent with our overall research strategy for the generation of a grounded theory (Glaser and Strauss, 1967). Moreover, analysis of self-help group activities holds out the promise of some immediate pay-off in allowing more easily for the development of training programs for enhancing the effectiveness of these groups. However, the virtue of dealing with processes is that they should possess a greater degree of generality and so should allow us to see better the similarities and differences between self-help groups and other forms of psychological care giving. Both activities and processes, however, should allow us to answer questions about differences among self-help groups and, ultimately, about how to enhance the effectiveness of self-help groups as well as other psychotherapeutic modalities, professional and nonprofessional. Also, and most importantly in our view, knowledge about both the activities and processes found in self-help groups should contribute to an empirically based comprehensive theory of psychotherapeutic intervention. Therefore, we have attempted to answer the question of how self-help groups work in both ways. In this section, we shall consider processes; in the next, activities.

The processes we shall describe were first formulated during the second phase of our work (Levy, 1976) and have been modified only slightly in the light of later observations and data. They represent our best attempt to account for the diversity of activities and methods that we observed in self-help groups in terms that might also account for their effectiveness. On the basis primarily of our own observations, we have also found them consistent with descriptions of a variety of self-help groups by other writers, thus providing us with some assurance of their generality. Since we view these processes as genotypical, however, we would expect that their functioning in any given group might take a variety of different forms, and we would not expect them all to be operative to the same extent in all groups. Indeed, we expect their salience to vary with the type of group, as will be apparent from the following description.

Behaviorally Oriented Processes. The first four processes are reflected in methods that focus directly on members' behaviors and are not unlike those that might be involved in one or another form of behavior therapy. But although the processes themselves may not seem unique to self-help groups, their operation within a peer-group context, and the fact that each group member serves as both agent in their operation as well as target, does give them a unique quality. And this quality may be essential in understanding the unique contribution that self-help groups can make in dealing with the mental health problems of society. The four processes are:

1. *Both direct and vicarious social reinforcement for the development of desirable behaviors and the elimination or control of problematic behaviors.* Viewed in its broadest sense, reinforcement is inherent in all social interactions. In self-help groups, we find that its operation is focused and guided by the purposes of the group and its conceptualization of members' problems and appropriate ways of dealing with them. Thus, reinforcement functions in self-help groups much as it does in the hands of mental health professionals: It serves both to indoctrinate members in the group's ideology and as a means of modifying its members' problem-related behaviors. And it seems quite likely that as it becomes effective on one of these levels, its effectiveness on the other level will be reciprocally enhanced. Thus, for example, as Recovery members learn the "spotting" methods advocated by the group and receive praise from the group's leader when they give a correct example of having used one of them, we would expect the likelihood of their use of these methods to increase and that this, in turn, would increase the likelihood of their subscribing to Recovery's entire body of precepts for the conduct of one's life.

Although reinforcement may function in a similar way in professionally conducted psychotherapy, there is good reason to believe that its operation in self-help groups may be potentially more effective. For as membership in the group itself becomes intrinsically more rewarding—many members we interviewed said they expected to remain members of their groups indefinitely—it seems likely that reinforcement within the group context will become increasingly potent, much more so than it might within the dyadic relationship of conventional individual psychotherapy.

Some groups utilize reinforcement in a most obvious fashion, as in TOPS meetings where all members weigh in and their gains and losses in weight are announced to the whole group and are met by either applause or small monetary penalties. (As a means of changing eating behaviors, it might be noted, this may not be the most effective use of reinforcement since it is being administered for changes in weight rather than behaviors.) Less obvious, but perhaps no less effective, are the verbal compliments members of other groups give one another when they recount how they are dealing with their problems, or the recognition of progress given AA members when they become eligible to engage in Twelfth Step work, helping other alcoholics to achieve sobriety.

2. *Training, indoctrination, and support in the use of various kinds of self-control behaviors.* This process is perhaps most clearly illustrated in Recovery meetings in which members practice "spotting techniques" (Low, 1950), which are intended to allow them to identify and avoid emotional responses that are likely to be disturbing to them, and in Recovery's emphasis on "muscle control" as a means of controlling both feelings and thoughts—a proposition not unfamiliar in behavior therapy (Stuart, 1977), although expressed in different terms. This process was found to operate particularly in behavior control groups. In Overeaters Anonymous, for example, members are given the following advice: "Don't allow yourself to either think or talk about any real or imagined pleasure you once got from certain foods." The emphasis on a "one day at a time" approach to controlling problematic behaviors, found in Gamblers Anonymous and many other groups, may also be expected to facilitate self-control through providing perceptually more easily achieved goals, rather than trying "to tackle your whole life's problems at once" (*Gamblers Anonymous*, 1976).

3. *Modeling of methods of coping with stresses and changing behavior.* Modeling has been used by mental health professions in dealing with a wide variety of problems (Bandura, 1971; Meichenbaum, 1977). Its use by self-help groups is also quite common. The testimonials by fellow members who have successfully coped with their problems by following the group's precepts, as found in most of the "anonymous" groups, and the "examples" presented by panel members at Recovery meetings are formalized instances of the use of modeling. This process can also be seen to be operating in the self-disclosure and

advice giving and sharing of coping techniques that are common to most self-help groups. A member of a Parents without Partners group who told a new member that she dealt with her loneliness either by phoning someone or by writing letters to relatives may thus also be seen as providing a model of coping for the new member.

Most groups offer their members both mastery models and coping models (Meichenbaum, 1977). Mastery modeling is provided by members who have successfully coped with their problem, as exemplified by the AA member who has been sober for seven years. As these members "tell their story," they offer hope to new members and also provide "proof" of the effectiveness of the group's methods and the validity of its precepts. Members who have not fully succeeded in dealing with their problem provide the group with coping models; they report on the methods they are using and on their successes and failures. In this way, they present other members with information about an array of methods they might try with some indication of their relative effectiveness. Coping models also serve to immunize members against the effects of occasional failures and relapses as they describe their own struggles and how they handled failures when they occurred. This may be important in preventing demoralization and dropouts.

The diversity of persons giving testimonials and serving as models in self-help groups such as AA and OA may be particularly advantageous in enhancing the effectiveness of this process relative to its use by professionals. For this diversity helps assure that every member will encounter a model with whom he or she can identify—a factor of prime importance in determining the effectiveness of modeling (Bandura, 1971).

4. *Providing members with an agenda of actions they can engage in to change their social environment.* Although most typically found in what we have referred to as survival-oriented groups, such as Gay Liberation and NOW consciousness-raising groups, this process was found operating to some degree in many of the groups observed by us. Thus, for example, by helping one of its members to recognize all the sources of pressure in her daily life, Parents Anonymous not only helped relieve

some of her guilt feelings about her treatment of her child but also laid the groundwork for effective problem solving. In this instance, this included arranging for a baby sitter for two hours each day so that she could have some time for herself, and appreciating the importance of learning to communicate better with her husband about her own needs and their relationship.

This process operates in two ways to aid individuals in distress. First, it externalizes the source of their distress so that they are less likely to experience feelings of guilt and inadequacy, and second, it can result in actual changes in their social environment so that it is more supporting and less stressful. When this process is an institutionalized part of the group's activities, as it is in many survival-oriented groups, it can also reduce the powerlessness some people feel regarding the world about them; they are united with others in confronting the source of their oppression. In actuality, for many troubled individuals, effectively dealing with their difficulties requires some consideration and modification of their social context, and so this process serves to counterbalance their tendency to think only in intrapersonal or intrapsychic terms—a tendency that is likely to be fostered by many traditional approaches to psychotherapy.

Cognitively Oriented Processes. Self-help group members, just as many other troubled persons, are concerned with the meaning of their experiences and with understanding what has happened to them, as well as with finding relief. One AA member told us in an interview that he considered the self-understanding and tolerance that he acquired by being in his group as the most helpful aspect of AA, and this claim was not uncommon among the people we interviewed. Thus, it is not surprising that a substantial proportion of the discussion and activities of self-help groups is concerned with fostering understanding by members of themselves and their problems, with examining their beliefs about themselves and others, and with the interpretation of various critical events in their lives. But we would hasten to point out that the aim of these discussions is not the achievement of insight as this is thought of in conventional psychodynamic terms. Its focus is as often situational and interpersonal as it is intrapsychic, and its aim is to equip members better to cope with their problems, to foster better problem solving, and to alter how they view themselves and their circumstances. We believe that the following seven processes best capture what appeared to be involved in the discussions that we observed:

1. *Removing members' mystification over their experiences and increasing their expectancy for change and help by providing them with a rationale for their problems or distress and for the group's way of dealing with it.* Although the truth value of this rationale may be impossible to determine or may be seriously challenged by existing scientific evidence, this is of less importance in determining its effectiveness than is its acceptance by group members as a framework within which they can see order and the possibility of change where previously they experienced only confusion and a sense of fixity—a sense of being trapped. Thus, for the alcoholic who subscribes to the AA view of the nature of alcoholism and its Twelve Steps as the pathway to control of his or her drinking, what is important is the hope and direction this provides rather than its scientific support. Similarly, although the language of Recovery in talking about emotional problems in terms of "temper" may seem quaint to professionals, for Recovery members who subscribe to it, this can provide as effective a rationale for understanding their problems and dealing with them as Ellis' (1962) rational-emotive therapy, into whose terms much of Low's (1950) language could be relatively easily translated.

Self-help groups vary in the extent to which they have an explicitly articulated body of precepts concerning the problems they are dealing with and in the extent to which indoctrination in these views plays a substantial role in their meetings, but we have found no group in which some kind of ideology could not be found that was imparted to its members, albeit at a very implicit level in some instances. The drive for meaning is so basic in humans that this should not be surprising.

2. *Provision of normative and instrumental information and advice.* We found this to be quite prevalent in all groups, sometimes as part of their formal meetings and sometimes dur-

ing the informal socializing that frequently occurs after meetings. Occasionally, this included the use of guest speakers, as at one PWP meeting at which a member of the staff of a local counseling center spoke on "mood management." More often, however, it takes the form of information exchange between members, as at one MTC meeting we attended in which several members discussed how they dealt with some of the side effects of the chemotherapy treatment they were receiving, and at a PA meeting at which several mothers assured a particularly distressed mother that her anger at her child was not unreasonable, given her circumstances, and then went on to discuss how she might better handle it in the future.

We have no empirical basis at present upon which to compare the effectiveness of the information exchange that occurs in self-help groups with that which occurs in professionally conducted individual and group psychotherapy. However, research in social psychology on the determinants of the effectiveness of persuasive communications in producing attitude change and on the role of reference groups in determining personal satisfaction with one's status along a variety of dimensions of one's life suggests that, in many instances, self-help groups may have the edge over professionals because their members perceive each other as being more like themselves than would be the case in the typical professional-client relationship.

3. *Expansion of the range of alternative perceptions of members' problems and circumstances and of the actions they might take to cope with their problems.* This appeared to be a frequent consequence of much of the sharing, advice giving, and self-disclosure that occurred at group meetings, although we cannot recall any group, with the exception of MTC, that explicitly stated it as one of the purposes of their discussions. Yet, the solution to many of the problems with which people are confronted rests upon their finding alternative ways of construing their circumstances and expanding the range of possible actions they might take (Kelly, 1955). Make Today Count was founded on the premise that becoming a cancer victim did not have to mean that one could not find joy and meaning in one's remaining life, that by being willing to talk about one's illness

and death one can learn to "not consider each day another day closer to death, but rather another day to live as fully as possible" (Kelly, 1975). But regardless of the focal problem, it would seem that discussing it with others who share their perceptions of it and how they might deal with it is bound to result in an increase in one's repertoire of alternative ways of construing it and dealing with it, which is an essential aspect of effective psychotherapy according to Kelly (1955), whether it is explicitly stated as a goal or not.

4. *Enhancement of members' discriminative abilities regarding the stimulus and event contingencies in their lives.* The sense of perplexity and helplessness that many people feel in the face of their personal afflictions, both physical and psychological, often results from their inability to place them within a functional context so that they can recognize that there is some orderliness in the web of circumstances in which they seem enmeshed. This process helps them adopt a more analytical perspective as they view their life condition and experience.

It is illustrated in the report of a woman at a PA meeting who said that one thing that had helped her feel more secure was the realization—as a consequence of the group's efforts—that her present husband was not like her previous one who had been unreliable and brutal toward her. Another example of this process occurred in a women's support group discussion about when it was appropriate to ask your husband to help around the house. And yet another example comes from an AA "closed meeting" in which a new member was being encouraged to talk about the circumstances that usually led to his beginning a drinking bout. In all of these cases, as group members attempt to understand and analyze one another's experiences, they begin to develop better analytic and discriminative abilities, thereby making it possible for them to gain better control over their behaviors and their environment.

Self-help group discussions illustrating the operation of this process bear a striking similarity to how behavior therapists might conduct a functional analysis of some troublesome behavior or experience. Where the two approaches differ most essentially is in the latter's being conducted in a more systematic fashion, reflecting the explicit theoretical rationale that guides the behavior therapist's practices.

5. *Support for changes in attitudes toward oneself, one's own behavior, and society*. This might be thought of as the cognitive counterpart of the behaviorally oriented process of social reinforcement, but we believe that it is discernibly different and of such vital importance that it warrants identification as a separate process. When, for example, a PA member told her group she had decided to ask her husband to stay home with the children one night a week while she went out with friends, and the group, responding to her vague expressions of uncertainty and guilt over the decision, told her in a variety of ways that she had a right to have some free time for herself, it was not only reinforcing the action she planned to take but was also supporting a new view of herself as a person with legitimate needs and rights of her own for which she should not feel guilty. The group was also supporting her in the more assertive role she was taking in regard to her husband.

As group members begin to see their problems and experiences in a new light and begin to try out new and more effective ways of coping, their previous views of themselves as ineffectual, powerless, and unworthy begin to give way to new ones in which they see themselves as capable of achieving mastery over their circumstances and as worthwhile individuals. And as members express these different views of themselves, the confirmation they receive from their peers within the group serves as a powerful reinforcement for them, especially since, in most instances, these changes are also consistent with the body of precepts to which the group subscribes.

It must be emphasized here that, with this process as with the others we have been describing, not every group will be found to utilize it to the same degree, and for a variety of reasons. For example, this process appeared to be essentially absent in one group's meetings largely because they seemed to be used as occasions for the conduct of one-to-one therapy in a group (this was a group that had a professional sponsor), and members seemed so involved with their own problems that they tended to express little interest in those of others in the group. In another group, the effectiveness of the process seemed undermined, in our judgment, by the absence of an explicitly stated body of group-sanctioned precepts to which it could refer in legitimizing either its own actions or those of its members. As with all the processes we have been describing, we have yet to discover the critical factors affecting the presence or absence of this process in any given group.

6. *Social comparison and consensual validation leading to a reduction or elimination of members' uncertainty and sense of isolation or uniqueness regarding their problems and experiences.* Festinger (1954) has postulated the existence of a strong need in people to evaluate their experiences accurately and has shown how social comparison processes can help satisfy this need. Research has further shown (Gerard, 1963; Schachter, 1959) how these processes can explain affiliative desires in individuals under a variety of conditions that might give rise to emotional uncertainty. This same line of research also strongly suggests that the operation of social comparison processes leads people to seek out others who have had experiences similar to their own. We would argue that the self-disclosure, which is so common in self-help groups, as well as the testimonials presented by recovering and recovered group members, foster the operation of these processes and that they are essential to the development of a group's cohesiveness and sense of community, both of which are intrinsically rewarding as well as important in enhancing the group's influence over its members (Bednar and Lawlis, 1971; Kirschner, Dies, and Brown, 1978; Lott and Lott, 1965; Yalom, 1975).

Perhaps the source of relief most frequently cited by group therapy members, as well as by the self-help group members whom we interviewed, is the discovery that they are not unique in having a particular problem or particular feelings. This realization helps reduce some of the fear, shame, guilt, and hopelessness they frequently experience. Members realize that they share a common problem and a common purpose and they receive consensual validation for the experience and feelings. As a consequence, they become more open to the shared experiences and coping strategies tried by other members, which, in turn, increases their own coping resources.

7. *The emergence of an alternative or substitute culture and social structure within which members can develop new definitions of their personal identities and new norms upon which they can base their self-esteem.* The phenomenon of the development of group norms as members work together, even over a relatively short period of time, has had a long history of study in social psychology and has been demonstrated in a wide variety of contexts (for example, Lieberman, Yalom and Miles, 1973; Sherif, 1935). In common with other social groups, self-help groups also develop their own social norms and may thus come to function as reference groups (Hyman, 1942; Kelley, 1952) that serve to govern their members' attitudes, values, and interactions with each other, as well as how they think and feel about themselves and their circumstances. With well-established, older groups, these norms are frequently explicit, as in AA's Twelve Steps and Twelve Traditions (Alcoholics Anonymous, 1953), whereas in others they tend to be implicit but not necessarily any less operative.

Although self-help groups adhere to a peer norm of equality of status and mutuality between members, there are, nevertheless, roles to be filled, sometimes on a strictly mechanical basis (for example, the round-robin basis upon which AA members take responsibility for leading meetings) and sometimes through achievement (for example, as when an OA member qualifies to be a "food sponsor" through having practiced abstinence for some determined period of time), so that each group also possesses a social structure. And this structure clearly provides members with the opportunity to experience responsibility and recognition of achievement, two nutrients of self-esteem that many of them have been sorely lacking.

Whether branded a mental patient, an alcoholic, or a child-abusing parent, many members of self-help groups suffer from what Goffman (1963) has called "spoiled identities." Through its norms and social structure, the group provides its members with an opportunity to build a new identity and increase their self-esteem, and thus provides them with

a new base from which they can face the world and their predicaments. Role theoretical considerations (Sarbin and Allen,
1968) also lead us to expect behavioral changes in self-help
group members as they begin behaving in ways consistent with
their newly fashioned identities and improved self-esteem.

By its very nature, this process seems the least likely of
all the processes we have postulated to occur in professionally
conducted psychotherapy, especially when it is conducted on
a one-to-one basis. Thus, if our speculations are correct about
the roles of self-help groups' social structure and norms in the
rebuilding of personal identities and self-esteem, this would suggest that they may be the "treatment of choice" for persons for
whom stigmatization and loss of self-esteem constitute major
components or consequences of their problems.

It may seem surprising that we have not postulated any
explicit emotionally oriented processes. There are two reasons
for this. The first is that although we noted a great deal of emotional expression in the groups we observed, we found no instances where any group engaged in behaviors that seemed to be
exclusively focused on fostering emotional expression for its
own sake, or where discussions emphasized feelings over content or behavior. One apparent exception to this was a PA group
whose sponsor would occasionally point out to the group that
they seemed to be primarily engaged in "head work." But even
in this group, the focus of discussions after emotions had been
expressed was on the cognitive and the behavioral levels.

The second reason for the absence of emotionally oriented processes is that the operation of each of the processes
that we have postulated may be seen to affect the person's emotional state as well as either behavior or cognition. Thus, for
example, the cognitive restructuring that occurred in one Emotions Anonymous meeting when the resentment expressed by
one member over her husband's treatment of her was relabeled
as self-pity seemed to affect both how she felt about the epi-
sode she had been describing as well as how she might alter the
way in which she related to her husband. We are, therefore, inclined to believe that the split between affect, on the one hand,
and behavior and cognition, on the other, commonly found in

the psychotherapy literature may rest more on the theoretical preconceptions of their authors than it does on the reality of human functioning. In this, we find ourselves in essential agreement with Beck's (1976) and Ellis' (1962) views, and also find empirical support in our analyses of help-giving activities engaged in by self-help group members, to be presented in the next section.

Help-Giving Activities*

As we pointed out earlier, the processes that we have postulated as operating in self-help groups are inferential, based upon a qualitative analysis of our observations. They provide one way of understanding how self-help groups function. We turn now to our second approach, an attempt to analyze quantitatively the actual behaviors engaged in by self-help group members, behaviors which presumably are manifestations of the processes we have postulated. This analysis should provide us with some insight into the "natural help-giving activities" found in everyday life or, at the very least, the preferred methods of giving and receiving psychological help as practiced by self-help groups. It should also give us an opportunity to compare self-help groups with each other and to assess the extent to which there is a relationship between the kinds of problems they deal with, their ideology, and how they conduct themselves as they deal with their members' distress. Finally, this analysis, together with the development of measures of the processes we have just postulated, could provide the basis for differentiating between effective and ineffective self-help groups, once criteria for identifying such groups are developed.

Unfortunately, logistical reasons as well as the constraints placed upon us by the self-help groups themselves, severely limited our ability to observe and reliably record sufficiently large and representative samples of their activities. Consequently, our

---

* A preliminary analysis of the data upon which this section is based was presented at the meeting of the Midwestern Psychological Association, Chicago, 1977.

analyses are of members' reports of the activities that occur at their meetings rather than our own observations. Nevertheless, despite the obvious methodological shortcomings of such reports, they are the best data yet available for our purposes and we shall present some data below which suggest that they may be reasonably reliable.

There were eight groups involved in this phase of our study. In terms of our typology, there were five Behavior Control Groups—one chapter each of AA, OA, and PA, and two chapters of TOPS—and three Stress Coping Groups—one chapter each of EA, PWP, and MTC. Although the particular groups involved in this phase were somewhat fortuitous, they provide us with an opportunity to compare these two main types of groups and also to compare the degree of similarity between two chapters of the same group (TOPS) with that between other groups of the same and different classification.

As we noted earlier, it is difficult to estimate the extent of sampling bias in studies of self-help groups, and because we chose to have the questionnaires distributed by group leaders, it is also difficult to estimate their return rate. Based on the average attendance at each of the group meetings, however, we estimate that there was an average return rate of approximately 67 percent overall, with a range of from 54 percent for PA to 84 percent for TOPS 2. Selected demographic data and the actual number of questionnaires from each group entering into our analyses are presented in Table 1. Although the small number of cases involved must necessarily make our conclusions tentative, it should be noted that the age, sex distribution, and level of education of respondents were consistent with our impressions of the larger number of members making up their respective groups. Both OA and PA did have a few male members, but the preponderance of women in all groups except AA is characteristic of most of the self-help groups that we have observed and of self-help groups described in the literature (for example, Wechsler, 1960; Weiss, 1973).

The wording of the definitions of the help-giving activities is presented in Table 2. We attempted to be as concrete as

Table 1. Demographic Characteristics of Self-Help Groups
Used in Questionnaire Analysis

	N	Mean Age	Sex M	F	Mean Years Education
Behavior Control Groups					
Alcoholics Anonymous	11	38.2	6	5	15.0
Overeaters Anonymous	4	30.2	0	4	12.0
Parents Anonymous	5	31.7	0	5	14.2
Take Off Pounds Sensibly #1	15	44.6	0	15	11.8
Take Off Pounds Sensibly #2	13	45.7	0	13	13.4
Stress Coping Groups					
Emotions Anonymous	7	35.3	1	6	14.6
Make Today Count	6	49.3	2	4	14.8
Parents Without Partners	11	35.2	2	9	13.0

possible in our definitions, taking into consideration the most likely form in which each activity might manifest itself and how members might describe it. The names of the activities did not appear in the questionnaire, only the definitions. Members rated each activity on a five-point scale, with *one* defined as "*an inaccurate description* (this process rarely occurs, is not something the group emphasizes, and is a misleading characterization of this group)" and *five* defined as "*a very accurate description* (this process occurs frequently, is something the group emphasizes, and gives a good idea of what the group is like)." Thus, the points on the scale were clearly defined in terms of frequency of occurrence.

Frequency of Occurrence. It seems reasonable to assume that members' reports of the frequency of occurrence in their groups of the twenty-eight help-giving activities reflect their groups' preferred modes of functioning in dealing with the problems of their members. Whether these preferences result from group members' differential comfort in engaging in the various activities or from their experience with these activities'

Table 2. Definitions Provided Self-Help Group Members of Help-Giving Activities and Means of Ratings of Their Frequency of Occurrence

Activity[a]	Definition	Overall means
1. Behavioral prescription	When a personal problem is brought up by a group member, other group members suggest things the person might do to overcome the difficulty. The group sometimes even makes very direct suggestions, such as "*Do this* and see what happens."	3.40
2. Behavioral proscription	When a personal problem is brought up by a group member, other group members often identify actions they believe are things that he or she shouldn't do. The group even makes the direct suggestion "*Don't do this.*"	2.62
3. Behavioral rehearsal	When a personal problem is brought up by a member, other group members often suggest how the person might act to handle the problem, and then ask the person to *practice these behaviors in the presence of the group.*	1.79
4. Positive reinforcement	When a member does something the group approves, the group often *applauds* this behavior or in some way *rewards* the member for acting in this way.	3.66
5. Punishment	When a member does something the group disapproves, the group often *criticizes* this behavior or in some way *punishes* the person for acting in this way.	1.65
6. Extinction	When a member says or does something the group disapproves, the group members often *ignore* the person's behavior.	2.17
7. Modeling	Group members often explain how they would go about handling a problem brought up by another member. In order to give this member a clear idea of what they have in mind, members often *demonstrate* just how they would react if they were faced with this person's problem.	2.25
8. Self-disclosure	Group members often disclose to other members experiences, fantasies, thoughts, or emotions that are very personal and that they normally *wouldn't tell other people.*	3.67

9. Sharing	Group members often share past and present experiences, thoughts, or feelings with other members. These things are not as private as those in #8, but serve to let other members know *what's going on* in each other's lives with respect to a whole range of areas, for example, coping with a problem, family life, financial matters, and past events of interest.	3.83
10. Confrontation	Group members often *challenge* one another, sometimes in a *demanding* or *threatening* way, to explain themselves or account for their behavior.	1.65
11. Encouragement of sharing	When a group member brings up a personal problem, other members often *ask the person for additional information* or explanation about this problem, but do so in a way that is *not challenging*.	3.57
12. Reflection and paraphrase	In order to clarify how a member thinks or feels about something, other members often put in other words what they believe the person has said; they may also make some statements to the person concerning how they believe he or she is feeling emotionally.	3.17
13. Requesting feedback	A group member often asks other group members how he or she impresses them and how they feel about him or her.	1.76
14. Offering feedback	Group members often disclose their feelings toward, and impressions of, another group member, and do so "face to face."	2.01
15. Reassurance of competence	Members often assure one another that they are *capable* of handling their problems.	3.41
16. Justification	Members often let other members know that they were justified in feeling or acting as they did in response to some situation.	3.35
17. Mutual affirmation	Members often assure one another that they are *worthwhile, valuable* people.	3.94
18. Empathy	When a person expresses emotions in the group, other group members let that person know that they *understand and share his or her feelings*.	4.20
19. Normalization	When a person describes his or her actions or emotions as somehow strange or abnormal, other group members often *assure him or her that this behavior is normal*.	3.39

Table 2. Definitions Provided Self-Help Group Members of Help-Giving Activities and Means of Ratings of Their Frequency of Occurrence (continued)

Activity[a]	Definition	Overall means
20. Morale building	Group members often reassure other members that their problems will eventually be worked out positively.	3.82
21. Personal goal setting	A group member often sets his or her own goals and checks the progress he or she has made toward these goals.	3.61
22. Establishing group's goals	Group members often discuss goals that they believe should be adopted by the group.	2.78
23. Reference to group's norms	The group seems to have rules concerning how members should feel and think and act. Group members often refer to these rules in one way or another during group meetings.	2.39
24. Consensual validation	Members often use the group as a way of determining whether their personal view of the world is the "best" or "most accurate" way of looking at the world. This process generally involves three steps: (a) a group member tells other members how he or she feels about certain issues, situations, or other people; (b) then, this group member learns from other group members how they feel about the things he or she has mentioned; and (c) the member evaluates his or her view. If other group members agree with this person's view, the person tends to feel that his or her opinions are right. If other group members disagree with this person's view, the person tends to feel that his or her views need to be corrected. In short, *the group helps the member determine whether his or her own point of view or way of seeing things is accurate or not.*	2.92

25. Functional analysis	Group members often try to understand a problem by *breaking it down* and determining such things as what went on before the problem situation arose, how the person reacted, and what happened after the difficulty arose.	3.30
26. Discrimination training	When a group member describes a situation happening at the present time as similar to situations that happened in the past, other group members often point out in what ways these situations or emotional reactions are different.	3.30
27. Explanation	Members provide explanations that help other group members to a *better understanding of* themselves or their reactions to a situation.	3.89
28. Catharsis	The group often emphasizes and encourages the *release of emotions*.	3.59

[a] Group members were not given names of activities in their questionnaires.

differential effectiveness, or both, are questions that clearly call for additional research.* But regardless of the answers to these questions, to the extent that the patterns of help-giving activity that emerge from our data are valid portrayals of what transpires in self-help groups, they provide us with yet another way of answering the question of how these groups work.

Because of the small number of cases in some of the self-help groups, it was decided that frequency data for individual groups would be too unreliable to warrant separate reporting. Thus, mean frequencies were computed for each group for each of the activities and then an overall mean frequency rating for each activity was computed based upon these group means. These means are presented in the last column in Table 2. Dividing this distribution of means into thirds, we find that the nine most frequently occurring activities are *empathy, mutual affirmation, explanation, sharing, morale building, self-disclosure, positive reinforcement, personal goal setting,* and *catharsis.* The third least frequent activities are *confrontation, punishment, requesting feedback, behavioral rehearsal, offering feedback, extinction, modeling, reference to group's norms,* and *behavioral proscription.* These two sets of activities differ from each other in a number of interesting ways.

Considering the activities in the upper third of the distribution, it would appear warranted to suggest that, on the whole, self-help groups focus the major portion of their efforts on fostering communication between their members, providing them with social support, and responding to their needs on both cognitive and emotional levels. Taken as a group, moreover, these activities appear to be noncoercive, nonthreatening, and likely to foster group cohesiveness (Kirschner, Dies, and Brown, 1978; Yalom 1975). Thus, they also suggest that self-help groups provide their members with safe, supportive, and noncoercive

---

* It is conceivable, of course, that group members' reports were also influenced by their beliefs about what *should* have occurred in their groups—by their own theories of self-help groups—but since there is no way of ascertaining the extent to which this might be so, and since our primary purpose here is the discovery of theory rather than its confirmation, we choose to ignore this possibility at this point.

environments—a conclusion also reached by Lieberman and Bond (1976) in their study of women's consciousness-raising groups.

By contrast with the most frequently occurring activities, those in the lower third of the distribution appear to be more overtly controlling and behaviorally manipulative and also more likely to be threatening or to elicit negative affect. Some of the activities, such as confrontation and those involving feedback, may also require a higher level of therapeutic competence for their effective use than is likely to be found among nonprofessionals. Together with the activities found in the upper third of the distribution of frequency of occurrence, these activities further confirm the view of self-help groups as essentially benign, and further suggest that they may generally be aware of the limits of their therapeutic competence and avoid exceeding them.

The contrast between the most and least frequently engaged in activities also suggests that self-help groups generally operate within the norms governing behavior in natural social situations. That is, the most frequent activities are those one might expect to find in any natural social setting, whereas the least frequently occurring ones are rarely found in such settings and are more characteristic of the "artificial" settings constructed by psychotherapists and other socially sanctioned care givers. As a consequence, this would suggest that the social reality within which a person joining a self-help group must function would require less readjustment and, hence, be less stressful than that of the professional care giver.

If the behaviors found occurring in self-help groups appear to be similar to those occurring in natural social situations, it is reasonable to wonder how self-help groups can bring about changes in their members which their normal social settings apparently could not. It would seem that self-help groups or other change-inducing settings should contain something more or different from that which is found in everyday life. We believe that this is true. But we also believe that the difference may be not so much in the inventory of processes and activities found in the two kinds of settings as it is in the systematic way in which they are marshaled in the service of specific, targeted changes in the case of professional and nonprofessional change settings as opposed to everyday life settings, and in the commitment to change which entry into a self-help group or professional treatment entails on the part of the person seeking help.

In this regard, it is also interesting to view our findings on help-giving activities in the light of Gurin, Veroff, and Feld's (1960) survey of Americans' attitudes toward their mental health. They found that less than one third of those who sought help with a personal problem consulted a mental health professional. This would suggest that fertile ground exists for the development of self-help groups. But more interesting in view of our data was their conclusion that most people who sought help with personal problems were looking for comfort, reassurance, and advice, rather than change in themselves (p. 323). Although no grounds exist upon which we can assess the change-producing effectiveness of the twenty-eight help-giving activities included in our study, in view of those activities self-help groups engaged in most frequently it would appear that their members are not very different from the population at large, and that perhaps self-help groups are giving their members what they most want—understanding (*empathy*), assurance of their worth as a person (*mutual affirmation*), and some advice and feedback (*behavioral prescription* and *positive reinforcement*).

However, although some professionals might believe that the self-help groups in this study made insufficient use of the most effective change-producing methods, there is no reason to conclude that self-help group members do not want change in themselves, their behavior, or their circumstances. For neither our findings, nor those of Gurin, Veroff, and Feld, necessarily imply that people do not desire to change; these findings are just as compatible with the view that they do want to change, but on their own terms and as a result of their own initiatives and efforts rather than those of others. Most people may believe that they can take charge of their own lives and be the agents of their self-change, if they are provided with the support and other resources they need—and it may be this belief that is expressed in the pattern of help giving we have found in self-help groups.

Comparison Between Groups. How do groups compare with each other in their patterns of help-giving activities? With groups dealing with such diverse problems as alcoholism and living with a life-threatening illness (as MTC members prefer to call it), and with corresponding widely different ideologies, we might expect widely differing care-giving approaches among them. Antze's (1976) analysis of the complementary relationship between the ideology of AA and what he believes to be the alcoholic's exaggerated sense of "his own authorship in the events of his life" (p. 331), as well as his similar analysis of Recovery, Inc., and Synanon, might lead us to expect to find such differences. Similarly, the conventional wisdom, probably reflecting the medical notion of disease-specific treatment, and expressed idiomatically as "different strokes for different folks," as well as in the current advocacy of a "prescriptive" approach to psychotherapy (Bergin and Strupp, 1972; Goldstein and Stein, 1976), suggests that we should find differences in the techniques used by different self-help groups. However, if there is a universal core of psychological processes involved in the effective treatment of psychological distress, as would be expected from the writings of Rogers (1957) and as fully implied in the literature of psychoanalysis, and if the various problems around which self-help groups have been formed can be meaningfully characterized as "problems in living," we might expect to find that the groups do not differ greatly from each other—their processes and activities may be similar and only their content may differ. What did we find?

One approach to this question is to compare the groups with each other in terms of their relative frequency of use of the twenty-eight help-giving activities. This would tell us how similar their *patterns* of activity usage are, and is obtained by computing the intercorrelations between all the groups on the basis of their mean ratings of the frequency of occurrence of the twenty-eight activities in their respective groups. These intercorrelations are presented in Table 3.

On the whole, these correlations suggest a substantial degree of similarity between the groups, although there is some variation in its magnitude. However, the variation in the magnitude between correlations does not seem to fit any easily dis-

Table 3. Correlations Between 8 Self-Help Groups' Mean Ratings of Frequency of Occurrence of 28 Help-Giving Activities

Groups	AA	TOPS #1	TOPS #2	PA	OA	PWP	EA
Taking Off Pounds Sensibly #1	.65						
Taking Off Pounds Sensibly #2	.70	.86					
Parents Anonymous	.64	.47[a]	.38(NS)				
Overeaters Anonymous	.80	.68	.65	.78			
Parents Without Partners	.77	.60	.55	.72	.67		
Emotions Anonymous	.79	.56	.48	.60	.72	.88	
Make Today Count	.67	.53	.43[a]	.78	.81	.64	.70

[a] $p < .05$; $p < .01$ for all other rs, except between PA and TOPS #2.

cernible pattern. The two TOPS chapters are highly correlated with each other, as would be expected, but not any more so than EA and PWP, two very dissimilar organizations in terms of both membership and ideology. Also, it is difficult to see what the problems of persons suffering from life-threatening illnesses might have in common with those people who have trouble controlling their eating—and yet MTC correlates .81 with OA. The pattern of correlations between groups does not correspond with our classification of them into Behavior Control and Stress Coping groups, nor does any other pattern appear to emerge, except for the fact that the two TOPS chapters' correlations with all other groups tend to be among the lowest. Thus, with the exceptions we have noted, we are inclined to interpret these data as suggesting that there is a reasonably substantial consensus among self-help groups in their preferred means of care giving. At the very least, this would seem to imply that the overall mean frequency ratings for the twenty-eight help-giving activities presented in Table 2 are a fairly reliable portrayal of their relative frequency of usage among self-help groups in general.

A second way of answering the question of how similar the various groups in this study were to each other is to compare them in terms of the extent to which they engaged in each of the help-giving activities. Although the correlations in Table 3 reveal an impressive degree of similarity between the groups in their relative usage of each of the twenty-eight help-giving activities, differences between them may still exist with respect to particular behaviors. *Explanation*, for example, may be the most frequent behavior found in two different groups, but one group may still manifest a great deal more of it than the other. Thus, groups were compared in terms of their mean frequency ratings for each of the activities.

Because of the small number of persons in several of the groups, as well as the unequal numbers among the groups, it was not felt that analysis of variance could be applied to these data. Instead, Mann-Whitney U tests were performed comparing the five Behavior Control groups with the three Stress Coping groups. This yielded only two statistically significant differences ($p = .04$): Behavior Control Groups reported greater use of *per-*

sonal goal setting and *positive reinforcement* than Stress Coping Groups.

Since at least one difference significant at the .04 level among the twenty-eight comparisons might be expected by chance, we do not feel it warranted to make too much of the two significant differences that were found. We cannot refrain, however, from pointing out that in both instances the direction of the differences seems to make sense since both activities are ideally suited for the modification of clearly defined, troublesome behaviors, behaviors that are more likely to be of concern to Behavior Control groups.

Our comparisons between groups suggest that, on the whole, they are more similar to each other than different in how they engage in the process of helping their fellow members. This conclusion is generally consistent with our observations, viewing the group at the process level only, and not considering differences in form or content. There are several caveats that must be acknowledged, however, before we pursue the possible implications of this conclusion. First, this finding is limited by the particular activities sampled in the twenty-eight that we studied; conceivably, we may have failed to include some other important activities in which the groups might have been found to differ dramatically. Second, this finding is limited by the small number of groups included in this study, and the small number of respondents in some of these groups. And finally, our data have nothing to say about possible differences between groups either in the skill with which they engaged in these activities or about the particular form they took. (On this latter point, for example, *positive reinforcement* could consist largely of verbal praise in one group and of applause and paralinguistic responses in another.) Yet, having entered these caveats, we believe that there may be some value in speculating on the meaning of our findings.

These findings appear to be most consistent with a broad-spectrum model of psychological care giving rather than a narrow-band, prescriptive, problem-specific conception. That is, they suggest that self-help groups may be drawing upon a fundamental core of interventions that may be therapeutically effective in dealing with a very wide range of personal problems. Of course, their effectiveness remains to be demonstrated, but that such a core may exist seems quite possible. Where the groups may differ from each other, and where, more generally, psychotherapy may become particularized, is at the level of the content of their help-giving transactions—what they choose to reinforce positively, how they explain their problems, the contents of their self-disclosures, and so forth. And it may be for this reason that groups as diverse as OA and MTC appear to be quite similar to each other when compared at the formal level of activities and processes. These are similar from group to group but they are operating in the service of different ideologies and the solution of different problems.

Should our findings be replicated, they would also provide the basis for the development of technical support materials for use by self-help groups wishing to enhance their effectiveness and for those wishing to establish self-help groups. They would also provide an empirical framework within which to compare self-help groups with other mental health resources, both as to how they function and their effectiveness, and this framework could also contribute to the development of an overarching theory of mental health delivery that would include self-help groups as one of its components.

Finally, it seems possible to view our findings concerning the similarity between different self-help groups' patterns of help giving as suggesting that self-help groups are not only trying to help their members deal with their identified personal problems but are also serving to meet their members' most fundamental human needs—needs for empathic understanding, for enhanced self-esteem, for meaning, and for an opportunity to express their feelings and share their experiences with another. If this view is correct, it may explain why self-help groups are continuing to grow in popularity and why, in another part of our study, we found that close to 70 percent of the members surveyed by us said they expected to remain in their groups indefinitely. More importantly, this view suggests that the study of self-help groups could be as important an avenue to knowledge about human nature in the second half of the twentieth century as the psychoanalyst's couch was in the first half.

CHAPTER 12

Role of Ideologies in Peer Psychotherapy Groups

Paul Antze

Of the many kinds of mutual help groups that exist today, those trespassing on the customary grounds of psychotherapy are perhaps the most interesting. In contrast to groups that seek only to educate members or the public about an issue or to advance the interests of a minority or to promote "growth" for its own sake, a peer psychotherapy organization tries to help its members to deal more effectively with shared "problems in living." Thus it is usually engaged in helping them to undergo some highly determinate form of change.

Despite the paucity of outcome studies on peer psychotherapy, there is a growing consensus among professionals that the idea works. A wide array of investigators (Grosz, 1972; Stewart, 1955; Strunkard, 1972; Sugarman, 1974; Tiebout, 1944; Volkman and Cressey, 1963) have presented informal evidence or case materials indicating the effectiveness of individual peer-helping organizations.

Note: Portions of the research for this article were supported by a grant from the Institute for Juvenile Research, Chicago, Illinois.

If we grant the efficacy of these groups, another problem arises. How does one explain it? Clearly most of the factors invoked to explain conventional dyadic psychotherapy (expertise of therapist, client-therapist empathy, handling of transference) are hardly appropriate here. Up to now most efforts to explain peer psychotherapy have leaned instead on a rough analogy to "group therapy." Observers ranging from Hobart Mowrer (1975) to Erving Goffman (1963) and Robert Bales (1944) have argued that there is something about sharing experiences or feelings with a body of like-minded others that reduces anxiety and promotes more constructive behavior. Viewed from this perspective, self-help groups achieve their results through a relatively simple cluster of social-psychological processes: confession, catharsis, mutual identification, and the removal of stigmatized feelings. Clinard's (1963, p. 647) text on deviant behavior offers a convenient summary of this approach: "In each case the group helps to integrate the individual, to change his conception of himself, to make him feel again the solidarity of the group behind the individual, and to combat social stigma. These group processes, it is felt, replace 'I' feelings with 'we' feelings, give the individual the feeling of being in a group, and redefine certain norms of behavior."

Despite its considerable merits, this common view of peer psychotherapy has one serious drawback: It neglects the very feature of these groups that their members take most seriously. Each self-help group claims a certain wisdom concerning the problems it treats. Each has a specialized system of *teachings* that members venerate as the secret of recovery. These are often codified in a book or recited in capsule form at the start of each meeting. I have chosen to call such teachings "ideologies." In the present context, however, this term includes not only the group's explicit beliefs but also its rituals, rules of behavior, slogans, and even favorite expressions.

Ideology and Therapeutic Change

One has only to read group literature or watch the induction of newcomers to recognize that, as far as members themselves are concerned, a group's teachings are its very essence.

274 Self-Help Groups for Coping with Crisis

Slogans like "Get with the program," "Try doing things our way," and "Just follow these simple steps" are the first exhortations and the ones most repeated. Why then have social scientists neglected them? On the surface, these ideologies often appear shallow or incoherent and thus of little importance, therapeutic or otherwise. Also, the central activity of peer therapy groups is the sharing of experience in a structured setting, an activity that lends itself well to the interpretation previously noted. Some writers (Bales, 1944; Clinard, 1949), in fact, have argued that all the key social characteristics of these groups (their specialization, use of mutual confessions, and quasi-religious style) may be understood as serving the same basically supportive or "integrative" purpose.

Persuasive Process. My objection to this supportive approach is that it is seriously incomplete. Social psychologists have been right in seeing peer therapy groups as arrangements for mutual support and the removal of stigma. They may be right in holding that such activities have therapeutic value. But in neglecting ideology they have missed another, equally crucial, function of these groups—a *persuasive function*. Whether by accident or unconscious design, most peer therapy groups also share an array of traits that make them highly effective in impressing their teaching on members. The result is that, with time, active participants tend to absorb group ideas not just as a creed or set of beliefs but as a living reality that is reconfirmed in each day's experience. No understanding of how these groups help their members can be complete without examining this persuasive process.

We may begin this examination by briefly considering the structural characteristics that make these groups so persuasive.

First, peer therapy organizations are like religious sects and, unlike most other forms of therapy, they are *fixed communities of belief*. To join is to enter a new group of others who are committed to certain very definite notions about the world, and to espouse those beliefs and share in the group on a long-term basis. (In group therapy, by contrast, the experience lasts a few weeks or months at best, and the beliefs imparted tend to come directly from the leader.) Studies of religious conversion have shown that such association is a powerful force in the induction and maintenance of new attitudes. As Berger and Luckmann (1967, pp. 158–159) have written: "To have a conversion experience is nothing much. The real thing is to be able to keep on taking it seriously; to retain a sense of its plausibility. *This* is where the religious community comes in. . . . The partners in significant conversation change. And in conversation with the new significant others subjective reality is transformed. It is maintained by continuous conversation with them, or with the community they represent." By the same token, peer therapy organizations draw much of their persuasiveness simply from placing the individual in close and lasting proximity to others committed to group beliefs.

Second, the sharing of experience plays a central role in this process. Stories that members tell become an object lesson, an illustration of certain ideas. In this sense, the sharing of experience runs well beyond confession or catharsis and operates as a subtle form of indoctrination. It becomes a way of giving depth and substance to the group's main ideas. Experimental evidence on the influencing process (Festinger, 1957) suggests that the persuasive effect here is likely to be strongest for the person telling the story, since that person is actively recasting his or her experience in the light of the group's ideas. Reworking experience in this fashion is a technique shared by such diverse systems of persuasion as Chinese thought reform and psychoanalysis (Lifton, 1961; Sarbin and Adler, 1971).

Experimental research (Hovland, Janis, and Kelley, 1953; Watts, 1967) has shown that the most effective forms of persuasion are those initiated by the subjects themselves. In trying to persuade someone else, they are likely to pick up just the arguments that they themselves find most convincing. Thus, when members of peer therapy groups work at counseling newcomers or at explaining the group's ideas to visitors, they are also working to deepen their own convictions. This may be one reason for the emphasis these groups place on externally oriented activities like "Twelfth Stepping" and "Open-House Night."

Third, because every peer therapy organization deals with a single and specialized problem, all those who join it tend to be alike in certain ways. In some cases, this likeness may be trivial (for example, in groups treating strictly medical problems), but where the problem has a social or psychological basis, it is often quite striking. In many of these groups, the uniformity of members is also enhanced by a natural sorting process that tends to exclude persons who feel out of place.

Because such uniformity makes mutual identification easier, it may help to reduce feelings of isolation. The uniformity of members helps to assure a high degree of group cohesion, and as experimental studies have shown (Bednar and Lawlis, 1971; Lott and Lott, 1965), cohesiveness is a major factor in any group's ability to influence its members. In addition, Festinger (1954) has argued that the strongest influencers are those whom the subject sees as like himself or herself but more successful.

Fourth, to some extent, peer therapy groups draw their persuasiveness from the kinds of problems they treat. A great many of these groups, though not all of them, address conditions of an extreme and terrifying kind (alcoholism, drug addiction, terminal illness), so that prospective members often arrive in states approaching despair. With their former lives in complete disarray, these sufferers are only too ready to embrace a new system of ideas that promises relief or comfort. The affective forces at work here are very close to those found in religious conversion, and so the resulting beliefs often attain a similar depth and tenacity.

Taken together, these four traits suggest that peer therapy groups are social forms especially well adapted to inducing standardized changes of outlook at a deep level among their membership. These changes are in each case defined by the group's ideology. Let us assume for present purposes that such changes occur. Do they have any therapeutic importance? Frank (1961) offers a sustained argument for the view that every effective therapy achieves its ends by changing the client's "assumptive world." The methods used may vary widely but, according to Frank, the crux of the therapeutic process is always some modification of "values, expectations, and images"—in short, a cognitive change. This view finds more direct and empirical support in a recent major study of the encounter movement conducted by Lieberman, Yalom, and Miles (1973), which concluded that the most helpful encounter group leaders were those who engaged extensively in "cognitizing" behavior. In practice, this meant that participants derived the greatest benefit from a group when the leader operated as an "interpreter of reality," by attempting "the translation of behavior and feelings into ideas" or by supplying "clear conceptual organizers" and "frameworks for how to change" (pp. 238, 442). "Cognitizing" in this sense comes very close to the persuasive process I have been describing in peer therapy groups.

Cognitive Antidote. To say that therapy entails cognitive change, however, is very different from showing that a given cognitive change is therapeutic. Peer therapy groups hold no patent on ideology, nor on the power of persuasion. Similar claims might be made for religious sects and social movements with little therapeutic value. What is more, the cognitive changes described by Frank and by Lieberman are usually imparted by a skilled practitioner to meet the special needs of an individual. How can we expect a standardized ideology to offer similar benefits?

The answer lies in the highly specialized nature of all peer therapy organizations. Within this framework, it may be possible for a group's ideology to function more precisely, working as a "cognitive antidote" to basic features of the specific condition shared by everyone who joins. Such a relationship is hard to prove, but if it does exist, then one should also find a fairly detailed correspondence between the peculiar teachings of the group and the peculiar dynamics of the problem it treats. Such connections would not only throw light on the therapeutic process but would also do much to explain the differences in philosophy that separate these groups.

The remainder of this chapter represents an attempt to apply this hypothesis to three prominent peer therapy organizations: Alcoholics Anonymous, Recovery, Inc., and Synanon. Before entering a substantive discussion of the teachings of these groups, I would like to offer a brief account of the general reasoning that guides my interpretations.

Most attempts to explain a therapeutic process begin by examining the etiology of the problem treated. The assumption is that effective therapy must counteract one or more of the causes behind a disease. However, the conditions treated by our three groups—alcoholism, mental illness, and heroin addiction—are exceedingly complex phenomena. Attempts to attribute these social ills to a single cause or even a plausible network of causes have been unconvincing. The same is true of efforts to locate underlying personality types behind the problems. Evidently, people come to each of these conditions from many avenues. For this reason, there seems no way of explaining the success of a group's uniform method by showing how it undoes uniform causal factors or meets the needs of uniform personality types among its membership.

When we look closely, however, another strategy appears. The conditions treated by these and many other peer therapy organizations have a curiously *intermittent* quality. The alcoholic, the former mental patient, and the drug addict may all experience periods of seeming normalcy. The trouble is that these periods are usually brief and are prone to ending in relapse. It seems possible to describe the work of peer therapy groups in rather simpler terms. They need not necessarily cure the conditions they treat by removing underlying causes (and in fact none of them claims to do so). Their achievement may be the more modest one of blocking the relapse process in some fashion, of maintaining the state of remission. To learn how peer therapy groups help their membership, then, we need not grasp the causes of the problems they treat but only the dynamics of relapse.

In our contemporary American social structure, each of these conditions places its victims in a *socially standardized situation*, one that runs far beyond the simple fact of the alcoholic's drinking problem or the mental patient's psychiatric history. Factors defining this situation are extremely diverse. Personality and biology may be involved, but so are a great many cultural, economic, and even legal conditions. Most problem drinkers in America are alike in having been chastised by others for their lack of self-control. Most heroin addicts share a common reliance on illegal activity to support their habits. As a result of factors like these, no matter how an individual comes to a given problem, once he arrives he is very much in the same boat with his fellow victims. He comes to cope with life in a similar fashion; he comes to think of himself and others in similar ways; and he faces identical problems in trying to change.

Parsons (1955) has argued that the social meanings and consequences attached to deviant acts usually serve the interests of control, by persuading and coercing the deviant back into the fold of normal society. In the cases before us, however, the relevant social effects do not seem to exert this benign influence, nor are they purely neutral. Rather, some of them actually serve to exacerbate the problem, locking the deviant more tightly into his or her marginal niche and rendering any attempts at recovery increasingly ineffective. The result, then, is a vicious circle: A central habit of deviant behavior has generated implications that intensify rather than diminish it.

The ideologies of peer therapy groups may be seen as extremely shrewd and insightful attacks on the most harmful of these standardized implications. If they have therapeutic value, it is because each manages to break some link in the chain of events maintaining a condition and to provide viable defenses against its renewal. Full evidence for my views, based on ethnographic study of all three groups and a close analysis of the conditions they treat, will be treated in a longer work now in progress. What follows here will be more heuristic in flavor—a series of reasoned conjectures linking the teachings of Alcoholics Anonymous, Recovery, Inc., and Synanon to the "standardized situations" faced by their clients.

Alcoholics Anonymous

Ideology of AA. AA's central teachings find a very clear presentation in a number of the group's publications but most notably in the "Big Book," *Alcoholics Anonymous* (1955). Drawing on these sources as well as on personal attendance at meetings, I have condensed the AA ideology into five essential points:

1. *Nature of Alcoholism.* AA takes a highly paradoxical view of the problem besetting its members. On the one hand, the group holds that compulsive drinking is the work of a *disease* for which there is no real cure. The alcoholic, according to AA, is constitutionally different from other persons. He suffers a physical quirk rather like an allergy that makes him unable to tolerate even small amounts of alcohol. AA views this disability as a permanent one. As the Big Book puts it: "We are like men who have lost their legs; they never grow new ones." Members reaffirm this belief in every meeting with the ritual confession, "My name is ___ and I am an alcoholic."

On the other hand, AA ascribes compulsive drinking to a kind of moral failing rooted in the drinker's own pride and selfishness. The Big Book contains a liberal sprinkling of statements like these: "Selfishness—self-centeredness! That, we think, is the root of our troubles." "The alcoholic is an extreme example of self-will run riot, though he usually doesn't think so." "Self, manifested in various ways was what had defeated us." At first, it seems hard to imagine any way of reconciling the disease concept of alcoholism with this moralistic language. However, the fact that the two are juxtaposed suggests that neither may quite mean what it seems.

2. *"Hitting bottom."* AA teaches that recovery begins only after a special experience of despair, an experience that finally compels the confession of illness. Ironically, members believe that the alcoholic is ready for change only when persuaded that all efforts at self-control are hopeless. To this end, AA "Twelfth Steppers" (members working with drinking alcoholics) often attempt to push their prospect toward despair. A favorite technique is challenging the candidate to "try some controlled drinking," the expectation being that he will fail miserably, and that in the depression that follows he will take the first of AA's Twelve Steps: "We admitted that we were powerless over alcohol—that our lives had become unmanageable."

3. *The Higher Power.* AA teaches that in order to recover, an alcoholic must come to accept the existence of a "power greater than himself." Officially, AA makes no statements about

the nature of this power. Members are encouraged to think of "God as you conceive Him." Yet when we read AA literature or talk with members, it becomes clear that this power is not in any respect a stern father, lawgiver, or punisher. He *asks* nothing. His role is much closer to that of a guide or protector. He is, as one member put it, "a friend who never lets me down and is ever eager to help. I can actually take my problems to Him and He gives me comfort, peace, and understanding" (Alcoholics Anonymous, 1955, p. 303).

Having accepted the Higher Power, the alcoholic asks Him "in His good time" to remove the desire to drink and also to remove various moral shortcomings. He begins to pray regularly for such personal qualities as humility and tolerance, making frequent use of the phrase "Thy will, not mine, be done." He relies especially on the famous AA Serenity Prayer: "God grant me the serenity to accept the things I cannot change, courage to change the things I can, and the wisdom to know the difference."

4. *The Moral Inventory*. The next step on AA's road to recovery is a searching self-scrutiny, conducted in the style of an accountant's yearly audit. Having completed this reckoning, the member then confesses his misdeed to another trusted person and makes amends to all whom he has wronged.

5. *"Twelfth-Stepping."* The final step of the AA plan calls on the member to carry AA's spiritual message to other alcoholics. Two reasons are implied: First, of all the people in the world, the alcoholic is uniquely gifted to help others like himself ("Only a drunk can help another drunk"). Second, helping others is thought essential to the member's own sobriety. To neglect this part of the program is to increase the danger of a "slip."

The Alcoholic Experience. AA's teachings take on added meaning when we consider them in the light of certain traits found among compulsive drinkers, at least among their male representatives in Anglo-American countries. These traits are well known and well sung in barroom folklore. Their presence has also been confirmed by a number of empirical studies (Jones, 1965; McClelland and others, 1972; McCord and McCord, 1960).

Although some would regard these as *personality traits*, it seems
at least likely that they are learned in the course of the addiction
process. They include great ambition, perfectionism, impulsiveness, narcissism and low frustration-tolerance, unreliability,
grandiosity, defiance and extreme defensiveness, and prone-
ness to bouts of remorse accompanied by resolutions to "do
better." At first, this seems an extremely mixed bag of tendencies and one quite unrelated to drinking per se. However, I think
that all of these traits can be shown to stem from a common
root, and that as a group they do much to explain why the alcoholic tumbles off the wagon and back into drink with such dis-
maying regularity.

These traits suggest that the alcoholic differs from the
ordinary person in one key respect: He exaggerates his own
authorship in the events of his life. Sober or drunk, he tends to
perceive his world as fashioned mainly by his own acts; somehow he always finds himself at center stage. The result of this
attitude is a growing isolation of self from world, an isolation
that is ultimately very painful.

For analytical purposes, the condition I am describing
may be broken into three distinct experiences of self. Each
plays its own part in disorganizing the alcoholic's life and driving him deeper into drink. Taken together, they embrace all the
tendencies previously noted.

1. *The omnipotent self.* The experience at work here is
best described in the phrase "I can do anything I want." It consists of an overblown sense of the world's malleability to one's
own decisions. This includes the alcoholic's insistence on "doing it now" (his notorious impatience, impulsiveness, and low
frustration-tolerance) as well as his insistence on "doing big
things" (his ambition, grandiosity, and perfectionism). These
two attitudes are themselves a dangerous combination, since
they mean that the alcoholic repeatedly sabotages his own ex-
travagant plan. As life begins to sour, a third attitude joins this
group: a dogged belief that "I can do better," yielding an inevitable string of false resolutions and broken promises.

This group of attitudes adds up to unrealistic volition.
Somehow the alcoholic's experience of "willing" has slipped

out of gear with events, so that he is constantly "intending" things he fails to do, or doing things that defeat one another. Given this broad tendency, it is easy to see why traditional exhortations to "use a little more willpower" are seldom of any avail, and the irony is that the alcoholic's false sense of omnipotence created an actual condition of growing impotence.

2. *The embattled self.* Here we meet the alcoholic in his aggressive or defiant mode. McClelland and others (1972) have shown that male problem drinkers have an unusually high need to assert power over people and situations. Working from a different body of data, Bateson (1971) reached a similar conclusion. He suggested that this need for power plays an especially important role in the relapse process. The problem drinker is marked by a distinctive style of action: He bends most of his energies against what he takes to be *challenges*. As his condition worsens, he begins to treat most of his life as a contest and sees everyone and everything as potential opponents, a tendency that may alone suffice to promote drinking ("She don't want me to drink, I'll show her"). However, it is most pernicious when the "worthy opponent" is drink itself. The problem is that the alcoholic works to abstain from drinking only so long as he perceives this task as a challenge ("I can leave it alone"). But as soon as he succeeds, the challenge dwindles and his motivation slackens. Eventually another challenge appears: to show he "can take a drink." The result is an endless series of binges followed by earnest attempts to reform.

3. *The accountable self.* Despite his defiance and aggressiveness, at some level the alcoholic feels enormous guilt over the havoc he has wrought. Just as he exercises his will alone and fights his battles alone, the alcoholic also feels himself to be sole author of his failures. These represent a terrible burden, one he seeks constantly to deny, hence the notorious "touchiness" of the alcoholic and his endless need for self-justifying excuses. Of course, guilt of this kind is hardly functional since, as the drinker soon learns, the best anodyne for its pain is more alcohol.

Some of these tendencies promote self-defeating behavior and continued drinking in their own right. When taken together, however, they have the added effect of driving the alcoholic into a kind of radical isolation. He comes increasingly to see himself as a solitary actor pitted against the world. He sustains his peculiar way of being with a kind of dogged pride but he can never bear it for long. Luckily (or unluckily) there always remains one way of softening the boundaries, of merging with the world for a while. This, of course, is drink—"the poor man's mysticism," as Aldous Huxley called it. Reports from recovered alcoholics suggest that this is the true appeal of the "bender." For a brief moment, every contradiction vanishes, all things are possible, and his old enemies (even his "worthy opponent") become friends.

Therapeutic Effects. My aim up to now has been to show that many of the key attitudes found among alcoholics reflect an exaggerated sense of personal agency in events and that these attitudes play a central role in the psychology of compulsive drinking. I would like to argue now that the AA ideology may be understood as a specific and thorough antidote to this way of being. Its prime therapeutic function is to induce a wide-ranging contradiction in the member's sense of agency. *To absorb the AA message is to see oneself much less the author of events in life, the active fighter and doer, and much more as a person with the wisdom to accept limitations and wait for things to come.* These changes provide the member both with a sound defense against alcohol and with a greater reduction in his need for it. A brief review of the ideological tenets noted earlier may show how they serve this end.

1. *Nature of Alcoholism.* Athough AA's two views of compulsive drinking may appear logically inconsistent, they harmonize very nicely when viewed from a practical or persuasive standpoint. In its own way, each of these views nudges the alcoholic to relinquish his sense of being "in charge" of his life and to accept a more limited assessment of his powers. The belief that alcoholism is a permanent disease does this in two ways which are both of great therapeutic importance. In the first place, it removes the whole issue of drinking from the voluntary sphere. The member who accepts his impaired status knows that he cannot drink in moderation. The issue is already decided. He *is* an alcoholic, and if he tries to drink he *must* fail. In addition, this realization lifts much of the guilt that plagues the account-

able self. If the alcoholic is the victim of a disease, then he is hardly to be blamed for his actions. In many cases, this discovery brings enormous relief. "The first chapters [of the Big Book] were a revelation to me. I wasn't the only person who felt and behaved like this! I wasn't mad or vicious. I was a sick person. I was suffering from an actual disease that had a name and symptoms like diabetes or cancer or TB—and a disease was respectable, not a moral stigma" (Alcoholics Anonymous, 1955, p. 227).

AA's contention that compulsive drinking arises from "selfishness" is not quite the moralistic attack that it seems. When we examine statements of this kind in context, either in the Big Book or in stories told by members, they almost always refer to something like the isolation and exaggerated sense of agency mentioned above. The Big Book speaks of the alcoholic, for instance, as a kind of stage director who tries to "arrange" everything in his life and thus meets constant frustration. He is "like an actor who wants to run the whole show; is forever trying to arrange the lights, the ballet, the scenery, and the rest of the actors in his own way. If his arrangements would only stay put, if only people would do as he wished, the show would be great. . . . What usually happens? The show doesn't come off very well. He begins to think life doesn't treat him right. He decides to exert himself more. He becomes on the next occasion still more demanding or gracious, as the case may be. . . . What is his basic trouble? Is he not really a self-seeker even when trying to be kind? Is he not a victim of the delusion that he can wrest satisfaction and happiness out of this world if only he manages well?" (Alcoholics Anonymous, 1955, pp. 60–61).

The kind of language that AA invokes against such behavior is distinctly religious in flavor but it also contains a major psychological insight. Its primary therapeutic benefit is to give the alcoholic a moral reason for letting go, for asking less of himself, and for putting his trust in forces that lie beyond his conscious effort.

2. *"Hitting bottom."* I have suggested that AA seeks to end the alcoholic's self-defeating battle for mastery over the events of his life. But a battle, especially a battle of this kind,

does not end without surrender. Only a deep-seated experience
of defeat will convince the alcoholic that he is *not* in control.
"Hitting bottom" provides this experience and readies the
drinker for a new and more modest view of his capacities.

   3. *The Higher Power* represents the positive side of this
change. If the self is to become less of an agent in daily life,
something else must take its place. For the AA member, the
Higher Power fills this role, gradually becoming the real author
of everything worthwhile. Where originally the alcoholic had
acted by trying to impose his will upon the world, now he tries
to live by the maxim "Thy will be done." Action ideally becomes a matter of trying, doing what one can, and leaving the
rest to God. (To the outsider, of course, the AA member may
seem more active than before he joined. The point is that action
is now *construed* very differently.) Because the Higher Power is
a warm, nonjudgmental figure, it also does much to relieve the
alcoholic's sense of isolation, replacing the supportive or "mys-
tical" role once played by drink. In this sense, the whole of AA
may function as a Higher Power for its members. In addition,
AA members contact the Higher Power daily in prayers asking
for humility, tolerance, and an end to resentments "in God's
good time." This exercise would seem an almost ideal therapy
for someone overly given to assertions of personal will. Its effect is nicely illustrated in a member's comment in the *Grapevine* some years ago: "Although my defects of character are
shrinking slightly as I try to practice the principles of Alcoholics
Anonymous, I am beginning to understand that if they are ever
removed completely, it will be because I allow the forces or
powers, or whatever this function is in a human being (which
most people call God) to take over and eliminate them for me.
It will not be my willpower or my 'strength' that will do it."

   4. *The moral inventory*, with its related steps of confession, forgiveness, and amends toward others is highly effective
as a release for the alcoholic's long-standing burden of guilt. It
also helps to arrest the endless stream of denials and alibis that
isolate him by poisoning his relations with others. In addition,
these steps provide the alcoholic with a modest, sober, and systematic way of putting his good intentions back in touch with
his actions, thus combatting his tendency to unrealistic volitions.

5. *Twelfth-stepping* offers at least two important benefits. In his efforts to help drinking alcoholics, the member receives constant object lessons in the seriousness of alcoholism and in the need for constant vigilance. Where his efforts succeed, they provide continuing personal demonstration of the power of AA, whereas failures are easily written off to the prospect's unreadiness.

Twelfth-stepping also has another, more interesting value: It represents a very nice exercise in "nonagentive" action. The twelfth-stepper can never *compel* his prospect to sober up or have a conversion experience (in fact, he is specifically enjoined against any such effort). All he can do is create opportunities, leaving the rest to his prospect, to fate, and to the Higher Power.

Recovery, Inc.

Ideology of Recovery. Recovery's teachings find their most important expression in the book *Mental Health Through Will-Training* (1950) authored by the group's founder Dr. Abraham Low. Unfortunately, the unusual language of the work and the apparent inconsistencies render a direct summary very problematic. Hence what follows is already an interpretation, an attempt to render Low's system as faithfully as possible into everyday English. Thus distilled, it comes down to four basic points:

1. *Authority of the doctor.* Most patients attending Recovery are also seeing a physician or psychiatrist at the same time. In early years, this figure was Dr. Low himself. Since Low's death in 1954, members have seen private doctors, and no professionals have played a direct role in the organization. It remains a crucial tenet of Recovery teaching, however, that *the doctor is always right*. To question the doctor's diagnosis is to take the first step in undermining health. There is an important hidden assumption here—that the member's psychiatrist, whatever his views, is offering a brand of supportive therapy that emphasizes his client's basic soundness. (Given Recovery's particular clientele, this assumption is not wholly unreasonable.) Thus to accept the doctor's "diagnosis" is to believe oneself essentially well, or at least getting better.

2. *The Will*. Dr. Low maintains that, no matter what stress he or she faces, every human being retains a certain autonomous power of choice. The seat of this choosing faculty is the Will, which lies within a kind of impregnable bastion at the center of each person. Despite appearances, Low maintains, no emotional force can unseat or even influence the vigilant Will. Thus nobody can capitulate to stress without secretly choosing to do so, and the person who succumbs has only himself to blame. The reason is that no stressful experience is every wholly real; properly tutored, we can learn to ignore it and go on acting.

3. *Illusions of illness*. Recovery offers two explanations for the *appearance* of illness that continues to beset group members. The first points to some mixture of habit and defeatist language. In many cases, the member is someone who has been ill (that is, hospitalized); as a result, he is still prone to using "sick" language about himself, to speaking of "setbacks," and "unbearable pains." Recovery teaches him a different language, a kind of "newspeak" that curtails unhealthy thoughts. Thus, "setback" becomes "lowered feeling" and "unbearable pain" becomes "bearable distress." In addition, Low maintains that if anyone practices Recovery methods for two months and still find that his troubles persist, the reason is that he *secretly indulges them*. Without realizing it, he is probably engaging in "self-diagnosis," and thus "sabotaging the physician's efforts" (the cardinal sin for Recovery).

4. *Will-Training*. This, as the title of Low's book indicates, is the way Recovery defines its main therapeutic activity. The "training" seems to be a matter both of alerting the Will against its possible complicity with symptoms and of giving it ways to "stay in charge" in the face of any crisis. There are two prongs to this strategy.

The first is the *devaluation of feeling*. In Dr. Low's view, the Will is assailed constantly by a welter of conflicting thoughts, sensations, and emotions, most of them highly untrustworthy. One of its basic tasks is to choose among these, rejecting some and accepting others. Low (1950, p. 136) puts the crucial feature of this task very forcefully: "Get it into your heads that a human being has the power to choose what to believe and what not to believe. This power to choose is called the Will. The main beliefs between which the Will must choose are that in a given condition you are either secure or insecure. If you accept the thought that your head pressure is the result of a brain tumor you have formed the belief of insecurity. If instead you choose to think of a mere nervous headache you have rejected the belief of insecurity and put in its place that of security." The mark of a well-trained Will, then, is an ability to "accept the secure thought and reject the insecure one." In actual practice, however, Recovery seems much more concerned with ways of rejecting perceptions and feelings than with ways of accepting them. The essential technique is termed "spotting," the art of identifying and curtailing insecure thoughts before they get out of hand. Most of the group's slogans and formulas are directed to this end. Some of these ("I can bear the discomfort"; "There's no right and wrong in family affairs") negate the importance of events in the *outer environment* of social life and personal relations. Others ("Feelings are not facts"; "That's just fearful temper"; "It's only a trigger symptom"; "It's distressing but not dangerous") are meant to combat threats from the *inner environment*, the realm of emotions and somatic symptoms. The actual uses of these formulas are extremely varied. However, all of them seem to be ways of softening disturbing perceptions by treating them either as meaningless or as unable to affect the self.

If Recovery seems bent at points on the devaluation of feeling, it is equally bent on the *promotion of action*. This is the second prong of Will-Training. Just as the Will is free to reject threatening perceptions, it is also free to initiate actions that benefit the patient, even in the face of great anxiety or depression. The secret of this freedom is a technique that Dr. Low cryptically labels "muscle control." It is based on the simple fact that anyone, even a person who has "lost the desire to do anything," retains the power to move the muscles of the skeletal frame. If he moves them in the right order, he can go through the motions of being a normal human being. And this is precisely what Recovery tells him to do. The assumption is that "the muscles can reeducate the brain." If the member acts normal for a long enough period, he will begin to feel normal too. Much the same strategy applies to the daily trials of social life. Here members counsel one another, when beset by strange impulses and unpleasant thoughts, to practice "wearing the mask" and "controlling the speech muscles"—in other words, to keep up a solid pretense of normalcy. Their guiding principle under such conditions is "group-mindedness," which means behaving in accord with social obligations in spite of anything they may feel. The key assumption is that *being* normal is fundamentally a matter of acting that way.

Clientele of Recovery. Earlier I described the AA ideology as functioning to reduce the alcoholic's sense of agency in events. It seems that Recovery pursues just the opposite strategy, augmenting its members' sense of personal volition while teaching them to ignore experiences lying beyond their control. AA holds willpower to be almost useless, whereas Recovery holds it to be the secret of mental health. AA teaches that its members are diseased and powerless, whereas Recovery teaches that they are well and strong. I tried to explain the therapeutic effect of AA by presenting the alcoholic as someone whose overinflated sense of agency generated patterns of behavior that trapped him in the world of drink. It seems to me that, in a very special sense, the typical client of Recovery suffers from the inverse of this problem. He too is trapped in a vicious circle, but the cause is a severely diminished sense of his own power to act.

Recovery has always presented itself as an organization open to every sort of "nervous and former mental patient." However, my own experience and some limited statistical evidence indicate that Recovery's clientele is restricted in several important ways. Despite surface differences, most members of this group face a roughly common phenomenology of illness. First, as Grosz (1972) notes in reporting the results of an extensive survey, Recovery's membership hardly represents the full spectrum of mental disorders in the United States. Most members, he noted, had been having depressive, psychosomatic, or anxiety symptoms. On the basis of my observation of the group, I would add phobias and obsessions to his list. All these problems are alike in two respects: All are distinctly unpleasant, and all fall into that broad class of disturbances that psychoanalysts call *ego-alien*. That is, in all cases the disturbance presents itself to the patient as something quite beyond himself and his wishes, an external force that "comes on" him or "takes over." At no time in my Recovery fieldwork did I find a member, for example, whose difficulty lay in the areas of the perversions, or megalomania, or hebrephrenic schizophrenia. In each case, the disorder manifested itself in discrete, unpleasant, and ego-alien experiences. Three additional factors serve to amplify and complicate this primary fact. First, according to Grosz, less than 20 percent of Recovery's clientele have had any education beyond high school. This puts the average member well beyond the circle that Kadushin (1969) identifies as "the Friends and Supporters of Psychotherapy," and squarely in the therapeutic class that Orlinsky and Howard (1972) have labeled Type II. Members of this client group typically lack a complex introspective vocabulary and so tend to project and somatize emotional problems. They are also more likely to seek help from physicians than psychotherapists. Furthermore, over 50 percent of Recovery's members have been hospitalized for a psychiatric illness at some point before joining (Grosz, 1972). This humiliating experience oftens leads patients to a lingering self-definition as "sick" (that is, permanently impaired by illness). Finally, because all Recovery meetings are held outside mental hospitals and because they follow a tight, semiformal set of rules, they usually manage to exclude persons too disturbed for normal social interaction.

Taken together, all these factors lead to the following profile of a typical Recovery member: His problems manifest themselves in unpleasant, ego-alien experiences, which he interprets in medical rather than interpersonal or dynamic terms. He often views himself as sick or prone to sickness—by definition a state beyond his control. At the same time, he retains enough ego control to behave almost normally. The nature of his symptoms and his preference for physicians makes it likely that he is receiving some combination of medication and supportive therapy (confirming Recovery's tacit assumption on this score). Grosz (1972) observed that the disorders troubling most Recovery members fall into the chronic or recurrent category. In other words, most persons joining this group have experienced not just a single traumatic attack but a continuing series of relapses. I would propose that in persons of this type, relapses take place in accord with a consistent pattern: Some stressful experience in daily life leads to a rise in the general level of anxiety. This anxiety is then projected into one or several phobic, obsessive, or somatic symptoms. These symptoms have dire associations because the subject cannot help ascribing them to his old illness (possibly an illness for which he was "put away"). This association brings an increase in anxiety that intensifies his symptoms and leads to an upward spiral of panic. Once again, the subject has been defeated by "that terrifying feeling that comes out of the blue and just overwhelmed" him. The whole experience confirms his prior suspicion, namely, that he is a sick person, liable at any moment to attack by a mental illness that renders him helpless.

Therapeutic Effects. The Recovery ideology combats this vicious circle on several fronts.

1. In stressing the authority of the doctor (who assures the patient that he is well), Recovery not only counters the member's "sick" self-conception but also helps relegate his symptoms to the realm of imagination, where they have less force.
2. Low's depiction of the Will as an impregnable bastion is the explicit rationale for this voluntarism. But more importantly, it provides members a place of symbolic refuge in times of stress. They learn that they can never really be overwhelmed, that one faculty, the crucial one, always retains its freedom to act.
3. In ascribing the persistence of illness to tacit "self-indulgence," Recovery carries this approach to its logical conclusion. Symptoms are shown to draw their power not from any external force (like a physical illness) but from the victim's own consent to them. (They aren't "its" doing, but "mine.") The gruff language ("malingering," "sabotage," "coddling," and the like) serves to drive this message home, employing mild shame as a way of exorcising old habits of fear.
4. In devaluing feelings while stressing the importance of action, Recovery makes shrewd use of an old phenomenological truth. The quality of subjective experience, especially its affective

dimension, is never amenable to direct control. We cannot be happy just by deciding to be. A therapy that seeks to augment volition must find ways of belittling experiences intractable to will, and Recovery does just this. Publicly visible action, however, is the province of the will par excellence; hence it is the ideal place to augment feelings of control and agency. There is no doubt that the experience of seeing oneself act normally in public situations and of being accepted as normal by others provides an enormous boost to self-confidence.

5. Finally, the formulas used to devalue threatening experiences help to check the vicious circle of relapse in two specific ways. Those treating "outer environment" give the member ways of writing off troublesome events before they can generate the kind of anxiety that leads to symptoms. Those treating "inner environment" help the member to sever the crucial link between the experience of symptoms and the conclusion that he or she is "ill again."

To show how these techniques work in practice, I offer the following example, originally given by one of Recovery's national spokesmen and based on his experience while speaking before a closed-circuit television camera at a state mental hospital.

> As I started to give the introductory talk about Recovery's history I had an uneasy feeling . . . because I was looking directly at the camera and the cameraman instead of . . . the audience as I am accustomed to do. I had the feeling that I was performing in a mechanical way, rather than in such a way as to clearly express my feelings of interest and concern for the patients, self assurance in my delivery, and so on. I began to work myself up.
>
> But I spotted this reaction as fearful temper —that is, self distrust. I spotted that I could command face muscles, my speech muscles, and the muscles of my body to demonstrate self-confidence. I endorsed myself several times for my con-

trol of the fearful temper. This was indicated by
commanding the eye muscles to keep looking into
the camera and [the neck muscles] to keep the
head in the correct position, with the shoulders up,
and commanding the speech muscles to modulate
the voice. . . .

As I practiced relaxation by bearing discomfort I began to *feel* that I really was spontaneously
talking to the patients out there in the wards. Later . . . the director of the TV program told me
I had good presence before the camera.

Before Recovery I would have been convinced that I could not act spontaneously if I did
not *feel* spontaneous. I would not have looked
directly into the TV camera but away from it, because of the fear that I might look again like I was
mentally ill. . . . I would have developed sweats,
severe difficulty in concentrating, . . . a continued
lack of spontaneity, and self-consciousness [Raiff,
1978, p. 10].

To conclude this very schematic summary, it should be
evident that the ideology of Recovery is directed against most
of the attitudes that seem to underlie the chronic relapses typ-
ifying this group's clientele. If these attitudes, in a special sense,
constitute a diminished experience of volition or personal agency, then the whole Recovery strategy is an attempt to augment
this experience. In this special sense, the ideologies of AA and
Recovery represent mirror images of each other, and their opposition is explained by an equally marked opposition in the
phenomenology of the problem they treat.

Synanon

Synanon is a much more complex organization than either
AA or Recovery, Inc. It has no Big Book, and its ideology has
shifted in important ways over the past two decades. Its program is a residential one; its members now include persons from
all walks of life—not only addicts and criminals but also many
respectable citizens. There have been recent indications, in fact,

that Synanon may be abandoning its original therapeutic aims in favor of a somewhat different role as an experimental community. For all these reasons, a full discussion of the group's current ideology would be both impractical and inappropriate here. However, since Synanon built its reputation on the rehabilitation of heroin addicts, and since in this capacity it has provided the underlying model for nearly all other antidrug communities in America, I would like to examine just a few of Synanon's most basic and permanent teachings, showing how they have helped the group's addict members to live free of drugs (members must abstain from alcohol and drugs as a condition of residence).

Ideology of Synanon. A cornerstone of the whole Synanon system is a distinction drawn within the organization between two separate fields of action: "the Floor" and "the Game." "The Floor" is Synanese for the world of everyday life among members, either on the organization's premises or elsewhere. "The Game" refers to the special sessions of attack therapy that engage all members several nights a week. These two fields are in many ways polar opposites.

1. *The Floor.* At Synanon the Floor is marked by a rigid and intricate set of standards for behavior. In spite of their demanding character, these standards do not usually take the form of rules. Instead, members are asked to "assume certain attitudes," and to carry these into the minutest particulars of conduct. One such attitude is: "This is your home and people here are your family." In practice, especially for the newcomer, this means saying "Hi!" to everyone encountered in the hallway, conversing soberly and pleasantly with others at meals, wiping up a bathroom sink each time one uses it, and "pulling up" (correcting) anyone else whose conduct is out of order. Another attitude is that "the job you're doing is the most important in the world." This means that performance on any task of Synanon—from fixing an engine to washing the dishes—must show a perfectionist's care for detail. Naturally, Synanon recognizes that these attitudes may not reflect the real feelings of members. The point is that on the Floor an individual's feelings, especially such negative ones as resentment, frustration, or boredom, do

not really matter. They are "garbage" and should be ignored. What matters is conduct. As leaders point out, Synanon asks only that the members "go through the motions," that they "act as if" they cared. At the same time, this act must be a thorough and persuasive one. (During my visit, I saw members upbraided in Games for such minor lapses of "attitude" as staring out a window briefly or failing to return a coffee cup.) Furthermore, since time is closely scheduled and space is organized to make most activities public, the Floor offers few opportunities to set the act aside.

2. *The Game*. Members view the Game as the Heart of Synanon and the secret of the organization's success. They believe that when properly played, the Game solves virtually all personal and social problems.

A typical Game lasts three or four hours and involves roughly twelve players seated in a circle. Strictly speaking, the Game has no rules; short of physical violence, players may say or do anything they wish. In practice, however, most Games consist of a series of "indictments" directed against individual players, each running fifteen to thirty minutes. The aim of an indictment, according to one Synanon regent, is "to push a person into a corner, to the point where his rationality fails him." Usually one player initiates the attack, but others soon join in, accusing, teasing, and provoking the target player until he "breaks," either by crying or by exploding in anger. This climax usually opens the way for a quieter period in which the target shares current feelings or problems with the group while others respond with constructive advice. Normally, this process continues until all present have been targets.

3. *Ideology Surrounding the Game*. When they speak of the Game, Synanon members tend to invoke a striking number of incremental images. They describe it as a place for "dumping garbage," "emptying your gut," and "blowing out the tubes." Charles Dederich, Synanon's founder, has portrayed the Game as an "emotional bathroom." Expressions like these leave the sense that the Game is mainly a place for discharging a toxic and dangerous substance that everyone accumulates.

The explicit rationale for this view lies in Synanon's conception of the Game's essence, an activity known as "breaking contracts." "Contract" here is Synanese for an agreement that anyone makes with himself or others, consciously or unconsciously, not to discuss something. The assumption is that all members in the course of daily life enter tacit contracts of various kinds. Two members working a common job detail, for instance, may develop a friendship that keeps them from reporting or correcting each other's mistakes. Or a subordinate may stifle his anger at a supervisor out of fear of reprisals. Or a newcomer, motivated by pride, may refuse to voice the frustration and loneliness he feels in his early weeks at Synanon. In all of these cases, someone is "contracted out"—he is concealing part of himself from others. Synanon teaches that contracts of any kind pose serious dangers. They rob the individual of energy and impose an increasing burden of anxiety, guilt, and depression that may eventually drive him to "split" (leave the community). Thus Synanon teaches its members that the secret of well-being and the cure for nearly all psychic ills is to "use your Game," "break your contracts," and "make your life public." Leaders explain this idea to newcomers with a kind of gastric or intestinal image. They speak of "red spots" that "build up inside the human gut" whenever feelings or problems go unshared. The point emphasized is that whenever a member feels unusually anxious, discouraged, or restless, he may be sure that "red spots" are the cause. The remedy, accordingly, is to "empty his gut" in a Synanon Game, sharing all unconfessed fears, resentments, and misdeeds with the group. Leaders insist that while this process is frightening at first, it inevitably brings relief and a new sense of lightness and ease. As a House Director in San Francisco explained to a group of relative newcomers: "Sure it's scary to cop out on yourself or someone else. But you'll never get hurt. You'll just have to take the plunge and trust the process. You'll be amazed at what happens. You'll come out of it feeling light as a feather. Of course you have to do it regularly. It's a bit like brushing your teeth. So long as you keep playing the Game and breaking your contracts, you'll feel great."

For Synanon members, the Game provides an almost daily exercise in the truth of these statements. One has only to witness the nervous silence that precedes a Game and the relaxed ebullience that follows it to understand why participants find Synanon's explanation of "red spots" and its teaching about "contracts" an accurate map of reality.

The Heroin Addict. The great puzzle of heroin addiction is not why people get "hooked" on the drug, but why so many of them (fully 97 percent according to one study) go back to it after complete detoxification. A variety of theories have sought to provide answers, but none has been wholly satisfactory. The view most widely accepted today asserts that prolonged heroin use brings certain changes in body chemistry that create a permanent "metabolic hunger" for opiates (Dole and Nyswander, 1967). As a result of these changes, even after he is fully detoxified the addict is subject to intermittent attacks of the "postaddiction syndrome," a shifting combination of anxiety, depression, and craving for the drug. For this reason, advocates have argued that the only effective therapy for addicts is regular administration of a substance like methadone that quells the metabolic hunger but still permits normal functioning.

There is an impressive body of evidence to support this theory. A number of very different studies testify to the strength and durability of the postaddiction syndrome (Martin, 1972; O'Donnell, 1969; Trussell, 1969). Research with detoxified addicts in a state of enforced abstinence (maintained by detention or by administration of a narcotic antagonist like cyclazocine) has shown that levels of anxiety and depression become so high as to impair normal functioning (Chappel and others, 1971; Freedman and others, 1967). Studies of the few ex-addicts who do abstain on their own have revealed an extremely high rate of alcoholism (Stevenson and others, 1956).

At the same time, important doubts remain. A growing body of research appears to argue for the influence of a psychological factor in the postaddiction syndrome (Martin, 1972; Martin and others, 1973; Wikler, 1965). The populations of Synanon and its various replicas (Gateway House, Daytop Village, and others) include many ex-addicts whose habits were extreme by any standard. And yet these members show remarkably few signs of the postaddiction syndrome. The energy and creativity of Synanon's addicts stand in sharp contrast to the depression and alcoholism found among heroin abstainers in other contexts.

For these and other reasons, some observers have suggested that the postaddiction syndrome may actually be the work of two distinct components. The first is a metabolic problem, but one that is very general in its effects. It simply reduces the addict's tolerance for stress, making him unusually prone to states of anxiety and depression. The second component is the result of a conditioning process built up over long years of heroin use. In the course of this process, the addict comes increasingly to experience pleasurable or tension-free states as directly caused by the heroin in his system. More importantly, however, he loses the ability to recognize the practical and interpersonal reasons for feelings of stress. His keen interest in avoiding withdrawal has taught him to attend closely to these feelings, but only as the first signs that his "fix" is wearing off. The strong association between emotional tension and impending withdrawal eventually yields a state in which any severe emotional strain may trigger a bout of withdrawal sickness, complete with chills, nausea, and muscular cramps. Clinical studies have shown that this effect may persist for years after detoxification (Goldstein, 1972; Wikler, 1965). And that it is even found occasionally among addicts whose metabolic needs are being met by methadone (Whitehead, 1974).

If the hypothesis described here is valid, then it provides the basis for a more flexible view of the relapse process. My understanding of that process draws on two additional facts. First, it is well known that the "high" provided by heroin is in essence a feeling of *insulation* or *detachment* from the environment (Chein, 1966; Gerard, 1968), a sense of "inviolability" as Trocchi (1960) called it. In the words of another addict whose biography has become a classic in the literature: "One of the biggest effects of horse is that you simply do not worry about the things you worried about before. You look at them in a different way. . . . Everything is always cool, everything is all right. It makes you feel like not fighting the world" (Hughes, 1961). The strong association between this feeling and the relief of stress tends to shape the addict's response to all stressful situations. Instead of confronting them directly, he tries to "tune them out" or minimize their importance (Chein,1964, pp. 201–208). Furthermore, owing to his criminal activities and to the notorious unreliability of his fellow users, the addict often drifts into a more literal detachment from his environment; he becomes a loner. He tends increasingly to view all transactions with others as "hassles" and to relish the solitary relief from hassles that heroin affords (Waldorf, 1973).

In effect, physiological, social, and cognitive factors have conspired to maximize the "pulls" toward renewed drug use while minimizing the countervailing "pushes." The pulls are a direct result of the addict's low tolerance for stress and his tendency to experience all stress as craving for heroin. Since the addict has trouble locating the interpersonal sources of stress, he is also less likely to confront them and take corrective action before they exceed his threshold of tolerance. At the same time, the addict's long-standing pursuit of emotional detachment and social isolation renders him singularly immune to institutional controls that might help to check temptation. He is unlikely to have a strong investment in family or career. And if by some chance he does, he is likely to cope with the demands they make in the same way that he copes with other forms of stress—by "tuning out" or trying to feel detached rather than by changing his behavior. Thus even without the pulls of the postaddiction syndrome, the addict stands in grave danger of simply drifting back into heroin use.

Therapeutic Effects. The elements of the Synanon ideology reviewed above may be understood as a concerted attack on all the features of this relapse process.

1. *The Floor.* The intricate and demanding standards of the Floor serve a number of important functions within Synanon. From the viewpoint of the addict, however, their greatest value may lie in their power to redirect attention. The addict is likely to be someone closely attuned to his own levels of stress and quite out of touch with his social environment. The Floor calls for a reversal of these habits. Unpleasant feelings are "garbage," and only behavior matters. Activity on the Floor is so tightly scheduled and requires such close attention to detail

(saying "Hi" to everyone; doing a job according to instructions) that there are few opportunities to brood upon inner states. Thus the Floor teaches that stress can be mastered by a simple process of ignoring it, doing one's job, and "acting as if" all is well.

2. *The Game*. While the regimen of the Floor provides a measure of control over tensions, it hardly eliminates them. The Game represents a superb device for purging these feelings, at least for a limited period. Its very structure seems contrived to generate cathartic expressions on a routine basis. The "indictment" system, with its wild teasing and unfair accusations, begins by locating hidden anxieties or tensions and then drives them to unbearable levels. Unable to deflect these feelings by taking a drug or by "tuning out," the target player is forced to vent them in a way that he never did as an addict—with a paroxysm of rage or tears. Doing so brings him sudden relief, of two kinds: The tensions within mysteriously subside, and his fellow players show him a new warmth and closeness.

I would hypothesize that the Synanon Game works as a functional alternative to heroin in relieving the chronic stress experienced by abstaining addicts. The Game may be the most important reason for the well-being found among Synanon's addict residents. However, whereas heroin relieves stress by a process of distancing or detachment, the Game relieves it by intensifying feelings until they find an expressive outlet.

3. *Ideology Surrounding the Game*. The effects of this cathartic experience, repeated over time, run well beyond the simple discharge of tension. Playing the Game regularly is also a learning process and a form of conditioning, and it has its own cognitive influence.

For Synanon's members, the Game functions as an exercise in a new theory of stress. They discover that playing the Game relieves feelings that once were remedied only by taking drugs. As a result of this discovery, which is strengthened with each successive Game, they begin to experience their intermittent anxiety and depression in a different fashion. Instead of pointing to the need for more heroin, these feelings come to indicate the member's need to "empty his gut," to play another

Game soon. Thus the Game experience gradually reshapes the whole meaning of stress. It helps to destroy the link between emotional tensions and withdrawal pains and to substitute a more benign perception.

Synanon does not teach that contracts are just vague feelings in need of expression. Contracts arise through someone's failure to confront a definite interpersonal problem. "Breaking a contract" means finding the problem and talking about it. "Indictments" are attacks against specific acts or habits of behavior. In launching them, accusers often break contracts of their own. Most important of all, when the target player finally "breaks," his outburst is usually a new admission of thought or deed. As a result of the contract idea, then, playing the Game does more than redefine feelings of stress. It differentiates them, gradually restoring a sense of their interpersonal origins, with the positive result that when experienced players feel tense or upset, they have little difficulty in ascribing their feelings to tangible causes. Often they use the Game itself to take corrective action.

Synanon teaches that "breaking a contract" is more than just confronting a problem; it is sharing it with the group. The Game, in fact, is an arrangement that allows a player to relieve his private tensions only in an act of opening himself to others. This arrangement has an interesting consequence. Whenever a player reveals some new truth about himself, he is also forging certain emotional bonds with those who hear him. As religious groups ever since the Essenes have known, mutual confession is a powerful source of mutual loyalty. The result is that a player emerges from an effective Game not only feeling refreshed and relaxed but also feeling a new closeness to his fellow players. Repeated over time, this process builds strong ties with the Synanon community at large.

The Synanon Game has harnessed the most basic need of the addict—his need to discharge stress—in a way that strengthens his relationships with others. The process that relieves his tensions also deepens his emotional investments. Viewed in this light, the Game is a perfect antidote to heroin and its long-range effects. Like heroin, the Game combats stress. But whereas heroin does so at the cost of emotional detachment and social isolation, the Game does so in a way that promotes a deeper engagement in the group and its values. This engagement in turn provides a strong bulwark against the temptation to "split" and return to the world of drugs.

Systems of Meaning and Their Importance

The foregoing discussion of AA, Recovery, Inc., and Synanon have been much too brief and skeletal to yield systematic conclusions. But even outlines of this kind permit certain inferences, and two of these deserve our parting attention. The first is simple and practical; the second, theoretical and rather less precise.

The main burden of this report has been to show that the benefits conferred by peer therapy groups are closely linked with the systems of meaning they generate. The precise nature and effect of these systems may be open to dispute. What should be clear by now, however, is that the connections between ideology and therapy are substantial, intricate, and often far from obvious. This point has a special importance for professionals and policy makers working in this area of peer psychotherapy. Whenever outsiders try to support or cooperate with one of these organizations, they run some risk of tampering with its ideology. This may happen quite inadvertently. Sometimes the mere involvement of a professional can weaken the meaning of certain teachings (for example, "Only a drunk can help another drunk"). Matters become worse if the observer should point out that a given belief runs against medical knowledge, or if he or she counsels changes to increase the group's acceptability in professional circles. If the view developed here has been valid, then meddling of this kind would do real harm to the therapeutic process. Thus the first rule for professionals working with these groups must be a scrupulous respect for their teachings.

My second point concerns the broad theoretical picture suggested by this investigation. We have seen that each of the organizations considered here achieves its effects by counteracting certain key attitudes that typify its client group. Thus,

AA counters the assertiveness of alcoholics by teaching surrender; Recovery, Inc. blocks the habitual surrender of former mental patients by promoting willpower; and Synanon reverses the addict's social and emotional detachment through a process that expresses feelings and strengthens social engagement. This pattern suggests that there may be identifiable logic that governs all peer therapy organizations: Every affliction has its typical attitude or style of action, every therapy group its countervailing ideology. Once this logic is understood, we may be able to construct a typology of afflictions based on a small number of basic attitudes that sustain them. Such a typology would provide a systematic explanation for broad similarities and differences found among the ideologies of successful groups. It might even yield some modest predictions about the viability of new organizations.

Given the current state of our knowledge in this field, however, such ambitions remain utopian. Our first and most pressing need is for more hard research on these groups—not just ethnographic work but quantitative studies on client characteristics, turnover rates, therapeutic outcome, and similar matters. It is only by amassing a solid fund of such information that we can hope to move beyond interesting conjectures and toward a verifiable theory.

CHAPTER 13

Emergence of Ideology in a Bereaved Parents Group

Barry Sherman

In the previous chapter, Antze asserts that self-help groups possess special systems of teaching which members believe to be the secret of recovery. He argues that such teachings or ideologies exert a persuasive function by inducing standardized changes of outlook at a deep level among the membership, and sees the victims of particular shared afflictions as being in a socially standardized situation where they develop common outlooks and attitudes. He speculates that a self-help group's ideology functions as a cognitive antidote to common, shared features of a condition, that the ideologies of peer therapy groups may be seen as extremely shrewd and insightful attacks on the most harmful of these standardized implications. The essence of Antze's statement is that self-help groups achieve their effects through an ideology that counteracts key attitudes toward an affliction shared by its victims. The benefits conferred by peer therapy are closely linked with the system of meaning generated and the prescribed norms.

Antze's conceptual schema has been applied only to Alcoholics Anonymous, Recovery, Inc., and Synanon. These groups can be characterized in Levy's terms as organizations whose objective is some form of conduct reorganization or behavioral control, as contrasted with groups that emphasize coping with a common stressful predicament (Levy, 1976). Behavioral control groups generally deal with a recurrent or chronic, debilitating personal problem that may be harmful to others. A stressful event where an individual, family, or group find themselves in a sudden unpredictable situation over which they have little control—such as the loss of a child—is a situational and social event that affects many people. This chapter attempts to extend Antze's paradigm beyond behavioral control groups and apply it to Compassionate Friends, a self-help group for parents who have lost a child.

The goal of most behavioral control groups is to eliminate or control problematic behavior. With an addictive disorder, the ideology attempts to counter habitual self-destructive attitudes and beliefs held by an individual. In coping with bereavement, the intention is not to eliminate grieving behavior but rather to reconceptualize it and put it in an adaptive perspective. Changing one's attitude about self is necessary, but for complete adaptation, one must reestablish and redefine relationships with others who may have been estranged. Bereaved parents particularly face challenges in internal family relationships and social reintegration. It is my assertion that for conditions such as bereavement, "cognitive antidotes" are required not only to counter the attitudes and feelings around one's own behavior but also to redirect the way one perceives and interprets the behavior of significant others.

This chapter aims to explore the ideology of a stress-coping self-help group and to compare and contrast its function with the ideology of behavioral control groups. In adapting Antze's model to this case, I shall follow a parallel method. On the basis of participant observations of five Compassionate Friends groups in the Chicago area and numerous personal interviews with members, I shall describe the experience of being a bereaved parent by identifying three major predicaments or "standardized situations" faced by them—maladaptive responses, family relationships, and social reintegration—and suggest how these situations are addressed by relevant tenets of the ideology. The categories of *maladaptive responses* and *social reintegration* are presented as specific examples of problem areas faced by a particular stress-coping group that are not as central in the focus of behavioral control groups.

Experience of Being a Bereaved Parent

In our society, the death of a child is a severely stressful event. It is a rare occurrence and is experienced as qualitatively different from the deaths of other close relatives or friends. One of the most frequent complaints voiced by bereaved parents toward professionals and well-meaning friends and relatives is their tendency to equate the death of a child with other losses. As one woman stated: "When I went to the local mental health center they didn't know how to handle me. They tried to tell me that the death of my daughter was similar to the death of a parent or a friend. They had no idea that Pam's death would *never* seem similar to any other death or loss. They drove me away from their 'help' by trivializing the meaning of my daughter's death by equating it to other deaths." Several widows in Compassionate Friends disclosed that coping with the loss of their child was much more difficult than adjustment to the loss of their husbands. One woman, whose husband had died a few years before her son died in an automobile accident, explicitly stated that she felt that the two losses were incomparable: "When a woman loses her husband, she feels alone and left with incredible sorrow, but when your child dies, it's as if you lose part of yourself—your future and your hope. In no way was my grief following my husband's death the same as my grief when my son died."

The magnitude of the loss creates a crisis situation in which the adaptive capacities of the individual are tested in totally unique ways. The death of a child is always an unexpected shock. There is absolutely no forewarning. The consequences for the parents are more devastating than from other traumatic and trying situations they have faced. Members whose children died of long-term illness reported feeling that they had been afforded the time for anticipatory grief work and even felt relieved by the eventual death. However, parents who experience the sudden traumatic loss of their child are denied this opportunity and may react in a more disquieted fashion. One bereaved father remembered his sudden trauma: "It was the occasion of a religious holiday. Everybody was in the house getting dressed for church. Johnny finished getting ready before anyone else so he went out in the front yard to play. Minutes later we heard a loud crash from inside the house. Everybody ran out to discover that a reckless driver had driven up on the lawn and stricken Johnny. He was instantly killed. We exploded in an outrage of disbelief. Our healthy, happy son was gone."

Although a multitude of problems face bereaved parents, most complaints surface around impaired functioning or communication problems in the areas of personal adjustment, family relationships, and social reintegration.

Personal Maladaptive Responses

Denial. Typically most bereaved parents experience a compelling propensity to deny that the death really happened. Lindemann (1944) and Parkes (1972) have documented that denial is part of normal grieving, particularly in the immediate aftermath of the death. A couple whose son was shot down in a helicopter in Vietnam, but never positively identified, exemplified this inclination by saying that they "could never give up the hope that their only son was still alive." Another woman, whose daughter died after a sudden rare viral disease, stated that even though she had sat by her daughter's bedside in the hospital for two days and had been with her daugher when she died, she still felt her daughter's presence around the house. These experiences persisted for years after the child's death.

Anger and Guilt. Where a person is apparently responsible for the death, that individual often becomes the object of intense rage. Outraged parents may attempt to seek revenge and even threaten the responsible person with violence. A woman

whose daughter had been raped and killed reported feeling even more anger when the criminal was sentenced to life imprisonment. For her, it simply was not a fair exchange for her daughter's life. The due process of law was not just enough in her eyes.

Bereaved parents also reported more generalized feelings of anger and rage. One woman reported: "If anyone even *looked* at me, I'd feel myself burning up, and if they spoke to me, I couldn't keep myself from snapping back—I despised everyone." A minister revealed: "My personal torment was when I despaired in the God I had always turned to. My love and reverence turned to bitterness and hate. I hated my life; I hated everything and everyone around me. I was sure God had forsaken me."

The problem is further complicated if one of the parents feels truly responsible for the child's death. Feelings of guilt and self-blame can be so overwhelming that they incapacitate day-to-day functioning. The parent feels vulnerable to accusations by others and plagued by preoccupying thoughts of "if only I had done something differently it wouldn't have happened." A young woman unveiled her continuing feelings of guilt and responsibility: "I had put the baby to bed for the afternoon and my girlfriend and I were chatting over a cup of tea in the living room. The baby began to cry so I gave him an old feather pillow which was on the sewing table awaiting mending of a hole. He went right to sleep. An hour or so later when I went in to check on him I discovered that he was not breathing. The autopsy report stated that he had inhaled down and suffocated. If only I had sewn the pillow before placing it in the crib, my baby would still be alive." Many bereaved parents discover that it is futile to blame uncontrollable external forces so they blame themselves, perhaps as an attempt to gain control over something that they do have power to influence.

Despair and Depression. Intense feelings of depression, uniqueness, and isolation from the rest of the world are common to most bereaved parents. Many disclose a lack of motivation to do anything and have difficulty just getting out of bed and performing daily tasks. They experience a sense of purposelessness and meaninglessness in life that precipitates a desire to be dead also, and frequently disclose suicidal wishes. They try to answer existential questions such as "Why my child?" and can come up with no satisfying answers. Newly bereaved parents frequently break down and cry at their first attempt to mention the child's name and cause of death. Their appearances are often affected: Faces are ashen with eyes sunk in dark circles, posture is slouched, and there is frequent lip-biting.

Problems of Family Relationships

Contrary to the popular myth that "tragedy brings a family together," bereaved parents find that tragedy separates parents and alienates them from surviving children. Marital problems are exacerbated. As one bereaved father put it: "With the death of a child, the parents experience the deprivation of a sense of competence. Since they cannot blame a tumor or virus, or the unknown, they look for scapegoats and blame each other. Bereaved parents are multiply victimized: by the loss of the child they love, by the loss of dreams and hopes they had invested in that child, and by the loss of their own self-esteem resulting from the experience of helplessness. Bereaved parents feel they should be punished; since their child will never love or be happy again, neither can they love or be happy again" (Freireich, 1978). Each parent becomes a constant reminder to the other of the pain and loss. Sexual problems may result from guilt over sensual pleasures or fear of recreating the pain by having another child. Responses to the trauma are varied, and each recognizes that the other is undergoing changes. Suddenly one's mate becomes almost a stranger. Ironically, when they need each other the most, depression, guilt, and grief create an emotional chasm.

Surviving siblings in the family have also suffered the loss. Yet the very personalized suffering of the parents often inhibits meaningful communication with their other children. Surviving siblings have reportedly confessed feeling inferior to a dead brother or sister, that they could never measure up to the ideal image that their parents now present. Frequently, younger siblings possess fears that they too may die of the same cause or at the same age as their brother or sister. The love, assurance, and attention they require are often denied them, or parents may overreact to any activity that entails some degree of risk: spending a night away, swimming, sailing, or even driving the family car.

The loss of a family member creates other unsettling situations. What shall be done with pictures, mementos, and personal possessions of the deceased? And some parents frequently catch themselves routinely setting an extra place at the dining table.

Problem of Social Reintegration

In our society, people generally treat death—especially the death of a child—as a taboo subject and fail to realize that bereaved parents frequently would prefer to talk about their child's death. "Around the time of the death of the child, the parents are usually surrounded by the activity of caring relatives and friends who bring flowers, prepare meals, and make decisions for them. The bereaved parents are allowed free expression of grief at the funeral and during the mourning period thereafter. However, after a few weeks or months the anesthetic of the initial shock begins to wear off and the reality of the pain sets in. The relatives and friends who came so quickly have gone home to their own concerns and daily obligations. The bereaved parents often find themselves alone, uncared for, depressed in feelings of abandonment, and unable to cope with the painful readjustment to life without their beloved child" (Shamres, 1975). This quote captures what bereaved parents experience as the "conspiracy of silence" (Stephens, 1972).

The grief process also disturbs normal interpersonal relationships (Lindemann, 1944; Pollack, 1961). This disturbance may range from well-intending friends who make insensitive remarks such as "You're lucky, because you have other children," or "If your child had lived, he could have been an invalid," or "It's God's will," to relatives and friends who avoid bereaved families.

Such dissonance often makes bereaved parents feel like outcasts from everyday society. They feel victimized and alone, with no easy opportunities to discuss their feelings and experi-

ences with others who could fully sympathize, for it would be
rare and unexpected that a bereaved parent would routinely
come into social contact with other bereaved parents. Even if
they met, most social situations would not allow the kind of
open, in-depth communication needed. Home-bound wives face
an especially difficult situation since they are home alone with
all the reminders of the lost child.

Compassionate Friends

Chapter Format. In most chapters of Compassionate
Friends, there is a leader and/or board of officers who share
the responsibilities of recruiting, keeping records, and planning
programs. It is typical of many chapters in the Chicago area to
hold two types of meetings each month, one evening meeting
and one afternoon coffee. Evening meetings tend to be larger
and frequented by both spouses, afternoon coffees generally
smaller and attended mostly by women. Meetings are usually
held in a community facility, a room in a YMCA, church hall,
lounge in a hospital, or town hall. Upon entering a typical
evening meeting, one is greeted by a host or hostess and asked to
fill out a name tag. Coffee, tea, and cookies are in sight and informal interchanges proceed as people drift in. The introduction
of newcomers is begun in an atmosphere of warm friendly hos-
pitality on the part of experienced group members, who attempt to make the new, potentially threatening situation as
comfortable as possible.

Once everyone is seated around the table, the meeting
begins with a standardized introduction process in which all
those present give their name, the name and age of their dead
child, and a brief description of the circumstances surrounding
the death. After everyone has spoken, including both new and
old members, a meeting may take one of two courses: either
a presentation by a guest speaker, such as a psychologist, doctor,
minister or rabbi, funeral director, or social worker; or open discussion focusing on a particular issue of the grieving process.
Typical subjects include medical or legal questions, day-to-day
concerns such as disposition of the deceased child's belongings
and pictures, and issues around marital strife, loneliness, guilt,

and suicidal feelings. After the formal meeting closes, many members remain and cluster in small informal discussion groups, often consisting of parents who have lost their children in similar circumstances.

Ideology. Specific tenets in the ideology of Compassionate Friends are still developing. As yet, there are no codified beliefs such as the *Twelve Steps and Twelve Traditions* of Alcoholics Anonymous (1953) or *Mental Health Through Will-Training* by Abraham Low (1950), the founder of Recovery, Inc. The ideology of Compassionate Friends is less uniformly articulated but, for many, it represents a system of teachings and beliefs that is seen as a constructive way for bereaved parents to respond to personal, family, and social problems. The overriding philosophy recognizes that the bereaved person's experience, however bizarre, is a normal part of the grief reaction. Even those who think they are "going crazy" are seen as responding normally to a devastating loss. Some characterize this process of providing mastery over the distressing personal and social experiences of bereavement as completing the "grief journey from presence to memory."

What follows is an attempt to describe the ways in which the specific ideological teachings of Compassionate Friends address particular problems of bereaved parents. The point-by-point relationship between the stressful condition and its corresponding teaching or belief will be outlined. Table 1 summarizes the developing ideology of Compassionate Friends.

Personal Maladaptive Responses

Denial. The group setting is purposefully presented as a place to remember the deceased child in an effort to facilitate acceptance and to undermine the inclination to deny that the death really happened. It provides time not otherwise set aside to grieve and think about the child. Bereaved parents are encouraged to display mementos such as pictures or trophies. At one afternoon meeting, snapshots of the deceased children were passed around and examined by all. Bereaved parents are encouraged to visit their child's grave as frequently as they like.

Table 1. Ideology of Compassionate Friends

Sphere of Difficult Problem in "Standardized Situation"	"Cognitive Antidote" or Ideological Teaching Aimed at Countering the Problem
I. *Maladaptive responses*	General belief that any aberrant feelings or behaviors are not intrinsic to the self but can be attributed to the external stress of grief
A. Denial	Maintain central focus on child in group
	Verbal introduction of nature of child's death
	Emphasis on neutralization of emotional engagement through a cognitive intellectual understanding exemplified in establishment and use of a library on death and grief
B. Anger and guilt	Forgiveness and nonresponsibility
	Replace feelings of despair by encouraging reconceptualization of the loss and gradual reinvestment in social and educational activities
II. *Family relationships* A. Marital strain	Belief that it is the external stress of child loss that precipitates acute marital difficulties and not something intrinsic to the relationship itself
	Spouses have different, often incompatible grieving styles and there should be tolerance of these differences
B. Surviving siblings	Do not neglect surviving siblings through a preoccupation with and overidealization of the dead child
	Do not overprotect the living children
III. *Social reintegration* A. "Conspiracy of silence"—isolation	Initiate social relationships; practice new expressive behaviors with others in group
B. Alienation by insensitivity of others	Courtesy and tolerance while expressing honest feelings

A second means by which many chapters attempt to counter denial and encourage acceptance is through a routine introduction procedure at the beginning of the meeting. Parents are asked to introduce themselves, give the name of their child, and the date and circumstances of the child's death. Whereas some of the old members may appear to give more controlled introductions, many of the newly bereaved are often moved and quite tearful. Frequently this is the first time they are saying these words aloud to people other than relatives or close friends.

Educational materials are the third important means by which acceptance and understanding of the loss are facilitated. Seventy-five percent of the chapters surveyed just prior to the first national convention in April 1978 had established lending libraries in an attempt to stress the importance of cognitive understanding of the grieving process. These libraries include books on death and grief, tape recordings of relevant talks and television shows, such as Harriet Schiff's presentation on the Phil Donahue television show, and copies of the first convention workshop sessions. Compassionate Friends places a strong emphasis on finding new insights in written materials, sharing information, and learning through identification with the experiences of those who have worked through their grief and made the transition to living normal lives again. Personal references to how individual parents adapted successfully to their grief are common during the meetings. The intellectual focus provides a common ground for sharing as well as a point of departure for conversation within the group. It is a link to the bereaved parents' affective-emotional experience as well as a structure on which new coping is built. Focus on an external issue, taken from a book or a speaker's address, is turned to one's own experience in dialogue with others concerning such issues as marital strain, sibling problems, or overidealization of the dead child. Through identification of one's feelings with the topic, which has gained legitimacy through outside recognition, the gradual process of adjustment may take a new and constructive turn. This cognitive framework is believed to provide parents with a sense of coherence and mastery over the personal devastation resulting from the death of their child. It neutralizes the intense feelings and makes acceptance of the loss possible.

Anger and Guilt. A second major challenge is to provide "cognitive antidotes" for the feelings of anger or guilt about responsibility for the death. Anger and guilt are considered to be a normal part of grieving. However, to continue to punish another person or oneself to the point of doing harm is discouraged. To counter these feelings, a belief in forgiveness of oneself

and others is wholeheartedly stressed as the only means of finding peace. One father recounted in several Compassionate
Friends meetings that he knew the adolescent boy who lost control of his car and killed his seven-year-old son. Although the
accident had occurred over a year ago, the man's face contorted
as he spoke of "the murderer." He said that hatred and rage
envelop him whenever he sees "the murderer." This man had
pressed charges against the teenager but was bitter about the
legal process. He angrily stated that the adolescent would probably get off with probation. "But even if I killed the one who
murdered my son, which I want to do every time I see him, this
would still not satisfy my wish for revenge, to show this boy the
pain and suffering he has shown me." Group members respond
by listening and tolerating the expression of even the most extreme feelings and wishes. This father's expressions were acknowledged and respected, but other group members (usually
the "helpers" who have resolved these feelings for themselves)
maintained that peace and resolution would come with time.
He was told that "ultimately there is no alternative but to for-
give, or else your rage will eat you alive."

Those enveloped in feelings of guilt around their degree
of involvement in the death of their child are listened to, but
are exonerated from self-blame. Helpers continually assuage
such feelings and thoughts by persuading these individuals that
they did all they possibly could. It was an accident. Period.
There is an emphatic attempt to dispel the bereaved parents'
dilemma of thinking that they could have prevented the death
"if only" they had or had not done something differently. One
woman, whose son died of carbon monoxide poisoning, recol-
lected how she was busy cooking a big dinner in the kitchen one
Saturday afternoon. Her son was tuning his car engine with the
garage door closed. She had planned to bring him a cold drink
sooner but couldn't leave the kitchen with so many things cooking on the stove. When she finally went out to the garage with
the drink, she found her son lying on the ground. To this day
that woman laments that "if only" she hadn't been cooking and
brought her son his cold drink just a few minutes sooner, he
might still be alive today.

In reality, whether the parent is truly responsible or not seems irrelevant. The ideological tenet here is to encourage an open expression of feeling and to instill a belief in forgiveness that approaches nonresponsibility. What is important and at times necessary for successful adaptation and survival is a personal conviction by bereaved parents that they are not ultimately at fault, and Compassionate Friends promotes this kind of thinking.

Debilitating feelings of despair and depression often result as a reaction to anger and guilt. These are countered by promoting a gradual reinvestment in the activities of life; the parents must restore their functioning in the parental, marital, and work spheres of life. The purpose of the group is to provide a bounded setting where persistent grieving is tolerated and the child can remain a central preoccupation. Bereaved parents are encouraged to grieve as long as they want privately or in the group. No time limit is ever set. However, preoccupation with the dead child must not permeate the person's life to the point where normal functioning is impossible. One intention here is to replace such traditional beliefs as "Children should survive their parents" with the belief that "We were lucky to have our son as long as we did." Bereaved parents are guided to avoid trying to answer such questions as "Why me?" Sometimes the emphasis on universality is comforting through a recognition of the inevitability of death for everyone. Others advocate religious rationalizations such as "It was his time to be called to heaven." This cognitive reconceptualization of one's experience coupled with reinvestment in activities is Compassionate Friends' formula for enabling the bereaved person to escape the incapacitating nature of the intense depression and to return to prior levels of adult functioning and even to experience the loss as growth producing.

Like Recovery, Inc., Compassionate Friends stresses the importance of activity and encourages feelings of control and agency. To dispel feelings of isolation, the reinvestment process is initiated by encouraging involvement in Compassionate Friends activities. The group goal is participation by all. Recognizing that not everybody feels capable of talking in front of groups, leaders in the Chicago area choose to close the formal meeting early. This provides an opportunity for those who did not verbally participate during the meeting to stay and visit in a more comfortable one-to-one sharing situation. For those not able to tolerate the group setting, a telephone line and a monthly newsletter keep them in touch with other bereaved parents and informed of the group's activities. Many chapters are actively engaged in "death education" programs and encourage bereaved parents to become involved. Keeping busy is strongly advocated as a means of escaping angry or depressed feelings. Educational activities include seminars, presentations, and workshops for professionals such as hospital staff, social workers, and funeral directors. Death education programs have been initiated for children in public schools. Many parents write about their experiences and are encouraged to publish; others appear on appropriate television talk shows.

Problems in Family Relationships

Compassionate Friends' ideology attempts to save marriages and prevent the dissolution of the family. The specific belief of the group focuses on the different, often apparently incompatible, grieving styles of parents. The ideology is predicated on the sanctity of the family and assumes that it is the external stress of the child loss that precipitates acute marital difficulties, and not something intrinsically characteristic of the relationship itself. To alleviate disharmony, the group attempts to teach specific understanding of these differences. For example, a wife wanted to keep pictures of their deceased son in every room. Her husband could not tolerate the idea and broke down crying every time he saw a picture. The disagreement was finally resolved with a compromise. They agreed to have one small snapshot in the corner of the living room and to keep the rest of the pictures in the basement. Whenever the wife wants to peruse the pictures she goes downstairs in the basement, eliminating anxiety for her husband.

Keeping the marriage together is also emphasized by encouraging both spouses to attend meetings. This allows both spouses equal exposure to the group's tenets. Absence of one's spouse is usually noted and explained by the one present. At one meeting, after introducing herself and the circumstances surrounding her daughter's death, a woman explained that her husband was not present because he was out of town on business. On another occasion, a father explained that it was impossible to get a babysitter that night, so his wife stayed home with the other children.

Modeling is an important mechanism provided by husband-wife teams, who frequently lead meetings in a joint effort to teach and epitomize the ideology. Very often these spouses will freely disclose the kinds of problems they have encountered in attempting to respect each other's different grieving styles. In this way, other spouses can learn that their problems are not unique, but something shared by all bereaved parents.

The group setting itself facilitates discussion and working through of stalemated family conflicts. Many bereaved parents utilize Compassionate Friends as a useful third party. The open communication provides a forum to express feelings, thoughts, and disagreements that may be difficult to share elsewhere. Tolerance of these differences is crucial, but equally important is finding a way to give expression to one's own needs, even if they conflict with one's spouse. One woman stated that what had distinguished her experience in Compassionate Friends from her experience in psychotherapy was that the knowledge she derived from other husbands helped her understand her own husband's grieving. The opportunity for both the husband and wife to participate in Compassionate Friends serves to open communication and to recognize not only differences but important commonalities in the couple. Men, especially, are liberated from their conventional stoic, unemotional role by being encouraged to express their feelings during meetings. One meeting was led by three men who initiated discussion on anger and guilt from their personal points of view as husbands and fathers.

A major concern in the developing ideology of Compassionate Friends is the manner in which the surviving siblings are regarded. The group attempts to raise parents' awareness of the fact that their other children have also suffered a loss and have needs of their own. The group advocates a strategy that counters extreme tendencies either to neglect the remaining children or to indulge or overprotect them. The ideological tenet that seems to apply here is belief in the positive value of "letting go"—letting go of the dead child and of the fear of losing one of the living children. Compassionate Friends reminds its members that they have surviving children who require their love and affection more than the deceased child. Overidealization of the lost child, either in conversation or by erecting shrines to his or her memory is to be avoided, for the surviving siblings may come to feel that they are being ignored in favor of an image of their brother or sister with which they cannot compete. One bereaved mother confessed forgetting all about her two children who were waiting to be picked up after school one day. She had gone to the cemetery to visit her dead son's grave. When this was presented at a group meeting, members suggested that next time she pick up her children first and take them with her to the cemetery so that they could see their brother's grave too. In contrast, other bereaved parents express an intense fear of letting their children out of their sight, because they are afraid something will happen to them too. One woman whose son died in a car accident reported how she was unwilling to let her teenage daugher go out at night in a car with her friends. Others in the group made her aware that not only was she being overprotective and should let go but also that she could never really exert ultimate control over her teenage daughter's life anyway.

The essence of the group's teachings is that surviving siblings should neither be neglected nor overprotected. They should be engaged in all of the activities around the death and the funeral and memorial ceremonies thereafter. Certain chapters in Compassionate Friends have, in fact, organized groups, workshops, and picnics for siblings where they are provided the opportunity to share and discuss, with other bereaved siblings, their painful feelings and memories of their dead brother or sister.

Problems of Social Reintegration

Members of Compassionate Friends are encouraged to take the first step to break the "conspiracy of silence" by taking an active role in teaching friends and neighbors that it is okay to talk about the dead child. The ideology teaches that it is the task of bereaved parents to reach out to those who are alienated by their fear of causing more pain. They are encouraged to begin by making new friends in the group. One must not be enraged at those who are insensitive but rather be open and honest with them. Bereaved parents must take responsibility for reaching out to friends if they do not want to compound their loss by losing them too. One couple recalled in a meeting how they had hardly been asked to dinner at any of their friends' homes since their child's death. After six months or so, the wife invited all of her closest friends to dinner for the same evening. Several of the guests remarked how they would have loved to get together sooner but did not know if the couple felt "ready" yet. In the following weeks, the couple's invitation was reciprocated and they began to socialize with their friends again on a more regular basis.

While the ideology stresses that bereaved parents should take the initiative in making social contacts, it simultaneously holds a value of maintaining courtesy toward and tolerance of the unintended foibles of friends and relatives. The group members attempt to teach acceptance through taking the role of the other and encouraging others to try to remember how they might have responded to bereaved parents before their own loss. Members are encouraged not to have unrealistic expectations of others, especially of doctors, ministers, or other professionals. The group believes that most of these professionals are uninformed.

Group meetings serve as settings where bereaved parents can simulate behaviors with each other in a supportive and fomative environment, where there is safety in numbers and considerable feedback. They also learn that it is all right to laugh again and express humor before others. The group gives them the chance to try out their beliefs and expressions with each other. One member captures the essence of this feeling by saying, "You cannot smile in front of anybody but a bereaved parent because people think you're getting over it."

This chapter has applied the model suggested by Antze for behavioral control groups to a case of a group coping with a stressful predicament. The beliefs and teachings of this group function as a "cognitive antidote" to counter personal maladaptation but are also important in dealing with family and social relations. The impact and consequences of bereavement—due, in this case, to the loss of a child—necessitate a more extensive ideology to contain, redirect, and reconceptualize the attitudes and values of affected parents in the larger contexts of their lives.

CHAPTER **14**

Problems in
Studying Outcomes

*Morton A. Lieberman &
Gary R. Bond*

Soon after we began investigating self-help groups, we began to struggle with the basic issue that has plagued research on all forms of intentional intervention: how to assess the effectiveness or outcome of the effort. In this chapter, we shall set out some of our first attempts to unravel the outcome question in studying self-help groups; the reader may well find us more articulate with regard to the dilemmas than the solutions. Our intent is not to revisit the multitude of technical issues surrounding evaluation. Instead we shall offer some thoughts on three pragmatic issues that have emerged from our investigations: what to measure, when to measure, and whom to measure. In subsequent chapters, we shall illustrate these issues by investigating three very different types of self-help groups: women's consciousness-raising (CR) groups, Mended Hearts, and SAGE (Senior Actualization and Growth Encounter).

Note: Portions of this chapter are reproduced by special permission from *Journal of Small Group Behavior* "Self-Help Groups: Problems of Measuring Outcome," by this chapter's authors, 9 (2), 1978.

What to Measure

The selection of outcome measures requires that the investigator set priorities according to several important criteria: reliability, validity, comparability to other studies, and relevance to the population under study. The struggle of psychotherapy researchers over the past decade to develop reliable and valid indexes and the slowly evolving consensus regarding such indexes provide a glimmer of hope in a field marked by frequent failure. In addition, the accumulation of information among groups of investigators using similar outcome indexes has slowly begun to provide a cumulative base of findings. Although the lessons so arduously wrought from experience with psychotherapy outcome research offer significant guideposts for investigating self-help enterprises, we believe, unfortunately, that much of the information developed by psychotherapy researchers cannot automatically be applied to self-help groups. Thus the instruments developed out of the long struggle to achieve reliability and standardization must be examined with caution by investigators of self-help groups. The differences in problems that self-help participants present and the differences in system level goals make many of the instruments used in assessing psychotherapy outcome inadequate for the self-help context. The continual development of new groups with different goals adds to the problem of standardization. Effort must be directed to the nature and character of the self-help groups themselves, with an outcome framework for assessing outcome developed out of such examinations and reconceptualizations.

Strupp and Hadley (1977) have proposed a heuristic framework for conceptualizing psychotherapeutic outcomes. They suggest that mental health can be assessed from three viewpoints: that of the client, who wants to be happy and feel less discomfort; that of the mental health professional, who wants the patient to develop a well-integrated personality; and that of society, which wants the patient to conform to certain normative standards. This formulation brings into focus the competing values involved in evaluating outcome that are especially prominent in nontraditional therapeutic groups. In a related manner, we shall examine three perspectives in discussing what to measure: the client's own perspective, the perspective of the group, and the external point of view represented by the researcher.

Ideographic Perspective. We have found the ideographic approach to outcome measurement, which recently has enjoyed a renaissance in the psychotherapy literature (Sloane and others, 1975; Waskow and Parloff, 1975), to be a useful guide for indexing the participant's perspective on improvement. The target complaint approach (Battle and others, 1966), in which the client provides the goals used to assess improvement, has proved readily adaptable to nontraditional systems. Our experience, however, has led us to be skeptical of client ratings of improvement on target problems. First, most people report improvement on target problems, even when they are in "control" groups, or when other criteria suggest a lack of improvement. One analysis also indicated high correlations between improvement ratings on specific goals and global ratings, which have generally been regarded as having low validity (Bond and others, 1979). Second, although there is considerable overlap in the problems targeted by clients of various types of helping systems, differences can be noted that suggest system-level influences. When the top three goals of clients entering group psychotherapy are compared with those of CR participants, "changing interpersonal relationships" is stated as a goal by 64 percent of the group psychotherapy clients, compared with 61 percent of the CR participants; "increasing self-esteem" is mentioned by 44 percent of the group psychotherapy clients, compared with 48 percent of the CR participants. However, whereas 61 percent of the psychotherapy clients mention at least one problem relating to internal feeling states (depression, anxiety, trouble expressing feelings, and so on), only 16 percent of the CR participants identify such problems. This difference is likely to be a result of "system characteristics" rather than distinctions among clients. As discussed in Chapter Seven, objective measures of psychological symptoms have indicated that CR members are more depressed and anxious than a normative sample and have been in psychotherapy more often.

Such observations make it impossible to determine if, for example, the lack of change CR participants registered in anxiety or depressive symptoms is accounted for by the ineffectiveness of the change process employed or by system properties that induce members to select against intrapsychic goals (see Chapter Fifteen). Although they experience anxiety or depression, CR participants may not see these problems as relevant to consciousness-raising groups and, in that context, do not place them high on their agenda for exploration and change. It is equally possible, however, that the particular processes of change used in consciousness-raising groups would not ordinarily yield high change in anxiety and depression.

The difficulty of disentangling system values from client goals and proselytizing character of many self-help groups suggests that alternative measurement approaches may be required to maximize the utility of ideographic assessment. As an alternative, we identified one of the more salient goals among the CR sample—increased self-esteem—and used it as a classificatory variable for comparing interactions between participant goals and outcome. The target problem approach by itself does not provide for the assessment of improvement on problems not included in the target list. Fortunately, we had correctly anticipated self-esteem as a major area of concern and had also administered a standardized self-esteem scale (Rosenberg, 1965). By using the nomothetic instrument, we hoped to obtain more reliable estimates of change. The application of this combination of instruments allowed us to assess whether self-esteem increased specifically for those women who targeted this goal, rather than simply whether self-esteem was generally altered by experience in the women's groups.

As anticipated, the subgroup of women entering CR with a target goal of increasing self-esteem had lower initial mean scores (mean = 2.9, s.d. = 1.6, N = 15) than those who did not target this as a goal prior to entering CR (mean = 1.8, s.d. = 1.9, N = 17, t = 1.8, p < .10). The difference in mean change scores (1.00 for the low self-esteem group; .65 for the remainder) was in the predicted direction, though not statistically significant. Our hope is that in larger samples and with batteries of nomothetic instruments used in conjunction with the target problem instrument, we can move toward more precise statements about the nature of change.

Obviously, there are a number of methodological problems to be ironed out. We have not yet addressed the problem of unequal N's. The method will not help for target problems that are truly idiosyncratic. But such goals have never been accurately reflected in nomothetic designs. The strategy suggested here works for goals that are well represented for clients of a selected self-help group.

We believe the dual strategy has the advantage of combining the best features of the ideographic approach—that is, the specificity of individualized goals—with the best features of a nomothetic approach—namely, standardization of language and comparability to other samples. Such a combination offers the investigator the possibility of using standardized instruments to measure goals that are relevant within the particular context under investigation. This advantage seems particularly important in the study of self-help groups, where so little is known regarding their hierarchy of goals and other aspects of their culture.

Our approach assumes that sorting of clients according to individualized problems and goals is necessary and useful. Clients differ in the relative emphases they place on the attainment of goals with a finite range of possibilities. We do not take the more extreme position of a completely ideographic approach, in which each person's outcome is evaluated solely on the basis of his or her own goals, because we have not found that wide a range of problems among clients. It may also be that individual differences in the desired direction for change are not as important as is sometimes assumed. For example, feminists have proposed that positive change for a woman may entail her becoming angrier and more hostile (with regard to the conditions in society). Therefore, it is reasoned, the goals of consciousness raising clash with the goals of traditional psychotherapy. However, we found no indication that CR participants sought to bring about any such intrapsychic change. A greater acceptance of self and others was as typical a desired outcome as it is in psychotherapy.

In a similar fashion, psychotherapists will sometimes suggest that certain clients need to become more depressed (that is, realize how depressed they really are) before they can start improving. A study that involved teams of expert clinical judges who defined ideographic goals for clients entering therapy (Bloch and others, 1977) was designed in part to determine to what extent clinicians would make such distinctions. The goals the experts defined for clients were not "tailor made" in the sense of movement in both directions. Instead, the direction of change was always the same—becoming *more* assertive, becoming *less* depressed, and so on.

The one area in which it is most difficult to evaluate whether the change is desirable is in the domain of values and life-style. (Dramatic changes in life-style may be viewed as withdrawal or failure in societal terms while quite explicitly considered a positive change by the individual (for example, see Lieberman, Yalom, and Miles, 1973). We found several instances in the CR study where a woman made a major decision and where the growth potential of the change was equivocal. In the value domain, therefore, the individual's evaluation of the direction of change is important.

Perspective of the Self-Help Group. Although the client's anticipation about a particular system shapes his or her conceptualization of a personal problem so that there is some fit between the person's view of the problem and the helping system's view, there is no reason to assume identity. (See Lieberman and Gardner, 1976, concerning the discrepancy between the ideological position of growth centers and the needs and goals of their clients.) Thus an understanding of the impact of self-help groups on their participants requires that the intent of the system be taken into account. Antze's (1976) framework, described in Chapter Twelve, based on a study of three self-help groups (Alcoholics Anonymous, Synanon, and Recovery, Inc.), portrays a highly articulated and specified belief system that characterizes each type of self-help group. He describes, for example, how the ideological tenets of AA, which emphasizes diminished agency, and Recovery, with its enhancement of agency, represent mirror images of each other. For Antze, although similar social-psychological processes characterize both of these groups, it is the close fit between the ideological tenets and the specifics of the disease that are the center of his framework.

Such a perspective suggests that the process of change induction in self-help systems involves a basic reorganization of beliefs and attitudes toward a particular problem or affliction in a predetermined direction. The values that usually underlie self-help organizations do not always fit comfortably or easily within more traditional views of change processes. This departure from standard beliefs may constitute a knotty problem for those trained to evaluate traditional psychotherapy, who are likely to bring implicit assumptions about change that are derived from traditional contexts and do not carry over automatically to newer mechanisms of help. The discrepancy between the psychotherapy researcher and the self-help system is perhaps most dramatically illustrated in the criticism of many mental health professionals—that self-help groups encourage denial, construct mythologies, and so on. Such criticisms may represent differences in philosophy or values about appropriate outcomes rather than differences in level of sophistication about what is required for "lasting" change.

Assessment of the impact of self-help groups on their participants requires outcome measures that reflect system-level criteria. Such issues have been confronted in the psychotherapy literature, for example, in the discussion centering around repair versus growth. Such considerations are even more critical for research on self-help groups in light of their diversity and their explicit commitment to ideologies that may be at sharp variance with that of the mental health investigator.

The researcher who approaches the measurement of effectiveness of self-help groups will soon discover that to understand the system from the perspective of the self-help group, outcome measures are not always the most crucial. The goal for an alcoholic, for example, is abstinence. Whereas this ultimate endstate is shared by Alcoholics Anonymous and professionals alike, AA presumes a particular route to that endstate. From the system's perspective, the particular set of attitudes adopted by the alcoholic is crucial. If members ever think that they can consider themselves ex-alcoholics, they are, from AA's perspective, not a success case, for it is assumed that this belief leads to recidivism. In this sense, the right attitudes and beliefs are a necessary component of successful outcomes. Behavioral change is only one component.

The richness and vividness of ethnographic detail illustrating the proper attitudes for members of a group are a far cry from showing that any noteworthy proportion of the members actually adopt these attitudes. Ethnographers can, under some circumstances, legitimately use a single informant to identify components of the cultural scene (Spradley and McCurdy, 1972). The outcome researcher's task is to assess how pervasive the proper attitudes are among members.

Two concrete examples from our own pilot work on Mended Hearts and women's consciousness-raising groups illustrate some of the dilemmas that outcome researchers face in examining self-help groups from the perspective of the system. Field observations and interviews in these two systems have enabled us to start developing hypotheses about their ideologies and how they might affect the members. A core issue for all self-help organizations is the way they deal with the stigma associated with their condition. Of course, neither being a woman nor having heart surgery elicits as strong a social response as many of the conditions around which other self-help groups have been organized. What is interesting about becoming "mended" in Mended Hearts or having one's consciousness raised in a CR group are the distinctive changes in the awareness of stigma. In examining the effects of participation in Mended Hearts groups, we hypothesized that such groups serve to destigmatize the heart surgery patient and provide the patient with the confidence to return to or exceed presurgical, non-self-conscious levels of activity. We developed a stigma questionnaire ("People treat heart surgery patients differently," "Employers are reluctant to hire someone who's had heart surgery" are illustrative items) based on field observations and interviews, and conducted a pilot survey of heart surgery patients. Some were members of Mended Hearts who had been involved in visiting others in the hospital about to have surgery; others were members of Mended Hearts who did not participate in this central activity; and a third group consisted of those who had had similar surgery but were not members of Mended Hearts. Members who had been official Mended Hearts visitors had a significantly less stigmatized view of their affliction than those who had not been visitors or than nonmembers. In contrast, women who participated in CR groups demonstrated a significant *increase* in believing themselves "stigmatized" (with regard to hiring, promotions, obtaining credit, and so on) as a result of participating in consciousness-raising groups.

Whether such changes as those noted in both these self-help groups regarding stigma are valued by the researcher is not a research question. It is possible to argue that the Mended Hearts group serves a "cooling out" function—that heart surgery patients, who certainly suffer from discrimination in employment, insurance, and so on, are not served by this change in their value system and their perceptions about society's view of their condition. Similarly, the change in women who have participated in CR may be evaluated contradictorily as a more realistic assessment of society or as a defensive maneuver interfering with meaningful personal learning. These simple examples underscore the necessity for those who would study the effectiveness of self-help groups to understand the particular ideological dimensions of each system and to take into account the perspective of the system being studied.

Perspective of the Researcher. Evaluators of traditional psychotherapy do not ordinarily face the dilemma we believe they will encounter in self-help groups. Change from the perspective of the psychotherapeutic system and change from the perspective of the researcher are usually one and the same, since the researcher represents the basic philosophical position espoused by most psychotherapy systems. Although those who deliver services and those who investigate services are frequently not the same persons, they do represent the same basic view of human nature, of what ails people, and of what is needed to rectify the ailment. Our comment on the relative homogeneity within psychotherapy research and practice needs, of course, to be placed in some perspective. Although there are increasingly broadening philosophical differences within the field of psychotherapy (the growing distinction between the view of psychotherapy as repair and psychotherapy as growth perhaps captures a portion of the current diversity), the ideological differences in traditional formulations are small compared to the diversity of views within the various self-help groups currently functioning in the United States. Although psychotherapy investigators may disagree on the importance of changes in symptoms, nearly all will see them as a relevant dimension of inquiry. Values such as insight, self-understanding, self-realization or actualization, no matter what specific conceptual terms are used to describe them, are shared by nearly all schools of psychotherapy.

In some self-help groups, however, such as women's consciousness-raising groups, Gay Liberation, or Synanon, the concept of distress as employed in a mental health perspective is not relevant. Although the individuals within such systems are acknowledged to experience inner distress, the aim of the movement is to relieve it by locating the source externally—in its social origins—rather than by processes directed at insight, self-understanding, actualization, and so on; in fact, a search for these is seen as inappropriate. It is "a sociological understanding" of the failures of society that is believed by the group's originators to provide the participant in such self-help groups with relief. Symptom reduction thus becomes a matter of altering external conditions or society; symptoms are seen as "false beliefs" rather than as accurate monitors of internal distress. Other groups, such as Recovery, Inc., rely on an elaborate ideology that encourages "denial-like" mechanisms as a source of salvation. The Mended Hearts ideology appears to support some mechanisms designed to permit avoidance of the psychological distress associated with the physical condition.

Given these realities with regard to the diversity of end-states valued by varying self-help groups, it is our view that assessment of effectiveness requires an additional perspective to those of the person and the self-help system. Particularly where one is interested in comparing diverse helping systems or in developing information to guide policy, psychosocial standards of a much broader nature than those typically used to evaluate traditional mental health programs must be entered into the consideration of what should constitute appropriate outcome criteria. Thus, for example, a traditional psychotherapeutic perspective would undoubtedly require the judgment that CR groups were a failure in the event of a pre-post design that revealed no appreciable symptom reduction among participants who entered the group with a higher than normative number of symptoms. With an alternative framework, however, in which a variable such as "social sensitivity" assumed priority among assessment criteria, the same group experience might be judged as a success.

Considerations of this sort have led us to explore a perspective for the establishment of appropriate criteria that depart somewhat from those that typify the evaluation of psychotherapy outcome. The approach involves the assessment of adequacy of functioning in marital, occupational, economic, parental, and analogous major social roles, rather than limiting criteria to measures of psychological functioning. Although a few self-help groups define their purpose to be the alteration of normative definitions of given social roles and, indeed, have set themselves the task of creating their own definitions of appropriate role performance, and others, as indicated, see their function as changing external society, most groups are directed toward recovery from or better adaptation to life crises caused by illness, role loss, and so on. For such groups, the assessment of the quality of life as it is reflected in the performance of members in their major life roles directly addresses the relevant outcome question: What are the consequences of participation on the psychological adjustment *and* social role performance of participants?

A recent large-scale study of adaptation in which the senior author has been engaged has illuminated our ideas on the development of measurement techniques of this sort. This survey, which assessed a probability sample of 1,100 adults in 1972 and again in 1976, attempted to assess the impact of various transitional events and crises on role functioning and psychological well-being. As researchers on self-help groups, we have begun to use these measures to evaluate outcome. Particularly in those circumstances where we cannot do pre-post research and cannot draw adequate control groups, our hope is to assess role functioning of individuals at various stages of membership in self-help groups using the normative data derived from the probability sample as a base for comparison. These normative data, adjusted for social structural variables (age, race, sex, and socioeconomic class), hold the potential of establishing norms of functioning to which we can compare an individual at different stages of membership in self-help groups. Our plan is to create a measurement matrix that also provides a way of assessing various factors that may affect role functioning. Thus, for example, we can begin to look at such transitions as retirement, the "empty nest," and so on, and assess the degree to which they affect role functioning. This will provide a framework to compare the effects of intentional efforts at change through self-help groups with certain life events that are also change inducing. We have barely begun examining the implications of these normative data for measurement of the impact of self-help groups. We are encouraged, however, by the possibility they appear to provide to look at the individual's performance in a major life role as an appropriate mechanism for examining and comparing the impacts of a large number of different self-help systems.

We recognize that the model of evaluation we are proposing flies in the face of conventional wisdom. Using Campbell and Stanley's (1963) terminology, the "static-group comparison," which the approach in the preceding paragraph approximates, suffers from internal validity problems. The thrust of the normative base of comparison to our investigations of outcome is to lend anchor points to findings that may otherwise be statistically significant but clinically irrelevant. The comparison with a normative sample provides additional information to strengthen the external validity.

Our study on the impact of consciousness-raising groups on women (Chapter Fifteen) serves as a small illustration of the method. It is not, however, a direct test of this perspective. We conducted this study on women, in the classical pre-post psychotherapy research design, to examine the mental health implications of women's consciousness-raising groups. Most of our measures were traditional psychotherapeutic ones—indexes of self-esteem, symptoms, and marriage. In the study, we were struck by the absence of changes in the marital area as a result of participating six months in women's consciousness-raising groups. The measures used were borrowed from marital therapy research. This lack of findings, given the anticipation that consciousness raising would impact on the marriage, led us to an examination of the sample from a status point of view. Essentially, we compared the women who participated in the consciousness-raising group with a sample drawn from our normative population matched for age and socioeconomic status. The status of the women who participated in CR subsequent to the consciousness-raising experience indicates that, as a group, at a statistically significant level these women were functioning more poorly in their marriages than comparable normative cohorts (on marital stress, strain, and two of the five marital coping scales—use of less expression and more passivity). This provided the investigators an indication that all of the other information we had about the pre-post changes or lack of them in marital relationships, using standard psychotherapy measures, was probably not in error and that, in fact, one could reasonably conclude that for this group of women, at the end of the consciousness-raising experience, their marital relationships contained considerably more stress and strain and less adequate coping strategies than comparative populations. One could reasonably conclude that marital relationships are not positively affected by consciousness-raising experience, although one could obviously not conclude that they are made worse. From a societal perspective, this particular type of self-help group would be unlikely to make a major impact on marriages that were in trouble. The small example serves only to illustrate the potentials of this method; problems of comparable samples are a major impediment, but it does help to place the group under study in some perspective with regard to the general functioning within particular areas of a normal cohort.

When to Measure

Traditional psychotherapeutic systems are generally temporary systems. Evaluation procedures are based on the expectation that people will enter, go through a set of experiences, and exit when they are "cured." Whether he or she continues for six weeks or six years, an individual in psychotherapy has an image of progressing from a starting point to an ending point. A person who remains too long in therapy may be viewed as becoming "overly dependent."

In contrast, self-help groups do not negatively sanction long-term involvement in the group. Members of addiction groups take pride in the number of years they have belonged, or more specifically, the number of days since they last partook of the undesirable behavior. While some groups, such as AA and the groups modeled after it, have "Twelve Steps" by which participants can note their progress, in most there is no graduation or termination; the problem or affliction is perceived as lifelong. One never loses one's status as an alcoholic or compulsive gambler or drug addict. The fundamental outcome in these groups is not any positive sign of recovery, but the negative information that something did not occur.

For the self-help groups organized around trauma or illness, a similar situation obtains. One does not "graduate" from Mended Hearts. Although there are various identifiable statuses within the organization (visitor-trainee, accredited visitor, local officer, national officer, and the like), these do not inform us of the outcome status of the members. In Compassionate Friends, expressions of grief are appropriate for the newly bereaved as well as for one who lost a child several years prior. The group does not apparently place time limits on this process. Thus, although these support groups encourage members to return to normal functioning, the recovery process is not used as a criterion that one is ready to leave the group, as it often is in psychotherapy. Self-help groups, not having the time boundaries typical of psychotherapy, create design problems for the researchers.

People who go to self-help groups may drop into meetings on a very sporadic schedule. They may choose to go to a meeting on a day that they feel especially depressed. The support from the group does not stay within the boundaries of a fifty-minute hour—members may talk to each other over the phone between meetings, or become involved in a number of activities that do not fit in the categories of traditional psychotherapy. Some self-help groups have more than one chapter in an area that a person can visit on different nights. All of these characteristics make the research goal of standardization of treatment difficult.

The conventional pre-post design is inappropriate for other reasons as well. In the case of unexpected trauma, we have no simple way of assessing the level of adaptation prior to the trauma event. We cannot measure the heart patient's level of stress and symptoms before learning of his surgery, or know the quality of the marital relationship for a couple before their son or daughter died. Many of the conditions addressed by self-help groups have a natural history of reaction and reintegration.

Research on self-help requires quasi-experimental methodology. The designs must take the following factors into account: the long-term and intermittent nature of the help giving, the "after only" requirement in the case of the unexpected events, the importance of the nonoccurrence of events in the case of the addictions, and "spontaneous" recovery.

Whom to Measure

The control group issue, which is difficult even when the research has some control over participant assignment, is exceedingly difficult for our topic of inquiry. The basic issue is that we have no way to control for self-selection.

One strategy we have not adopted is direct experimental intervention where some approach favored by the researcher, such as behavior modification, is compared to self-help efforts, using some conventional research design (Jordan and Levitz, 1973; Levitz and Strunkard, 1974). Our interest is more in the discovery of new knowledge and the evaluation of natural systems. We must therefore consider all the problems inherent in comparisons between subjects who are not randomly assigned.

If we cannot control self-selection, we can at least examine how members and nonmembers differ. There are several important categories of nonmembers: persons who live in areas where a self-help group for their problem has not yet been formed, persons invited to join but who never attend a meeting, persons who attend only one meeting, and so forth. Statistical control is one possible strategy for making groups equivalent. We should not rule out the possibility that the principle of self-selection may, in some cases, be overestimated. Our pilot study of Mended Hearts suggests fewer demographic differences between members and nonmembers than we expected.

We have already spoken of the sporadic and unpredictable time of involvement for members of a self-help group. Members may also differ in their *kinds* of involvement, and we may indirectly determine the active ingredients of help giving for a group by distinguishing among member status. So, for example, accredited visitors in Mended Hearts appear to be functioning much better than members who attend monthly meetings, suggesting that it is the act of visiting others that brings about the most improvement. These within-group comparisons, as an indirect strategy for evaluating outcome, are subject to the same criticisms about possible confounding effects.

A characteristic of self-help participants that further confounds outcome assessment is that, frequently, they are users of multiple forms of help. Although this is certainly also characteristic of psychotherapy patients (Bergin, 1971), the types of afflictions from which self-help group participants suffer and the often emergency nature of their problems make them even more likely to enter general helping systems. We see no easy solution to this problem, except to underscore that in studying the impact of self-help groups on their participants, the researcher must attempt to use large sample designs because of all the "uncontrolled factors."

Separate from design problems, the use of multiple help arouses investigative curiosity about the impact on the individual of help-providing systems which on the surface look ideologically disparate. Perhaps the most common example of this is the clinician who reports struggles with a patient who is also a member of AA. Both patient and therapist experience dissonance created by the competing views of the curative process and the endstate which are embodied in the psychotherapeutic system

and in AA. Although this problem is rarely studied, the findings
at hand suggest lower levels of disruptive dissonance than both
clinician and researcher anticipated. In our pre-post study of
women in consciousness-raising groups, we found that a significant portion also were in traditional psychotherapy. We anticipated that women in these two systems would experience
dissonance because of the different ideologies, but on the
contrary those who were in both psychotherapy and consciousness-raising groups improved more (with regard to self-esteem
and on other target problems) than those who were in consciousness raising only. Possibly, we incorrectly assumed a greater
need for consistency in humans than such findings portray. The
ability to be involved in helping systems that use different diag-
nostic tools may offend the researcher's need for order, but not
the client's.

　　We expect to find increasing documentation by researchers of professional and nonprofessional systems alike of this
multiple help-seeking phenomenon. For example, Yalom and
others (1978) concluded that professional group therapy was
complementary, and not antagonistic, to Alcoholic Anonymous.
Whereas AA was instrumental in maintaining sobriety, therapy
provided a context for interpersonal change. As with the preceding example, it appeared that clients had little trouble moving back and forth between change-induction systems with
disparate goals, values, and systems of belief.

　　Ideally, research should attempt to sort out the relative
effects of concurrent change-induction systems when it is apparent that many of the clients under study are seeking out
more than one form of help. It is in practice a formidable task
even to specify the universe to which one is generalizing. Traditional problems with sample attrition are multiplied when the
research considers more than one system. Yet if researcher findings are to represent accurately the realities of the clients under
study, we must begin to address this issue.

　　Returning to the larger issue of control groups, we have
no unique solution to propose. As described earlier, we are at
present exploring the use of a large normative sample as the
standard against which to measure the quality of life of mem-

bers of self-help groups. The normative sample is, of course, not to be confused with the conventional control group. We would not expect cancer victims to experience the same quality of life as comparison groups, even if they had the support of self-help. Conversely, there is no reason to assume that some groups do not enhance the quality of life beyond conventional standards. The normative sample is not a true control group, nor a statistical standard that the members of a self-help group must achieve in order to say that the group is effective. It may, however, give us some perspective on what effects the group is having.

Our experience in the evaluation of the impact of self-help groups leads us to believe that appropriate models for research design will not be found among those employed in psychotherapy research, but are more likely to be derived from the experiences and perspective of evaluation research. Researchers must pay attention to factors ordinarily not conceptualized or noted in classical psychotherapy research. They must become more sensitive to system properties. For example, most psychotherapy researchers do not face the complex issue of negotiations with groups of individuals like those who control the resources of self-help groups, who frequently do not share the values of the researcher. Unlike psychotherapy research, those who are interested in evaluating self-help must begin to construct designs based on assumptions of community involvement. Entrance to and collaboration with self-help groups involves the researcher in a new matrix of relationships and issues and, in this sense, such a researcher is closer to the traditions of macro-evaluation research than he or she is to psychotherapy research. As researchers, we must realistically share with those who are influential in the self-help movement decisions about how research is done and what it is done about. Without such an approach, which radically alters the conventional stance of the researcher, we believe it may be impossible to study the self-help movement adequately.

CHAPTER 15

Effectiveness of Women's Consciousness Raising

Morton A. Lieberman,
Gary R. Bond, Nancy Solow
& Janet Reibstein

One consequence of the women's movement has been to direct attention to widespread dissatisfaction with traditional sex role structures and attitudes toward women. As an early outgrowth of the women's movement, consciousness-raising (CR) groups provided women with a setting in which they could draw upon the commonalities underlying personal experiences to analyze and understand their discontent (Allen, 1970). The precursors of CR groups were political discussion groups for women involved in the civil rights and antiwar protest movements during

Note: Portions of this chapter are reproduced by special permission from *Archives of General Psychiatry*, "The Psychotherapeutic Impact of Women's Consciousness-Raising Groups" by this chapter's authors, 1979, *36*, 161–168.

the 1960s (Carden, 1974). Since then, CR groups have generally evolved into support groups serving a psychotherapeutic function (Freeman, 1975; Warren, 1976). This change probably reflects the fact that CR groups lacked the structure and clear-cut objectives of task-oriented political action groups. In Chapter Seven we described a national survey of women entering CR in which it was found that CR attracts a sizable proportion of psychologically distressed women with psychotherapeutic goals.

The present study assessed the psychotherapeutic effectiveness of CR by investigating four general areas of impact: (1) mental health status and psychological functioning; (2) life-style decisions and personal values; (3) marital relationships; and (4) feminist attitudes and orientation.

Method

Two women's centers located in an Eastern metropolitan area were contacted. Both held open meetings during which CR "starters" (women who help coordinate and advise CR groups) organized a number of smaller CR groups. The research was presented to women attending the organizational meeting. Packets containing self-administered questionnaires were distributed to women interested in the study. To insure anonymity, the questionnaires were number-coded and cross-indexed with a postcard identifying the respondent. The postcard was mailed back to the women's center. About 100 questionnaires were distributed in this manner, and an additional 50 distributed to other newly forming groups known to women at the centers. In all, seventy-three women returned questionnaires.

Six months later, respondents were mailed a follow-up questionnaire. Eighteen respondents not providing addresses were lost from the sample. In all, forty-three women (76 percent of those contacted at follow-up) completed the second questionnaires, thirty-two had continued in the group for four months or more. The evaluation of changes was based on this subsample.

Thirty women indicated that they would participate in a telephone interview; we were able to contact twenty-four of them. In these twenty- to ninety-minute interviews, we asked each woman to discuss her most and least positive meetings, examined specific changes and decisions in her life occurring during the time of her CR participation, and clarified and amplified questionnaire responses.

Outcome Measures

Outcome measures listed in Table 1 reflect the hypothesized areas of change in CR. Measures of psychological functioning, personal value systems, and the quality of marital relationships were drawn from the psychotherapy and encounter group literature, whereas the feminist attitudes scales were used in the aforementioned CR survey. The questionnaires also examined reasons for joining, expectations, and experiences in the group. In the follow-up questionnaires, we included additional scales of marital stress, strain, and coping.

Reliability coefficients for internal consistency were computed on scales for which such information was not previously available. Using the scores from the initial sample of seventy-three women (fifty-one married), Cronbach's alpha coefficients were as follows: self-reliance, .56; marital satisfaction, .77; marital communication, .89; marital discord, .81; and discrimination index, .69. The coefficients of reproducibility and scalability were taken from the Guttman procedure for the feminist orientation scale and were .93 and .51 respectively.

Sample

CR Participants. Our previous survey, described in Chapter Seven, found that CR attracted well-educated, white, upper-middle-class women between twenty and fifty years of age. The seventy-three women who completed the initial questionnaire resembed this survey sample. Respondents in the current study ranged in age from twenty-one to sixty-two, with a mean age of thirty-seven. Sixty-nine percent were married, 23 percent were divorced or separated, and 8 percent were single. Those who were married had been so for a median of fourteen years (range one to thirty-one years); the median number of children was be-

Table 1. Outcome Battery

	Instrument	Chief Source	Format	Content
Mental health status	Target problems	Battle and others, 1966	3-item open-ended	Ideographic problems and goals in group
	Self-esteem	Rosenberg, 1965	10-item scale	Feelings about self
psychological functioning	Hopkins Symptom Checklist	Derogatis and others, 1974	35-item checklist	Symptom distress (e.g., depression, anxiety)
	Coping strategies	Lieberman and others, 1973	19 Likert scales	Coping styles: defensive, adequate subscales
	Personal resources	New	8-item open-ended	Source of social support for stressful events; self-reliance subscale
Personal value systems	Life space	Lieberman and others, 1973	12-item open-ended	Personal values; life-style goals and decisions; orientation toward growth
Marital relationship	Marital satisfaction	Landau, 1976	6-item checklist	Extent of satisfaction
	Marital communication	New, adapted from Jourard 1961	15-item checklist	Degree of disclosure to spouse
	Marital discord	Landau, 1976	17-item checklist	Frequency and areas of disagreements
	Decision making	Landau, 1976	6-item checklist	Actual and ideal ratings
Feminist attitudes and orientation	Feminist identification	New	7-point Likert scale	Identification with women's movement
	Discrimination index	Lieberman & Bond, 1976	6-item checklist	Perception of personal discrimination
	Feminist orientation scale	Lieberman & Bond, 1976	7-item scale	Attitudes on feminist issues: ERA, day care, abortion, etc.
	Feminist affiliations	Lieberman & Bond, 1976	9-item checklist	Membership in women's groups

tween two and three. The women were well-educated: 44 percent were college graduates, and another 40 percent had attended college. The majority of women were employed outside of the home: 21 percent held professional or managerial positions; 36 percent worked in secretarial or administrative capacities; and 4 percent were skilled or unskilled workers. The remaining 39 percent were either students (6 percent), unemployed (9 percent), or housewives (24 percent). Students were underrepresented in the current sample (16 percent of the women in the national survey were students), whereas housewives were overrepresented (24 percent as compared to 14 percent in the national survey). On the whole, however, the women in the current study were fairly similar demographically to the survey sample.

The motivations for joining CR offered by the women in the present study also were similar to those described by the survey sample. In both samples, the predominant reason for entering a CR group was an "interest in women's issues" (for example, to share thoughts and feelings about being a woman; to learn about other women and their experiences; to examine problems women have with their traditional roles). Often such motivations were accompanied by "help-seeking" concerns, as manifested in the desires "to get relief from things or feelings troubling me," "to solve personal problems," and "to bring about some change in myself." Political motivations, only slightly evident in the national survey, were virtually absent in the current sample. The current sample was less involved in political activity: Whereas 40 percent of those in the survey were members of women's political organizations, only 21 percent in the present study had such affiliations.

The interests of the women in the present study thus seemed to reflect a trend, extending from the late 1960s to the early 1970s, noted in the survey: Women increasingly join CR for the enhancement of their personal well-being rather than to induce social and political reform. This preoccupation with self-improvement was also reflected in the women's widespread utilization of professional mental health services. In the present study, 74 percent (55 percent for the national survey) had received psychotherapy within the past five years; of these, 44

percent were in treatment at the time they entered a CR group.
The current sample had higher psychiatric distress scores on the
Hopkins Symptom Checklist than the women in the national
survey; both samples, however, were well above the average distress ratings reported for a normative sample of demographically
similar women.

The CR Group. The groups were small (six to fifteen),
leaderless groups structured along a set of guidelines provided
by the women's centers. These guidelines merit special attention,
for they help to distinguish CR group process from that of traditional group therapies. Each weekly CR meeting centered
around the discussion of a specific topic chosen by the group
members; mothers, fathers, sexuality, self-image, and husbands
were topics covered by most groups. The guidelines recommended that each woman address the chosen topic from the
first person perspective. Further, while recounting her personal
experiences, a woman was not to be interrupted nor criticized
by other group members, nor was the speaker herself to solicit
advice or comments.

From the interviews we determined that the sample included women from at least fifteen different groups. Three of
these groups disbanded after meeting for less than four months.
In one group, a depressed, suicidal woman demanded considerable individual attention; the others decided to disband rather
than to continue to deal with the distressed member's suicide
threats. A second group experienced two sources of tension:
ambivalence about getting involved with the problems of a more
distressed member, and conflicts between the interests of older,
separated, or divorced women and younger, married participants.
The third group appeared to have multiple difficulties: The
members had subgrouped by age and religious affiliations;
further, levels of disclosure may have been ill timed, with wom-
en revealing intimate details of their lives (lesbianism, having an
abortion) early in the group's existence. Problems of composition and inability to resolve conflict, then, may have contributed to the difficulties of groups that disbanded.

Dropouts. The mean number of women initially in a CR
group was eleven (range seven to fifteen), and most groups
maintained a steady membership of approximately nine active

members. In the twelve ongoing groups, on the average about three women dropped out (based on questionnaire information of all respondents). Available follow-up information on nine dropouts and thirty-two continuers revealed that the only demographic characteristics distinguishing dropouts from continuers was marital status: Half of the dropouts were separated or divorced (all within nineteen months prior to joining CR) as compared to one fifth of the continuers. Initial mean level of symptom distress, self-esteem, and coping styles did not distinguish the two groups, nor did attitudes on feminist issues. The dropouts cited reasons for leaving their CR group that were linked either to general group conditions ("dull," "too large," "polarized—older versus younger women") or to an incompatibility of goals ("the women in the group were about five years behind me in their awareness of women's rights," "others used the group as an adjunct to their psychotherapy") or to the discomfort with their own quality of participation ("too frightened," "unable to participate," "felt left out").

Dropouts, not surprisingly, had much lower evaluations of their CR experience than continuers, as indicated by percentage of positive responses to the testimony scales: "met goals"— 0 percent of dropouts, 59 percent of continuers; "learned a great deal"—13 percent of dropouts, 69 percent of continuers; "enjoyed" the group—13 percent of dropouts, 86 percent of continuers. Dropouts, although less likely than continuers to encourage others to join CR, did not actively discourage others from participation.

Changes After Six Months in CR

The impact of CR was assessed for a sample of thirty-two women who participated in a CR group for at least four months. Besides the nine participants just described who voluntarily dropped out, two others were eliminated from the analysis since one had contracted hepatitis and never actually attended a meeting and the other was asked to leave by the other group members early in the group's history. The results of the analysis of change, therefore, are limited to the outcome for those women who participated meaningfully in their CR group.

Table 2. Target Problems

Category	No. (%) of Women Mentioning Problem
Self concept	
Self-esteem	16 (50)
Role dissatisfaction	7 (22)
Autonomy	6 (19)
Identity	5 (16)
Interpersonal	
With women	7 (22)
With men	5 (16)
Marital	3 (9)
Family	4 (13)
Loneliness	5 (16)
Isolation	3 (9)
Skills	6 (19)
Symptoms/affective	
Anxiety	3 (9)
Handling of feelings	2 (6)
Depression	0 (0)
Other	
Career	5 (16)
Women's Movement	3 (9)
Situational	3 (9)
Weight reduction	2 (6)
Sexuality	1 (3)
Physical complaints	1 (3)
Growth	1 (3)
Total	88[a]

[a] Based on 32 women: 29 women mentioned three problems, one woman mentioned two problems, and two women mentioned one problem. In three instances, a woman mentioned two similar problems, which have been counted only once.

Target Problem. Prior to their participation, the women indicated three "target" problems or goals (Table 2). The majority reflected concerns about the self-concept and interpersonal functioning, with 72 percent of the problems concerning either the self-concept or interpersonal functioning.

Self-concept problems included concerns about self-esteem, assertiveness, and identity. Some women complained that they lacked the self-confidence to be assertive, whereas others hoped to become more self-reliant and independent of their husbands. Some women felt inadequate and incapable of making changes in their lives. Others seemed to be experiencing identity confusion. Common goals were: "to discover who I am," "to explore my identity as a women," or "to find a direction in life." Some were reevaluating their social roles; one woman described her target problem as "confusion on happy marriage—I love my home life, yet feel guilty for accepting 'home, wife, mother' as total."

Interpersonal problems centered on a desire to explore marital, family, and female relationship issues. Several felt isolated and lacking in interpersonal relationships; they believed that CR would give them an opportunity "to develop closer relationships with women," as well as "to hear how other women feel," "to learn how others cope with similar problems," and "to like women more." Still others anticipated improving general interpersonal skills by reducing "impatience with others" and by learning to "speak more freely and deal with people in a more relaxed manner."

Problems concerned with affect (depression, anxiety, affect control) were rare, despite the high scores on the Hopkins Symptom Checklist. Here the target goals differed markedly from those reported in psychotherapy studies, which typically find that more than half of the patients mention such problems (Sloane and others, 1975; Yalom and others, 1978). For the most part, they hoped to explore their attitudes and feelings toward the self and significant others and did not expect to deal with symptomatic distress.

Changes in Mental Health Measures. The results presented in Table 3 suggest that CR aided the women by improving self-attitudes, but it was limited in promoting other changes in psychological functioning. Of the seven measures in this area, significant levels of improvement were found for only two indices: Mean distress on target problems was significantly decreased ($p < .001$) and mean level of self-esteem significantly increased ($p < .003$). There was also a trend toward an increased reliance on the self rather than on significant others or informal helping networks in dealing with problematic situations ($p < .06$). No appreciable changes were evident for symptom distress or the adequacy of coping styles.

The questionnaire data thus portrayed a specific pattern of change: Feelings about and attitudes toward the self improved, whereas symptoms and coping styles remained unimproved. Since most women had indicated that at least one of their target problems centered on their self-concept, this pattern of change was consistent with their goals. The lack of symptom reduction in spite of relatively high initial levels was surprising.

Accompanying this increased self-esteem were modest changes in behavior, such as asserting one's right to take the night off from preparing dinner and taking separate vacations from one's family. Changes were also found in the area of self-reliance, as indicated by responses to a series of dilemmas (for example, "making an important decision," "facing an embarrassing situation"). Contrary to theoretical expectations, women did not expand their range of utilization of significant others. Rather, they increased in the average number of dilemmas they would deal with on their own, without outside help.

Although such self-reliance is congruent with changes in self-esteem, peer self-help systems would be expected to increase use of such networks. Perhaps their increased self-reliance was part of a general feeling of greater mastery and control over their situation—to assert their needs despite what others thought or felt about them. For one woman, this change involved "becoming more choosey with the type of person I spend my time with. Before, I wanted everyone to like me—especially my husband's friends. Before, I used to trail along. Now, I'm just as happy to be alone. Now, if my husband invites some people over who I don't like, I'll go into another room. Other times, I just won't go out with my husband. I do what I want to do, which is selfish, but it's good for me."

Life-style Decisions and Personal Value Systems

Were changes in feelings about the self translated into decisions that altered the women's life-styles? In all, 35 percent reported an important change in their career or interpersonal situations. Four returned to college and three previously nonworking women were employed at follow-up. Changes in marital status included one marriage, one separation, and a reconciliation between a separated couple. One woman became engaged, and two single women terminated long-term relationships with men. The woman who separated, whose change scores suggested substantial gains from the CR group, said this about her relationship: "I felt strong enough to question his attitudes and feelings and decided we were getting nowhere together. . . . I got the strength to make the break in my group. I realized I don't have to let someone physically and verbally abuse me. I had a right to leave." For the most part, however, the women did not consider their CR experience to play a primary role in initiating such decisions, although groups generally did support the women after they had made their decisions.

Analysis of the women's "life space" values further supported our impression that CR itself generally did not initiate life-style changes. The women decreased in their desire for growth, change, and learning ($p < .01$), which may indicate that CR lowered rather than raised expectations about how much change was feasible and/or desirable. Some women appeared to have moved toward greater acceptance of their current situation. One woman, whose initial target problem centered on difficulties in trusting her husband and in feeling close to her family, described her CR experience as having been significant because: "I felt that I have the happiest life of all the members—a reasonable husband, interesting job, relative freedom, and I have a feeling of being able to cope with whatever may come. . . . It made me feel more content with me."

Nor did CR have any dramatic impact on the ordering of priorities in the life space. Using the first five life space values mentioned by each woman, we determined a hierarchy of values both for individuals and for the sample as a whole. The sample hierarchy prior to CR (1. Personal growth; 2. Family; 3. Instrumental—career, education, and the like; 4. Interpersonal; 5. Hedonistic) was the same at follow-up, except for an increased emphasis on the family at the expense of interpersonal relationships outside the family. Overall then, values remained fairly stable with some suggestion of a slight shift toward a more traditional view of the family.

Table 3. Outcome Results (N = 32)

Scale	Pre-CR Group	6-Month Follow-Up	p
Mental health status and psychological functioning			
Target problem distress			
(1, low; 9, high)	5.9	4.8	.000
Self-esteem			
(6, low; 0, high)	2.3	1.5	.003
Symptom distress			
(.00, low; 1.00, high)	.29	.25	NS
Coping strategies			
Adequate (1, least;			
8, most adequate)	5.6	5.7	NS
Defensive (1, least;			
8, most defensive)	5.2	4.9	NS
Personal resources			
Self-reliance (0, low;			
8, high)	1.1	1.5	.06
Personal value systems			
Growth orientation, % of			
values growth-oriented			
(0, none; 100, all)	65	48	.01

		6-Month Follow-Up		
		More Important	Less Important	No Change	
Value hierarchy, relative importance of each area					
Personal growth	—	9	11	12	NS[a]
Family	—	19	5	8	.01
Instrumental	—	10	11	11	NS
Interpersonal	—	3	16	13	.07
Hedonistic	—	8	13	11	NS

Scale	Pre-CR Group	6-Month Follow-Up	p
Marital relationship (N = 21)			
Marital satisfaction			
(1, high; 5, low)	2.3	2.2	NS
Marital discord			
(0, low; 17, high)	1.8	1.8	NS
Marital communication			
(0, low; 15, high)	6.7	6.4	NS

Marital decision making (0, low discrepancy from ideal; 4, high discrepancy from ideal)	.39	.29	NS
Feminist attitudes and orientation Feminist identification (1, positive; 7, negative)	3.4	2.9	.05
Discrimination Index (0, low; 6 high)	1.4	2.3	.001
Feminist orientation scale (0, low; 7, high)	4.97	5.0	NS
Feminist affiliations (member of at least one women's group)	22	37	NS[b]

Note: All statistical analyses were calculated using *t* tests between pre-CR group and six-month follow-up means, unless otherwise indicated.

[a] Sign test.

[b] McNemar test for the significance of changes.

Marital Relationships. CR seemed to have no impact in enabling the women to establish more effective communication, reconcile differences in various conflict areas, or adopt decision-making processes closer to their ideals. As is indicated by Table 3, the women did not manifest significant decreases in marital conflicts or communication, nor did they change their patterns of decision making. Further, no consistent changes were discernible in marital satisfaction or dissatisfaction. Nearly all women who were initially dissatisfied with one or more aspects of their marriage (this included 71 percent of the sample) remained dissatisfied at the six-month follow-up. However, those women who were initially satisfied were also generally not affected.

Testimonials about the impact of CR on marriages gave a different picture. Over half of the married women indicated greater acceptance, if not renewed appreciation, of their marriages. The most prevalent response (N = 7) was that the women felt more trusting and closer to their spouses. In several cases, the opportunity for comparisons with other women's marriages provided a new framework in which the woman could assess her own marriage. The result of such comparative evaluations was often an increased appreciation of the marriage. Other women (N = 5) indicated that their CR group helped them become aware of their husbands as individuals with their own strengths and weaknesses.

Still others seemed to have reconceptualized the meaning of marriage to themselves and to have reevaluated their roles within the marital relationship. Echoing the general increase in self-assertion, several women (N = 6) assumed greater responsibility for their own happiness while decreasing dependence on their husbands. For example, a woman married for twenty-two years recognized that participating in CR "verifies that my relationship with my husband is not what I would want it to be or not on a par with what other women expect and receive. But the point is that I have stopped blaming and come to a new point of actively making more of myself and relying less on him for meaning in life."

Finally, two young women came to the conclusion that they had to give more to the marital relationship; as one self-described feminist explained: "I now realize that I have to give a little too. I was very nervous about going into a marriage as a feminist. I thought I would either have to give up everything or stand so firmly that we would get nothing done as partners. Through CR, I've seen that I have to give a little, I don't have to give up everything nor do we have to battle constantly."

Many would view this testimonial evidence with some skepticism, especially since it was not corroborated by other evidence. Nonetheless, we conjecture that some women may have adopted different and more functional attitudes about their marriages in ways the scales did not measure.

In order to gain greater perspective on the nature of the women's marriages at follow-up, we took advantage of an alternative frame of reference by comparing the CR women to a demographically similar group of women (white, married, college educated, age twenty-five to forty-five) drawn from a probability sample of adults living in an urban area (Pearlin and Lieberman, 1979). The results of these comparisons between the CR and normative samples on standardized scales of marital strain, stress, and adjustment are shown in Table 4. This approach, although not addressing the issue of change, does clarify questions concerning the quality of marital relationships at follow-up.

Table 4. Marital Comparisons Between CR Group
and Normative Samples

	CR Group Sample (N = 21)	Normative Sample (N = 76)	p
Marital stress (1, low; 4, high)	2.2	1.6	.002
Marital strain 1, low; 4, high)	2.0	1.6	.01
Marital coping levels (1, maladaptive; 4, adaptive)	2.9	3.0	NS
Emotionality	2.4	3.1	.002
Social comparison	3.2	3.2	NS
Negotiation	3.0	3.2	NS
Passivity	2.8	3.1	.05
Selective ignoring	3.0	3.1	NS
Comparison with other people's marriages, %			NS[a]
Much better	48	29	
Somewhat better	33	37	
Same	10	32	
Not quite as good	9	1	
Much worse	0	1	
Own marriage over time, %			NS[a]
Gets better	81	79	
Stays same	10	29	
Gets worse	9	0	
Preoccupation with marital problems, %			.02[a]
Very often	33	5	
Fairly often	14	8	
Once in a while	38	40	
Never, almost never	14	47	

Note: All statistical analyses were calculated using *t* tests between sample means, unless otherwise indicated.
[a] Kolmogorov-Smirnov test.

The findings clearly demonstrate that the CR sample had significantly greater stress and strain in their marriages ($p < .002$ and $p < .01$, respectively) than the women in the normative sample and were also more likely to utilize maladaptive coping strategies such as avoidance and emotionality. Thus, the CR participants' lack of change on the marital scales is probably not explained by the supposition that their marriages were unstressful. Based on the evidence available, it appears that CR had little discernible impact on marriages.

Feminist Attitudes and Orientation. Concern with changes in ideology are somewhat outside the usual interest of psychotherapy researchers. However, because of the ideological component of CR groups and their historical development within the feminist movement, several indexes reflecting changes in feminist orientation and attitudes were included in our battery.

After participating six months in a CR group, the women reported having experienced significantly higher levels of discrimination than they had prior to their CR experience ($p < .02$). There was also a significant increase in perceiving themselves as identified with the women's movement ($p < .03$), and eight women who previously had no affiliation with women's organizations joined such associations.

Over half of the women we studied remained uninvolved in any formal political organization after six months' participation in CR. Most of the women were reluctant to convert the consciousness-raising group into a political forum. For example, when a woman tried to get her group involved in a chapter of NOW that was being formed, she was ignored by other group members. In some respects, participants become more sympathetic to the feminist viewpoint, particularly in seeing their own lives as being shaped by discrimination. This identification, however, did not result in activist political involvement in the feminist movement.

Conclusions

Our findings should be viewed in light of the strategic and technical problems facing investigators interested in assessing the impact of nonprofessional helping systems. Paramount are the problems of adequate control groups; managing outcome assessment on a turf that is in no way controlled by the investigator; and dealing with ideological differences that emerge when the organization controlling the treatment resources holds values distinct from those of the researcher.

How representative of CR participants is this small sample of middle-class women from a suburban Eastern area? Obviously, they do not represent American women in general, but the sample does appear to mirror the demographic, stress levels, and motivations of our 1974 survey of 1,669 women who were consciousness-raising group participants. How representative was the consciousness-raising experience for the participants in this sample? The basic format used by the National Organization for Women, which emphasizes guidelines for topics of discussion and procedures, was followed by the groups studied. More direct evidence that this sample of consciousness-raising groups was similar in method of operation to most other consciousness-raising groups is provided by a direct comparison between the several hundred groups studied in the survey and the twelve groups used in the present study. Identical instruments, which asked respondents to indicate meaningful group experiences that impacted on their learning or change, were administered in both studies. This instrument consists of five factor-analyzed scales representing major therapeutic mechanisms of change. The sample means and standard deviations for the current study and the national survey on these five dimensions were: Sharing Commonalities, 1.60 (.58), 1.59 (.58); Involvement, 1.70 (.71), 1.81 (.75); Risk Taking 1.87 (1.00), 1.96 (.74); Insight, 1.99 (.72), 2.07 (.72); Role Analyses, 2.58 (.80), 2.21 (.73). The rank order of importance is identical, with Sharing Commonalities being the most important, Role Analyses the least. The fact that similar guidelines for conducting the groups were followed in both the sample studied here and the large sample studied in the survey, as well as the reported significant properties by the participants both in the present study and in the national survey, suggests that the current study did examine women who are in groups "typical" of CR groups in general.

The preliminary and exploratory nature of this study notwithstanding, a number of important and interesting findings have emerged. CR appears to have a unique impact that distinguishes it from other helping systems. Unlike psychotherapy, in which symptom reduction nearly always occurs, CR did not decrease depression or anxiety. Unlike encounter groups, CR did not lead to increasing emphasis on personal growth and change. Rather, the impact involved reassessment of the self, reflected typically in increased self-esteem, renewed self-respect, and acknowledgment of self-importance.

The specificity of outcome results, as well as information from the interviews, suggests several important group process considerations. CR groups are not social microcosms; they do not rely on the examination of the interactive here-and-now that is prototypical of almost all psychotherapy. Rather, they are environments that provide support, attention, and direction for the exploration of personal problems. High disclosure about past experiences, accompanied by minimal expression of current feelings toward group members—what could be labeled "introspection within a group"—may promote the specific changes found: higher self-esteem and greater reliance on self. A common existential theme, often expressed as "I am responsible for my own happiness," emerged from the interviews. Participants linked this new awareness to the opportunity to examine their personal experiences on chosen topics without the distractions of suggestions, interruptions, and advice giving.

Another element highlighted in CR groups is comparative judgment. Frequently women reported gaining a new perspective or a new view on themselves or their marriages, such as "after having heard others talk about their problems, I realized I was in a much better position than I had previously thought." More often than not, these comparative judgments led to perceptual reorganizations of the life space rather than to decision making. Instead of confirming the feminist imagery of radical life changes, CR discussions reinforced modest expectations of self, career, and spouse. Private fantasies about major changes in lifestyle were modified by the sharing of experiences.

A major concern among professionals about self-help groups is their psychological safety. Several CR groups did have difficulty when confronted with participants in severe emotional distress. One group asked a severely depressed woman to leave their group (providing her with a transparently false pretext). The woman in question survived the incident and subsequently sought professional treatment, as suggested by the group; but potentially harmful effects of explicit rejection by one's peers are well documented. This anecdote suggests that such rejections do occur in CR groups.

Another incident involved the sabotage of a group by a suicidal woman. The group disbanded rather than contend with the suicidal threats. The suicidal woman could hardly have benefited from the experience, and the others undoubtedly felt bruised by it. Another group, by disbanding after several sessions, left members who exposed their vulnerabilities with unresolved feelings. The consequences were especially adverse for a fifty-two-year old divorcee, who described herself as an isolated woman with a "tendency to hide." She summarized her group experience: "I was able to reveal that I had an abortion many years ago. This was significant because I was unmarried and at that time that situation was a disgrace—and I made up my mind at that time I'd never tell anybody about it. I have since regretted telling the group since shortly thereafter the group disintegrated."

Although such unfortunate incidents occur in professional treatment as well, the responsibility for screening applicants and for following up clients, especially after negative experiences, is much clearer for professionals. Backup for peer-led groups is often ambiguous. As already mentioned, NOW has been giving attention to the quality control of feminist CR groups. Such self-monitoring of self-help activities is fairly typical of national self-help organizations. Efforts to increase the psychological safety of participants in nonprofessional groups usually involves setting limits on appropriate content and behavior. Within CR groups, time-limited, uninterrupted turn-taking is one step toward greater safety. The approaches of such organizations as Alcoholics Anonymous and Gamblers Anonymous suggest that highly ritualized formats can be fruitful. Yet ultimately, such constraints result in a concomitant loss in spontaneity and free expression of feeling, so valued in psychotherapy.

Even if psychotherapists experience dissonance as they try to understand CR and other self-help activities, participants themselves do not. Clients often move back and forth, with no apparent conflict in loyalty, between change-induction systems with radically differing ideologies about the causes and solutions of problems. Although professional mental health services and peer-led self-help groups are often viewed as antagonistic helping networks, in actuality many women in the present study were receiving professional psychotherapeutic treatment concurrent with their participation in CR. Their experiences lend support to a "synergistic" model to describe the relationship between professional and self-help services, since those participating in both changed significantly more than the others, who received no professional help. (However, this finding must be interpreted cautiously. The women receiving professional treatment were initially more distressed, as measured by the symptom checklist, the target problems, and the self-esteem scale.)

The interviews amplified the adjunctive role that CR played in psychotherapy. Several women found that the CR group provided important sources of material for later therapy sessions. One woman became aware of a tendency to compete with other women, a problem which her therapist had discussed with her but which she did not recognize until she participated in CR. For another, a CR discussion of childhood sexuality stimulated material for "a major breakthrough in therapy."

In addition to opening up new areas and providing new insights into old problem areas, the CR group seemed to play an important role in bolstering changes that had already been initiated in therapy. One woman commented: "My CR group gives very strong reinforcement of the self-confidence that gets built up in therapy. Every week I always get a compliment from someone; someone in the group will comment how I've thought something out well. The group really reaffirms my therapist who always tells me, 'You can do it.' "

Bearing in mind the need for more research to illuminate the issues raised by this modest study, we venture a number of preliminary conclusions. CR is not a substitute for psychotherapy for those women whose problems are long-standing and involve severe neurotic or character problems. Rather, the groups in the present study provided a forum in which mildly depressed women with low self-esteem could explore their feelings about themselves and their life situations. The major impact of such an experience was a revised self-image. These changes did not lead to modification in life-styles. The lack of change in areas of symptom distress, coping styles, and marital relationships supports our prior speculation (based on the survey of CR groups described previously in Chapter Seven) that CR experiences serve a limited, although valuable psychotherapeutic function.

CHAPTER **16**

Psychosocial Adaptation in a Medical Self-Help Group

Lynn M. Videka

This chapter presents the results of a study of the impact of Mended Hearts, a medical self-help group for heart surgery patients and their spouses. Ethnographic and survey data were used to explore the effects of membership in Mended Hearts on the psychosocial adaptation of heart surgery patients. The study of Mended Hearts seemed a reasonable place to begin a study of the effectiveness of medical self-help groups. That heart surgery is a stressful life event to which individuals differentially adapt has been documented by a number of studies (Abram, 1965; Kimball, 1969; Kimball and others, 1973). Mended Hearts, established in 1951, is one of the oldest and most successfully organized of all self-help groups.

An impact study of medical affliction sharply contrasts the few empirical investigations conducted on self-help groups.

Heretofore, outcome research in self-help has centered around a few organizations: notably, Alcoholics Anonymous, Synanon, and a few other Anonymous groups (Emrick, Lassen, and Edwards, 1977). Mended Hearts differs from these groups by helping individuals cope and adapt to life crises and role transitions rather than encouraging behavioral control or modification.

Methodology

Our investigation of the impact of Mended Hearts rested on the interplay of several methodological approaches: ethnographic observations, interviews, and quasi-experimental survey methods. These diverse research methods enabled us to maintain a collaborative relationship as researchers with Mended Hearts, to gain an understanding of the ideology, purposes, and goals of this organization from both the organization's and the members' points of view, and to integrate and reciprocally build our qualitative and quantitative knowledge base of this organiation's impact on its members.

We chose four geographically diverse chapters of Mended Hearts for intensive study. The first chapter (MW) was chosen because of its proximity to the Chicago area. The other three chapters (SE, SW, W) were chosen as exemplars of Mended Hearts chapters, as identified by the national organization: They had been in existence for at least five years, had continued to attract new members, and had won awards from Mended Hearts' national organization for their furtherance of the purposes and functions of the national organization (this included maintenance of a successful hospital visitation program).

In each of these geographic areas, field visits preceded the survey of heart patients. These visits included observation of the chapter's monthly meeting and of hospital visits by Mended Hearts visitors, as well as interviews with chapter leaders, rank-and-file members, and involved health personnel (cardiologists, hospital administrators, and cardiac care nurses). Data obtained on these visits familiarized us with the needs expressed by heart patients and with Mended Hearts' approach to dealing with these needs. This knowledge became the foundation upon which the survey instrument was built.

Through field observations and interviews it became clear that Mended Hearts is built upon its hospital visitation program, where accredited Mended Hearts visitors visit preoperative and postoperative heart patients in local hospitals. Mended Hearts carefully selects and screens its official visitors, and this sub-sample (25 percent of membership) constitutes the active core of membership (and an important subclass of membership for our study). As Chapter Eight documents, adoption of the visitor role leads to a long-term involvement in Mended Hearts. Visitors attend more meetings and occupy a greater number of leadership roles in the organization than do nonvisitor members. Visitors also testify more strongly to the relevance and helpfulness of Mended Hearts in their lives.

It is worth noting here that *definition of membership* may be a vexing problem for researchers evaluating the impact of self-help groups. Whereas many self-help groups (for example, Compassionate Friends) have no set boundaries for membership other than meeting attendance, Mended Hearts has a dues-paying criterion. The questionnaire data, however, revealed that 32 percent of this dues-paying membership had not attended a single meeting in the past year.

Survey Design. The major strategy of the survey was to compare heart surgery patients belonging to Mended Hearts with nonmembers living in the same geographical areas. The survey proceeded in two waves. The MW chapter was studied first, using a complete list of heart surgery patients in its semirural area. The W, SE, and SW chapters were surveyed in the second wave. In these locations, complete listings of heart patients were not available and the sample was based on lists of heart patients identified and visited by Mended Hearts visitors. Nonmembers were randomly selected from these lists to compose a control group stratified for years of surgery, whereas the complete roster of Mended Hearts members was sampled. This sampling procedure equalized the proportion of nonmembers by year of surgery within each location. A total of 1,293 questionnaires were mailed; fewer than 6 percent were returned because of an incorrect address or lack of a forwarding address. Seven hundred seventy-nine completed questionnaires were returned (64 percent of those delivered) from 473 of 689 members (69 percent) and 306 of 529 nonmembers (58 percent).

Survey Instrument. The questionnaire mailed to each respondent included a range of indexes designed to generate information about selection factors, group process, and the impact of the group on the individual. The impact, or outcome, indexes included measures of mental health, styles of coping, perceived health, functioning in major adult roles, and attitudes toward heart surgery patients.

Specific mental health indexes included a psychological symptom checklist (Derogatis and others, 1974) which measured overall symptom levels, as well as indexes of depression, anxiety, interpersonal disturbance, and somatic symptoms. Other mental health measures included self-esteem (Rosenberg, 1965), a projective (sentence completion) test of negative affect developed by Tobin and Lieberman (1976)—items included "The strongest part of me . . . ," "When I think of the future, I . . . ," and "My health . . . ")—using a scoring system developed by Gottschalk and Gleser (1969), and a measure of positive-to-negative affect balance (Bradburn, 1969) indicating psychological well-being. Measures of generalized coping (Pearlin and Schooler, 1978) included dimensions of a masterful orientation toward environment, denial, escape, self-disclosure, and use of psychotropic medications.

Health status was measured by a scale of physical symptoms associated with cardiovascular disease (for example, "respiratory congestion or cough," "swelling of ankles or fingers," "pains in heart or chest"—reliability for this scale using Cronbach's alpha = .83), how often health gets in the way (for example, "How often does your health get in the way of what you want to do?"), health compared to others of the same age, health compared to other heart patients, and activity level since surgery (more, the same, or less as compared to presurgery activity level). Strain in the marital, work, retirement, and homemaker roles was assessed through scales developed by Lieberman and Pearlin (1977) for a longitudinal study of adaptation in a normative population.

Attitudes toward heart patients were measured by a scale constructed for this survey. It consisted of two dimensions: the degree to which heart patients were perceived as stigmatized or discriminated against by others (for example, "People treat heart surgery patients differently when they find out they've had heart surgery," "A person who has had heart surgery is sexually unappealing," and "Co-workers feel uncomfortable around a person who's had heart surgery," Cronbach's alpha = .72), and the degree to which heart patients were perceived as bonded by mutual understanding (for example, "No one understands a heart surgery patient like another heart surgery patient," and "Heart surgery patients should help one another," Cronbach's alpha = .62).

The instruments used in this survey represented a mixture of nomothetic, standardized instruments used in other research programs and specially developed instruments pertinent to this population. This balance of instruments was designed to remain close to the phenomena under investigation (Mended Hearts and the heart surgery population) while couching the study in a broader context of research on general adaptation and effectiveness of other treatment forms.

Survey Findings

Description of the Sample. By and large, demographics did not distinguish members and nonmembers. The mean age of heart surgery patients was 56.5 years with 91 percent of the respondents 45 or older. Seventy-eight percent of the respondents were males. This statistic reflects a higher incidence of heart surgery for men, rather than differential rates of respondence or differential patterns of membership in the organization between sexes. Eighty-nine percent of the respondents were married at the time of the survey. (See Chapter Eight for a fuller description of the sample.)

A large number of the respondents were retired. The percentage of respondents who were employed full or part time postsurgery as compared to presurgery dropped from 78 to 56 percent. This decrease was accounted for by the number of respondents who retired after their surgeries (28 percent as compared to 12 percent who were retired presurgery). Of all the retired respondents, 75 percent directly related their retirement to their heart problem.

Comparison of Members and Nonmembers. Specific questions addressed included: Does membership in this self-help group make a difference in terms of amount of psychological distress experienced by the heart patients? Do members show higher levels of self-esteem and psychological well-being? Does membership lead to adoption of particular coping styles? Does membership lead to differences in physical symptoms experienced or in perceived health status? Does it distinguish respondents in terms of strain in the role areas? And lastly, do members of Mended Hearts perceive the status of heart patients differently than do nonmembers?

The knowledge of two "membership" statuses within the organization led to the following analytic strategy. Three distinct groups were compared: visitor members, nonvisitor members, and nonmembers of Mended Hearts. A series of one-way analyses of variance was performed. Post hoc contrasts were used to determine which of these groups differed on dimensions of psychosocial adaptation. More specifically, these analyses addressed two questions: Does *membership* in Mended Hearts lead to better psychosocial adaptation in heart surgery patients in terms of these outcome measures? And, do *visitors*, representing a special membership status with greatest involvement in this organization, show better adaptation than either nonvisitor members or nonmembers on these outcome dimensions?

The results of this analysis are shown in Table 1A. As we can see from this table, few differences existed between groups. Members could be distinguished from nonmembers on mean retirement strain and perceived mutuality among heart patients. Members in Mended Hearts showed no differences in any of the mental health indexes surveyed. Visitors showed higher levels of masterful coping than either nonvisitor members or nonmembers. No differences existed on the other coping styles. Visitors less frequently perceived their health as getting in the way of what they wanted to do and saw themselves as more active than

Table 1A. Comparison Among Heart Patients in Psychosocial Adaptation by Membership Status

	Membership Status			Significance	
Dimensions[a]	Visitor N = 123	Nonvisitor Member N = 349	Nonmember N = 306	Overall[b]	Post Hoc Contrasts
Mental Health					
Overall psychological symptoms	1.6	1.6	1.6	NS	
Depression	1.5	1.6	1.6	NS	
Anxiety	1.5	1.5	1.5	NS	
Interpersonal	1.8	1.8	1.7	NS	
Somatic	1.6	1.6	1.7	NS	
Self-Esteem	5.2	5.0	5.0	NS	
Negative affect	1.9	1.9	1.8	NS	
Well-Being	-2.2	-2.0	-2.2	NS	
Coping Styles					
Mastery	5.3[c]	4.9	4.8	**	V>NVM & NM
Denial	3.7	3.7	3.7	NS	
Escape	1.6	1.5	1.4	NS	
Self-Disclosure	1.7	1.7	1.8	NS	
Psychotropic medication	2.0	2.0	1.9	NS	

Health Status					
Physical symptoms	1.5	1.6	1.6	NS	V>NVM & NM
Health gets in way	2.5[c]	2.7	2.7	NS	
Health compared to others same age	1.8	1.8	1.8	NS	
Health compared to other heart patients	1.6	1.6	1.6	NS	V>NVM & NM
Activity level since surgery	1.9[c]	1.7	1.7	**	
Role Strain					
Marital	1.7	1.7	1.6	NS	
Work	1.8	1.9	1.9	NS	
Retirement	1.8	1.7[c]	2.0	*	V & NVM>NM
Homemaker	2.0	2.0	2.0	NS	
Attitudes Toward Heart Surgery Patients					
Perceived discrimination	15.1	14.7	14.9	NS	
Mutual understanding	4.0[c]	4.6	5.0	***	V>NVM>NM

[a] Entries are mean scores.
[b] Significance level (ANOVA): * $p < .10$, ** $p < .05$, *** $p < .01$.
[c] This group had the best outcome on this dimension.

Table 1B. Comparison Among Retired Heart Patients in Psychosocial Adaptation by Membership Status

Dimensions[a]	Membership Status			Significance	
	Visitor N = 41	Nonvisitor Member N = 93	Non-member N = 85	Overall	Post Hoc Contrasts
Mental Health					
Overall psychological symptoms	1.7	1.7	1.8	NS	
Depression	1.6	1.6	1.7	NS.	
Anxiety	1.6	1.6	1.7	NS	
Interpersonal	1.8	1.8	1.9	NS	
Somatic	1.7[c]	1.7[c]	1.9	*	V & NVM>NM
Self-Esteem	5.1[c]	5.0	4.6	*	V & NVM>NM
Negative affect	2.2	1.9	2.0	NS	
Well-Being	-1.9	-2.0	-1.8	NS	
Coping Styles					
Mastery	5.0[c]	4.8	4.2	**	V & NVM>NM
Denial	3.4	3.6	3.8	NS	
Escape	1.5	1.6	1.5	NS	
Self-Disclosure	1.3	1.8	1.9	***	V<NVM & NM
Psychotropic medication	2.0	2.6	2.2	NS	

Health Status				
Physical symptoms	1.6^c	1.6^c	1.8	*	V & NVM>NM
Health gets in way	2.8^c	3.2	3.3	*	V>NVM & NM
Health compared to others same age	2.0	2.0	2.0	NS	
Health compared to other heart patients	1.9^c	1.9	1.8	NS	
Activity level since surgery	1.9^c	1.5	1.5	**	V>NVM & NM
Role Strain				
Marital	1.7	1.6	1.7	NS	
Work	—	—	—	—	—
Retirement	1.8	1.7^c	2.0	***	V & NVM>NM
Homemaker	—	—	—	—	—
Attitudes Toward Heart Surgery Patients				
Perceived discrimination	14.5	14.0	13.2	NS	
Mutual understanding	4.0^c	4.6	4.6	*	V>NVM & NM

[a] Entries are mean scores.
[b] Significance level (ANOVA): *p < .10, **p < .05, ***p < .01.
[c] This group had the best outcome on this dimension.

either nonvisitor members or nonmembers. There were no differences in the other health dimensions. Agreement with the attitudes of mutual understanding among heart patients seemed to depend on level of involvement with Mended Hearts. Visitors more strongly agreed with the attitude that there exist mutual understanding and empathy among heart surgery patients than did nonvisitor members. But, in turn, nonvisitor members of Mended Hearts showed a higher level of agreement with this attitude than did nonmembers. In terms of role areas, no differences existed among these groups in the strain experienced in the marital, work, or homemaker roles. All retired members of Mended Hearts (both visitor and nonvisitor members) indicated lower levels of retirement strain than did nonmember heart patients.

Exploration of the Lack of Differences. Despite the large sample (N = 779) and consequent statistical power, few differences were found among visitors, members, and nonmembers. This number of statistically significant findings is no larger than that expected by chance alone. The subsequent strategy in the data analysis was to explore variables other than membership status that might be associated with adaptation to heart surgery. It was expected that time passed since surgery would exert an influence on psychosocial adaptation. Heart surgery constitutes a crisis (Caplan,1964; Moos, 1977) and it was therefore expected that patients who had had surgery most recently would evidence poorer levels of psychosocial adaptation, with an increase and then leveling off of psychosocial adaptation in our indicators. In addition, differences among Mended Hearts chapters may have obscured the overall results. Perhaps some chapters were more effective than others in helping their members adapt.

To test these ideas, a series of three-way analyses of variance was performed using geographic location, time passed since surgery, and membership status as factors in the design.

Whereas differences in location did not account for the nature of these findings, time since surgery proved to be an important variable in understanding the functioning of heart surgery patients. Time since surgery was divided into four categories: less than one year post-op, one to two years post-op, two to three years post-op, and over three years post-op. Time was found to affect significantly (p < .05) levels of self-esteem, somatic symptoms, and physical symptoms. Respondents who had had surgery less than one year ago showed the *lowest* symptom level and the *highest* self-esteem.

A trend analysis was used to explore the effects of time more closely. For this analysis, categories of membership status were collapsed since there was no indication in the three-way analysis of variance that time effects interacted with membership effects. The results of this analysis are shown in Table 2. A clear picture emerged from these data. There was evidence of a linear trend over time in overall psychological symptoms, depression, anxiety, interpersonal symptoms, somatic symptoms, physical symptoms, activity level since surgery, health compared to other heart patients, self-esteem, use of psychotropic medication, and work strain. For each of these measures, *level of functioning was best for those respondents who had surgery within the last year*. These respondents showed the lowest levels of overall psychological symptoms, depression, anxiety, interpersonal symptoms, somatic symptoms, physical symptoms, and use of psychotropic medication; they showed the highest levels of self-esteem and resumption of activities since surgery; they tended to compare their health more positively to other heart patients. For each of these indexes, increasing time passed since surgery was associated with increasing level of distress. Styles of coping (except for use of psychotropic medication), negative affect, well-being, and attitudes toward heart surgery patients showed no indication of this variability over time. Despite a cross-sectional design, these findings suggest that time exerts an important influence in the psychosocial adaptation of heart surgery patients.

Because our design was cross-sectional and the incidence of cardiac bypass surgery has increased dramatically in the last five years, a greater proportion of respondents who had had surgery more than three years ago had valve-replacement surgery compared to those who had surgery in the last year or two ($x^2 = 27.0$, d.f. = 6, p < .01). But an analysis of the outcome measures by type of surgery disconfirmed the alternative hypoth-

Table 2. The Effects of Time on the Psychological Adaptation of Heart Patients

	Time Since Surgery				Significance
Dimensions[a]	<1 yr. N = 180	1–2 yrs. N = 229	2–3 yrs. N = 171	>3 yrs. N = 198	Linear Term[b]
Mental Health					
Overall psychological symptoms	1.6c	1.6	1.7	1.7	**
Depression	1.5c	1.6	1.6	1.6	*
Anxiety	1.4c	1.5	1.5	1.5	**
Interpersonal	1.7c	1.8	1.8	1.8	*
Somatic	1.5c	1.6	1.7	1.7	***
Negative affect	1.9	2.0	1.8	1.8	NS
Well-Being	-2.2	-2.2	-2.2	-1.9	NS
Self-Esteem	5.2c	5.0	5.0	4.8	**
Coping Styles					
Mastery	4.9	5.1	5.0	4.8	NS
Denial	3.7	3.7	3.8	3.6	NS
Escape	1.5	1.4	1.6	1.5	NS
Self-Disclosure	1.7	1.7	1.8	1.8	NS
Psychotropic medication	1.6c	1.8	1.9	2.3	*

Health Status					
Physical symptoms	1.4[c]	1.6	1.6	1.6	***
Health gets in way	2.6	2.7	2.6	2.8	NS
Health compared to others same age	1.6	1.6	1.6	1.7	NS
Health compared to other heart patients	1.7[c]	1.8	1.8	1.9	***
Activity level	1.8[c]	1.8	1.7	1.7	*
Role Strain					
Marital	1.6	1.6	1.7	1.6	NS
Work	1.9	1.9	1.9	1.9	*
Retirement	1.8	1.8	2.0	1.8	NS
Homemaker	2.1	2.0	2.2	2.0	NS
Attitudes Toward Heart Surgery Patients					
Perceived discrimination	15.0	15.0	14.7	14.8	NS
Mutual understanding	4.7	4.6	4.6	4.8	NS

[a] Entries are mean scores.

[b] Significance level (ANOVA): * p < .10 ** p < .05 *** p < .01.

[c] This group had the best outcome on this dimension.

esis that the results in Table 2 were due to the effects of different surgeries rather than time. It seems reasonable that the
findings in Table 2 are basically a result of effects of time and,
therefore, that time since surgery is an important variable in
studying the psychosocial adaptation of heart patients.

These results suggest that a downward trend in some
areas of psychosocial functioning for heart surgery patients is
likely and that psychosocial adaptation does not improve over
time as predicted by the crisis model of adaptation. In this
study, members of Mended Hearts had surgery earlier than
nonmembers, but an analysis of covariance using time as a covariate and membership status as the design factor revealed that
the effect of time was not strong enough to reveal differences
among the membership groups. Although time elapsed since surgery was a statistically significant covariate, group means were
not adjusted enough to conclude that differences in the time
passed since surgery obscured evidence of Mended Hearts' effectiveness.

Thus, even statistically controlling for effects of time, the
lack of demonstration that Mended Hearts effects better psychosocial adaptation in its members as compared to nonmember
heart surgery patients stood. We still are faced with a large discrepancy between interview and testimonial data collected from
Mended Hearts members and the survey findings. For example,
in this same survey, members rated their involvement in Mended
Hearts on a seven-point semantic differential on dimensions of
relevance/nonrelevance to one's needs, enjoyable/nonenjoyable,
helpful/not helpful, and informative/not informative. In addition, each member rated his or her chapter on a six-point scale
from "could not be better" (1) to "very unsatisfactory" (6).
Members were overwhelmingly positive about their involvement
in Mended Hearts. Sixty percent rated the group as relevant to
their needs (on the top three scale points of the differential), 70
percent rated it as enjoyable, 68 percent as helpful, and 71 percent rated it as informative. Fifty percent rated their chapter
as "very satisfactory" or "could not be better"; another 36 percent rated it as "satisfactory."

Interviews with members corroborated this positive testimony of involvement in Mended Hearts. Many visitors reported

that visitation was also helpful to them because it "kept me active," "helps keep me from feeling sorry for myself," and "makes me feel that this surgery has had a purpose—now I can be of some help to other heart patients." Members (visitors and nonvisitors alike) testified to the importance of the monthly meetings in learning about surgery and the technical medical care (both in the hospital and in day-to-day living as a post heart surgery patient) which is part of the long-term medical regimen for heart patients. In one meeting visited, members eagerly sought information from the guest speaker, a cardiac surgeon, about postoperative depression and the use of anti-depressants or minor tranquilizers to control it. In several chapters, core members reported that they frequently got together apart from scheduled meetings and activities and shared their feelings and concerns with one another (which is discouraged in hospital visits and occurs infrequently in the monthly meetings) and that this alleviated some of the depression or worries they had. The discrepancies between these testimonials and our indexes of functioning is puzzling. Our information indicates that members perceive their involvement in Mended Hearts as personally beneficial, although the survey findings show much less effect of membership.

Were we misreading the avowed goals and purposes of Mended Hearts? Chapter Two documents that Mended Hearts emphasizes its service to preoperative heart patients, not primarily to its members. Perhaps the impact of Mended Hearts would be best assessed in comparing heart patients visited by a Mended Hearts visitor to those not visited, regardless of membership status. In order to focus on the time near surgery, we selected those who had had their heart surgeries in the last year. T-tests comparing those visited to those not visited were performed on our indexes of psychosocial adaptation. No differences were found between these groups on our measures. Thus, we had no evidence on which to conclude that we had missed the impact of Mended Hearts by concentrating on the wrong target group.

Were the appropriate dimensions tested? Were we correct in using measures focused on psychological symptoms, strain in role areas, and coping styles? In other words, the outcome variables used in this study assume that psychological symptoms, self-esteem, coping styles, and functioning in the role areas are the appropriate indicators of impact in a self-help group serving heart surgery patients. Our orientation to studying Mended Hearts rested on the assumption that these psychosocial dimensions were pertinent in studying this self-help group's impact on the psychosocial adaptation of its members. This lack of findings led us to question whether this was a sample who experienced distress on these dimensions as a result of their heart surgery. Was this sample distressed as compared to "average" functioning of the non-heart surgery population? How does the psychosocial functioning of heart surgery patients compare to that of the demographically similar population at large?

To test this assumption, the heart surgery sample was compared to a demographically matched normative population. To obtain a picture of a "normative population," data from a study surveying a probability sample of urban Americans (Pearlin and Lieberman, 1979) were utilized. This study used the same measures of depression, anxiety, self-esteem, coping mastery, use of psychotropic medication, and strain in the role areas as had been used in the survey of Mended Hearts. A subsample was randomly selected from this normative sample to match the heart surgery sample on sex by age distribution. This normative sample did not differ from the heart surgery sample in terms of socioeconomic status as measured by educational attainment (x^2 = 6.43, d.f. = 6, p > .25). Thus, with a sample matched on sex by age distribution and comparable in terms of education, the question was posed: Is the heart surgery sample more distressed on the above-mentioned indicators than a demographically comparable sample of individuals who have not had heart surgery?

The results of this analysis indicated that the heart surgery sample was more distressed than the "normative" sample. The heart surgery sample (Mended Hearts members and nonmembers alike) was associated with more depression (p < .01) and anxiety (p < .01) than its demographically matched nonheart surgery counterpart. Heart patients showed lower self-esteem (p < .01), more use of psychotropic medication (p < .05), and greater strain at work (p < .05), and greater strain in retirement (p < .05) than the normative sample. Heart patients did not differ from the normative sample in coping styles or marital strain. Indeed, the experience of being a heart patient seems likely to result in psychosocial distress. And it is clear that indicators of psychological distress and social functioning in work and retirement roles are pertinent dimensions in the heart surgery population.

Mean scores of members and nonmembers were very close in all measures except retirement strain. In mean retirement strain, Mended Hearts members scored identically with the matched normative sample. The nonmembers evidenced higher strain in the retirement role, accounting for the difference between this sample and the matched normative sample.

The fact that Mended Hearts members *did not* show higher levels of retirement strain than the matched normative sample, and that nonmember heart patients *did* evidence greater strain in retirement as compared to both retired Mended Hearts members and the matched normative sample, suggested that heart surgery patients who have also lost their work role might be the population most likely to benefit from membership in Mended Hearts.

Retirement rates after surgery more than doubled compared to the number of respondents who were retired prior to surgery. Seventy-five percent of these respondents directly related retirement to their heart problem. Retired respondents also showed the highest level of distress. Compared to nonretired respondents, retired respondents showed more symptoms overall, including more depression, anxiety, interpersonal, and somatic symptoms (p < .01). Retired heart patients also showed a lower level of coping mastery (p < .01), greater use of psychotropic medication (p < .05), more frequent perception that their health gets in the way (p < .01), more physical symptoms (p < .01), and more strongly believed that heart patients are discriminated against (p < .01).

These findings, as well as those portrayed earlier (Table 1A) that showed lower levels of strain in the retiree role for Mended Hearts members as compared to nonmembers, may signal a highly specific impact of this self-help group. Retirement necessitated by their health is a reality for many heart patients. Participation in Mended Hearts may aid in functional adaptation to retirement. To examine this possibility, retired respondents were selected from the sample. Outcome among retired visitors, nonvisitor members, and nonmembers, was compared. Paralleling the first analysis of impact, a one-way analysis of variance design was used. Post hoc contrasts of retired visitors versus retired nonvisitor members versus retired nonmembers were tested. These findings are displayed in Table 1B. They indicate that Mended Hearts members (visitors and nonvisitors) experienced fewer somatic symptoms, higher self-esteem, higher levels of coping mastery, fewer physical symptoms, and less strain as retired persons (including strain experienced in fewer areas of retired life).

Retired visitors were distinguished from retired nonvisitor members and retired nonmembers by demonstrating even less coping through self-disclosure, their health was perceived to get in the way of what they want to do less often, and they were more active since surgery. In addition to the resumption of pre-surgery activity levels, a greater number of retired visitors picked up at least one *new* activity since their surgeries as compared to retired nonvisitor members and retired nonmembers ($x^2 = 10.9$, d.f. = 2, p < .01), and they more strongly agreed that heart patients are bonded through mutual understanding. Thus, in this sample, retired visitors were more active and perceived their health as less limiting in day-to-day activities than did retired nonvisitor members or retired nonmembers. But overall, retired visitors *and* nonvisitor members fared better than retired nonmembers in psychosocial adaptation.

Given the importance attached to the visitor role in this organization, why, among retired respondents, doesn't visitor status lead to better adaptation? Retired members were more active in Mended Hearts regardless of whether or not they were visitors than were their nonretired counterparts. Retired members attended an average 5.4 meetings in the last year as compared to the average 3.9 meetings for nonretired members (p < .02). Retired respondents were also more likely to be visitors (31 percent of all retired members) than were nonretired members (only 24 percent of nonretired members are visitors). The difference in degree of involvement in Mended Hearts found previously between visitors and nonvisitor members did not pertain to those who are retired.

Thus, retired members of Mended Hearts, regardless of whether they were visitors, showed better psychosocial adaptation. Members had fewer physical and somatic complaints, had higher levels of self-esteem, experienced less strain in their retired roles, and made greater use of a coping style of mastery, with less use of coping through self-disclosure.

Conclusions

This study raises two major issues. The lack of findings in the overall comparison of visitors, nonvisitor members, and nonmembers of Mended Hearts necessitates an explanation. Is Mended Hearts ineffective in aiding adaptation as a heart surgery patient? Is the psychosocial impact of heart surgery too great to be affected by this group? What are the design artifacts that blur effects of membership? The second issue raised by this study is the need for an explanation of the demonstrated effects of group membership on retired heart patients. How are we to understand these findings in the context of the lack of demonstrated impact for all heart patients? How might involvement in Mended Hearts lead to better functioning on the part of retired heart patients?

There may be several reasons for the lack of differences in adaptation among Mended Hearts members and nonmembers. These reasons may be subsumed under general headings of *nature of the affliction, nature of the self-help group,* and *nature of the research design.*

One explanation of the lack of demonstration of more adaptive functioning in Mended Hearts members may have to do with the affliction itself. In comparison of the heart surgery sample with a demographically matched sample of the normative population, the heart surgery sample demonstrated substantially poorer psychosocial functioning. These findings suggest that the experience of heart surgery (and chronic cardiovascular disease) results in levels of psychosocial distress greater than that expectable in the normal population, and corroborates the body of research on the psychosocial impact of heart surgery (Kimball, 1969). This raises the possible interpretation that the affliction (the heart disease and the resultant surgical treatment) results in psychosocial distress so profound that even an adaptive stance toward one's status as a heart surgery patient (such as involvement in an information-oriented, optimistic group) cannot ameliorate the psychological effects of this stress.

While recognizing the speculative nature of construing a longitudinal argument from cross-sectional data, the findings of the analysis of psychosocial adaptation over time elapsed since surgery (Table 2) suggest that what may be expectable in samples of heart surgery patients is that some psychosocial indexes show a slight *deterioration over time*. These findings are congruent with the conclusion that heart surgery results in psychosocial distress and, in addition, suggest a pessimistic prognosis for psychosocial functioning over time for this population. This finding stands contrary to that expected from crisis theories of adaptation (Caplan, 1964), which assert that the individual's psychosocial functioning drops in response to the crisis with a gradual restoration of functioning as time passes after the crisis. Perhaps these results indicate that heart surgery patients experience a progressive letdown as time passes after surgery; perhaps the expectation that surgery would alleviate the health impairment did not occur; perhaps these patients experience disillusionment and discouragement when they discover that their health impairment remains, even after the drastic treatment of cardiac surgery. In sum, the lack of demonstration of the effectiveness of Mended Hearts may be a result of the magnitude of distress resulting from the heart condition and the heart surgery.

A second explanation of the lack of evidence of the effectiveness of Mended Hearts for its overall membership may lie in characteristics of the organization. It is not surprising that a group in which 32 percent of the dues-paying members do not attend a single meeting in a year shows minimal effects when effects are averaged over all the members. Many Mended Hearts members are minimally involved with the group; it would be more difficult to explain that group involvement does impact on these members than it is to explain that it does not. It is no surprise that low-intensity involvement results in no impact, particularly when the magnitude of the distress resulting from the heart condition and the heart surgery are considered.

What is more difficult to explain is why visitors, who demonstrate greater involvement in the group, show no better functioning than nonmembers of the group. We find no evidence for Riessman's (1965) "helper therapy principle" in the psychosocial adaptation of Mended Hearts visitors. Testimony of the relevance and helpfulness of Mended Hearts is strong among visitors (see Chapter Two for details), but we find no consistent evidence that visitors benefit in terms of their own psychosocial functioning from involvement in the group.

As Chapter Two documents, the primary goal of Mended Hearts is to provide service to the preoperative heart surgery patient. Although the main thrust of this study was to investigate the effects of membership in Mended Hearts on the psychosocial adaptation of heart surgery patients, we found no evidence of differential adaptation when we compared heart patients who had surgery in the past year and were visited by a Mended Hearts visitor with those comparable heart patients who were not visited. Thus, although we approached the "impact" of this organization in a manner tangential to its explicit goals, it does not seem likely that our approach missed the mark of discovering the impact of Mended Hearts in terms of its self-stated goals.

In terms of artifacts of the research design, our quasi-experimental design (necessary in studying self-help groups), with one postsurgery sampling, makes it impossible to tease out definitively effects of the group. There is no way to determine the equivalence of the experimental and control groups prior to surgery and prior to their involvement in Mended Hearts. Although members and nonmembers are demographically similar and seem to represent one population (see Chapter Eight), whether more distressed heart patients self-select into the group is not answerable. Perhaps an additional control group of heart patients who had no access to such a group would have clarified the potential effects of this group.

The second major issue to be discussed is why retired
heart patients emerge as the target population most likely to
benefit from involvement in Mended Hearts. Adapting to retirement in addition to a heart condition and heart surgery is a reality for many patients. In addition, these two life events are not
independent. Seventy-five percent of our respondents retired
because of their heart problems. That the retired subsample was
more distressed across most of these psychosocial indexes is not
surprising. In essence, they may be viewed as facing a double-
barreled crisis—that of heart surgery with its concomitant health
problems, and that of retirement. Our findings that retirement
strain in Mended Hearts members is close to the level experienced by a similar "normative" sample of adults, whereas nonmembers show higher levels of strain as retired persons, as well
as survey findings that show retired members experience less
psychosocial distress and higher self-esteem, suggest that involvement in Mended Hearts may play an important part in
adapting as a *retired heart patient*, even though such effects do
not prevail for Mended Hearts membership as a whole.

First of all, *retired persons tend to become more active in
Mended Hearts* (visitors and nonvisitors alike) than do their
nonretired counterparts. This increased participation in the organization is likely to increase the potency of the group's influence on these individuals; it makes sense that the more involved portion of the membership demonstrates greater benefit
from the group. Nonretired visitors, also active in the organization, did not show these positive effects of membership. Perhaps
retired members invest more meaning and salience in their
participation in Mended Hearts since they no longer sustain
a work role in day-to-day life. This line of reasoning leads to
the conclusion that *involvement in Mended Hearts functions
as a replacement for the lost work role* for these respondents.
Therefore, although Mended Hearts' model of influence is not
traditionally psychotherapeutic in terms of high self-disclosure
(congruent with the low use of self-disclosure as a coping style
in retired visitors) and small group interaction, it is therapeutic
for these respondents in terms of easing a stressful role transition by replacing the lost work role with another pertinent,

meaningful, and valued activity. With this explanation in mind, it makes sense that Mended Hearts members evidence less strain as retired persons.

In addition to functioning as a replacement for the lost work role, this *activity itself may serve a function in adapting to the dual predicaments of heart surgery and retirement*. Gal and Lazarus (1975) explain the efficacy of activity in stressful situations as the instillation of a feeling of mastery even when control over the situation is not possible. This explanation suits retired Mended Hearts members well. Although no ultimate control can be established over the heart condition and the changes it imposes on one's life (such as early retirement), involvement in Mended Hearts, through the activity it entails, enhances the retired heart patient's sense of mastery and self-esteem. Retired members also show higher levels of coping mastery, which supports this model of activity as an important coping mechanism insofar as it leads to a sense of mastery of the heart condition.

Mastery of the heart problem is encouraged through the monthly educational meetings as well as through the intensive medical training that prospective visitors must undergo. As Moos' (1977) model explicates, mastering the essential skills to maintain one's health is an important component in adaptation to a chronic disability. Mended Hearts certainly promotes this kind of mastery over the heart condition, which may explain why retired members experience fewer somatic and physical symptoms and perceive their health only sometimes to get in the way of what they want to do.

There is another component to the activity in Mended Hearts that may further illuminate its beneficial impact on retired members. Not only does activity in Mended Hearts replace the work role and not only is it concerned with mastery of one's health condition, but also this activity is *altruistically oriented* in the visitation program and in the overall service orientation of the organization (as documented by Chapter Two). Mended Hearts' motto, "It's great to be alive and to help others," articulates its altruistic orientation. We may posit that this altruistic focus lends a sense of importance and worthwhileness to activities in the organization and thus raises the retired heart patient's self-esteem. Adams and Lindemann (1974) emphasize self-esteem maintenance as crucial in adjustment to a disability. Indeed, low self-esteem is a characteristic shared by retired heart surgery patients. But a self-help group like Mended Hearts, with its emphasis on learning about and mastering one's physical problems, and the opportunity it provides to replace the lost work role with service-oriented activity may serve to enhance the self-esteem of retired heart patients. Not only is the activity in the organization geared toward the individual's own problems but it is also service-oriented and seen as purposeful in a larger, other-directed context.

Thus, we may conceptualize the model of helping in self-help groups such as Mended Hearts *not* as reform or control of self (as in groups like AA or Synanon), and *not* as emphasizing introspection or interpersonal learning or self-disclosure (such as in traditional psychotherapy groups), but as promoting *mastery* of one's affliction and *maintenance* of a sense of worthwhileness. Self-help groups such as Mended Hearts may be particularly beneficial when usual sources of self-esteem and self-worth (such as the work role) are no longer available.

CHAPTER 17

Effects
of Change Groups
on the Elderly

Morton A. Lieberman &
Nancy Gourash

This chapter stresses the impact of the SAGE experience on the lives of its elderly participants. SAGE (Senior Actualization and Growth Explorations) is not a traditional self-help group. It was developed by a small group of lay and professional people who wanted to create a growth setting for the elderly. In neither the ideology of the program nor the behavior of the leaders are the participants treated as adults who are winding down and whose primary needs are comfort and security.

Technically, SAGE combines a wide range of "change activities" that have been borrowed from a diversity of sources—group therapy, encounter groups, Zen, biofeedback, meditation,

Note: Portions of this chapter are reproduced by special permission from *International Journal of Group Psychotherapy*, "Evaluating the Effects of Change Groups on the Elderly: The Impact of S.A.G.E.," by this chapter's authors, in press.

and various physical programs that resemble classical relaxation techniques. Each group consists of about fifteen elderly people and two or occasionally three leaders. It is an intensive experience involving weekly three- to four-hour sessions for approximately nine months. In addition to being guided through exercises that involve the whole group, members are paired with one another to work on interpersonal tasks of sharing and exploration. They also are given homework assignments generated by topics discussed in the weekly meetings. Informal contacts among SAGE members are encouraged beyond the formal group meetings. In short, the SAGE program offers a wide range of physical, spiritual, intrapersonal, and interpersonal activities in a climate of strong support. It is a relatively structured setting in which participants move from one series of activities to another over the nine-month program. But it is more than that; friendships are formed, support is given, relationships are explored, and issues in living (both past and present) come to the fore. SAGE has moved increasingly, during the past five years, toward a more traditional self-help organization, with the elderly taking more responsibility for conducting both the governance of the organization and change activities for other aged.

Framework for Assessing Outcomes

In our study, sixty people aged sixty or over were recruited either by word of mouth or through publicity generated by the organization. The first thirty people were randomly assigned to two SAGE groups. The remaining thirty were asked to enter a delayed group who would begin their SAGE experience approximately ten months later and would serve as a control group. Prior to the onset of the groups (Time 1), a three- to four-hour interview was conducted for each of the sixty participants in the study. At the end of the nine months of group sessions (Time 2), both participants and those waiting were reinterviewed. The second interview repeated the measures used in Time 1.

Included were measures within the following perspectives: (1) ideographic, (2) mental health, (3) physical health, (4) social functioning, and (5) developmental. The interview first asked individuals to describe their major goals and objectives (Battle and others, 1966). At the end of the group program, each individual was asked to rate on a nine-point scale the degree to which he or she accomplished these target goals. This technique provided information on the issues that brought people to SAGE and allowed an assessment of the value of the group experience from the perspective of the individual. In addition, all participants were asked to generate a list of activities in which they would like to be involved but which were not included in their present routine. They were then asked, during the Time 2 interview, to rate their involvement in each activity on a four-point scale.

Mental health measures included: the Hopkins psychiatric symptoms scale (Derogatis and others, 1974); the Rosenberg (1965) self-esteem scale; the Gottschalk-Gleser anxiety and depression ratings of sentence completions (Tobin and Lieberman, 1976); and measures of various coping strategies adapted from Pearlin and Schooler (1978). These self-report and projective measures provided procedures for determining changes in levels of psychological distress and alterations in strategies for coping with potentially stressful situations.

Changes in physical status frequently accompany old age and have a negative effect on aged persons' attitudes about themselves and their bodies as well as their psychological well-being. The SAGE program focuses many of its group sessions and individual exercises on health issues in order to achieve several goals: improving the individual's physical condition through exercise; fostering a positive self-image; developing awareness of the individual's full range of physical capacities; and reducing the use of health props (particularly psychotropic medication). Attitudinal indexes included self-ratings of health status, health status compared to peers, the extent to which health interfered with activities, and preoccupation with health matters. In addition, sentence completion items were rated for illness and physical deterioration anxiety. Health behavior was evaluated on the basis of the number of physician visits, days spent indoors, and days spent bedridden in the last year due to illness, and also on the number and kinds of medications taken in the previous week.

The fourth perspective for assessing the impact of SAGE developed out of concern with the changing social life space of the elderly. Spouses and friends become ill and die, work roles change, children are grown and involved in their own lives, and negative societal attitudes about aging come to the fore. These are issues that SAGE asks its group members to address. To evaluate changes in social functioning, we compiled three sets of measures: (1) the person in relation to his major social roles; (2) the person in relation to his social support network; and (3) his evaluation of his social world. In evaluating social roles, measures were adapted from Pearlin and Lieberman (1979) to assess the amount of strain associated with the marital and parental roles as well as the mechanisms used to cope with these strains.

Would the SAGE experience, with its emphasis on closeness and intimacy, alter the ways individuals use these significant others to provide support? The social network of relatives, friends, and neighbors used for coping with stress was assessed using the Social Resources Scale developed by Tobin and Lieberman (1976) to determine both the size and breadth of the available social network.

Other indications of social functioning included the person's own evaluation of his or her social surroundings as measured by the Life Satisfaction Index (Neugarten, Havighurst, and Tobin, 1961), which provides a subjective appraisal of a person's life. In addition, the Srole Anomie Scale (Srole, 1956) was used to determine degree of detachment from the social world. The individual's orientation toward others was assessed using a sort task based on a checklist of phrases describing such interpersonal reaction patterns as "I can reproach people when necessary" and "I am timid and shy."

Finally, we investigated two intrapsychic processes that reflect important developmental themes: maintenance of self-image and the use of one's personal past. Maintenance of self-image was measured by asking the participants to give examples that supported their selection of phrases describing interpersonal orientations. A rating scheme developed by Rosner (1968) was used to determine if the examples were rooted in the past, in the present, or in a sense of conviction, were wishes, or were based on sheer mythology. Use of personal past was assessed from self-ratings of reminiscence which focused on the frequency of reminiscence, its associated affect, its use in problem solving, and its importance in the rater's life.

Sample

The fifty women and ten men interviewed were generally between the ages of 60 and 70 (60, 2 percent; 60–65, 40 percent; 65–70, 32 percent; 70–75, 13 percent; 75–80, 10 percent; 80+, 3 percent). Forty-two percent were married; 25 percent were widowed; 30 percent were divorced or separated, and 3 percent were single. They composed a very well-educated sample of the elderly: 2 percent had some high school experience; 18 percent were high school graduates; 27 percent attended college; 33 percent were college graduates; and another 20 percent held advanced degrees.

Over three-fourths of the sample reported good health, and close to that number felt they were healthier than their peers; 33 percent had made five or more physician visits in the past year but spent less than five days indoors due to illness ($\bar{x} = 4.55$) and between one and two days bedridden ($\bar{x} = 1.40$). Most participants felt that physical problems had not significantly affected their lives and spent little time thinking about health matters. Despite this positive portrayal of health, 73 percent reported using some form of medication in the previous week.

The overall evaluation of life was generally positive within this sample and the majority had relatives and friends ($\bar{x} = 3.55$) available for assistance and support. Stress was reported in the marital and parental role areas, but mean levels were usually equivalent to or lower than those of their age-mates (Pearlin and Schooler, 1978). The people coming to SAGE, however, reported experiencing some forms of distress. The mean symptom level on the Hopkins Symptom Checklist was higher than that reported in a random sample of people over sixty living in the

Greater Chicago Metropolitan Area (Pearlin and Schooler, 1978). Analyses of the twenty-two-item Sentence Completion test yielded a mean of 8.55 scorable responses, with over half rated on a depression subscale and the remainder scored for anxiety. In addition, 37 percent of the sample reported seeking professional help within the previous year for a nervous or emotional problem.

Self-reported motivations for joining SAGE were: to implement personal changes, to begin new activities, and to establish new interpersonal relationships. Many participants wanted assistance in coping with physical, emotional, and marital problems. Still others hoped that the SAGE experience would help them overcome negative personal and societal attitudes about growing old.

Methods of Analysis

The Student t statistic or chi-square for categorical variables was used on Time 1 measures to examine the comparability of the participants and wait controls prior to the start of the SAGE program. Analysis of covariance was used to assess the difference in the degree of change on various measures between the participants and control groups. Covariance statistics were calculated on the Time 2 scores, using Time 1 scores as the covariant to control for possible bias due to group differences in Time 1 scores.

We were also interested in the overall impact on participants. Each case was analyzed in order to place the individual in a category of change or no change. We assumed that the best way to study individual change was to examine the direction of change across a number of indexes. Eight indexes representative of the various perspectives were selected (symptoms, self-esteem, life satisfaction, overall coping, anomie, anxiety, depression, and percentage of present feedback support self-concept). The raw change scores for the entire sample were used to calculate a 95 percent confidence interval for each of the eight indexes. The scores that fell within the confidence interval were divided into thirds. Each person was assigned a plus or minus on each index if his or her score on that measure was in the top or bottom third of scores. A zero was assigned if it fell in the middle third or was outside the range of the confidence interval. A plus indicated positive change (for example, fewer symptoms, higher self-esteem) and a minus indicated negative change (for example, greater anxiety, increased anomie). Classifications were then made according to the number of changes: positive changer, four or more pluses; negative changer, four or more minuses.

Findings

Despite the similarity in recruitment procedures and the demographic equivalence of the participants and those waiting to enter, the first analysis yielded significant Time 1 differences between the groups. The control group had significantly higher depression and anxiety scores (see Table 1), higher scores on anomie and parental strain, and lower scores on life satisfaction (see Table 3). Participants were more invested in reminiscence activity, saw it as more functional in problem solving, and thought it was more important in the management of their daily lives (see Table 4).

The evaluations of the target goals indicate that participants felt they had accomplished their desired goals to a greater extent than those in the wait control group (t = 3.68, p < .01). Group members also described themselves as becoming somewhat more engaged in desired activities than people in the nine-month waiting period (t = 1.83, p < .07).

Analyses of mental health variables yielded significant differences between participants and controls in symptoms and self-esteem (see Table 1). Psychiatric symptoms, particularly obsessive and depressive symptoms, diminished more among SAGE participants than among members of the control group. Self-esteem increased more for SAGE participants, although both groups showed an appreciable increase on this measure.

No significant changes were found on any of the measures of attitudes toward physical status or health behavior (see Table 2). Some comparisons, however, approached statistical significance and are worthy of comment. Participants showed more change than the control group in perceptions of the degree to which health problems affected their lives (p < .07). They rated health problems as having less impact in changing their lives following the group experience than before it. A comparison between participants and controls on changes in anxiety about health (p < .09) showed that SAGE group members exhibited a reduction in anxiety about illness and physical deterioration in contrast to the controls, who exhibited a slight increase in health anxiety over the nine-month wait period.

Significant changes in social functioning were found in the way participants coped with marital strain (see Table 3). Group members were more likely, at the end of the SAGE experience, to sit down and talk problems out and to express their feelings directly in order to let off steam.

Within the developmental perspective, the impact of SAGE could be seen in the mechanisms used to maintain a consistent self-image (see Table 4). Subsequent to the group experience, participants emphasized current interactions as a source of feedback in maintaining their self-image. In contrast, the controls tended to shift toward an emphasis on the past. It is interesting to note that, following the SAGE experience, group members also consistently decreased their investment in reminiscence activity, their use of reminiscence for problem solving, and the level of importance attached to reminiscence (see Table 4).

We found that 44 percent of the SAGE participants compared to 35 percent of the controls could be classified as positive changers, whereas 32 percent of the participants and 41 percent of the controls could be classified as negative changers. The differences between the participants and controls was not statistically significant ($\bar{x} = 1.19$, d.f. = 2).

Conclusions

At the end of nine months of group meetings, those who participated felt they had substantially met their initial goals. They also experienced fewer psychiatric symptoms and had a marked increase in self-esteem. The age-related findings were equivocal. No consistent evidence of change in health behavior

Table 1. Mental Health

	Means						Significance Test[a]	
	Exper. Pre	Exper. Post	Control Pre	Control Post	Change Score Exp	Change Score Con	E/C Pre	Covariance
Symptom Checklist Total	1.55	1.48	1.64	1.64	-0.07	-0.00	0.24	0.02*
a) Somatic	1.45	1.34	1.44	1.36	-0.11	-0.08	0.90	0.51
b) Obsessive	1.80	1.60	1.88	1.85	-0.20	-0.03	0.56	0.01**
c) Interpersonal	1.70	1.60	1.90	1.79	-0.10	-0.10	0.11	0.44
d) Depression	1.53	1.41	1.77	1.72	-0.12	-0.05	0.03*	0.06*
e) Anxiety	1.43	1.33	1.50	1.41	-0.10	-0.10	0.52	0.64
Anxiety-Sentence Completion	2.74	3.17	3.98	2.68	0.36	-1.24	0.03*	0.15
Depression-Sentence Completion	5.30	4.85	5.57	5.86	-0.42	0.22	0.67	0.17
Self-Esteem	1.76	0.96	2.10	1.93	-0.80	-0.17	0.41	0.01**
Coping Strategies								
a) Adequacy	2.48	2.57	2.53	2.62	0.08	0.09	0.65	0.58
b) Self-Disclosure	2.45	2.33	2.38	2.26	-0.12	-0.12	0.55	0.79
c) Denial	2.67	2.46	2.52	2.46	-0.22	-0.06	0.35	0.35
d) Escape	2.25	2.07	2.49	2.40	-0.18	-0.10	0.22	0.25

[a] Significance levels: * p < .10 ** p < .01.

Table 2. Physical Health

	Exper. Pre	Exper. Post	Means Control Pre	Control Post	Change Score Exp	Change Score Con	Significance Test[a] E/C Pre	Covariance[a]
Evaluation of health (good and excellent)	72.0%	76.0%	86.2%	86.2%	-.04	.04	0.49	0.60
Health compared to others (better)	75.0%	56.0%	69.0%	59.3%	-.21	-.15	0.85	0.73
Health status interference (never & rarely)	48.0%	44.0%	48.3%	51.7%	-.16	-.14	0.49	0.92
Health problems changed life (little, somewhat, very)	61.9%	36.0%	44.8%	44.8%	-.57	.00	0.30	0.07*
Think of health problems (occasionally & never)	61.9%	76.0%	65.5%	69.0%	.07	.03	0.73	0.29
Physician visits 5+	20.0%	34.0%	38.0%	28.0%	-.16	.10	0.54	0.11
Medication use (yes)	68.0%	76.0%	82.8%	79.3%	-.08	.03	0.61	0.36
Number of indoor days	8.50	12.00	7.94	7.31	-3.33	-1.46	0.89	0.73
Number of bedridden days	2.83	6.25	4.43	4.91	2.68	0.67	0.29	0.54
Health anxiety	1.76	1.28	1.86	1.96	-0.48	0.10	0.79	0.09*
Memory	12.14	11.04	12.72	13.59	-1.25	0.70	0.61	0.20

[a] Significance level: * p < .10.

Table 3. Social Functions

| | Means | | | | | | Significance Test[a] | |
	Exper. Pre	Exper. Post	Control Pre	Control Post	Change Score Exp	Change Score Con	E/C Pre	Covariance
Life Satisfaction Index	12.88	13.60	11.28	11.66	0.72	0.38	0.07*	0.36
Anomie	3.53	3.46	3.17	3.21	0.08	0.07	1.00*	0.61
Marital Strain-Total	1.90	1.81	1.97	1.85	0.04	0.04	0.82	0.47
a) Reciprocity	2.33	2.17	2.30	2.10	-0.91	-0.93	0.93	0.85
b) Role expectancy	1.64	1.64	1.69	1.64	0.11	-0.03	0.84	0.34
c) Accepting self	1.75	1.69	2.05	1.89	0.07	-0.03	0.42	0.60
Single Strain	2.19	2.12	2.36	2.39	-0.12	-0.00	0.41	0.35
Marital Coping								
a) Positive comparison	3.20	3.08	3.40	3.33	-0.20	-0.22	0.64	0.84
b) Selective inattention	2.51	2.37	2.06	2.00	-0.09	-0.11	0.04*	0.14
c) Emotionalism	1.75	1.92	2.40	1.67	0.18	-0.56	0.07*	0.02*
d) Negotiation	3.09	3.12	2.85	2.44	0.05	-0.39	0.34	0.04*
e) Passive avoidance	2.47	2.22	2.07	2.22	-0.18	0.19	0.16	0.17
Parental Strain	1.55	1.57	1.89	1.82	0.02	-0.07	0.03*	0.93
Parental Coping								
a) Selective inattention	2.30	2.41	2.42	2.24	-0.00	-0.16	0.47	0.51
b) Passive avoidance	3.14	2.95	3.31	2.85	-0.20	-0.39	0.56	0.74
Size-Resource Network	3.58	3.79	3.79	3.45	0.44	-0.35	0.63	0.25
Number of different types of personal resources	2.25	2.48	2.31	2.38	0.21	0.07	0.76	0.58
Interpersonal Orientation								
a) Dominance	1.43	-1.78	3.34	-1.83	1.92	6.96	0.30	0.33
b) Affiliation	1.58	1.59	1.01	-1.62	0.01	1.19	0.85	0.84

[a] Significance level: * p < .10.

Table 4. Developmental Perspective

	Means				Change Score Exp	Change Score Con	Significance Test[a]	
	Exper. Pre	Exper. Post	Control Pre	Control Post			E/C Pre	Covariance[a]
Adequacy of maintenance of self-concept								
Use of present	0.63	0.70	0.66	0.58	.05	-.08	0.53	0.03*
Use of past	0.16	0.15	0.21	0.25	-.02	.03	0.23	0.09*
Use of conviction	0.14	0.09	0.05	0.11	-.03	.06	0.05	0.24
Use of wish	0.003	0.00	0.002	0.00	-.003	-.002	0.91	—
Use of distortion	0.07	0.07	0.07	0.06	.002	-.01	0.97	0.61
Reminiscence activity								
a) affect (yes and sometimes)	52.4%	41.7%	37.9%	32.1%	-0.05	.07	0.11	0.85
b) problem solving (yes and sometimes)	66.7%	50.0%	32.1%	32.1%	0.25	.00	0.04*	0.57
c) importance (very)	28.6%	16.7%	21.4%	35.7%	-0.10	.05	0.33	0.57

[a] Significance level: * p < .10.

Table 5. Number of Changes: Experimental vs. Control

Variable Name	Group	Change-Better	No Change	Change-Worse
Hopkins symptoms checklist	Exp.	9	8	8
	Control	7	7	15
Rosenberg self-esteem	Exp.	8	7	10
	Control	15	7	7
Life satisfaction	Exp.	10	9	6
	Control	9	9	11
General coping	Exp.	9	6	10
	Control	10	8	11
Srole anomie scale	Exp.	11	2	12
	Control	13	6	10
Sentence completion anxiety	Exp.	8	7	10
	Control	9	13	5
Sentence completion depression	Exp.	9	7	9
	Control	9	4	14
Memory task	Exp.	5	13	2
	Control	9	12	6
Self-concept present	Exp.	13	3	8
	Control	8	6	14

was found, with only scattered trends suggesting that perhaps the program affected attitudes about health. The group experience did, however, influence the way participants dealt with marital strain but did not have the same impact on strategies for coping with parental role strains, use of the social network, or evaluations of the social surroundings. Participants shifted toward the use of more present-oriented mechanisms for maintaining a consistent concept of self and appeared to decrease their involvement in reminiscence.

The case analysis of change suggests that the impact is area-specific rather than facilitating major personal reorganization. Many made significant alterations in their lives, but few showed consistent changes in overall functioning.

What do these findings tell us about the efficacy of the SAGE approach to change in the elderly? An answer to this question requires an understanding of the program goals as well as SAGE's assumptions about aging. The SAGE program draws a distinction between "growth" and "repair" and offers to its clients not psychotherapy, but experiential learning designed to maximize their potential as elderly. SAGE assumes that many of the problems experienced by the elderly are the result of accepting negative stereotypes or "myths" about aging. They do not believe that physical and cognitive decline are inevitable concomitants to growing old, nor do they pay tribute to society's adulation of youth. They reject the disengagement model of aging and disavow theories that purport the necessity of an introspective, past-oriented focus in order to deal with the psychological reality of impending death. Instead, SAGE follows a doctrine that distinguishes the effects of illness and disease from the process of aging. Through physical exercises, meditation, and yoga, they encourage participants to exorcise self-images of fragile, deteriorating old people and to discover the full range of their physical and spiritual potential. They believe that the qualities attributed to youth and revered by society— vitality, curiosity, openness to new ideas and experience, expressivity, beauty, creativity—are present throughout the life span and are enhanced in old age by a past filled with rich and varied experience. SAGE provides the opportunity to establish and explore new interpersonal relationships and promotes active participation in a variety of social roles. Finally, SAGE encourages participants to focus on the present rather than the past in order to be fully aware of and explore the options and new experiences available to them in their last decades of life. In short, the primary goals of SAGE are twofold: (1) to dispel, in the minds of participants, the myths of aging, and (2) to provide novel experiences and teach new skills in order to facilitate physical, spiritual, intrapersonal, and interpersonal improvement.

Our findings suggest the dichotomy of growth versus repair may be false. People came to SAGE with goals reflecting themes of growth. But many, as reflected in their target goals, also had mental health concerns. For some, these concerns were revealed in the desire to alleviate feelings of anxiety and depression; for others, they were expressed in terms of lifting a sagging self-esteem, changing ways of interacting with others, and learning new strategies for coping with stress. These "reparative" goals did not match the primary values of SAGE, and yet, from the point of view of many participants, they were the focus of the nine-month experience and the most important aspect of change. Perhaps for old people (or all people), growth means, first, the alleviation of psychological distress and then the actualization of human potential.

In light of the programmatic emphasis placed by SAGE on health issues, our findings in this area are particularly disappointing. No changes in health behavior were reported. Only slight reductions in fears about physical illness and minor changes in attributions about the impact of health problems were observed. One possible explanation is that a nine-month experience covering the wide array of topics is too short and unfocused a time period to have other than a minor impact on a lifetime of attitudes and behavior. Another possiblity is that the elderly experience realistic fears about the effects of major illness, and concern with health matters is a viable means of coping with their fears. Although SAGE participants are selected for health, many see friends and relatives become sick and die. Visits to the doctor and medication use may reflect anticipatory socialization into a sick role that conceivably will

soon be a salient one in their lives. The SAGE promise to dispel
the "myth" of decline may be a false one, and thus the elderly
are resistant to efforts that are counterintuitive to their own
sensitivity to physiological change.

It appears that interpersonal skills learned in the group
were employed by participants when coping with marital strain.
Similar results were not found in the parental role area. Many
people remarked during the interviews that the parenting questions seemed inappropriate now that their children were adults.
Thus, it is likely that comparable effects were not found in coping with parental stress simply because it is a less salient role
area at this stage in the life span. It should be recalled, however,
that no measurable impact on other aspects of social functioning was found. No changes were found in the perceived availability of network members in times of stress. Those mentioned
as available were primarily relatives and friends. It is possible
that no changes were observed because no new intimate relationships were formed through SAGE.

The impact of SAGE viewed developmentally indicates
that both participants and controls were able to maintain a consistent self-image. Participants, however, shifted from an emphasis on the past to a focus on current interaction as a source of
feedback in maintaining the self. Previous research (Lieberman
and Coplan, 1969; Lieberman, 1975) has found a positive association between the ability to support a consistent self-image
and successful adaptation under conditions of high stress. The
relationship between maintenance mechanisms and well-being,
however, is not as clear. Lieberman (1971) reported that the use
of current feedback to support the self-image is important in
maintaining homeostasis among old people experiencing relocation. In contrast, we found a small, but significant correlation
between shifts toward present mechanisms and increases in psychiatric symptoms ($r = .23$, $p < .05$). One can explain this contradiction by noting that successful coping under conditions of
extreme stress may require behaviors that are normally considered maladaptive. Under severe stress, a present-oriented
focus that allows the individual to attend to the immediate environment may be the key to adaptation; but in everyday cir-

cumstances, changes toward the present may be disruptive. Erikson (1950) has proposed that accepting one's own life history is a primary task if one is to age successfully and come to terms with death. Butler (1963) has posited "a universal occurrence in older people of an inner experience or mental process of reviewing one's life." Although the universality of such a process has come under question (Gorney, 1968; Lieberman and Falk, 1971), it has been reported in clinical populations (Butler, 1963) and in people residing in the community (Gorney, 1968). It is possible that the SAGE experience with its focus on present functioning has, for some people, interrupted the life review and resulted in an increase in symptoms. Reminiscence or life-review therapy (Butler, 1975) may be more appropriate for those seeking therapeutic assistance while systematically reviewing their pasts.

Finally, we found in the analysis of individual cases that the impact of SAGE was not to induce major personal reorganization but to affect functioning in only a few areas. The expectations of the SAGE staff with regard to facilitating self-actualization across many domains may be unrealistic. However, that is not to say that important improvements did not take place. Perhaps the wide variety of issues explored and change techniques presented in the SAGE program allowed participants to be selective in what they attended to and incorporated into their lives. Another possibility is that the effects of all change-induction systems, no matter how focused on specific problems and techniques, are limited to only those areas that initially motivated the client to seek assistance.

Clearly, the SAGE program has demonstrated its effectiveness in dealing with psychological distress. It did not appear to have the same impact on functioning in other aspects of life; nor did it produce far-reaching changes in the individuals who participated. Are the goals of the program unrealistic? Is the nature of aging such that one can only offer comfort and support for inevitable cognitive, physical, and social losses rather than attempt to stimulate further growth and development? Is psychological distress so widespread among the elderly that programmatic goals should focus initially on repair? Are there intrapsychic processes specific to the last decades of life that must be considered when doing psychotherapy with the elderly? Further explorations into the nature of the aging process will certainly illuminate these questions. But only systematic, comparative research investigating the effectiveness of various change strategies for elderly will provide a meaningful perspective for evaluating SAGE.

The design used in assessing the impact of SAGE resembles the methods of classical psychotherapy research more than it does self-help research strategies. The unusual circumstances of a center in which these activities were offered and a paid staff supported by a National Institute of Mental Health grant that mandated an evaluation component made such a design possible. The lack of an immediate crisis, though often a psychologically and socially painful accompaniment of the "affliction of aging," as well as the limited resources available to the program, provided an ethically reasonable setting for a research design that used randomization of assignment to provide a control group. The rapid spread of both the SAGE ideology and technology, the use of the elderly in providing leadership, as well as the formation of SAGE communities—individuals who have gone through the experience and have now voluntarily associated themselves—make this particular study of SAGE unique for a setting that now shares many similarities with the more traditional self-help groups. As the central resource of leader-conducted groups, so characteristic of professional systems, becomes readily available, neither practically nor ethically can such a random design assigning participants to control and intervention groups be accomplished.

What the design does illustrate is that some of the method problems encountered in the previous two chapters describing consciousness raising and Mended Hearts outcomes are minimal. The problem of interpreting outcome results among Mended Hearts and CR participants and distinguishing them from the effects of selection were not paramount in our study of SAGE. Thus, although illustrating, in any practical sense, the possibilities of self-help outcome research, the study does provide a unique example of the assessment of a self-help group under controlled conditions.

The SAGE study also illustrates our response to the what-to-measure question described in this section's introductory chapter. The importance of studying self-help groups from a variety of perspectives is empirically underscored by the SAGE study. If we had examined the impact of SAGE from a traditional "mental health perspective," we would have missed much of what SAGE has to offer. Similarly, if we had utilized only the client's perspective, we would have erred on the side of overly positive conclusions. The specific and limited impact of SAGE is clearly demonstrated by use of the multi-outcome perspective.

Conclusion: Contributions, Dilemmas, and Implications for Mental Health Policy

Leonard D. Borman &
Morton A. Lieberman

Self-help groups are currently viewed as a helping resource for vast numbers of the population faced with afflictions or conditions for which existing forms of help—whether derived from professional services, natural networks, or personal resources—appear to be insufficient. In this final chapter, we shall explore some issues bearing on the wider use of self-help groups. We shall consider some existing myths and misconceptions, issues relevant to the national developmental organization of self-help groups, problems concerning the acceptance or legitimacy of self-help groups in the wider society, and, finally, in the light of our findings, some recent recommendations of the President's Commission on Mental Health concerning community support systems and self-help groups.

Myths and Misconceptions

Self-help groups are often erroneously believed to be anti-professional. The findings reported in this volume indicate not only that seasoned professionals have been involved in the founding and support of most self-help groups but also that most participants utilize professional help to a greater extent than do nonmembers of self-help groups and, in a number of cases (CR groups, Naim, and Mended Hearts), indicate fairly high satisfication in their experience with professionals. It is also true that most of the professional founders and supporters of self-help groups have been dissatisfied with limitations in their own professional disciplines: theoretical disputes, new views on the nature of afflictions, the appropriate role of the professional, issues concerning fees, auspices, and so forth. Nonetheless, all of these professionals have attempted to maintain communication with their colleagues by publishing papers or books, or in other ways attempting to elucidate the value of self-help group resources for particular afflictions. Admittedly, from the traditional professional perspectives, self-help groups' resources are unconventional or novel and move in some new directions. The articulation between self-help forms and the usual professional forms may be complex and puzzling, but it would be inappropriate to characterize self-help groups as anti-professional.

Many of the misconceptions about self-help groups stem from a polarity that views them either in highly romanticized terms or as completely worthless. From one point of view, groups are glorified or seen as panaceas for all human suffering. The other side speaks of pathological dependencies, escapes from reality, and needless isolation of stigmatized populations. It may be trite to suggest that the truth lies somewhere in between.

The studies reported in this volume pinpoint specific ways in which self-help groups provide important benefits for some of their members. Our findings with Mended Hearts, for example, indicate that those heart patients who are forced into early retirement seem to benefit the most from their service responsibilities as Mended Hearts visitors. At the same time, from the perspective of those about to undergo heart surgery, such visits from those who have had the experience seem to be most welcome. To characterize the visitors' activities as an unfortunate dependency or a kind of escapism would be inappropriate. Nor would these terms accurately characterize the activities of long-term widowed members of Naim. The pilot study of Naim reported in this volume indicates the important value placed on sociability and social linkage by members of this group. Yet we have found that many of those who were invited to join Naim have chosen not to, relying perhaps on personal resources in meeting social linkage needs. Our findings indicate that the most pressing problem of isolation or separation lies not with the group participants but with those segments of the population—in this case, Catholic widowed—who are unaware of helpful resources or find them inaccessible. We shall say more later about these neglected pockets in our population.

What can we say concerning any possible harm that may be done as a result of participation in a self-help group? We are continuing to explore the impact of self-help groups but have thus far uncovered only a few casualties as a result of self-help group participation, unlike the results of outcome studies in psychotherapy and encounter. Although our survey findings of Mended Hearts reveal that the group has little effect on psychological adaptation and other measures—such as coping styles, health status, and role strains—there was little indication that participation in the group did any harm. A few casualty cases in the CR outcome were found, however.

Another prevalent conception of self-help groups, especially among some professionals, is that such groups serve to supplant or even reject society's responsibility for dealing with the needs of special populations. Our findings indicate that this is a premature conclusion, and the recommendations of the

President's Mental Health Commission, to be considered later, concur that self-help groups represent an additional resource—in some cases an alternative to professional services, and in some an adjunct to other natural helping networks. But in either case, the Commission does not advocate the withholding of professional or formal institutional services, and few self-help groups suggest that the functions of professionals or families should be abnegated. Rather the obverse is more true: Many self-help groups contribute to the stability of the family by improving relationships that may be deteriorating. Compassionate Friends, for example, faces the common myth that tragedy brings a family together by providing opportunities for group discussion, the use of relevant literature, and special convention workshops focusing on marital and parental issues. Through the stimulus of Alcoholics Anonymous, Al-Anon and Alateen have been formed to deal with the family problems of alcoholics. Moreover, we can identify a considerable roster of groups, from Families Anonymous for the parents of drug addicts to Parents of Gays, where the membership consists of parents and other family members attempting to maintain stability in the face of a condition that has affected one of their own.

Such groups as Alcoholics Anonymous (AA) and Synanon have stimulated considerable interest on the part of both the public and private sectors in alcoholism and drug abuse. Since AA does not endorse extraneous interests, many AA members wearing other hats have played a considerable role in the activities of the National Council on Alcoholism, which has established voluntary associations in over a dozen states. The influence of federal initiatives in the field of alcoholism has also been prompted from similar sources. Parents Anonymous, a self-help group for child abusers, has received nearly $1 million from federal sources and credits this support for the spread of its programs nationally in a relatively short period of time and for the resulting impetus to public and private efforts in the child abuse field. A dramatic example of drawing societal interests to a little-known disease is the success of the Committee to Combat Huntington's Disease. Begun as a small self-help group effort, the committee, over a twelve-year period, has succeeded in spearheading an effort to establish a federally funded program to conduct research and develop service programs for Huntington's and related disorders. We would anticipate that analogous activities would be stimulated as a result of the formation of newer groups, such as those in epilepsy, cancer, and a myriad of others not discussed in this volume.

Finally, we should like to address the general conception that self-help groups are for "everyman." Self-help, as with most newly discovered resources, may be promoted far beyond the limits of its usefulness. The use of many of the self-help groups reported in this volume seems highly selective; women's consciousness-raising groups, Mended Hearts, Compassionate Friends, and so forth, represent the more educated, less disadvantaged members of society. Although the more educated Catholic widows prefer not to participate in Naim, those who do are still more advantaged than the matched population that had no access to information about the group. Our findings seem to indicate that those who utilize self-help groups are pretty much the same population that use professional services. This was also found to be true in a recent study of Recovery, Inc., which also revealed that the use of physicians' services was markedly reduced after a patient's involvement with the self-help group (Raiff, 1978). We suspect that epilepsy groups, as well as the increasing numbers utilizing Parents Anonymous, likewise represent users of professional services. These characteristics of self-help group users should not blind us to the fact that self-help groups address enormously diverse conditions, meet needs that are neglected by those rendering professional services, and are available at little or no cost. The self-help form potentially may be useful to the others not currently being reached, but these more disadvantaged populations are not currently utilizing some of the prominent national groups. We should point out, at the same time, that there appears to be a host of other more localized self-help groups, some short-lived, that as a whole reach a more diversified population than many of the national or regional groups addressed in this volume. These would include groups formed under the auspices of the National Council of Negro Women, Native American and

Mexican American groups formed in urban areas, and groups formed for ex-offenders. Our historical analysis reveals that self-help groups as common interest groups or voluntary associations are not the special province of some sectors of society, although they may emerge more fully and more rapidly among some segments than others. But surely, as this form of grouping becomes understood and recognized, its utilization among a broader spectrum of society is to be anticipated. As with other forms of innovation in society, such as occurs in language, music, clothing styles, and so forth, self-help groups can form among marginal populations and find their way eventually among other more remote or central segments of the social spectrum. For example, the Lamaze method of childbirth that began among working-class mothers in France found its greatest acceptance in the United States among educated middle-class women.

Organizational Issues

During the past several years, our study of self-help groups has provided us with a fair share of unexpected impressions and findings. We have been constantly surprised at the ability of such organizations to stabilize themselves and ensure continuity in the face of what, on theoretical grounds, would seem to be a reasonable prediction of early demise. Despite apparent chaos, most organizations have endured. The groups presented in this volume are, from an organizational point of view, success stories. When we initially began our studies of self-help groups, we cast a wider net and found a number of groups whose demise was imminent as well as groups that were never able to organize for even brief periods of continuity. Some of these failed because they developed no means of outreach—of recruiting new members to their system—others because the sufferers of the particular affliction they addressed, such as victims of rape, apparently wished to put the trauma rapidly behind them. We need to distinguish between the failure of a particular self-help group and of a larger self-help organization that has given rise to a number of groups. For all of the organizations discussed in this volume, some self-help groups in particular locations have failed, despite the success and growth of the larger organization. What are the requirements, then, for the maintenance, organization, and stability of the self-help organization? How is continuity ensured? We have come to believe that without the addition of new members self-help groups cannot long maintain their original purpose. At first glance, the issue of continuity seems contradictory, for the kind of self-help groups we have studied are fellowships of the afflicted and clearly have as their goals aiding the afflicted to the point where they no longer need the services of the group. The range of solutions to this apparent contradiction, to heal and yet maintain a fellowship of affliction, is illuminating. Alcoholics Anonymous, the largest and most visible self-help organization in the United States, redefines the affliction so that lifelong membership in AA is seen as a signal that the individual has coped with alcoholism in spite of the fact that he continues to be possessed by it. The "twelfth-stepping" of AA, which carries the message to other alcoholics, also provides for continuity. Compassionate Friends has also redefined the affliction. In contrast to the prevailing culture, Compassionate Friends has considerably lengthened the "appropriate" period of mourning, so that one can be a bereaved parent without the sharp time limitation specified by societal norms. Moreover, the loss and its consequences can be openly felt and discussed. Mended Hearts has taken a different course to ensure its continuity. Its prevailing ideology is altruism and one is not "truly mended" until the trauma of surgery can be put behind so that reaching out to the similarly afflicted is possible. The ideology of Mended Hearts provides the mechanisms for its survival and continuity as an organization.

Some of the other self-help organizations we have studied have not been as successful in maintaining continuity. For example, we have seen that women's consciousness-raising groups are more akin to professional treatment systems in that they are conceived of as, and in fact are, temporary structures lasting usually no more than a year to a year and a half. They use proselytizing rather than the organizational means of recruitment characteristic of Compassionate Friends and Mended

Hearts. Furthermore, they are closed systems spinning off a number of new cells rather than absorbing new members into their already existing structures. Some other groups that we are just beginning to study, such as groups of new mothers, share many of the characteristics of consciousness-raising groups. They are closed systems generated out of a parent organization, and appear to have a temporary life span. Perhaps some common afflictions are such that the groups must, of necessity, be temporary systems and can only exist over time under the egis of another system or organization.

A scan of most college campuses, for example, will find a myriad of self-help groups for students based on shared ethnic, racial, or religious backgrounds, living conditions, or other common interests. Rarely do these groups persist in the same form after their members graduate. Some become institutionalized, receiving university support and recognition after a few years. Small groups of patients that form in hospitals, some under the auspices of professionals, provide another example of short-lived self-help groups that develop in relationships to a more enduring organization. In large, long-term mental hospitals, such as those operated by the Veterans Administration, patient self-help groups have been initiated by the patients themselves and eventually have obtained some staff and institutional support (see Borman, 1970). Other examples are provided by the women's consciousness-raising groups, the women's movement, and particularly the National Organization for Women (NOW), which has become the parent organization of women's consciousness-raising groups.

In some preliminary exploration of widowed groups, we find that professional systems provide the organization with continuity over time, but that the afflicted move on and do not remain in the system itself. Widowhood is perhaps the most obvious example of an affliction that responds to two different forms of self-help groups. One form is seen in the Coordinating Council of Widowed Services (CCWS) in Detroit, and the other is the classic widow-to-widow program described by Silverman (1976). These are temporary systems whose continuity is dependent on external organization and/or professionals. The central purpose of these groups is to help the bereaved through a particular period of time, and they see as their goal "graduation" into the larger community rather than maintenance of widowhood status. Our description of the transformation of Naim provides an instructive contrast. Although begun by widows and clearly directed toward issues of bereavement, Naim has maintained its continuity and stability over time and has grown into a large multigroup organization by becoming a system that redefined the affliction and the needs of the afflicted so that members could maintain themselves in it indefinitely.

These reflections do suggest that self-help groups can maintain a degree of continuity only if they are open systems. The closed-systems group must be a temporary one or, if not, must become a group that radically transforms its purpose. We believe, but do not yet have the range of information available to suggest, that the nature of the affliction to some extent affects the choice of closed versus open systems. If the choice is for continuity, unless there is a superstructure provided either by professionals or by an overarching central organization, closed systems cannot long maintain themselves.

Some groups may come to resemble small, secret societies or friendship groups that may persist for a good deal of the lifetime of their original members but admit no new members. Some organizations have devised an arrangement whereby individual chapters or cells may restrict new members, becoming closed in fact, while the larger, parent organization remains open and continues to recruit. In this case, as with Epilepsy Concern, members of closed groups become active with the parent organization and help in the formation of new chapters for the new recruits.

The mark of a successful self-help group is a functional recruitment procedure. A major mechanism of recruitment in the early history of many self-help groups has been the mass media. In all the systems, if it were not for mass media and their portrayal of particular self-help groups, many would never have grown to their current size. Yet publicity has often brought large numbers of new members with which the self-help groups were not prepared to deal. The clearest example of this problem was found in Naim, whose goals and structure were radically changed by an influx of new members due to media publicity. Alcoholics Anonymous, however, developed the Twelve Traditions or guidelines to allow for organizational persistence in the face of widespread group development and membership influx. We have no easy solution to this problem. In order to maintain themselves, self-help groups must grow and recruit new members, and in their early stages the most successful recruitment is public exposure.

The development of centralized functions for the purpose of group growth and development also presents some knotty problems. Where the key helping mechanisms lie within the local, face-to-face group, requests and requirements from "national" may be seen as intrusive. Accordingly, most of the successful national groups have developed a finely honed system of representation so that centralized functionaries do not usurp local prerogatives. The national office takes on clearinghouse-convener-convention functions and minimizes top-down control. But the strain upon local group commitment and self-sufficiency that centralized functions impose may never be satisfactorily resolved. Most national organizations, at least in the corporate and government arena, developed centralized procedures for establishing corporate goals, relating budgetary decisions to these goals, defining measurable results, allocating resources appropriately, and monitoring performance. Clearly, these bureaucratic or hierarchical characteristics are alien to most self-help organizations—yet they may be tempted to emulate these successful organizational examples that stand in their midst.

The Problem of Legitimization

As self-help groups are increasingly being viewed as alternative helping resources, they must deal with issues of societal sanctions regarding their role and place in offering aid. Historically, many of what we now view as traditional sources of help have faced a long and arduous task in achieving such legitimization. More often than not, they have gained such status through identification with previously legitimized structures in society. The early history of psychiatry and its need to distinguish itself from religious healers and cloak itself with the legitimization of medicine and science illustrates this process. How have self-help groups sought to achieve legitimization? One pathway is illustrated by Naim, which embedded itself in a traditional structure, the Catholic church, as a basis of legitimization. Of all the groups we have studied, Naim provides perhaps the clearest example of the utilization of the status of a traditional organization in order to legitimize itself. Traditionally, the role of the church in dealing with death is paramount. It is an easy step to see such a structure providing a vehicle for a self-help group dealing with the widowed.

Another pathway for legitimization observed among those groups studied was the use of professionals for sanctioning. We noted that one of the founders of Alcoholics Anonymous frequently referred to the support of the physicians and psychiatrists who not only gave the group ideas and encouragement but also presented scientific papers on its therapeutic mechanisms before scientific audiences. The history of Mended Hearts is instructive. Considerable effort by the members of this self-help organization to generate friends and allies within the medical profession is amply documented in this volume. Testimonial letters, associate membership, the use of hospital resources for meetings are all mechanisms developed by this self-help organization to utilize traditional sources for legitimization. Despite early attempts, Mended Hearts did not gain the recognition of the National Heart Association, a well-established, fund-raising group concerned with matters of heart disease. This is more the rule than the exception. Organizations concerned with fund raising and lobbying regarding particular afflictions have rarely served to legitimize self-help groups. Perhaps because their status is itself precarious within the larger society, they perceive a possibility of risk in taking such a step. However, we cannot be sure that they would provide legitimization even if they were to give their "blessings." Mother's Groups, another group currently being studied, have derived their legitimization from an ongoing, educationally oriented, prenatal care group—

Lamaze. Lamaze itself, not so long ago, had its own struggle with legitimization. It has, however, developed into a structured professional organization that can now provide a source of legitimization for other organizations associated with it. The official name of the Lamaze organization, the American Society for Psychoprophylaxis in Obstetrics (ASPO), was selected in order to give the organization a "medical" designation.

The pathway used by Compassionate Friends is less clear than that of the aforementioned self-help groups. Compassionate Friends developed its legitimization through a variety of sanctioning bodies: the church-related activities of its founder, central members who were clergymen, the support of various professionals interested in death and dying, and, to some extent, the mass media. Three major sources of news coverage were Barbara Walters and Phil Donahue on television and Ann Landers in the press. These illustrate how well-known public media figures can provide the potential for legitimation. There certainly is a difference between having an information article appear in the paper and having well-known media figures call attention to a group's "good works." A book about the organization also added to the recognition of Compassionate Friends. On the local level, individuals such as clergy, funeral directors, and coroners, who are legitimized by society to deal with death, are among the sources of referral to Compassionate Friends. However, compared with other pathways we have described, it is clear that a degree of legitimization for Compassionate Friends is less certain. We say this fully cognizant of the fact that Compassionate Friends may be one of the fastest-growing self-help groups in the country.

Women's consciouness-raising groups provide the most complex and least clear case of self-help legitimization. Although they have increasingly become part of NOW, a clearly legitimized women's organization, many of the groups have little or no affiliation with NOW or other women's movement organizations. They are free-standing affiliative associates, assembled in small groups of women who may share, in addition to their womanhood, friendship networks, networks in work settings, or geographical propinquity. Can an ambiguous social movement, recruited through word of mouth and the public media, serve as a source of legitimization? It is unusual, certainly, compared to the characteristic processes for the legitimization of professional helping resources. We can, however, find no clear-cut evidence that women's consciousness-raising groups, in contrast to the other self-help groups we have described, have the same degree of legitimization. There is plentiful evidence of resistance by kith and kin toward participation, of the transitory nature of such groups, and of the fact that women's consciousness raising is perceived as ambiguous in purpose, goal, and function. Consciousness-raising groups exist on two levels: an articulate ideology of purpose and a shared, perhaps covert, goal of the majority of participants that is clearly in opposition to the "official goals."

Prior to examining the implications of legitimization and its sources for self-help groups, we should mention another major source of legitimization. When we move from an organizational to a group level, one of the major functions of the national organization that characterizes Mended Hearts and Compassionate Friends and the citywide organization that characterizes Naim is to provide important sources of legitimization for the growth of new groups. In other words, the national or regional organizational level of self-help groups plays a critical role in helping with problems of legitimization for any given self-help group. This critical function in itself provides sufficient rationale for supporting, from a policy point of view, the development of self-help groups in this direction. Again, consciousness-raising groups are illustrative since, until very recently, the majority of them were not linked to any national or larger than group-size body. They were free-standing entities, which would imply that the growth and development pattern would be distinct in contrast to self-help groups that partook of larger self-help organizations. It might not be too farfetched to suggest that larger entities, such as affiliations of self-help groups themselves within major geographical areas as well as on a national basis, could serve such a function for a diversity of self-help groups. Implied in this suggestion is the assumption that legitimization is required for the growth, maintenance, and stability of self-help groups. Here our evidence is only partial at best. At the initiation of our study, we did, however, examine a large variety of self-help groups and found some, such as Divorce Anonymous, despite its long history, to be a disintegrating group. The problems for this group were many but they did include the fact that there was no source of legitimation available.

At the very least, being legitimized as a helping resource does provide for ease of entrance by participants since they have to overcome less resistance on an individual level to entering such a system. They receive support from society in general and from significant representatives in their own lives, who may include both friends and family as well as relevant professionals. There is no question that self-help groups themselves view legitimization as a critical element. The effort and energy spent on this issue by such organizations as Mended Hearts amply demonstrate, from the perspective of the self-help organization, the importance of societal support.

Another important source of legitimization for many groups has been the support and recognition received from charitable foundations. Whereas professionals, voluntary associations, and government agencies have been reluctant to recognize the helpful role of self-help groups, foundations have not been hesitant. Alcoholics Anonymous received a considerable boost from John D. Rockefeller, Jr. in its early years, not so much from the limited funds provided but from the hosting of luncheons and the introductions to influential citizens in society. The W. Clement and Jessie V. Stone Foundation played a similar role with Parents Anonymous many years later when it facilitated the development of the Chicago chapter, organized press conferences, and provided organizational fund raising consultations, in addition to some monies. Such support from private prestigious donors often signals to other segments of society that a group is legitimate, not a superficial flash in the pan, and deserves the opportunity to demonstrate its value.

We have, unfortunately, no clear idea beyond these speculative comments of how to assess the degree of legitimization possessed by each group and from what sources it is derived. It does not seem farfetched, however, given the history of the self-help groups we have studied as well as the larger context of helping resources and their requirement for legitimization in their early history, to suggest that this is an issue that must be confronted by self-help groups in order for them to maintain continuity over a reasonable period of time. Unlike some social movements that arise in clear-cut opposition to society, the organizing intensity of self-help is not to be found in this mechanism. Self-help groups do not parallel the growth of many social movements—religious, protest, and so forth. Self-help groups are not in opposition to society and they seek its legitimization in order to maintain themselves over time.

Despite the efforts that self-help groups may make to seek wider acceptance in society—through the use of professionals, the media, a national organization, foundation support, and so forth—they may nonetheless be rebuffed by some prestigious sources of legitimacy. Recovery, Inc., for example, in its early years received considerable support from psychiatric and academic circles, especially in Illinois where its founder had a distinguished reputation. But as the group began to grow and spread and developed a national organizational structure, it met with increasing coolness by psychiatrists. So long as Recovery was seen as a professionally supervised adjunct to psychotherapy, as it was under Dr. Low in its early years, it was accepted. But once it became a layman-run self-help group, especially following the death of its founder in 1954, it lost much of its psychiatric credibility. The 1957 Joint Commission on Mental Illness and Health (1961) agreed to review the work of Recovery and other self-help groups, but in its final report devoted only two pages to its findings on "ex-mental patient organizations," concluding that the groups were not increasing in number and were remarkably unstable and short-lived. In striking contrast is the 1978 report of the President's Commission on Mental Health, to be considered in the next section, which highlighted the work of Recovery and other self-help groups.

Some Policy Implications

What had changed over the seventeen-year interval between the two commission reports that generated an about-face in the consideration of the role that self-help groups might play in the mental health of society? One document that provides a valuable glimpse into the basis for this shifting viewpoint is the *Forward Plan For Health*, published by the Public Health Service of the U.S. Department of Health, Education, and Welfare in 1976. It presents a coherent frame of reference for the examination of major health issues to inform those engaged in federal budgetary and legislative decisions. The plan identifies three critical areas for attention. These recommendations obviously set the stage for the new consideration of self-help groups and other community resources that followed.

The first recommendation focused on containing the cost of health care and noted that aspirations far outdistance resources. Two suggestions relevant to self-help groups were the importance of strengthening local planning and of developing greater health service capacities in local communities. A second recommendation concerned the need for implementing an aggressive strategy for prevention. It recognized that greater health benefits are more likely to accrue as a result of improving the health habits of citizens than through the expansion of health care programs, and recommended the expansion of consumer participation in all health activities. The third basic recommendation was for increasing the quality of health care. One central feature bearing on self-help groups was the priority placed on reducing institutional care while, at the same time, exploring noninstitutional forms of care, especially access to care.

In a special issue of the *Journal of Applied Behavioral Sciences* (JABS), which we edited in 1976, several courses of desirable public policy were reiterated, including the need for greater professional and public understanding of the self-help phenomenon, the availability of skillful, sympathetic, professional technical assistance, and the need for collaboration between self-help groups and professionals in areas of research, service, and development. (For additional discussion of policy, see Borman, 1976b.)

These recommendations and others have since been incorporated in a major report submitted to the President's Commission on Mental Health (1978). In considering self-help groups as one of several community support systems, the report

recommends that the federal government undertake some new
initiatives in community mental health that would achieve the
following objectives:

> Recognize and strengthen the natural net-
> works to which people belong and on which they
> depend—families, kin, kith, friendship, and neigh-
> borhood social networks; work relationships; reli-
> gious denominations and congregations; and self-
> help groups and other voluntary associations based
> on principles of intimacy and mutual aid.
>
> Identify and strengthen the potential social
> support functions of formal caregiving institutions.
>
> Improve the linkages between natural helping
> networks and the more formal sources of help—pro-
> fessional and institutional.
>
> Develop educational strategies to inform the
> general public and caregiving professionals on the
> nature and function of natural helping networks
> and on the importance of attachments and mutual-
> ity for well-being.
>
> Initiate research to provide national data
> periodically on social support and on natural help-
> ing networks in American society, to monitor the
> direction and magnitude of changes in these as-
> pects of American life, and to increase knowledge
> of how best to attain the above objectives (p. 144).

These were the report's general recommendations. It
might be useful, in the light of the research findings presented
in this volume, to comment on what the report identifies as its
recommended action strategies and policy options. Since the
report focuses on a variety of community support systems, including neighborhoods, community organizations, religious
institutions, and schools, we shall only comment on those recommendations most pertinent to self-help groups.

Recommendation 13: "Mandate that community mental
health centers provide directories of mutual help groups and
similar peer-oriented support systems as part of their resource
base and encourage other community organizations, both public
and private, to disseminate these directories in order to make

such groups more accessible to the public" (President's Commission on Mental Health, 1978, p. 178).

One of the common problems faced by the groups discussed in this volume has been that of reaching others who might benefit from group participation or services. Some of the problems faced by groups that suddenly become inundated with new members have already been considered. Since our studies indicate that most of those who avail themselves of self-help group services utilize professional services as well, other segments of the population may need to be reached. Our finding on those who did not use Naim, for example, indicated that those widowed Catholics in the population who were most in need of help, and who might most benefit from self-help groups, either had no access to the groups or were uninformed of their whereabouts. Although the media have played an enormous part in bringing self-help groups to the attention of those who would benefit, additional means are needed. Directories available in community mental health centers might be helpful to many, but we should be aware of the fact that those who may desperately need such help are not the clients of mental health centers, nor of other professional agencies. The recommendation suggests that other community organizations be involved in the dissemination of directories—and it may be that this option should be emphasized. Professional agencies could play an important role in identifying, updating, and retrieving information on the whereabouts of self-help groups. Clearly, new chapters come and go, new phone numbers and addresses appear, and new groups continually form. Thoughtful effort needs to be directed to such retrieval and dissemination issues.

Let us reiterate a caution raised earlier—that the sudden inundation of groups with requests for information, membership, group attendance, and so forth, can place strains on the existing resources of many self-help groups. They require the capacity to respond in a responsible way. Professionals and agencies who would accelerate access to groups should also be responsive to group requests for assistance, when these are forthcoming.

Recommendation 14: "Develop clearinghouses on mutual help groups and peer-oriented support systems in each federal region throughout the country to integrate information, to publish newsletters and other materials, to provide training and technical assistance, to sponsor periodic regional conferences on self-help, to enable professionals and members of self-help groups to learn from each other" (President's Commission on Mental Health, 1978, p. 178).

As indicated earlier, many of the initial contacts with some of the groups studied in this volume were made through the Self-Help Institute of Northwestern University, established as one of the first clearinghouses of its kind in the country. Such a multipurpose clearinghouse has not only facilitated our research efforts but has also provided a two-way vehicle: On the one hand we can translate our findings and understandings into language and programs ultimately useful to self-help groups; on the other hand, self-help groups are able to communicate their findings, needs, and problems to professionals as well. In addition, as a clearinghouse, the institute has facilitated communication between self-help groups and the public through the printing and dissemination of directories and other publications, providing information for the media, arranging for panel presentations of self-help group representatives before a variety of organizations, and responding to inquiries by phone and correspondence. Regional conferences and workshops may be extremely useful, as the institute itself was an outgrowth of the Self-Help Workshop convened in 1974. Such conferences can spawn new practical and scholarly endeavors, as with the epilepsy self-help group workshop. This workshop has been based on an "action-learning" model in which self-help group leaders (who all have epilepsy) meet one day a month with a small group of researchers and students. On the one hand, a national communications network is being facilitated through the publication of a newsletter (*Epilepsy Self-Help Workshop Newsletter*, 1979), and on the other hand, the entire group is learning about epilepsy groups nationwide. Often the group leaders and researchers will conduct site visits together in cities where such groups meet, reporting their findings to the entire workshop. The planned publications will also reflect this collaboration. Clearly, the multiplication of such clearinghouses throughout the country, would serve to strengthen local capacities of both professionals and self-help groups for improving health conditions.

There may be an important organizational basis for developing such clearinghouses independently of existing mental health agencies or clinics. One of the problems of tacking on an added function, such as clearinghouse, to an existing large organization, such as a mental health center, is that the new task may be neglected or simply overwhelmed by other more important purposes of the organization. A clearinghouse is not a treatment facility. This fact alone suggests clear separation from clinical-treatment agencies. At the same time, conventional service agencies and clinics might explore ways in which they can provide additional help to their clients, for example, by encouraging self-help groups to meet on their premises and/or serving as professional sponsors of such groups. Ways also need to be developed for self-help groups to tap professional skills that may be available at agencies (and elsewhere) around the myriad of problems such groups face. A clearinghouse could serve as such a "talent bank," utilizing a voucher system to provide a range of technical assistance to groups, as demonstrated in a project conducted recently at Northwestern University (Pitts, 1975).

Moreover, as we have noted, the successful national self-help organizations have developed an organizational style that places heavy emphasis on local autonomy, diminishing controls and directives from above. We need to be sensitive to these important dimensions of self-help group sustenance as we explore innovative approaches to be helpful. We may need to place some checks on our own professional and bureaucratic tendencies that might lead us to develop a "bureau of self-help groups." From all indications, this would be a disastrous outcome. Clearinghouse, yes; bureaucracies, no. A helpful analogy would be a comparison of telephones as clearinghouses or linkage mechanisms to television, which is top-down, one-way communication. Self-help clearinghouses might well follow the telephone model, which has provided the basis for the rapidly developing "learning exchanges" throughout the country.

Recommendation 15: "Develop curricula in all undergraduate and graduate programs in the social, behavioral, educational, and medical sciences and professions relating to mental health services delivery on the nature and function of community support systems, natural helping networks, and mutual help groups. The inclusion of such curricula should be considered an essential element in the accreditation process for approval status for graduate professional training programs in medicine, psychology, social work, nursing, pastoral counseling, rehabilitation, psychiatry, and other related disciplines" (President's Commission on Mental Health, 1978, p. 178).

Our studies clearly indicate the diversity of professionals involved with self-help groups, the paucity of the knowledge base around such phenomena in their particular disciplines, and the need to find ways to incorporate the gradually cumulative findings into graduate training programs. While academic disciplines are known to be conservative, they are also responsive to new empirical findings. All of us who have teaching responsibilities, and who have been involved in research reported in this volume, are finding ways to infuse these findings into course offerings. The issues of accreditation are more delicate and need to be addressed by the appropriate bodies. A balanced perspective is needed that would weigh the various educational and training components necessary for accomplished practice in specific disciplines. It is hoped that the studies reported here will help us move the field of self-help group studies out of the realm of speculation and onto a plane of empirical findings that would delimit the issues of argument. The findings reported in Part Three of this volume indicate that professionals have a propensity to emphasize only those group processes that they can determine and control. These findings may call for major revisions in our understanding of the effect of professionals in group settings. The role of professionals in the development of many self-help groups, outlined in Chapter One, may also provide some new clues for training directions that might be incorporated and required in new curricula.

On the issue of accreditation, we might reiterate the point made in the JABS special issue that professionals refrain from uninvited efforts at accreditation or certification of self-help group leaders. This is a process that the groups must monitor and control on their own. If some seek advice and suggestions, fine. But we should be restrained in our efforts to remake their groups and programs into images more consonant with professional skills or therapeutic ideologies. Recall Antze's warning (Chapter Twelve) on the risks assumed by outsiders, who may tamper with a self-help group's ideology.

Recommendation 2: "Experimentation, with program evaluation, to develop new mechanisms for reimbursement of social support services and for community support systems programming as a legitimate part of health and mental health services delivery" (President's Commission on Mental Health, 1978, p. 155).

Obviously, the issue of financial support of self-help and other community support systems needs careful scrutiny, for some of the same reasons given in the previous section: namely, the consequences of outside control, direction, accreditation, and so forth. However, we have already identified some tasks that have been supported in the development of self-help groups, or various stages at which outside financial support was essential. Some start-up funding was required, as in the development of epilepsy self-help groups through a federal grant. Some self-help group coordinators employed by epilepsy chapters continued to be supported through Title XX and other funding. Often they serve to facilitate the formation of self-help groups, although how they determine the eligibility of their "clients" and report on their group activities continues to be problematic. Evidently, such problems were not insurmountable in Australia, where GROW was able to increase its groups immeasurably with the support for chapter coordinators and group facilitators provided by the Australian government.

Parents Anonymous continues to be supported by government funds in its efforts to develop chapters in fifty states, disseminate a national newsletter, hold training sessions, and maintain a toll-free national hotline. These may suggest kinds of organizational support for specific programs that may be applicable to other groups as well. Other areas of support, at this general level, have included funds for research and evaluation, workshops, development of technical assistance manuals, and so forth. Obviously, more reimbursement experimentation needs to be undertaken, and some might well be developed around directory development and dissemination and the clearinghouse recommendation outlined previously, including the voucher system for technical assistance. The ways in which individuals might be assisted in their use of self-help groups requires additional experimentation. Transportation has frequently been seen as a problem, as we have found in Mended Hearts and Epilepsy groups. Obviously, we need to know more about those segments of the population who might well benefit from group participation but currently have little access to or information about appropriate groups.

Recommendation 16: "Federal monies should be made available to state mental health associations to help catalyze a citizen-controlled statewide strategy for the development of locally based peer-oriented support networks, to give technical assistance in the implementation to their local affiliated associations, and to develop information and referral sources of mutual help groups" (President's Commission on Mental Health, 1978, p. 178).

Recommendation 17: "Convene a national conference of directors of volunteer programs in health, mental health, educational, and social welfare programs to identify ways that volunteer programs can be creatively linked to the community's natural support networks and the formal caregiving institutions" (President's Commission on Mental Health, 1978, p. 179).

Both of these recommendations touch importantly on the voluntary sector of society. Our findings indicate that there has been a very uneven relationship between voluntary associations and self-help groups. On the one hand, many voluntary associations have evolved from self-help groups. On the other hand, the child may not recognize the parent and, in this case, place little emphasis on the qualities of self-help, mutual aid, and support that were most characteristic of founding peer-oriented groups. The lay component has often given way to professional expertise. Furthermore, it may be all too easy to gloss over important distinctions between voluntary agencies and self-help groups. As previously indicated, most of those voluntary associations that are affliction oriented have been hesitant in recognizing and supporting the work and activities of those self-help groups that share their focal concern.

These differences dramatize the importance of strengthening understanding between voluntary associations and self-help groups. National conferences may not be as productive as more systematic and sustained activities that would clearly inform both volunteers and self-help group members about each other's interests and perspectives. A clarification of these issues, with appropriate respect for each other's prerogatives, should precede, or become a part of, any effort to catalyze a citizen-controlled statewide strategy.

Finally, the report of the President's Commission on Mental Health (1978) recommends at several points the importance of research in increasing knowledge of the mechanisms whereby social support is effective in reducing mental distress. At the same time, the report recommends that procedures and instruments be made available to communities to permit them to evaluate their own progress in enhancing the giving and receiving of social support.

These recommendations touch very closely on the nature of the work reported in this volume. We have attempted to develop instruments that would provide a better understanding of the participants in self-help groups, the processes that make these groups effective, and the basis that can be used for assessing outcome. We need to reiterate the value we have placed on combining learning and the development of procedures and instruments with working together with self-help groups—this requires the utmost of mutual understanding. Often a back and forth interaction process has prevailed. As we have indicated throughout this volume, collaboration between researchers and self-help groups has been essential. Not only has this cooperation been crucial in advancing our understanding, in developing procedures, instruments, and so forth, but in the dissemination and utilization of our findings as well. We have continually provided feedback to the groups themselves, through reports, presentations, and informal contacts that we hope were intelligible to them. As research specialists, we tend to communicate primarily with our colleagues, through a language and concepts not always clear to the public or, in this case, self-help group members. If the commission's recommendations on this point are implemented, meaningful communication between researchers and community groups is essential for strengthening a community's capacity for evaluating social support.

As Havelock and Lingwood (1973) have indicated, the classic model of applied science that is usually divorced from user involvement may need modification. Our experience in learning about and working with self-help groups has convinced us of the values of such collaboration. We hope that other professionals find additional ways for reducing mental distress by combining learning with helping.

References

Abram, H. S. "Adaptation to Open-Heart Surgery: A Psychiatric Study of Response to the Threat of Death." *American Journal of Psychiatry*, 1965, *122*, 659–688.

Action for Mental Health: Final Report of the Joint Commission on Mental Illness and Health. New York: Basic Books, 1961.

Adams, J. E., and Lindemann, E. "Coping with Long-Term Disability." In G. N. Coelho, D. A. Hamburg, and J. E. Adams (Eds.), *Coping and Adaptation.* New York: Basic Books, 1974.

Al-Anon/Alateen Fact Sheet. New York: Al-Anon Family Group Headquarters, 1976.

Alcoholics Anonymous. *Twelve Steps and Twelve Traditions.* New York: Alcoholics Anonymous World Services, 1953.

Alcoholics Anonymous. *Alcoholics Anonymous.* New York: Alcoholics Anonymous World Services, 1955. (Originally published 1937.)

Alcoholics Anonymous. *Alcoholics Anonymous Comes of Age.* New York: Alcoholics Anonymous World Services, 1957.

Allen, P. *Free Space: A Perspective on the Small Group in Women's Liberation.* New York: Times Change Press, 1970.

Anderson, R. T. "Voluntary Association in History." *American Anthropologist*, 1971, *73*, 209–222.

Antze, P. "The Role of Ideologies in Peer Psychotherapy Organizations: Some Theoretical Considerations and Three Case Studies." In M. A. Lieberman and L. D. Borman (Eds.), "Self-Help Groups—Special Issue." *Journal of Applied Science*, 1976, *12* (3), 323–346.

Arnold, J. "Consciousness Raising." In S. Stambler (Ed.), *Women's Liberation: Blueprint for the Future*. New York: Ace Books, 1970.

Bach, K. W., and Taylor, R. C. "Self-Help Groups: Tool or Symbol?" *Journal of Applied Behavioral Sciences*, 1976, *12* (3), 295–309.

Baekeland, F., Lundwall, L., and Kissin, B. "Methods for the Treatment of Chronic Alcoholism: A Critical Appraisal." In R. J. Gibbins and others (Eds.), *Research Advances in Alcohol and Drug Problems*. Vol. 2. New York: Wiley, 1975.

Baker, O. V. "Effects of Social Integration on the Utilization of Mental Health Services." Paper presented at the annual meeting of the American Psychological Association, San Francisco, September 1977.

Bales, R. F. "The Therapeutic Role of Alcoholics Anonymous as Seen by a Sociologist." *Quarterly Journal of Studies on Alcohol*, 1944, *5*, 267–278.

Bandura, A. "Psychotherapy Based upon Modeling Principles." In A. E. Bergin and S. L. Garfield (Eds.), *Handbook of Psychotherapy and Behavior Change*. New York: Wiley, 1971.

Banton, M. "Voluntary Associations: Anthropological Aspects." *International Encyclopedia of the Social Sciences*, 1968, *16*, 357–362.

Barrett, C. J. "Effectiveness of Widows' Groups in Facilitating Change." *Journal of Consulting and Clinical Psychology*, 1978, *46*, 20–31.

Bassin, A. "Taming the Wild Paraprofessional." *Journal of Drug Issues*, 1973, *3*, 333–340.

Bateson, G. "The Cybernetics of Self: A Theory of Alcoholism." *Psychiatry*, 1971, *34* (1), 1–18.

Battle, C. C., and others. "Target Complaints as Criteria of Improvement." *American Journal of Psychotherapy*, 1966, *20*, 184–192.

Bauer, R. A. "The Communicator and the Audience." *Journal of Conflict Resolution*, 1958, *2*, 67–77.

Beck, A. T. *Cognitive Therapy and the Emotional Disorders*. New York: International Universities Press, 1976.

Beck, D. F. "Patterns of Use of Family Agency Service." Paper presented to biennial meeting of the Family Service Association of America, 1961.

Bednar, R. L., and Lawlis, G. F. "Empirical Research in Group Psychotherapy." In A. E. Bergin and S. L. Garfield (Eds.), *Handbook of Psychotherapy and Behavior Change*. New York: Wiley, 1971.

Berger, P. L., and Luckmann, T. *The Social Construction of Reality*. New York: Anchor Books, 1967.

Bergin, A. E. "The Evaluation of Therapeutic Outcomes." In A. E. Bergin and S. L. Garfield (Eds.), *Handbook of Psychotherapy and Behavior Change*. New York: Wiley, 1971.

Bergin, A. E., and Strupp, H. H. *Changing Frontiers in the Science of Psychotherapy*. Chicago, Aldine, 1972.

Biase, D. V., and DeLeon, G. "The Encounter Group: Measurement of Systolic Blood Pressure." In G. DeLeon (Ed.), *Phoenix House: Studies in a Therapeutic Community*. New York: MSS Information Co., 1974.

Bloch, S. T., and others. "The Evaluation of Psychotherapy by Independent Judges." *British Journal of Psychiatry*, 1977, *131*, 410–414.

Blood, R. B., and Wolfe, D. *Husbands and Wives*. New York: Free Press, 1960.

Bohannon, P. J. *Social Anthropology*. New York: Holt, Rinehart and Winston, 1963.

Bond, G. R., and others. "A Target Problem Approach to Outcome Measurement." *Psychotherapy: Theory, Research, and Practice*, 1979, *16*, 48–54.

Booth, A., and Babchuk, N. "Seeking Health Care from New Resources." *Journal of Health and Social Behavior*, 1972, *13*, 90–99.

Borman, L. D. "A Revitalization Movement in the Mental Health Professions." *American Journal of Orthopsychiatry*, 1966, *36* (1), 111–118.

Borman, L. D. "The Marginal Route of a Mental Hospital Innovation." *Human Organization*, 1970, *29* (1), 63–69.

Borman, L. D. *Exploration in Self-Help and Mutual Aid*. Evanston, Ill.: Center for Urban Affairs, Northwestern University, 1975.

Borman, L. D. "Barn-Raising Revisited: The Upsurge in Self-Help Groups." *Center Report*, 1976a, pp. 16–17.

Borman, L. D. "Self-Help and the Professional." *Social Policy*, 1976b, 7 (2), 46–47.

Borman, L. D. "Black Institutions and Potential Social Change In the United States." In D. Shimkin, E. Shimkin, and D. Frate (Eds.), *The Extended Family in Black Societies*. Hawthorne, N.Y.: Mouton, 1978.

Borman, L. D. "Action Anthropology and the Self-Help/Mutual-Aid Movement." In R. Hinshaw (Ed.), *Currents in Anthropology: Essays in Honor of Sol Tax*. Chicago: Aldine, 1979a.

Borman, L. D. "Belief Systems and Self-Help: Kalmuk Resettlement in America." In G. H. Weber and L. M. Cohen (Eds.), *Belief Systems and Self-Help: A Cross-Cultural Perspective*. New York: Human Sciences Press, 1979b.

Boswell, D. M. "Personal Crises and the Mobilization of the Social Network." In J. C. Mitchell (Ed.), *Social Networks in Urban Situations*. Manchester, England: Manchester University Press, 1969.

Bradburn, N. *The Structure of Psychological Well-Being*. Chicago: Aldine, 1969.

Brown, B. "Social and Psychological Correlates of Help-Seeking Behavior Among Urban Adults." *American Journal of Community Psychology*, 1978, 6 (5), 425–439.

Brown, B. "Predicting Patterns of Help-Seeking in Coping with Stress in Adulthood." Unpublished doctoral dissertation, University of Chicago, 1979.

Brownmiller, S. "Sisterhood is Powerful." In S. Stumler (Ed.), *Women's Liberation: Blueprint for the Future*. New York: Ace Brooks, 1970.

Burchinal, L. G. "Comparisons of Factors Related to Pregnancy-Provoked and Non-Pregnancy-Provoked Youthful Marriages." *Midwest Sociologist*, 1959, 21, 92–96.

Butler, R. N. "The Life Review: An Interpretation of Reminiscence in the Aged." *Psychiatry*, 1963, 26, 65–76.

Butler, R. N. *Why Survive? Being Old in America*. New York: Harper & Row, 1975.

Campbell, D. T. "On the Conflicts Between Biological and Social Evolution and Between Psychology and Moral Tradition." *American Psychologist*, 1975, *30* (12), 1103–1126.

Campbell, D. T., and Stanley, J. C. *Experimental and Quasi-Experimental Designs for Research*. Chicago: Rand McNally, 1963.

Caplan, G. *Principles of Preventive Psychiatry*. New York: Basic Books, 1964.

Caplan, G., and Killilea, M. (Eds.). *Support Systems and Mutual Help: Multidisciplinary Explorations*. New York: Grune & Stratton, 1976.

Carden, M. L. *The New Feminist Movement*. New York: Russell Sage Foundation, 1974.

Carnegie, D. *How to Win Friends and Influence People*. New York: Simon & Schuster, 1936.

Casriel, D. *So Fair a House: The Story of Synanon*. Englewood Cliffs, N.J.: Prentice-Hall, 1963.

Chappel, J. N., and others. "Cyclazocine in a Multi-Modality Treatment Program: Comparative Results." *International Journal of Addictions*, 1971, *6*, 509–523.

Chein, I. *The Road to H*. New York: Basic Books, 1964.

Chein, I. "Psychological, Social, and Epidemiological Factors in Drug Addiction." In S. B. Sells (Ed.), *Rehabilitating the Narcotic Addict*. New York: Arno Press, 1966.

Clinard, M. "The Group Approach to Social Reintegration." *American Sociological Review*, 1949, *14*, 257–262.

Clinard, M. *Sociology of Deviant Behavior*. New York: Holt, Rinehart and Winston, 1963.

Croog, S., Lipson, A., and Levine, S. "Help Patterns in Severe Illnesses: The Roles of Kin Network, Nonfamily Resources, and Institutions." *Journal of Marriage and the Family*, 1972, *34*, 32–41.

Dean, S. R. "Self-Help Group Psychotherapy: Mental Patients Rediscover Will Power." *International Jounral of Social Psychiatry*, 1971, *17*, 72–78.

DeLeon, G., and others. "Therapeutic Community for Drug Addicts: Long Term Measurement of Emotional Changes." In G. DeLeon (Ed.), *Phoenix House: Studies in a Therapeutic Community*. New York: MSS Information Co., 1974.

Derogatis, L., and others. "The Hopkins Symptoms Checklist (HSCL): A Self-Report Symptom Inventory." *Behavioral Science*, 1974, *19*, 1–15.

Dole, V. P., and Nyswander, M. E. "Heroin Addiction—A Metabolic Disease." *Archives of Internal Medicine*, 1967, *120*, 19–24.

Drakeford, J. W. *Farewell to the Lonely Crowd*. Waco, Texas: Word Books, 1969.

Duval, H., Locke, B., and Brill, L. "Follow-up Study of Narcotic Drug Addicts Five Years After Hospitalization." *Public Health Reports*, 1963, *78*, 185–193.

Ellis, A. *Reason and Emotion in Psychotherapy*. Secaucus, N.J.: Lyle Stuart, 1962.

Emrick, C. D., Lassen, C. L., and Edwards, M. T. "Nonprofessional Peers as Therapeutic Agents." In A. S. Gurman and A. M. Razen (Eds.), *Effective Psychotherapy: A Handbook of Research*. Elmsford, N.Y.: Pergamon Press, 1977.

Epilepsy Self-Help Workshop Newsletter. Evanston, Ill.: Self-Help Institute, Center for Urban Affairs, Northwestern University, 1979.

Erikson, E. H. *Childhood and Society*. New York: Norton, 1950.

Evans, G. *The Family Circle Guide to Self-Help*. New York: Ballantine Books, 1979.

Ferber, A., and others. "Current Family Structures: Psychiatric Emergencies and Patient's Fate." *Archives of General Psychiatry*, 1967, *16*, 659–667.

Festinger, L. "A Theory of Social Comparison Processes." *Human Relations*, 1954, *7*, 117–140.

Festinger, L. *A Theory of Cognitive Dissonance*. New York: Harper & Row, 1957.

Forward Plan for Health. Washington, D.C.: Public Health Service, U.S. Department of Health, Education, and Welfare, 1976.

Frank, J. *Persuasion and Healing: A Comparative Study of Psychotherapy*. New York: Schocken Books, 1961.

Freedman, A. M., and others. "Cyclazocine and Methadone in Narcotic Addiction." *Journal of the American Medical Association*, 1967, *202*, 191–194.

Freeman, J. "The Origins of the Women's Liberation Movement." In J. Huber (Ed.), *Changing Women in a Changing Society*. Chicago: University of Chicago Press, 1973.

Freeman, J. *The Politics of Women's Liberation.* New York: McKay, 1975.

Freidson, E. "Client Control and Medical Practice." *American Journal of Sociology*, 1969, *65*, 374–382.

Freireich, E. "Bereavement and Marriage Stress." Paper presented at the First National Convention of the Society of Compassionate Friends, Oak Brook, Illinois, April 1978.

Freud, S. *Group Psychotherapy and the Analysis of the Ego.* New York: Boni and Liveright, 1940.

Gal, R., and Lazarus, R. S. "The Role of Activity in Anticipating and Confronting Stressful Situations." *Journal of Human Stress*, 1975, *1*, 4–20.

Gamblers Anonymous. Los Angeles: Gamblers Anonymous, 1976.

Gartner, A., and Riessman, F. *Self-Help in the Human Services.* San Francisco: Jossey-Bass, 1977.

Gerard, D. L. "Some Comments on the Opoid Addiction Process." In A. Wikler (Ed.), *The Addictive States.* Baltimore: Williams & Wilkins, 1968.

Gerard, H. B. "Emotional Uncertainty and Social Comparison." *Journal of Abnormal and Social Psychology*, 1963, *66*, 568–573.

Glaser, B. G., and Strauss, A. L. *The Discovery of Grounded Theory: Strategies for Qualitative Research.* Chicago: Aldine, 1967.

Glick, I. O., Weiss, R. S., and Parkes, C. M. *The First Year of Bereavement.* New York: Wiley, 1974.

Goffman, E. *Stigma: Notes on the Management of Spoiled Identity.* Englewood Cliffs, N.J.: Prentice-Hall, 1963.

Goldstein, A. "Heroin Addiction and the Role of Methadone in Its Treatment." *Archives of General Psychiatry*, 1972, *26*, 291–297.

Goldstein, A. P., and Stein, N. *Prescriptive Psychotherapies.* Elmsford, N.Y.: Pergamon Press, 1976.

Gorney, J. "Experiencing and Age: Patterns of Reminiscence Among the Elderly." Unpublished doctoral dissertation,

University of Chicago, 1968.

Goss, A., and Morosko, M. I. "Relation Between a Dimension of Internal-External Control and the MMPI with an Alcohol Population." *Journal of Consulting and Clinical Psychology*, 1970, *34*, 189–192.

Gottschalk, L., and Gleser, G. C. *The Measurement of Psychological States Through Content Analysis of Verbal Behavior*. Berkeley: University of California Press, 1969.

Gourash, N. "Help-Seeking: A Review of the Literature." *American Journal of Psychology*, 1978, *6* (5), 413–423.

Grapevine (Alcoholics Anonymous newsletter), Jan. 1968, *24* (8).

Grosz, H. J. *Recovery, Inc., Survey*. Chicago: Recovery, Inc., 1972.

Guidelines for the Establishment of New Branches of the Compassionate Friends. Hialeah, Fla., 1977.

Gurin, G., Veroff, J., and Feld, S. *Americans View Their Mental Health: A Nationwide Survey*. New York: Basic Books, 1960.

Gussow, A., and Tracy, G. S. "The Role of Self-Help Clubs in Adaptation to Chronic Illness and Disability." *Social Science and Medicine*, 1976, *10*, 407–414.

Hammer, M. "Influence of Small Social Networks as Factors on Mental Hospital Admission." *Human Organization*, 1963, *22*, 243–251.

Hansell, N. *The Person-in-Distress: On the Biosocial Dynamics of Adaptation*. New York: Human Sciences Press, 1976.

Harken, D. E. "Letter in *Pro-Time*." Boston, Mass.: Mended Hearts, Inc., 1975.

Havelock, R. G., and Lingwood, D. A. *Research and Development Utilization Strategies and Functions: An Analytical Comparison of Four Systems*. Ann Arbor: Center for Research on Utilization of Scientific Knowledge, Institute for Social Research, University of Michigan, 1973.

Hessler, R. M., and others. "Demographic Context, Social Interaction, and Perceived Health Status: Excedrin Headache #1." *Journal of Health and Social Behavior*, 1971, *12*, 191–199.

Hill, N. *Think and Grow Rich Action Book*. New York: Hawthorn, 1972.

Hole, J., and Levine, E. *Rebirth of Feminism*. New York: New

York Times Book Co., 1971.

Hollingshead, A., and Redlich, F. *Social Class and Mental Illness*. New York: Wiley, 1958.

Holton, J. T. *Therapy and Alcohol: The Collected Works of Harry M. Tiebout*. New York: Hawthorn, in press.

Horowitz, A. "The Pathways into Psychiatric Treatment: Some Differences Between Men and Women." *Journal of Health and Social Behavior*, 1977, *18*, 169–178.

Hovland, C. I., Janis, I. L., and Kelley, H. H. *Communication and Persuasion: Psychological Studies of Opinion Change*. New Haven: Yale University Press, 1953.

Hughes, H. M. (Ed.). *The Fantastic Lodge: The Autobiography of a Girl Drug Addict*. Boston: Houghton Mifflin, 1961.

Hunt, J. D. "Voluntary Associations as a Key to History." In D. B. Robertson (Ed.), *Voluntary Associations: A Study of Groups in Free Societies*. Richmond, Va.: John Knox Press, 1966.

Hurvitz, N. "Peer Self-Help Psychotherapy Groups: Psychotherapy Without Psychotherapists." In P. Roman and H. Trice (Eds.), *The Sociology of Psychotherapy*. New York: Aronson, 1974.

Hyman, H. H. "The Psychology of Status." *Archives of Psychology*, 1942, *38* (269), 1–95.

Joint Commission on Mental Illness and Health. *Action for Mental Health*. New York, Basic Books, 1961.

Jones, M. C. "Personality Correlates and Antecedents of Drinking Patterns in Adult Males." *Journal of Consulting and Clinical Psychology*, 1965, *32* (1), 2–12.

Jordan, H., and Levitz, L. S. "Behavior Modification in a Self-Help Group." *Journal of the American Dietetic Association*, 1973, *62*, 27–29.

Joreen [pseudonym]. "The Tyranny of Structurelessness." In A. Koedt, E. Levine, and A. Rapone (Eds.), *Radical Feminism*. New York: New York Times Book Co., 1973.

Jourad, S. "Self-Disclosure Patterns in British and American College Females." *Journal of Social Psychology*, 1961, *54*, 315–320.

Journal of Applied Behavioral Science, 1976, *12* (3).

Jung, C. G. *Modern Man in Search of a Soul*. New York: Harcourt Brace Jovanovich, 1933.

Kadushin, C. *Why People Go to Psychiatrists*. New York: Atherton, 1969.

Kammeyer, K., and Bolton, C. "Community and Family Factors Related to the Use of a Family Service Agency." *Journal of Marriage and the Family*, 1968, *30*, 488–498.

Kasl, S. V., Gore, S., and Cobb, S. "The Experience of Losing a Job: Reported Changes in Health Symptoms and Illness Behaviors." *Psychosomatic Medicine*, 1975, *37*, 106–121.

Katz, A. H. "Self-Help Organizations and Volunteer Participation in Social Welfare." *Social Work*, 1970, *15* (1), 51–60.

Katz, A. H., and Bender, E. I. "Self-Help Groups in Western Society: History and Prospects." *Journal of Applied Behavioral Sciences*, 1976a, *12*, 265–282.

Katz, A. H., and Bender, E. I. *The Strength in Us: Self-Help Groups in the Modern World*. New York: New Viewpoints, 1976b.

Kelley, H. H. "Two Functions of Reference Groups." In G. E. Swanson and T. M. Newcomb (Eds.), *Reading in Social Psychology*. New York: Holt, Rinehart and Winston, 1952.

Kelly, G. A. *The Psychology of Personal Constructs*. (2 vols.) New York: Norton, 1955.

Kelly, O. E. *Make Today Count*. New York: Delacourt, 1975.

Keogh, C. B. *Readings for Mental Health*. Sydney, Australia: GROW Publications, 1975.

Keogh, C. B. "Report of the First Four Weeks of GROW Activity on Mainland USA in the State of Illinois." Unpublished manuscript, 1978a.

Keogh, C. B. "Who Works Out a Community's Mental Health Program?" Unpublished manuscript, 1978b.

Kerri, J. N. "Studying Voluntary Associations as Adaptive Mechanisms: A Review of Anthropological Perspectives." *Current Anthropology*, 1976, *17* (1), 23–35.

Killilea, M. "Mutual-Help Organizations: Interpretations in the Literature." In G. Caplan and M. Killilea (Eds.), *Support Systems and Mutual Help: Multidisciplinary Explorations*. New York: Grune & Stratton, 1976.

Kimball, C. P. "Psychological Responses to the Experience of Open-Heart Surgery." *American Journal of Psychiatry*,

1969, *126*, 348–359.

Kimball, C. P., and others. "The Experience of Cardiac Surgery: Psychological Patterns and Prediction of Outcome." *Psychotherapy and Psychosomatics*, 1973, *22*, 310–319.

Kirschner, B. J., Dies, R. R., and Brown, R. A. "Effects of Experimental Manipulation of Self-Disclosure on Group Cohesiveness." *Journal of Consulting and Clinical Psychology*, 1978, *46*, 1171–1177.

Kleiman, M. A., Mantell, J. E., and Alexander, E. S. "Collaboration and Its Discontents: The Perils of Partnership." *Journal of Applied Behavioral Sciences*, 1976, *12* (3), 403–409.

Kravits, J. "Attitudes Toward and Use of Discretionary Physician and Dental Services by Race, Controlling for Income and Age." Unpublished doctoral dissertation, University of Chicago, 1972.

Kroptkin, P. *Mutual Aid: A Factor of Evolution*. Boston: Extending Horizons Books, 1914.

Kübler-Ross, E. *On Death and Dying*. New York: Macmillan, 1969.

Landau, I. "Sex-Role Concepts and Marital Happiness in Middle-Aged Couples." Unpublished thesis, University of Chicago, 1976.

Leary, T. *Interpersonal Diagnosis of Personality: A Functional Theory and Methodology for Personality Evaluation*. New York: Ronald Press, 1957.

LeBon, G. *The Crowd: A Study of the Popular Mind*. New York: Viking, 1960.

Lee, N. *The Search for an Abortionist*. Chicago: University of Chicago Press, 1969.

Lennard, H. L., and others. "The Methadone Illusion." *Science*, 1972, *176*, 881–884.

Lentz, R. G. "Personality Correlates of Alcoholic Beverage Consumption." *Character and Personality*, 1943, *12*, 54.

Leutz, W. N. "The Informal Community Caregiver: A Link Between the Health Care System and Local Residents." *American Journal of Orthopsychiatry*, 1976, *46*, 678–688.

Levine, F., and Preston, E. "Community Resource Orientation Among Low-Income Groups." *Wisconsin Law Review*, 1970, *1*, 80–113.

Levitz, L. S., and Strunkard, A. J. "A Therapeutic Coalition for Obesity: Behavior Modification and Patient Self-Help." *American Journal of Psychiatry*, 1974, *131*, 423–427.

Levy, L. H. "Self-Help Groups: Types and Psychological Processes." *Journal of Applied Behavioral Sciences*, 1976, *12*, 310–322.

Libbee, M. "Diffusion and the Women's Movement." Unpublished paper, University of Oklahoma, 1978.

Liberman, R. "Personal Influence in the Use of Mental Health Resources." *Human Organization*, 1965, *24*, 231–235.

Lieber, L. L. "Mothers Anonymous: A New Direction Against Child Abuse." Paper presented at the first biennial conference of the Society for Clinical Social Work, San Francisco, 1971.

Lieberman, M. A. "Issues in Studying Psychological Predictors of Survival." In F. C. Jeffers and E. Palmore (Eds.), *Prediction of Life Span*. Lexington, Mass.: Heath, 1971.

Lieberman, M. A. "Adaptive Processes in Late Life." In N. Datan and L. Ginsberg (Eds.), *Life-Span Developmental Psychology: Normative Life Crises*. New York: Academic Press, 1975.

Lieberman, M. A., and Bond, G. R. "The Problem of Being a Woman: A Survey of 1700 Women in Consciousness-Raising Groups." *Journal of Applied Behavioral Sciences*, 1976, *12*, 363–380.

Lieberman, M. A., and Bond, G. R. "Self-Help Groups: Problems of Measuring Outcome." *Small Group Behavior*, 1978, *9*, 221–241.

Lieberman, M. A., and Borman, L. D. (Eds.). "Self-Help Groups—Special Issue." *Journal of Applied and Behavioral Science*, 1976, *12* (3), 261–463.

Lieberman, M. A., and Coplan, A. S. "Distance from Death as a Variable in the Study of Aging." *Developmental Psychology*, 1969, *2*, 71–84.

Lieberman, M. A., and Falk, J. "The Remembered Past as Data for Research on the Life Cycle." *Human Development*, 1971, *14*, 132–141.

Lieberman, M. A., and Gardner, J. A. "Institutional Alternatives to Psychotherapy: A Study of Growth-Center Users." *Archives of General Psychiatry*, 1976, *33*, 157–162.

Lieberman, M. A., and Pearlin, L. D. "Everyday Life Experience." Study in progress, University of Chicago, 1977.

Lieberman, M. A., Yalom, I. D., and Miles, M. B. *Encounter Groups: First Facts*. New York: Basic Books, 1973.

Liem, J. H., and Liem, R. "Life Events, Social Supports, and Physical and Psychological Well-Being." Paper presented at the annual meeting of the American Psychological Association, Washington, D.C., September 1976.

Lifton, R. J. *Thought Reform and the Psychology of Totalism: A Study of "Brainwashing" in China*. New York: Norton, 1961.

Lindemann, E. "Symptomatology and Management of Acute Grief." *American Journal of Psychiatry*, 1944, *101*, 141–149.

Litman, T. J. "The Family as a Basic Unit in Health and Medical Care." *Social Science and Medicine*, 1974, *8*, 495–519.

Little, K. L. "The Role of the Secret Society in Cultural Specialization." *American Anthropologist*, 1949, *51*, 199–212.

Litwak, E., and Szelenyi, I. "Primary Group Structures and Their Functions: Kin, Neighbors, and Friends." *American Sociological Review*, 1969, *34*, 465–481.

Lopata, H. Z. *Widowhood in an American City*. Cambridge, Mass.: Schenkman, 1973.

Lott, A. J., and Lott, B. E. "Group Cohesiveness as Interpersonal Attraction: A Review of Relationships with Antecedent and Consequent Variables." *Psychological Bulletin*, 1965, *64*, 259–309.

Low, A. A. *Lost and Found*. A Bulletin of the Association of Former Patients of the Psychiatric Institute of the University of Illinois and the State Department of Public Welfare. Chicago: Recovery, Inc., 1938.

Low, A. A. *The Historical Development of Recovery's Self-Help Project*. Chicago: Recovery, Inc., 1943a.

Low, A. A. *Lectures to Relatives of Former Patients*. Boston: Christopher, 1943b.

Low, A. A. *Mental Health Through Will-Training*. Boston: Christopher, 1950.

Lowenthal, M. F., Thurnher, M., and Chiriboga, D. *Four Stages of Life: A Comparative Study of Women and Men Facing Transitions*. San Francisco: Jossey-Bass, 1975.

Lowie, R. H. *Primitive Society*. New York: Liveright, 1947.

Lurie, O. R. "Parents' Attitudes Toward Children's Problems and Toward Use of Mental Health Services: Socioeconomic Differences." *American Journal of Orthopsychiatry*, 1974, *44*, 109–120.

MacAndrew, C. "The Differentiation of Male Alcoholic Outpatients from Nonalcoholic Outpatients by Means of the MMPI." *Quarterly Journal of Studies on Alcohol*, 1965, *26*, 238–246.

McClelland, D., and others. *The Drinking Man*. New York: Free Press, 1972.

McCord, W., and McCord, J. *Origins of Alcoholism*. Stanford, Calif.: Stanford University Press, 1960.

McGrath, E. "Guide to Developmental Journey: Power of Women's Groups." Symposium presented at the annual meeting of the American Psychological Association, Toronto, Canada, September 1978.

Machover, S., and Puzzo, F. S. "Clinical and Objective Studies of Personality Variables in Alcoholism." *Quarterly Journal of Studies on Alcohol*, 1949, *20*, 505–519.

MacIver, R. M. *Society and Its Structure and Changes*. New York: Long and Smith, 1931.

McKinlay, J. B. "Social Networks, Lay Consultation, and Help-Seeking Behavior." *Social Forces*, 1973, *51*, 275–292.

Martin, W. R. "Pathophysiology of Narcotic Addiction: Possible Roles of Protracted Abstinence in Relapse." In C. Zarafonetis (Ed.), *Drug Abuse: Proceedings of the Second International Conference*. Philadelphia: Lea and Febiger, 1972.

Martin, W. R., and Jasinki, D. R. "Physiological Parameters of Morphine Abstinence in Man—Tolerance, Early Abstinence, Protracted Abstinence." *Journal of Psychiatric Research*, 1969, *7*, 9–17.

Martin, W. R., and others. "Methadone: A Reevaluation." *Archives of General Psychiatry*, 1973, *28*, 286–295.

Martinez, T. "Alternative Mental Health Resources for the Spanish-Speaking: Latino Helping Networks." Paper presented at the annual meeting of the American Psychological Association, San Francisco, September 1977.

Mayer, J., and Timms, N. *The Client Speaks: Working-Class Im-*

pressions of Casework. Chicago: Aldine, 1970.

Meichenbaum, D. *Cognitive-Behavior Modification: An Integrative Approach*. New York: Plenum, 1977.

Menninger, K. A. "Self-Help, Money, and Psychoanalysis." In L. D. Borman (Ed.), *Explorations in Self-Help and Mutual Aid*. Evanston, Ill.: Center for Urban Affairs, Northwestern University, 1975.

Moos, R. (Ed.). *Coping with Physical Illnesses*. New York: Plenum, 1977.

Mowrer, O. H. *The Crises in Psychiatry and Religion*. New York: D. Van Nostrand, 1961.

Mowrer, O. H. *The New Group Therapy*. New York: D. Van Nostrand, 1964.

Mowrer, O. H. "Integrity Groups: Basic Principles and Procedures." *Counseling Psychologist*, 1972, *2*, 7–33.

Mowrer, O. H. "Small Groups Movement in Historical Perspective." In L. D. Borman (Ed.), *Explorations in Self-Help and Mutual Aid*. Evanston, Ill.: Center for Urban Affairs, Northwestern University, 1975.

Mowrer, O. H. "The Growing Impact of Mutual-Help Groups on Professional Psychotherapy and Counseling." Unpublished manuscript, 1978a.

Mowrer, O. H. "Is Much Psychotherapy Still Misdirected or Misapplied?" Unpublished manuscript, 1978b.

Mowrer, O. H., and Vattano, A. J. "Integrity Groups: A Context for Growth in Honesty, Responsibility, and Involvement." *Journal of Applied Behavioral Sciences*, 1976, *12* (3), 419–431.

Neugarten, B., Havighurst, R., and Tobin, S. "The Measurement of Life Satisfaction." *Journal of Gerontology*, 1961, *16*, 134–143.

Nuckolls, K., Cassel, J., and Kaplan, B. "Psychosocial Assets, Life Crises, and the Prognosis of Pregnancy." *American Journal of Epidemiology*, 1972, *95*, 431–441.

O'Donnell, J. A. *Narcotics Addicts in Kentucky*. U.S. Public Health Service Publication No. 1881. Washington, D.C.: U.S. Government Printing Office, 1969.

Orlinsky, D., and Howard, K. "Psychotherapeutic Processes." *Annual Review of Psychology*, 1972, *23*.

Parents Anonymous Frontiers. Torrance, Calif.: Parents Anonymous, 1979.

Parkes, C. M. *Bereavement: Studies of Grief in Adult Life.* New York: International Universities Press, 1972.

Parsons, T. *The Social System.* New York: Free Press, 1955.

Paykel, E. S., Prusoff, B. A., and Uhlenhuth, E. H. "Scaling of Life Events." *Archives of General Psychiatry*, 1971, *25*, 340–347.

Payne, C. "Consciousness Raising: A Dead End." In A. Koedt, E. Levine, and A. Rapone (Eds.), *Radical Feminism.* New York: New York Times Book Co., 1973.

Pearlin, L. D., and Lieberman, M. A. "Social Sources of Emotional Distress." In R. Simmons (Ed.), *Research in Community and Mental Health.* Greenwich, Conn.: JAI Press, 1979.

Pearlin, L. D., and Schooler, C. "The Structure of Coping." *Journal of Health and Social Behavior*, 1978, *19*, 2–21.

Perl, H., and Abarbanell, G. "Guidelines to Feminist Consciousness Raising." Manual prepared for the National Task Force on Consciousness Raising of the National Organization for Women, 1835 S. Bentley, Los Angeles, Calif., 1976.

Pitts, J. P. *The Community Service Voucher Program: An Experiment in Community Access to University Resources.* Chicago: Center for Urban Affairs, Northwestern University, 1975.

Pollock, G. H. "Mourning and Adaptation." *International Journal of Psychoanalysis*, 1961, *42*, 341–361.

President's Commission on Mental Health. *Commission Report.* Vol. 1. Washington, D.C.: U.S. Government Printing Office, 1978.

Pro-Time. Boston, Mass.: Mended Hearts, Inc., 1975.

Quarentelli, E. L. "A Note on the Protective Function of the Family in Disasters." *Journal of Marriage and Family Living*, 1960, *22*, 263–264.

Raiff, N. R. "Recovery, Inc.: A Study of a Self-Help Organization in Mental Health." Unpublished dissertation, University of Pittsburgh, 1978.

Redstockings Manifesto, July 7, 1969. Reprinted in *Notes from the Second Year: Women's Liberation*, 1970. Notes, Box AA, Old Chelsea Station, New York, N.Y. 10011.

Reibstein, J., and others. "A Psychotherapy Group for Women." Unpublished paper, 1979.

Riessman, F. "The 'Helper' Therapy Principle." *Social Work*, 1965, *10*, 27–32.

Robinson, D., and Henry, S. *Self-Help and Health: Mutual Aid for Modern Problems*. London: Robertson, 1977.

Rogers, C. R. "The Necessary and Sufficient Conditions of Therapeutic Personality Change." *Journal of Consulting Psychology*, 1957, *22*, 95–103.

Rosenberg, M. *Society and the Adolescent Self-Image*. Princeton, N.J.: Princeton University Press, 1965.

Rosenblatt, A., and Mayer, J. E. "Help-Seeking for Family Problems: A Survey of Utilization and Satisfaction." *American Journal of Psychiatry*, 1972, *28*, 126–130.

Rosner, A. "Stress and Maintenance of Self-Concept in the Aged." Unpublished doctoral dissertation, University of Chicago, 1968.

Sarachild, K. "A Program for Feminist 'Consciousness Raising.'" In *Notes from the Second Year: Women's Liberation*, 1970. Notes, Box AA, Old Chelsea Station, New York, N.Y. 10011.

Sarbin, T. R., and Adler, N. "Self-Reconstitution Processes: A Preliminary Report." *Psychoanalytic Review*, 1971, *57* (4), 599–615.

Sarbin, T. R., and Allen, V. L. "Role Theory." In G. Lindzey and E. Aronson (Eds.), *The Handbook of Social Psychology*. (2nd ed.) Reading, Mass.: Addison-Wesley, 1968.

Schachter, S. *The Psychology of Affiliation: Experimental Studies of Sources of Gregariousness*. Stanford, Calif.: Stanford University Press, 1959.

Schiff, H. S. *The Bereaved Parent*. New York: Crown, 1977.

Shamres, A. "No Death So Sad." A paper presented to the Foundation of Thanatology, New York, November 7, 1975.

Sherif, M. "A Study of Some Social Factors in Perception." *Archives of Psychology*, 1935, *27* (187), 1–60.

Silkworth, W. D. "A New Approach to Psychotherapy in Chronic Alcoholism." In *Alcoholics Anonymous Comes of Age*. New York: Alcoholics Anonymous World Services, 1957. (Originally published 1939.)

Silverman, P. R. *If You Will Lift the Load I Will Lift It Too:*

A Guide to Developing Widow-to-Widow Programs. New York: Jewish Funeral Directors of America, 1976.

Silverman, P. R. Personal communication, 1977.

Sloane, R. B., and others. *Psychotherapy Versus Behavior Therapy.* Cambridge, Mass.: Harvard University Press, 1975.

Smith, C., and Freedman, A. *Voluntary Associations: Perspectives on the Literature.* Cambridge, Mass.: Harvard University Press, 1972.

Smith, D. H. "The Importance of Formal Voluntary Organizations for Society." *Sociology and Social Research,* 1966, *50,* 483–494.

Spradley, J. P., and McCurdy, D. W. *The Cultural Experience: Ethnography in Complex Society.* Chicago: Science Research Associates, 1972.

Srole, L. "Social Integration and Certain Corollaries: An Exploratory Study." *American Sociological Review,* 1956, *21,* 709–716.

Srole, L., and others. *Mental Health in the Metropolis.* New York: McGraw-Hill, 1962.

Stephens, S. *Death Comes Home.* New York: Morehouse-Barlow, 1972.

Stevenson, G. H., and others. "Drug Addiction in British Columbia: A Research Survey." Unpublished paper, 1956.

Stewart, D. A. "The Dynamics of Fellowship as Illustrated in Alcoholics Anonymous." *Quarterly Journal of Studies on Alcohol,* 1955, *16,* 251–262.

Stone, W. C. *The Success System That Never Fails.* Englewood Cliffs, N.J.: Prentice-Hall, 1962.

Strunkard, A. J. "The Success of TOPS: A Self-Help Group." *Post Graduate Medicine,* 1972, *40,* 743–746.

Strupp, H. H., and Hadley, S. W. "A Tripartite Model of Mental Health and Therapeutic Outcomes." *American Psychologist,* 1977, *30,* 187–197.

Stuart, R. B. (Ed.). *Behavioral Self-Management: Strategies, Techniques, and Outcomes.* New York: Brunner/Mazel, 1977.

Sue, S., and others. "Delivery of Community Mental Health Services to Black and White Clients." *Journal of Consulting and Clinical Psychology,* 1974, *42,* 794–801.

Sugarman, B. *Daytop Village: A Therapeutic Community.* New

York: Holt, Rinehart and Winston, 1974.

Sullivan, T. A. "The Naim Conference of the Archdiocese of Chicago." Chicago: The Naim Conference, 1964.

Sussman, M. B. "Intergenerational Family Relationship and Social Role Changes in Middle Age." *Journal of Gerontology*, 1960, *15*, 71–75.

Synanon Fact Sheet. Marshal, Calif.: Synanon, 1976.

Thomsen, R. *Bill W*. New York: Harper & Row, 1975.

Tiebout, H. M. "Therapeutic Mechanisms of AA." *American Journal of Psychiatry*, 1944, *100*, 468–473. (Reprinted in *Alcoholics Anonymous Comes of Age*. New York: Alcoholics Anonymous World Services, 1975.)

Tischler, G. L., and others. "Utilization of Mental Health Services: Patienthood and the Prevalence of Symptomatology in the Community." *Archives of General Psychiatry*, 1975, *32*, 411–415.

Tobin, S., and Lieberman, M. A. *Last Home for the Aged: Critical Implications of Institutionalization*. San Francisco: Jossey-Bass, 1976.

Tolsdorf, C. "Social Networks, Support, and Coping: An Exploratory Study." *Family Process*, 1976, *15*, 407–417.

Tracy, G. S., and Gussow, A. "Self-Help Health Groups: A Grassroots Response to a Need for Services." *Journal of Applied Behavioral Sciences*, 1976, *12*, 381–396.

Trice, H. M., and Roman, P. M. "Delabeling, Relabeling, and Alcoholics Anonymous." *Social Problems*, 1970, *17*, 538–546.

Trocchi, A. *Cain's Book*. New York: Grove, 1960.

Trussell, R. E. "Second National Conference on Methadone Treatment." Unpublished paper, 1969.

Uhlenhuth, E. H., and others. "Symptom Intensity and Life Stress in the City." *Archives of General Psychiatry*, 1974, *31*, 759–764.

Volkman, R., and Cressey, D. R. "Differential Association and the Rehabilitation of Addicts." *American Journal of Sociology*, 1963, *69*, 129–142.

Waldorf, D. *Careers in Dope*. Englewood Cliffs, N.J.: Prentice-Hall, 1973.

Warren, L. W. "The Therapeutic Status of Consciousness-Raising Groups." *Professional Psychology*, 1976, 7, 132–140.

Waskow, I. E., and Parloff, M. B. *Psychotherapy Change Measures*. DHEW Publication No. (ADM) 74–120. Washington, D.C.: U.S. Government Printing Office, 1975.

Watts, W. "Relative Persistence of Opinion Change Induced by Active Compared to Passive Participation." *Journal of Personal and Social Psychology*, 1967, 5, 4–15.

Wechsler, H. "The Self-Help Organization in the Mental Health Field." *Journal of Nervous and Mental Disease*, 1960, *130* (4), 297–315.

Weiss, R. S. "The Contributions of an Organization of Single Parents to the Well-Being of Its Members." *Family Coordinator*, 1973, *22*, 321–326.

Wellman, B. "Community Ties and Support Systems: From Intimacy to Support." In L. Bourne, R. McKinnon, and J. Simmons (Eds.), *The Form of Cities in Central Canada*. Toronto, Canada: University of Toronto Press, 1973.

Wellman, B. *Urban Connections*. Research Paper #84. Toronto, Canada: Center for Urban and Community Studies, University of Toronto, 1976.

Westberg, G. *Good Grief*. Philadelphia: Fortress Press, 1962.

Whitehead, C. "Methadone Pseudo-Withdrawal Syndrome: Paradigm for a Psychopharmacological Model of Opiate Addiction." *Psychosomatic Medicine*, 1974, *36* (3), 189–198.

Wikler, A. "Conditioning Factors in Opiate Addiction and Relapse." In D. M. Wilner and G. G. Kassebaum (Eds.), *Narcotics*. New York: McGraw-Hill, 1965.

Wilson, B. "Dr. Jung, Dr. Silkworth, and AA." *AA Grapevine*, January 1968, pp. 10–15.

Wolff, K. H. *The Sociology of Georg Simmel*. New York: Free Press, 1950.

Wollert, W., Knight, R., and Levy, L. H. "Make Today Count: A Collaborative Model for Professionals and Self-Help Groups." Unpublished manuscript, Indiana University, 1978.

Yablonsky, L. *Synanon: The Tunnel Back*. New York: Macmillan, 1965.

Yalom, I. D. *The Theory and Practice of Group Psychotherapy*. (2nd ed.) New York: Basic Books, 1975.

Yalom, I. D., and others. "Alcoholics in Interactional Group Therapy." *Archives of General Psychiatry*, 1978, *35*, 419–425.

Zimbardo, P., and Formica, R. "Emotional Comparison and Self-Esteem as Determinants of Affiliation." *Journal of Personality*, 1963, *31*, 141–162.

Index

452